JEWS MAKE THE BEST DEMONS

"Palestine" and the Jewish Question

Jews
Make the Best
Demons

"Palestine" and the Jewish Question

Eric Rozenman

Published by New English Review Press
a subsidiary of World Encounter Institute
PO Box 158397
Nashville, Tennessee 37215
&
27 Old Gloucester Street
London, England, WC1N 3AX

Cover Art and Design by Kendra Mallock

ISBN: 978-1-943003-20-4

First Edition

NEW ENGLISH REVIEW PRESS
newenglishreview.org

For Renana, Ayala, Eitan and all their generation.

"[W]e must recognize much more clearly than before that since 1975 (with the passing of the scandalous U.N. resolution condemning Zionism as racism) hatred of Israel has increasingly mutated into the chief vector for the 'new' anti-Semitism."

—Historian Robert Wistrich, 2015.

"We will never surrender to the expressions of hatred; we will not surrender to anti-Zionism because it is a reinvention of antisemitism."

—French President Emmanuel Macron, July 16, 2017, the 75th anniversary of the deportation of more than 13,000 Parisian Jews to Nazi death camps.

"It happened, and therefore it can happen again. This is the core of what we have to say."

—Author and survivor Primo Levi. The words are inscribed at the entrance to Berlin's Holocaust Memorial.

Contents

INTRODUCTION

What's Old is New Again

J EWS AND NON-JEWS who wish them well believe the Holocaust ended in 1945. But if the Holocaust began with ideas and words, only ending in round-ups and gas chambers, then more to the point it was interrupted until it could be resumed with ideas and words.

Israelis and non-Israelis who support the Jewish state think Israel emerged victorious from several major Arab-Israeli wars. Therefore, they seek to "correct" rather than quash anti-Zionist, anti-Jewish prejudices in Diaspora and open the way to peaceful Arab-Israeli coexistence in the Middle East.

But more accurately, Israel won large, even existential battles. Yet the war itself, now in its tenth decade, continues. Enemies still undefeated, still confirmed or reconfirmed in anti-Israel, antisemitic mythology, continue to fight. By non-military as well as armed means they conduct a relentless a war of attrition aimed at eventual destruction.

If all this were not so, Israel would not have been the only one of the world's approximately 200 countries whose capital city hosted no foreign embassies until 2018; which periodically has issued gas masks to all its citizens (small tent-like protectors for infants); given endless incitement and terrorism against it feels compelled to wall itself in, ghetto-like, from neighbors; and is openly and repeatedly threatened with destruction by an Iran intent on nuclear weapons and bolstered by international trade.

Hatred of Israel, of the Jewish state, reanimates hatred of the Jewish people. In fact, the old hatred of the Jewish people compels much of the newer hostility to the Israeli state. In that sense, anti-Zionism is antisemitism and can hardly be otherwise.

9

"The Palestinian narrative," historical revisionism leading to denial of the Jewish people's past, incites hatred of Israel. In that way, it functions as the new blood libel. To the significant extent it complements Sunni Islamic imperialism, it also denies the Jewish present and, by implication, future. This imperialism rejects Judaism (not to mention Christianity) as a religion on equal footing with Islam.

The original blood libel—the fantastic charge that Jews murdered non-Jews and used their blood for religious purposes—began among ancient Greeks, was well-established in medieval Christianity, current in czarist Russia and revived by Nazi Germany. Today it circulates widely in Arab-Islamic lands. It does so at times independently, but often as part of the lie of Palestine.

Ahad Ha'am (Asher Ginsburg—his Hebrew pen-name means "One of the People"), was a late 19th century cultural Zionist. He termed the blood libel accusation "the solitary case in which the general acceptance of an idea about ourselves does not make us doubt whether all the world can be wrong, and we [the Jews] are right, because it is based on an absolute lie, and is not even supported by any false inference from particular to universal."

Actually, there have been more than a few cases in which the Jews, or the Jewish state, have been right and "all the world wrong." These include but are hardly exhausted by claims Jews control international finance, run the world's communications media, concocted the HIV-AIDS virus to attack their enemies, that Israel welcomed the 1967 Six-Day War as an opportunity to conquer Arab land, and that Zionism is racism.

Today, the primary case in which the Jews are right and much of the world wrong is the Palestine lie. It falsely charges that the Jews, as Zionists, ethnically cleansed an indigenous people from the land of Palestine, there established an imperialist, racist regime and that the Jewish state—Israel—undermines Middle Eastern and even world-wide stability. In fact, the Palestine lie has a) camouflaged antisemitism as anti-Zionism and b) promoted as justified a resurgence of antisemitism. In this way it functions as the direct descendant of the original blood libel. By no coincidence it repeatedly invokes the original to reanimate it if not return it to respectability. Calls for Jewish destruction on the streets of Europe and colleges campuses in North America have followed.

For those acquainted with the history of the blood libel and familiar with the inversions and fabrications of "the Palestinian narrative," re-examining either topic may seem tedious. The falsifications are similar.

But reexamining both the libel and the narrative have become inescapable. In increasingly "post-modern" Western culture, facts are decreasingly determinative. Which is to say, post-modern becomes pre-modern, empirical rationality yielding once more to romantic superstition.

For many, but perhaps now a minority, the Hebrew Bible's civilizing ethical monotheism remains a social-cultural cornerstone. In the West's none-too-distant past a majority including, for example, John Adams and Winston Churchill, took the Bible's civilizational centrality for granted. Members of Britain's Peel Commission went to Mandatory Palestine to investigate the Palestinian Arabs' anti-British, anti-Jewish rebellion in 1936—a rebellion armed and funded by Nazi Germany and fascist Italy.[1] Commissioners asked Zionist leader and later Israel's first prime minister, David Ben-Gurion, by what right the Jews claimed the Holy Land. The secular but Jewishly knowledgeable Ben-Gurion pointed to a copy of Scriptures and reminded them, "the Bible is our mandate." Sacrificing a Jewish state—and sacrifice it would be, in the original sense of ritual offering—the West would sacrifice its ethical anchor.

However, a large and growing number imagines post-modern, secular materialism can survive untethered from traditional values short-handed as "Judeo-Christian ethics." Whereas the blood libel once made Jews agents of Satan, the Palestine lie now casts them as agents of racism, equivalent to the anti-Christ in the secular fundamentalist catechism. "Racist!" like "heretic!" before it, as some have noted, is the ultimate malediction and authorizes the ultimate sanction.

So the West once again finds itself at a perversely familiar junction. The Jews, the Zionists, the Israelis are right, and much of the world is wrong. But such elevated outlier status for the Jews is intolerable. Therefore, the position of their enemies can be tolerated, even embraced. André Gide—who won the Nobel Prize for Literature when it still mattered—observed, "Everything that needs to be said has already been said. But since no one was listening, everything must be said again." So it is about the Jews, Israel and their enemies.

The Holocaust did not begin with concentration camps and gas chambers. Steven Blaney, public safety and emergency preparedness minister in the cabinet of staunchly pro-Israel Canadian Prime Minister Stephen Harper, felt compelled in 2015 to repeat a truism: "[The] Holocaust did not begin in the gas chambers, it began with words."[2]

---

1 *Nazis, Islamists, and the Making of the Modern Middle East*, by Barry Rubin and Wolfgang G. Schwanitz, Yale University Press, 2014, pages 4, 97.

2 "'Holocaust did not begin in the gas chamber, it began with words': Minister in de-

Those words led from slander to marginalization, from marginalization to isolation, and from isolation and dehumanization to the death camps. Blaney's observation, not new, was again necessary. Obfuscation aside—and it is limitless on the subject of the Jews and their state, whether intentional or unintentional, informed or ignorant—such words again enter common conversation, especially via the Internet.

The first words were those of the pagan blood libel. They gathered force with the early Christian charge of deicide. They then combined elements of both in the medieval blood libel. These words alleged that the Jews, who had denied, then sacrificed the son of God, did the same to his followers. Repeated massacres of Jews resulted.

Then came the 19th century's *Protocols of the Learned Elders of Zion*, a fantasy not of individual ritual murders but rather a Jewish conspiracy to destroy nations—mass politicide, in Israeli statesman Abba Eban's term—and rule the world. These enduring anti-Jewish indictments culminated in the Nazi delirium of an Aryan super race threatened by oxymoronically sub-human but particularly cunning, Jewish-capitalist-Bolsheviks in a battle to the death.

The words ended in Auschwitz, Bergen-Belsen, Sobibor and 42,500 other places big and small—more were still being discovered at this writing—with the enslavement and murders of six million Jews, one of every two in Europe, one of three world-wide.[3] After the cities of Jerusalem, Athens and Rome, the continent of Europe itself became the locus of Western civilization. From 1500 to 2000 that civilization influenced and even dominated much of the rest of the planet. And near the end of that epoch a blood-soaked Europe became the world's largest Jewish cemetery.

Many people are tired of hearing about the Holocaust, not a few of them Jews. Many others, as a poll in Italy a few years ago found, don't even recognize the term. Either way, the syndicated columnist George F. Will wrote decades ago, the Holocaust is the black hole at the center of modern civilization into which Americans in particular—with their defining and revolutionary national belief in life, liberty and the pursuit of happiness—ought to stare.

Stare, and listen. And doing so, recognize that the Holocaust indeed has resumed with words. The words are at times disguised, initially and temporarily substituting Zionism for Judaism, insisting Zionism is

fense of new anti-terrorism bill," *National Post* [Canada], March 10, 2015.
3 "Researchers uncover vast numbers of unknown Nazi killing fields," *Times of Israel*, Jan. 25, 2017.

racism, the all-purpose "Christ-killer!" condemnation of our time. At others—dismayingly if not surprisingly—they are heard again in their original forms.

Some words are high-sounding, if one ignores the corruption of their sources. For example, the United Nations Security Council—the global body which was created by victorious World War II Allies largely to prevent future wars with new eruptions of Holocaust-like genocide—declared on Dec. 23, 2016 that Jewish communities in the West Bank (Judea and Samaria) constituted "flagrant violations of international law." The Obama administration, denying charges it orchestrated the resolution behind the scenes, abstained. If not directly culpable, it nevertheless side-stepped an opportunity to tell the truth.

The U.N. Charter, Chapter 12, Article 80 (sometimes known as "the Palestine article") continues the League of Nations' Palestine Mandate. The Mandate's Article 6 encouraged "close Jewish settlement" on the land, meaning the land between the Jordan River and Mediterranean Sea, especially open, government or "waste lands." But anti-Zionist antisemitism conducts "lawfare" against the Jewish state and people. It transforms the original purpose of the United Nations into a variation of its opposite.

Turtle Bay's font of Israel-hatred and Jew-hatred—not to mention historical revisionism—overflows. The U.N. Educational, Scientific and Cultural Organization has determined that Jerusalem's Temple Mount, site of Judaism's First and Second temples, both of which predated Mohammed by many centuries, the Second of which figures prominently in the story of Jesus, is an Islamic-only shrine.[4] In May, 2017, UNESCO's governing board went further, declaring in full Orwellian mode that Jerusalem has no connection to Jews. The Torah, the Hebrew Bible, mentions Jerusalem and its synonym, Zion, more than 400 times; Islam's scripture, the Quran, refers to Jerusalem not once. Muslims at prayer face Mecca. Jews face Jerusalem, and have for more than 2,000 years.

When, early in 2017, the U.N.'s new secretary-general, Antonio Guterres, affirmed Jews' historic connection to the city and the fact that the Temple destroyed by Rome was indeed a Jewish one, the Palestinian Authority's minister for Jerusalem affairs, Adnan al-Husseini, rebuked him. Guterres, al-Husseini claimed, had "violated all legal, diplomatic and humanitarian customs, overstepped his role as secretary-general" and "must issue an apology to the Palestinian people." Reality being un-

---

4 "Palestine Wins Victory Against Israel; Jerusalem Holy Site Declared Muslim, Not Jewish in U.N. Resolution," *International Business Times*, Oct. 13, 2016.

kind to the Palestinian narrative, facts like those acknowledged by Guterres cannot be allowed to matter.

Delinquents not only in Europe but also the United States, as in Philadelphia and St. Louis in 2017, knock over headstones in Jewish cemeteries. They test whether desecrating the memories of dead Jews means it's safe to return to brutalizing the bodies of live ones. Diplomats signal that if it's not always permissible quite yet, it soon may be. As Daniel Bernard, then France's ambassador to the United Kingdom, told a London dinner party in 2001, "all the current troubles of the world are because of that shitty little country Israel." Probably unconsciously, he amplified while echoing the message of signs along German roads in the 1930s. They lamented, "The Jews are our misfortune." The signs themselves echoed an expression of Martin Luther's 400 years earlier and revived by the Nazi weekly, *Der Sturmer.* Bernard added, "Why should the world be in danger of World War III because of those people?" Why indeed? Cannot humanity finally be done with all its misfortunes caused by that troublesome people, those Jews?

Mad self-parodies underpin attitudes like those of the late French ambassador. Zionism as racism, Israelis as new Nazis, Palestinian Arabs as new Jews—are historical inversions. By consigning factual history to *1984*'s memory hole, they would erase essential elements of Judaism and the Jewish people's story. By doing so they would grease the way to a new erasure of the Jewish people. Zionism being the national liberation movement of the Jews and Israel being the Zionist project made manifest, anti-Zionism would and does ghettoize the Jewish state as antisemitism ghettoized pre-state European Jews. Hence, not only is Israel the only country in which every citizen may be issued a gas mask, noted above, but also every house or apartment built since Saddam Hussein's 1991 Scud missile attacks must have a "safe room" constructed to withstand both small rocket and chemical-biological weapons attacks. If one doesn't mind the steel doors and window shutters with their black, rubber-like seals, safe rooms can make, as I've seen, cozy bedrooms or studies. It's taken for granted that Jews should live thus. In the process of attacking Israel, anti-Zionist words invoke, in antisemitic fashion, Jews everywhere. They resurrect Jew-hatred on the "progressive," post-liberal left as fascism employed Jew-hatred on the reactionary, anti-democratic right.

Anti-Zionism functions as antisemitism in accordance with Natan Sharansky's "three 'D's'": Double standards, delegitimization and demonization. The United Nations and those who manipulate it as well as those who follow its lead deny the Jewish people its right to a sovereign state on a portion of its ancient homeland. They do so while accepting such a right axiomatically for many other peoples—but not all, ask the Kurds or Tibetans, for e xample—and insisting on it for a Palestinian Arab people of new and largely negative provenance. This double standard helps expose anti-Zionism's antisemitic compulsion.

CHAPTER ONE

Frenzied Scribblers, Madmen in Authority

T HE MOST USEFUL LEVER in antisemitism's "return to the norm," incorporating demonization and delegitimization as well as double standards, has been the lie of Palestine, the "Palestinian narrative."

"Practical men who believe themselves to be quite exempt from any intellectual influence, are usually the slaves of some defunct economist. Madmen in authority, who hear voices in the air, are distilling their frenzy from some academic scribbler of a few years back." So believed John Maynard Keynes, the influential early 20th century British economist. If so, then the history of ideas is one of the most important, though often minimized, branches of the discipline. It is true especially in our age, surfeited with academic scribblers whose distilled frenzies go from fads to lethal movements, accelerated by Web-enabled digital democracy. Democracy in this sense perhaps is understood best as the electrified version of what Edmund Burke, John Adams and other 18th century liberal conservatives feared as mobocracy. Regardless, today's virtual polity regularly features dilution of content but intensification of emotion via social media. Twitter, one key social media platform, is aptly named.

Where do our beliefs, our ideas that we imagine are simultaneously fresh and enduring, originate? Like coins worn by long use, they often come to us through many hands and over a span of time sufficient for superstition to reemerge as fact. Hoary notions—daubed with the rouge of contemporary jargon and sped along digitally—appear as new. If not from madmen in authority, then via ideologues who scribble as madmen's handmaidens, relentlessly mainstreaming what otherwise would be marginalized.

So it has been with the lie of Palestine, with antisemitism veiled by anti-Zionism. It turns out Theodore Herzl, Leon Pinsker and Max Nordau were wrong. They and other fathers of political Zionism believed the antisemitism flooding Europe at the end of the 19th century resulted from Jewish statelessness. Return them to their ancient status as a sovereign people and the Jews too, like Europe's re-emerging independent nationalities including Greeks, Italians and Germans in their newly sovereign or newly unified nation-states, no longer would be suspect strangers in lands not their own. Instead, they would be "normalized" in their old-new land, the *Altneuland* of Herzl's seminal Zionist work. The Jews' more than 1,800-year history of exile and wandering—stereotyped, belittled, scapegoated, ghettoized and ultimately slaughtered—would be ended.

But it didn't work that way. Rather, indigenous Middle Eastern antisemitism, particularly that rooted in Arab, Sunni Muslim imperialism, found itself reinvigorated by an incipient Islamism promoted during World War I by Imperial Germany to bolster Ottoman Turkey's fight against Great Britain and France. It received a more thorough accelerant via World War II propaganda, funding and training from fascist Italy and Nazi Germany. This European imperialism manifested itself in an Arab nationalist form in mid-twentieth century with Egyptian leader Gamal Abdel Nasser's pan-Arabism and competing Syrian and Iraqi branches of the Ba'ath (Renewal) Party. Renewal, in Arabic, was used commonly in Nazi propaganda to Arab audiences during World War II. Ba'ath Party founders acknowledged the inspirational example they found in the Third Reich, especially its strong man leadership principle, highly organized society and genocidal hatred of the Jews.

> Aside from the Muslim Brotherhood, the Young Egypt Party; the monarchs and military officers in Egypt and Iran; the grand mufti as leader of the Palestine Arabs; Iraq's government; and the Saudi monarchy, additional pro-German forces were arising in the region. The most durable of these would prove to be the Ba'ath, a pan-Arab nationalist party based on the fascist model. One branch would rule Iraq for forty-five years after the war, brought down only by an American led-invasion in 2003; another would rule Syria for a half-century. ... [Party co-founder and former Syrian Prime Minister] Sami al-Jundi, recalled those early days: 'We had been racist admirers of Nazism. We ... were among the

first who liked to translate Hitler's book [*Mein Kampf*]. In
Damascus, we felt admiration for Nazism.[1]

Arab-Islamic imperialism reappeared in a puritanical religious
manner early in the twenty-first century in the Islamic State's murderous "caliphate." The concept had been seeded world-wide through Sau-
di-funded, Wahhabi-influenced mosques and schools from Indonesia
to northern Virginia. Much of that funding came from the West in the
1970s and after as petro-dollars. Wahhabi supersessionism went back
several centuries in the Arabian Peninsula. From the 1890s through
World Wars I and II the roots of Sunni militancy were nourished by
German Arabists, beginning with Kaiser Wilhelm II's Arabist advisor,
Max von Oppenheim. Those von Oppenheim mentored played an even
larger role in German Middle East policy during World War II, always
hoping to promote *jihad* against the British and French.

The "Palestinian George Washington," Haj Amin al-Husseini—the
Nazis' most important non-European World War II collaborator—also
exercised a widely recognized and highly influential pan-Arab and
pan-Islamic leadership. Taking up where the Third Reich ended, the Soviet Union and its satellites stepped in with subsidies, indoctrination
and training. Thus enhanced, bolstered by Soviet anti-colonial agitation
and attaching itself to Western far-left movements, a "new-old" antisemitism soaked back into increasingly receptive European societies
as anti-Zionism after Israel's miraculous 1967 Six-Day War victory. It
increasingly became a universal antidote to European guilt over both
pervasive Jew-hatred that led to the Holocaust and colonial crimes in
Africa, the Middle East and other parts of Asia. Legendary Nazi-hunter
Beate Klarsfeld, for example, saw one instance of the tendency after the
Six-Day War in leftist German students finding it more convenient "to
demonstrate on behalf of Palestinians than to reckon with the crimes of
their own fathers."[2]

Anti-Zionist antisemitism spread from the Near East through Europe to North America, particularly through academia, some Protestant
churches and communications media by the end of the 20th century.
American Jewish defense organizations, self-disarmed by uncritical di-

1 *Nazis, Islamists and the Making of the Modern Middle East*, Rubin and Schwanitz,
pages 128-129.

2 "Militants of Memory," Bookshelf review by Benjamin Balint of *Hunting the Truth*, by
Beate and Serge Klarsfeld, Farrar, Straus and Giroux, 2018, *Wall Street Journal*, March
21, 2018.

versity worship, imaged that Jews as a free and independent people held membership like other peoples in a multi-cultural rainbow. As a result, they too often recognized and confronted the new/old antisemitism belatedly and half-heartedly.

But anti-Zionist antisemitism illustrated how Herzl's old-new Jewish state, Israel, conveniently had become the *Neualt Jude*, the new-old Jew. The collective, or collected, Jew replaced the individual, wandering Jew as target—not that individual Jews outside Israel would remain shielded. The U.S. Holocaust Memorial Museum, despite having examined post-World War II genocides elsewhere, as of this writing has yet to present an exhibit or symposium forthrightly addressing the renewed potential—fomented particularly by Islamists and the post-liberal left—of the specific catastrophe it commemorates. George Will might recommend staring into the black hole of the Holocaust to achieve a realistic appreciation of the depths as well as heights inherent in society and politics, but even for some of those most familiar with the Shoah, the possibility that it remains a process rather than having been an event mutes critical speech.

In the mid-1960s, Elie Wiesel wrote *The Jews of Silence*, about Soviet Jewry brutally repressed by the communist regime. Today's functional equivalent are those Jews emotionally unwilling or psychologically unable to speak for Zionism and Judaism, for Jewish peoplehood. When not silent they sometimes sublimate and, seeking protective coloration in an increasingly threatening environment, rhetorically impugn Israel and its advocates for violating standards no other country is held to.

From classical antiquity through medieval Christianity to the 19th and 20th centuries many people have believed the worst about Jews: Killers of non-Jews, killers of Christ, of children, of nations. When those superstitions have lain dormant, Jews, though almost everywhere and at all times a minority, often tiny, not only survived but also prospered. When those beliefs led to action, forced conversions, expulsions, pogroms and the Holocaust resulted.

Today Jews and non-Jews again live in a time of intensifying, spreading antisemitism. Anti-Zionist antisemitism strives to make intellectually respectable, even mandatory, hatred of the Jewish state. It thereby returns to acceptability open hostility to the Jewish people. The falsehoods entwined in the Palestinian narrative reopen "the Jewish question," as in "what crimes have the Jews committed now and what must we do about, with and to them?"

Journalist Jonathan Rosen observed, shortly after al-Qaeda's destruction of the World Trade Center and attack on the Pentagon on Sept. 11, 2001 that Jews—the Jews—had become a question mark again, as in, "What, are you still here?"

> I had somehow believed that the Jewish Question, which so obsessed both Jews and antisemites in the nineteenth and twentieth centuries, had been solved—most horribly by Hitler's 'final solution,' most hopefully by Zionism. But more and more I feel Jews being turned into a question mark once again. How is it, the world still asks—about Israel, about Jews, about me—that you are still here? I have always known that much of the world wanted Jews simply to disappear, but there are degrees of knowledge, and after September 11 my imagination seems more terribly able to imagine a world of rhetoric fulfilled.

> There are five million [now more than six and a-half million] Jews in Israel and eight million more Jews in the rest of the world. There are one billion [approximately 1.5 billion] Muslims. How has it happened that Israel and 'world Jewry,' along with the United States, is the enemy of so many of them? To be singled out inside a singled-out country is doubly disconcerting. There are a lot of reasons why modernizing, secularizing, globalizing America, whose every decision has universal impact, would disturb large swaths of the world; we are, after all, a superpower. Surely it is stranger that Jews, by their mere presence in the world, would unleash such hysteria.[3]

No, not strange at all. Its "normality" is made clear by the recurrent vitriol against a central—and chronically, often intentionally misrepresented—Jewish concept, that of the Chosen People with a Promised Land. Chosen people, not by virtue of being somehow superior, but rather exactly because of their comparative insignificance in numbers and raw power. That is, as the rabbinic sages taught, selected just so, to carry a message much greater than themselves. Promised land as in a stage, a platform from which to exemplify Judaism's message, rather than as an unmerited reward. Promised "because from Zion shall go forth Torah, and the word of God from Jerusalem" (Isaiah 2:3).

---

3 "The Uncomfortable Question of Anti-Semitism," *The New York Times Magazine*, Nov. 4, 2001.

And what is that Word? A Hebrew prophet summarized some-time late in the eighth century B.C.E. or very early in the seventh—long before Jesus, longer before Mohammed: "It has been told you, O man, what is good, And what the Lord requires of you; Only to do justly, and to love mercy, and walk humbly with your God" (Micah, 6:8). Justice, mercy (compassion), and humility, in that order. How often much of mankind finds those three instructions—that Torah, for one meaning of Torah is instruction—burdensome. And especially that emphasis on justice. Can we not do as we will, do what gives pleasure, and if someone else happens to be hurt, that's life, isn't it? Judaism, the Jews, say no, life has a higher purpose. Not by original sin, but by this original insistence they painted a bull's-eye on themselves.

Yet Jews as the bearers of Judaism have been from the start also a sort of superpower, a spiritual one, carrying this universal—if often unwelcomed—divine message of individual ethical responsibility. But even when unwelcomed, the message has been so inescapably influential that both Christianity and Islam were compelled to present themselves *ab initio* not as something completely new but rather as inheritors and completions of Judaism, branches superseding the trunk. The former grew as "the new Israel," the latter as "the final revelation."

When oppressed, the Jews—at least a critical mass of them—preserved that universal spiritual message. Most Jews, like most non-Jews, are in the historic sense quite ordinary people. But when relatively free, they—or at least individual members of their tribe—have been astonishingly productive, inexplicably disproportionate contributors to civilization. Those contributions extend over three millennia, from some of the greatest poetry ever written, epitomized by the "Song of Songs," to the fundamentals of the computer age as developed by Johann van Neumann and advanced by his students and disciples. They were often Jewish, many of them Israeli. They are closely analyzed by George Gilder as both examples of individual Jews' disproportionately high creativity and the benefit to mankind at large from free, liberal capitalistic societies.[4] One advantage of such societies is the opportunity they offer to that sliver of unusually creative Jews. The Jews amount to less than 0.25 percent of the world's population. Yet from among them have emerged 25 percent of all Nobel Prize winners—100 times more than "proportionate." No other people, large or small, comes close. Reason enough to hate them and their exceptional state.

---

4 *The Israel Test: Why the World's Most Besieged State is a Beacon of Freedom and Hope for the World Economy*, Richard Vigilante Books, 2009.

Prof. B.Z. Sobel of Haifa University (by way of Ohio's Miami and Massachusetts' Brandeis universities) used to say that of all peoples who were influential beyond their own borders in antiquity, only two remained so and basically intact in modern times—the Chinese and the Jews. The Chinese, of course, were never exiled from their homeland and constitute roughly one-fifth of humankind, not a fraction of a fraction of one percent. Of the scores of nations born or re-born since the end of World War II, few have begun with less and none achieved more, democratically, economically, scientifically, culturally and militarily, and none under such unrelenting threats, as Israel. Envy and resentment being constants of human nature, here lies emotion enough to revive antisemitism through anti-Zionism. But a pretext, a trigger, is required to transform emotion into action. That trigger has been the lie of Palestine.

So the resurgence of antisemitism via anti-Zionism is not strange after all. Rejection, supersession, envy, fear, scapegoating long have found in Jews, as a small tribe, and in the Jew, isolated or isolatable, the prototypical object and ideal target. Instead of strange, resurgent antisemitism—at times wearing and at other times discarding the cloak of anti-Zionism—amounts to a regression to the mean. In 2016, Prof. Alvin Rosenfeld of the University of Indiana, a specialist in the study of antisemitism, admitted he'd been wrong for many years to believe that after the Holocaust hatred of Jews would not reappear as a major trend throughout the West.

Israeli novelist Aharon Appelfeld, writing as had Rosenfeld, shortly after the Sept. 11, 2001 horrors and one year into the Palestinian Arabs' second intifada that would murder 1,100 Israelis and visitors before sputtering out in 2005, put it this way:

> I used to feel that those of us who had suffered in the Holocaust were immune to fear. I was wrong. We are more sensitive to danger. We can smell it. A few days ago, a Holocaust survivor came over to my table [at a Jerusalem coffee shop where Appelfeld often wrote] and enumerated the dangers ahead of us. During the war, he had been in three death camps. He was a master of dangers. There wasn't a danger that he didn't know in the most minute detail.

> The daily disasters evoke images of the Holocaust. Fifty-six years have passed, and the images don't go away. Last night, a

man approached me and said that he reads all my books with great diligence. Like me, he was an orphaned child during the war, roaming the forests and taking refuge with farmers. He, too, arrived in Israel. He is an engineer, and he is worried about Jewish destiny. Why do the Jews arouse such hatred? he asked. We had naively thought that all the anger and hatred toward us would disappear once we had our own state. I didn't know what to say. I have never dealt in abstract questions—I try to see the world in pictures. And so I kept quiet while he, dismayed, also kept quiet.[5]

At first glance, it might seem odd that Jews should have been, and are again in many quarters—in the Middle East and Europe, and increasingly in North America—the subject of a question, the "Jewish question" or even "the Jewish problem" that requires a "solution." The query is not new. The Enlightenment stimulated, among other things, "local learned societies" that brought the movement "down from the realm of books and ideas to the level of concrete reforms," according to historians Lynn Hunt, Thomas Martin, Barbara Rosenwein and Bonnie Smith. These societies often sponsored essay contests, such as the one in Metz in 1785 which asked, "Are there means for making the Jews happier and more useful in France?" The society "approved essays that argued for granting civil rights to Jews."[6] Two decades later Napoleon Bonaparte would adopt such means, though historian Berel Wein has argued that the emperor was interested more in the Jews' ultimate disappearance through assimilation than their continuance as a distinct people. In any case, Napoleon's emancipation of Jews from their ghettos and social and economic restrictions was opposed by monarchs across the continent.

Enlightenment fathers, including Denis Diderot and Voltaire, disdained the Jews. The former said they bore "all the defects peculiar to an ignorant and superstitious nation." As for the latter, Voltaire's antisemitism was criticized by America's second president, John Adams, in an 1808 letter. Adams famously wrote, "How is it possible [that he] should represent the Hebrews in such a contemptible light? They are the most glorious nation that ever inhabited this Earth. The Romans and their Empire were but a Bauble in comparison of the Jews. They have given

---

5 "Talk of the Town, Tuesday and After," *The New Yorker*, Sept. 24, 2001.
6 *The Making of the West: Peoples and Cultures, A Concise History*, by Hunt, Martin, Rosenwein and Smith, Bedford/St. Martin's, 2013, page 576.

religion to three quarters of the Globe and have influenced the affairs of Mankind more, and more happily, than any other Nation ancient or modern."[7]

Adams' philosemitism led him to pre-Zionism. He wrote in 1819 that he desired the Jews marching "into Judea & making a conquest of that country. ... For I really wish the Jews again in Judea an independent nation." His wish was not unconditional. Adams believed that "once restored to an independent government & no longer persecuted" Jews "would soon wear away some of the asperities and peculiarities of their character & possibly in time become liberal Unitarian christians [sic.] for your Jehovah is our Jehovah & your God of Abraham Isaac and Jacob is our God." But even in their prickly, pre-liberal Unitarian Christian condition the Jews were, in Adams's eyes, "a glorious nation" that "more happily" influenced humanity than any other.

Mark Twain's portrait of the Jews is better-known and less conditional than Adams'. Twain had shed anti-Jewish stereotypes common in the United States by the time of his famous 1898 Harper's magazine essay, "Concerning the Jews." In Vienna two years earlier he had witnessed numerous antisemitic attacks, political and physical. Twain identified the cause of Jew-hatred as economic envy more than religious difference and wrote, "The Egyptian, the Babylonian, and the Persian rose, filled the planet with sound and splendor, then ... passed away. The Greek and the Roman followed. The Jew saw them all, beat them all, and is now what he always was, exhibiting no decadence, no infirmities of age, no weakening of his parts . ... All things are mortal but the Jew; all other forces pass, but he remains. What is the secret of his immortality?"

Rather than try to answer his own question by exploring the Jews' understanding of their chosen people, promised land divine mission to live by and spread God's word, Twain commented somewhat facetiously on the first World Zionist Congress just held in Switzerland. Of Herzl's plan for a Jewish state in Palestine, Twain said, "I am not the Sultan [Turkey's Ottoman Empire still ruled much of the Middle East, including the Holy Land], and I am not objecting; but if that concentration of the cunningest brains in the world are going to be made into a free country (bar Scotland), I think it would be politic to stop it. It will not be well to let that race find out its strength. If the horses knew theirs, we should not ride anymore."[8]

---

7 "John Adams embraces a Jewish homeland," by Michael Feldberg, director, Jewish Historical Society, http://www.jewishworldreview.com/jewish/adams_israel.asp.
8 "Concerning the Jews," by Mark Twain, *Harper's New Magazine*, September, 1899

Winston Churchill, as his official biographer, historian Sir Martin Gilbert noted in *Churchill and the Jews: A Lifelong Friendship* (Henry Holt & Co., 2007), lived and worked in an environment in which antisemitism was rampant among Europe's ruling elites, including the English. Churchill said, "Some people like Jews and some do not, but no thoughtful person can doubt the fact that they are beyond all question the most formidable and most remarkable race which has ever appeared in the world." In 1921, Prime Minister David Lloyd George gave Churchill, as colonial secretary, responsibility for developing policies by which Britain would implement its 1917 Balfour Declaration. The declaration supported reestablishment of the Jewish national home in Palestine. In his 1922 White Paper on the subject, Churchill stated "the Jews are in Palestine of a right; not on sufferance."

As Gilbert observed in an interview, Churchill and many of his contemporaries were deeply versed in the Bible. But unlike most others, for Churchill the Bible stories were real, including those about Moses, God's promise to the Jews, and Jewish values. Visiting Jerusalem in 1921, the colonial secretary gave a speech in which he said "we owe to the Jews in the Christian revelation a system of ethics, which, even if it were entirely separated from the supernatural, would be incomparably the most precious possession of mankind, worth in fact the fruits of all other wisdom and learning put together. On that system and by that faith there has been built out of the wreck of the Roman Empire the whole of our existing civilization."

During Churchill's short visit to British-controlled Palestine that year, he was struck by "the contrasts between the extraordinary negative points of view put forth by the Palestinian Arabs and the equally positive ones put forth by the Zionists," Gilbert said. "Churchill didn't like negativism and he couldn't comprehend why the Palestinian Arabs were being so negative. It's quite curious. If you have a look" at what they told him, "you'll find that three or four [assertions] are actually in the Hamas Charter today, such as the world Jewish conspiracy and so on. ... When Churchill spoke to the Palestinian Arabs, he actually said to them, 'You've got to help the Zionists. They're people of quality and inasmuch as they'll succeed, you'll succeed. Without them, you won't succeed.'"[9]

If false, that statement would have been fatuous irrelevance. If

---

(written in 1898).

9 "Churchill and the Jews: One of his finest hours," by Amy K. Rosenthal, *World Jewish Digest*, www.worldjewishdigest.com and www.aish.com.

true, easily heard as a condescending reproach. In any case, Churchill told Parliament that "the Jews have developed the country, grown orchards and grain fields out of the desert, built schools and great buildings, constructed irrigation projects and water power houses [electricity generating plants], and have made Palestine a much better place to live than it was before they came a few years ago. To Jewish enterprise, the Arab owes nearly everything he has." But "fanaticism and a sort of envy have driven the Arabs to violence."

Religious and ethnic fanaticism and a sort of envy are elements bleached from the Palestinian narrative by Western proponents but enduring in Palestinian rejectionism. For example, Hamas (the Palestinian Islamic Resistance Movement), to which Gilbert referred, is a U.S. government-designated terrorist organization. It has dominated the Gaza Strip and contends strategically, though at times cooperates tactically, with Fatah, the main component of the Palestinian Authority that administers the West Bank. Though funded by Iran's Shi'ite Muslim Islamic Revolutionary Republic, Hamas is a branch of the Egyptian-based, anti-Western, anti-Christian and anti-Jewish Muslim Brotherhood. Founded in 1928, the Brotherhood became the incubator of Sunni Islamic extremist movements eventually including al-Qaeda.

The Brotherhood's credo was and is: "Allah is our objective. The Prophet [Mohammad] is our leader. The Quran is our law. Jihad is our way. Dying in the way of Allah is our highest hope." Western journalists and academics periodically discern what they believe are noteworthy divisions between Hamas's "armed" and "political" wings—as if it were not a unitary organization.

Envy and hatred of the Jews, including on the part of Palestinian terrorists, at times may be muted by immediate personal self-interest. Hamas leaders including Ismail Haniyeh, Palestinian Authority "prime minister" after the 2006 elections, have sent family members to Israel for medical treatment while their organization simultaneously prepared to murder Israelis.[10] And not just family members. During a mass hunger strike by Palestinian Arabs jailed on terrorism charges in 2017, the former head of Israel's bureau of prisons claimed Israeli care saved the life of Hamas' new leader in the Gaza Strip. Orit Adato (Lt. Gen., Res.) "pointed to Yahya Sinwar, the hard-line Hamas leader in Gaza, who, she said, is alive today only because of brain surgery he received, reportedly for a tumor, while in Israeli prison.

---

10 "Hamas leader's daughter treated in Israel hospital," *The Telegraph* (U.K.), Oct. 20, 2014.

'When they say they are not being treated well, I would ask you and others to give a phone call to one specific person, Yahya Sinwar, who is alive nowadays just because of life-saving surgery he was given,' she said. The terror group leader served 22 years after being sentenced to multiple life terms for masterminding the kidnapping and murder of two Israeli soldiers in 1988. He was one of more than 1,000 Palestinian terrorists and terrorism suspects exchanged for one captured Israeli soldier, Gilad Shalit, in 2011.

In March, Sinwar was elected Gaza leader of Hamas, a terror group publicly committed to the destruction of Israel by violent means which has fought three wars with Israel since it seized control of the Strip [from Fatah] in 2007.[11]

Hamas (as an Arabic word, the acronym Hamas means "zeal") does not conceal but rather spotlights its Islamic fanaticism. Its fervor is inculcated in Gaza's children—at early ages they are costumed by adults as suicide bombers and shown cartoons of Israelis as rats and spiders, Israel and the United States as vultures—and celebrated at mass rallies by the "resistance's" adults. Israel's humanitarianism toward believers such as Sinwar may reflect a Jewish obligation—Micah's injunction to love mercy—to fellow human beings. It may reflect Israeli policy, or perhaps Jewish foolishness. Maybe all three. What it does not demonstrate is racism toward Palestinian Arabs, including their worst representatives.

Asked about parallels between early 21st century radical Islam and 20th century Nazism, Gilbert said "what they have in common, for whatever reason, is that both of them have decided that the most effective demon is the Jew. All I can say is that Churchill was a persistent opponent of antisemitism." Radical Islam—better, Islamic supremacism—and Nazism do have demonization of Jews in common, and not by accident. Cross-pollinizing between the two ideologies intensified early in the Third Reich with a key Palestinian Arab-Nazi connection. This tie, and a close parallel, between Palestinian Arab movements and the Soviet Union and its clients, such as Cuba, in the 1960s and '70s, are discussed below. It was not Zionism and the Jewish state that was born in ideological sin, but rather its enemies, Palestinian Arab rejectionism

---

11 "We saved the life of Hamas' Gaza leader, says Israel's ex-prison chief, dismissing strikers' complaints," *Times of Israel*, May 11, 2017.

in particular.

Demonization is central to antisemitism, and to Islamist anti-Americanism. For that reason, leaders of Iran's Islamic Republic long have labeled Israel "the little Satan," the United States "the great Satan." The phrases are not rhetorical flourishes but rather expressions of core belief and motivation. At mass rallies organized by the Iranian government and its supporters, mentions of "the little Satan" and "the great Satan" have been and continue to be followed by shouts of "Death to Israel!" and "Death to America!" Sometimes the rallies feature parades of military units and equipment, including missiles draped with banners emblazoned with vows to fulfill those shouted demands. For example, when Iranian-backed Houthi rebels in Yemen attacked a Saudi frigate in the Red Sea—perhaps mistaking it for a U.S. vessel—killing two Saudi sailors and wounding three, a voice narrating a video tape recording of the attack shouts the Houthi battle cry: "God is great, death to America, death to Israel, a curse on the Jews and victory for Islam!"[12] The words, theatrics and deeds resonate far from Iran and not only among Shi'ite Muslims.

The Nazi Holocaust made antisemitism—Jew-hatred—disreputable in the West. For two generations. But the oldest hatred is back, revived and recertified by the lie of Palestine. Hence the Hamas Charter calls for the destruction of Israel, the establishment of a Sunni Muslim theocracy over it, the West Bank and Gaza Strip, and genocide of the Jews. Even so, Hamas has Western apologists, including leading members of the British Labor Party. And demonstrators outside the White House in 2003, who opposed the U.S.-led war against Iraqi dictator Saddam Hussein. They also denounced Israel in solidarity with the terrorist organization. "We're all Hamas now!" some declared.

Some insist they do not hate Jews as individuals and would tolerate them as members of a religious minority, one perhaps quaint, obsolescent or irrelevant. But simultaneously they are convinced by the Palestinian narrative and so believe the Jewish state to have been the wrong, even criminal answer to the Jewish question, a question reopened and clamoring once again for "the right" answer.

---

12 "Exclusive: Pentagon Believes Attack on Saudi Frigate Meant for U.S. Warship," *Fox News*, Jan. 31, 2017.

CHAPTER TWO

Denial, Revisionism and Narrative

"In 2007, a 22-year-old man who called [Elie] Wiesel's account of the Holocaust fictitious pulled him out of a hotel elevator in San Francisco and attacked him."[1]

The attacker's name was Eric Hunt, who, when convicted on false imprisonment-felony hate crime charges one year later, was described as a "troubled" New Jersey man. He had yanked Wiesel out of the elevator in an attempt to "persuade" him "to renounce the Holocaust." But metaphysically, his name could have been Haj Amin el-Husseini, or that of el-Husseini's relative and ideological heir Yasser Arafat, or Arafat's successor as leader of the Palestine Liberation Organization, Mahmoud Abbas. Not to mention many other "troubled" people, including the countless followers of al-Husseini, Arafat and Abbas, their apologists, enthusiasts or competitors—Arab, Muslim, European, North American, Christian, secular or even Jewish. Any passionate subscriber to the Palestinian narrative would do.

"Narrative" is the post-modern literary, historical or psychological term of art for a tightly held, highly personalized substitution and often partial if not complete falsification of factual history. Can history be factual? Isn't it an artificial construct by those with "hegemonic" power in any given society?

Is medicine fact-based, or is what one physician's biopsy reveals to be a malignant tumor just another doctor's wart? Are metallurgy and

---

1 "Elie Wiesel, Auschwitz Survivor and Nobel Peace Prize Winner, Dies at 87," *The New York Times*, July 3, 2016.

alchemy branches of the same discipline, or does the former rest on science, the latter on superstition? On Dec. 7, 1941 did Japan bomb Pearl Harbor, or was it the other way around, with the United States launching a surprise attack on Tokyo?

If reality hangs, Rashomon-like, on one's personal, subjective perspective, on a gaggle of conspiracy theorists' Web sites, then even though one person's blizzard is never another's heat wave, non-existent tunnels under a real Washington, D.C. pizzeria could be the site of a fictitious child sex abuse ring connected to Hillary Clinton—as asserted by the Internet-deluded in the fall of 2016. If those pizzeria tunnels were real, or at least virtually real, then one person's terrorist could be another's "freedom fighter"—as apologists for Palestinian terror have asserted for decades. This gossamer foundation of moral relativism constitutes an imagined shield for those who believe lofty sentiments immunize them against at least passive complicity in terrorist murder. By such pretexts they excuse, if not justify, the slaughter of Israelis and, if necessary, their Jewish and non-Jewish backers. They cover their excuse with the academic gloss of post-modernism, which in this case amounts to not only Holocaust revisionism and Zionist demonization but also Jewish obliteration. Such obliteration is epitomized, as noted, by the United Nations Educational, Social and Cultural Organization's repeated denials in 2016 and 2017 of Jerusalem's Jewish identity. First the word, then the deed. But if theft is not shopping, if rape and romantic sex, murder and execution describe opposites, then fact and fancy do diverge. Fancy, that is, narrative, can displace truth, including the Jewish people's 3,000 year connection to Jerusalem, including the fact of old Jew-hatred made new again by anti-Zionism. It just cannot do so honestly. First one must yank Wiesel out of an elevator, and prepare to again expel the Jews from their state.

Recovering truth

In reality, "truth is the only merit that gives dignity or worth to history." Thus declared Lord Acton, the British historian best known for his dictum that "power corrupts, and absolute power corrupts absolutely." And not just for history is truth the essential merit, but also much else in human life, including journalism, medicine, psychology, and even art worth cherishing. The Palestinian narrative—the lie of Palestine—corrupts, and the more homage paid it, the more absolutely it corrupts. It does so by confiscating Jewish, particularly Israeli, history. Hence the otherwise ludicrous intention by the Palestinian Authority in late 2016 to insist on the "return" of the Dead Seas scrolls—as if Arabs, Muslims or anyone else except Jews living in Judea 2,000-plus years ago had anything to do with them.[2]

Hence also the charge reported by the official PA daily that U.N. Secretary-General Guterres "clearly and explicitly sinned against peace and the Palestinian-Israeli political agreement when he claimed ... that he 'believes in the connection between Jerusalem and the Jews.'"[3] Like PA Jerusalem affairs minister al-Husseini, the authority's grand mufti and its official newspaper demanded Guterres apologize for stating the obvious. They repeated the PA's narrative fiction that "Jerusalem and all of Palestine—from the [Jordan] River to the [Mediterranean] Sea—are the land of the Palestinian people, and their history is its history... Jerusalem is Palestinian Arab. It belongs only to the followers of Islam and Christianity, and not Judaism."

By insisting on this nihilistic and annihilationist fantasy, the mufti and newspaper were not breaking with PA President Mahmoud Abbas. Rather, they echoed his claim three years earlier on PA Television that assertions of Jewish history in Jerusalem and the land of Israel (*eretz Yisrael*) were "delusional myths." It should be noted that Abbas, repeatedly described by Western and Israeli officials as a Palestinian "moderate," received his doctorate from a Soviet-era university in Moscow for a conspiracy theory dissertation, *The Other Side: The Secret Relationship Between Nazism and Zionism*, which put the number of Jewish Holocaust victims at less than 1 million. Call Abbas a slightly more subtle version of Eric Hunt, the man who attacked Elie Wiesel.

Unconnected to—in fact in aggressive denial of—facts, the Palestinian narrative advances the aim of returning the Jewish people, by force when possible, by diplomacy, lawfare and mass psychological abuse when not, to their pre-state, pre-Holocaust status of powerless scapegoats. Through anti-Zionism, it renormalizes antisemitism and with it the Jews' "usual" position from the Roman expulsions to Israel's rebirth—nearly 2,000 years—as inferiors. For many in the Sunni Muslim majority of the Middle East, that means returning Jews to the status of *dhimmi*, a "protected" member of the "people of the Book" (Jews and Christians who hold to the Hebrew or Christian Bibles). The *dhimmi* may live safely—"protected"—among Muslims but only so long as he or

---

2 "Palestinians to Demand 'Return' of Dead Sea Scrolls," *The Algemeiner*, Nov. 8, 2016.

3 "The [Palestinian Authority] Grand Mufti: Guterres' statements are severe violations," *Al-Hayat al-Jadida*, Jan. 31, 2017.

she pays the *jizya* tax on non-believers and accepts second-class standing. That's in theory. In reality, protected only so long as the tax is paid, inferiority accepted and the Muslim ruler determines it is politically or economically useful to keep chronic Jew-hatred in check.

Egypt's beleaguered and periodically murdered Coptic Christians—10 percent of the population and an indigenous, pre-Islamic people—exemplify the reality of *dhimmi* life. Implicitly if not quite yet explicitly, anti-Zionist antisemitism reopens "the Jewish question." If not for all Jews everywhere, then it does so for all Jews anywhere who insist on equality and especially from within a sovereign state. That is, for Jews who reject dhimmitude.

I did not fully understand this, sitting high in the visitors' gallery at the U.N. General Assembly hall one day late in 1988. I was listening to Farouq Qaddoumi—far away and small at the rostrum—declaim on "the Question of Palestine." Qaddoumi (Abu Luft) was, with Arafat (Abu Ammar), Khalid al-Wazir (Abu Jihad), Salah Kalahf (Abu Iyad), Mahmoud Abbas (Abu Mazen) and one or two other Abu's a founding member of Fatah in 1959. That is, eight years before Israel conquered the West Bank, Gaza Strip, Sinai Peninsula, Golan Heights and eastern Jerusalem in the 1967 Six-Day War. So to paraphrase Bill Clinton's 1992 presidential campaign focus on the economy, it wasn't the occupation, stupid, not fundamentally. Not the occupation of the West Bank, Gaza Strip, Golan Heights and Sinai Desert at any rate. It was the occupation of Israel by Israelis, of a sliver of the original British Mandate for Palestine by Jews. Fatah would become the major faction in the PLO, the establishment of which was orchestrated by Egypt's Nasser in 1964. After the 1993 Israeli-Palestinian Oslo accords, Fatah emerged as the dominant movement in the Palestinian Authority.

Fatah is a reverse acronym for Palestinian National Liberation Movement and an Arabic word meaning, in Islamic terms, "opening" or "conquest." The Palestine it sought to open and "liberate" by conquest was Israel.

Qaddoumi served as the PLO's de facto "foreign minister." Considered a hard-liner, he later would reject Oslo and even personal meetings with Israelis. Qaddoumi droned on that day to a nearly empty hall about Israel's sins, numerous and irredeemable. Palestine had been created by the League of Nations soon after World War I primarily to enable re-establishment of the Jewish national home. Prior to conquest by Great Britain in 1917 during the war, the territories that became Mandate Palestine had been for 500 years part of the Turkish Ottoman Empire. Never had there been a country called Palestine or an Arab people known as Palestinians.

Mandatory Palestine was maintained by the League's successor, the United Nations, after World War II and administered by the British through a League/U.N. mandate. But Palestine as a legal, territorial entity had ceased to exist decades before Qaddoumi spoke. It had been replaced by two successor states, one Arab—Jordan (originally Transjordan)—in 1921 and one Jewish—Israel—in 1948 in an incomplete "two-state solution."

Technically, while Qaddoumi talked, the remaining "question of Palestine" applied only to allocation of sovereignty over the disputed West Bank and Gaza Strip, the remaining five percent—Jordan comprising 77.5 percent, Israel 17.5 percent—of the lands originally intended for the Mandate. But for Qaddoumi, and most of the United Nations, dominated as the world body was by the Soviet bloc and partially overlapping Arab League, Organization of the Islamic Conference and "Non-Aligned Movement" countries, the question of Palestine really meant the question of Israel. That is, the question of how Israel best might be reduced, then erased. This much I did understand, and commented on as editor of *Near East Report*, a weekly newsletter on U.S. Middle East policy. (*NER* was published in association with the American Israel Public Affairs Committee [AIPAC], the largest registered U.S. pro-Israel lobby.)

What I did not quite recognize at the time was how insistence on examining "the question of Palestine," that is, the inadmissibility of the Jewish state, would lead to reopening "the Jewish question," the inadmissibility of free, equal and sovereign Jews. Where were debates, let alone obsessions, over the questions of Kenya, Yugoslavia, Indonesia, the United States or any other country, for that matter? The question of Palestine would, through the half-way house of anti-Zionism, help revive antisemitism, *de facto* if not *de jure*. The resurrection of antisemitism would, in turn, impel consideration among some of a renewed drive to provide a final solution to the Jewish question, or as often put before the Holocaust, the Jewish problem.

A year later, on Connecticut Avenue in downtown Washington, D.C., I passed a young black man wearing a *kefiyeh*, originally the traditional headscarf of Arab herdsmen. It was the first time I'd seen a *kefiyeh* worn in the United States. Introduced to Western television audiences by Arafat at his 1974 U.N. General Assembly speech, the *kefiyeh* by the end of the 1980s was becoming a fashion statement, like a Che Guevara

T-shirt, for those compelled to signal their revolutionary hipness. Guevara was, of course, Fidel Castro's enthusiastic executioner who once, while at the United Nations, boasted of his firing squads and pledged to continue operating them. A wary Fidel dispatched him from Cuba to spread, at arm's length, "the revolution" in South America. Conveniently for Castro and his long reign, Guevara would die at the hands of American-supported Bolivians. No matter. The revolutionary hipness, the fashion statement signaled by U.S. and European kefiyeh wearers survived. The statement was this: People who kill Jews were again fashionable.

Semiotically, the *kefiyeh* was a cloth swastika, but with a critical advantage: While lingering anti-antisemitism of the World War II generation still made the Nazi symbol taboo among respectable Westerners, anti-Zionism sanitized and sanctified the *kefiyeh*, culturally and ideologically. For those who chanted "Death to Israel!"—which by the time of al-Qaeda's Sept. 11, 2001 attacks against New York City's World Trade Center and the Pentagon in Washington had become "Death to the Jews!" in European mass marches and on American campuses such as San Francisco State University—the *kefiyeh*-as-swastika worked perfectly. Its elevation as a revolutionary totem trumped—yet simultaneously advanced—its blatantly reactionary demand. Death to Israel. Death to the Jews.

Hitler didn't finish the job!" "Go back to Russia!" and "Get out or we'll kill you!" a mob of students and other putatively enlightened, self-validated, anti-racist racists screamed as they surrounded pro-Israel classmates at San Francisco State in 2002. Prof. Laurie Zoloth, director of Jewish studies at the school, said "I turned to the police and to every administrator I could find and asked them to remove the counter-demonstrators from the plaza. ... The police told me that they had been told not to arrest anyone, and that if they did, 'it would start a riot.' I told them that it already was a riot." Eventually, the pro-Israel students "were marched to the campus Hillel House under police protection and a guard was posted at the door."[4]

"Zoloth also described what life is like for Jewish students and faculty at SFSU, noting her despair at the emergence of posters around campus equating Zionism with racism and Jews with Nazis, and pictures of cans of soup labeled 'Canned Palestinian Children Meat, slaughtered according to Jewish rites under American license.'" The blood libel, hardly updated, as if by Andy Warhol.

---

4 "Antisemitic riot at San Francisco State University," *The Jerusalem Post*, May 16, 2002.

"This is not civic discourse, this is not free speech, and this is the Weimar Republic with brown shirts it cannot control," the professor told *The Jerusalem Post*. Or chose not to control, in the case of administrators at San Francisco State and campuses elsewhere. Since then, similar incidents—including shouting down pro-Israel speakers, excluding pro-Israel student groups, intimidating and even attacking Jewish students—on campuses across the United States, Canada and in England have become numbingly repetitious.

Before the Holocaust, American universities often sought to suppress the number of Jews admitted as students. "Gentlemen's agreements" or "*numerus clausus*," implicit when not explicit, operated discreetly. Antisemitism faced by those Jews who were admitted as students was frequently less than discreet. After World War II, the number and percentage of Jews at universities, as students and faculty, exploded and remains what "social justice warriors" might consider disproportionately high. Nevertheless—or perhaps just so—via anti-Zionist antisemitism powered by the Palestinian narrative, by the lies of Palestine, a new version of the "Gentlemen's agreement" operates to intimidate and censor supporters of Israel. It does so not with discretion, but rather an often naked vehemence.

In June 2017, conditions at San Francisco State only having deteriorated over the previous 15 years, Jewish students filed a federal civil rights suit against the university for enabling the creation of a hostile environment. That is, condoning a reign of antisemitism on campus. Referring to an April, 2016 campus appearance by Jerusalem Mayor Nir Barkat, the suit charged that protesters used bullhorns to drown out the mayor's speech and yelled and chanted "Intifada," "Get the [expletive] off our campus," and "From the river to the sea, Palestine will be free" while university administrators allowed the disruption to continue and instructed campus police to "stand down."[5]

"SFSU has not merely fostered and embraced anti-Jewish hostility—it has systematically supported ... student groups as they have doggedly organized their efforts to target, threaten, and intimidate Jewish students on campus and deprive them of their civil rights and their ability to feel safe and secure as they pursue their education," the law suit charged. It asserted this was consistent with SFSU administration behavior over the years, including the 2002 riot and 1994 10-foot mural on the student union building "that featured yellow Stars of David inter-

5 "Lawsuit claims San Francisco State, university leaders, have history of cultivating campus environment hostile to Jews," *Los Angeles Times*, June 19, 2017.

twined with dollar signs, skulls and crossbones, and the words 'African Blood.'" Such legal action could have been taken against numerous other such former institutions of higher learning.

There were straws in the wind aplenty even earlier, hinting at the dismissal and ostracizing to come. A small one: One evening in 1981 my friend Steven L. Joseph, a young lawyer, was attending a reception in New York City and found himself conversing with a junior diplomat from what was then termed a "third world" country. Once his interlocutor realized Joseph was Jewish, he was made to defend Israel.

"Look," asked the foreign service officer, "why don't the Israelis just give the Palestinians the land they want and be done with the conflict?"

Joseph answered the question with a question. "How far do you think it is from Jerusalem to Tel Aviv?"

"Oh, 300 or 400 miles," the diplomat guessed.

"It's just 35 miles," Joseph corrected him.

The fellow—from a geographically and demographically large country—chortled. "You Zionists will say anything." Actually, from Ramallah to the United Nations to American campuses, it's been the anti-Zionists who've said and will say, will insist, on anything, anything to undermine the Jewish state and marginalize the Jewish people.

In American law, since the trial of printer John Peter Zenger in colonial times, truth has been a defense against libel. But when it comes to refutations of anti-Zionist and antisemitic libels, truth often is irrelevant.

CHAPTER THREE

The Lie Martyrs Truth

H OW WAS THE reemergence of open antisemitism possible when the Palestinian narrative rested on a chain of fairly obvious falsehoods and fabrications? I had the opportunity to help itemize and expose those allegations as editor (under the supervision of Leonard Davis, later Lenny Ben-David) of the 1985 and 1989 editions of *Myths and Facts: A Concise Record of the Arab-Israeli Conflict*, published by Near East Research, Inc. Alan Dershowitz's widely-selling *The Case for Israel* (John Wiley & Sons, 2003) updated the exposé's effort. Ben-Dror Yemini more recently and thoroughly dismantled the anti-Zionist, anti-Israel indictments of dispossession, ethnic cleansing, aggression and racism in his *Industry of Liles: Media, Academia, and the Israeli-Arab Conflict* (Institute for the Global Study of Antisemitism and Policy, 2017). So even for those not inclined to study tomes like Howard M. Sachar's *A History of Israel from the Rise of Zionism to Our Time* (Alfred A. Knopf, 1996, Second Edition), *Israel: A History,* by Martin Gilbert (Doubleday, 1998) or *The Siege: The Saga of Israel and Zionism,* by Conor Cruise O'Brien (Simon and Schuster, 1986) the facts "are out there." They always have been. But as the poet T. S. Eliot observed, "humankind cannot bear very much reality." Especially about itself, emphatically about the Jews and their state.

So Eric Hunt felt driven to pull Elie Wiesel from an elevator and try to threaten him into denying the Holocaust. So people—beginning with many Arab Muslims, Palestinian Arabs in particular—feel driven to deny the Jews their unique connection to an ancient homeland and to see them expelled once more from *eretz Yisrael*. So they are indulged in that emotion by many non-Muslims, non-Palestinians the world over. Hence when Palestinian leader Mahmoud Abbas in his Sept. 22, 2016 U.N. General Assembly speech denied the Jews' 3,000-year connection to the land of Israel, he was neither laughed at nor jeered from the rostrum. Instead, he found the United States and European Union recommitting themselves to the presumed necessity of a Palestinian state on the West Bank, Gaza Strip and eastern Jerusalem, as if that were Abbas' or Palestinian nationalism's objective.

Weeks after Abbas' 2016 General Assembly speech, UNESCO's governing board—squinting through the wrong end of reality's telescope—approved its monocular resolution recognizing only the historic-religious ties of Muslims to al-Aqsa mosque on Haram al-Sharif in Jerusalem's Old City. Nothing about that sacred space being the Temple Mount of Jews and Judaism, nothing about the site's pre-Islamic Christian connections. In fact, before conversion to al-Aqsa in the eighth century C.E., the mosque had been the Byzantine Church of St. Mary of Justinian. The New Testament's most dramatic moments in Christ's life take place on Temple Mount. Beyond that, UNESCO erased the original Jewish links that rendered the site religiously sacred and historically significant in the first place. Temple Mount, after all, was the location of the biblical First and Second Temples. UNESCO might as well have noted the cultural centrality of Paris to Western civilization while ignoring the city's French nature. The U.N. body's sins were those of omission, though silent erasure by anti-Zionist antisemitism can be as efficient as vehement inversion.

Also in 2016, former University of California President Mark G. Yudof and Michigan State University history professor emeritus Ken Walzer updated Prof. Zoloth's 2002 observations about anti-Zionist antisemitism on American college campuses:

> Anti-Israel sentiment mixed with age-old anti-Semitism has reached a fever pitch at Vassar College.... In the spring of 2014, the boycott of a course in the International Studies Program—because it involved a trip to Israel—included heckling students and picketing the class. During the fall of 2015, attempts were made to boycott Sabra hummus because the maker of this popular food is partly owned by an Israeli food company.

The most recent incident was a talk on February 3 by Jasbir Puar, a Rutgers associate professor of women's and gender studies. The address, 'Inhumanist Biopolitics: How Palestine Matters,' was sponsored by eight Vassar departments and programs, including Jewish Studies and American Studies.

Ms. Puar began by exhorting the students to support a boycott of Israel as part of 'armed' resistance. As reported by several in attendance at the speech—the professor introducing her requested that it not be recorded—Ms. Puar passed on vicious lies that Israel had 'mined for organs for scientific research' from dead Palestinians—updating the medieval blood libel against Jews—and accused Israelis of attempting to give Palestinians the 'bare minimum for survival' as part of a medical 'experiment.'

When asked, she agreed with a questioner that Israeli treatment of Palestinians amounted to genocide but objected to the term itself, which she said was too 'tethered to the Holocaust.'

Ms. Puar's speech was co-sponsored by the Jewish Studies Program, yet faculty members of the program remained silent in the audience during the event. This is a testament to the spell that anti-Israel dogma, no matter its veracity, has spread over the campus.

That is, "true" lies can be so powerful, so orthodox as to pass uncontested when asserted.

Wild charges against Israel have often been aired on U.S. campuses over the past several years, and their moral perversity pointed out. But Ms. Puar's calumnies reached a new low. She spoke of Jews deliberately starving Palestinians, 'stunting' and 'maiming' a population. The false accusation that a people, some of whose members were experimented on at Auschwitz, are today experimenting on others is a disgrace.

Yet characterizing Israel and Zionism in ways that antisemites formerly characterized Jews has become a stock in trade among anti-Israeli activists on college campuses. And it exposes the real motivation of those who profess to criticize only the Israeli government's policies with regard to the West Bank, not Jews themselves.[1]

One should not say "genocide" since that might recall the Holocaust. One should not say Holocaust since that might recall the Jews and what was done to them on the basis of lies, old and new, small and big. And if examined too closely, Nazi destruction of European Jewry would expose Palestinian Arab collaboration then, and the adoption and incessant dissemination of Nazi-like propaganda subsequently.

Puar's anti-Zionist antisemitism was rewarded in 2017 with publication by Duke University Press of *The Right to Maim: Debility, Capacity, Disability*. It alleges that Israeli forces shoot "to maim rather than to kill" violent Palestinian Arabs. This "ostensibly humanitarian" policy really disguises Israel's intention of "creating injury and maintaining Palestinian populations as perpetually debilitated, and yet alive, in order to control them."

An organization called Scholars for Peace in the Middle East, friendly toward Israel, called Puar's own variation on the blood libel "pseudo-scholarship, with no data to back up the fallacious theories." Blogger Peter Reitzes pointed out that Puar sits on the advisory board of the U.S. Campaign for the Academic and Cultural Boycott of Israel. The campaign has posted "such vulgarities as 'Israel-Nazi collaboration today echoes Zionist-Nazi collaboration in the 1930s-1940' and that Israel has turned Gaza into an 'extermination camp' and a 'concentration camp.'"[2]

Of course, it was Palestinian Arab leadership that collaborated closely with Nazis before and during World War II and with Moscow and its satellites afterward. And if Israeli control of the Gaza Strip turned it into an "extermination camp," the Zionists made a poor job of it, allowing the population to more than triple after the 1967 Six-Day War, and living standards to rise significantly from Egyptian-occupation levels as well.

Questioned as to how the school's press could publish such a grotesquery, University President Vincent Price pointed to the operation's

---

1 "Majoring in Antisemitism at Vassar," *Wall Street Journal*, Feb. 17, 2016.
2 "Why Did Duke University Press Publish Jasbir Puar's Fraudulent Anti-Israel Book?" *The Algemeiner*, Dec. 6, 2017.

academic peer review process, as if that attested to the work's intellectual rigor. But according to Reitzes, at least six members of the Duke University Press editorial advisory board had signed anti-Israel boycott, divestment and sanctions (BDS) initiatives and two were "endorsers of the USACBI." Two members of the press' book acquisitions group publicly support BDS. Regardless, Puar seemed to understand her time and audience; a book tour took her to Stanford, Dartmouth, Columbia and New York University, among other once-reputable institutions of higher learning. So the Palestinian narrative corrupts American education, at least its Middle East studies divisions and the umbrella humanities or liberal arts departments that indulge them.

And sometimes the narrative similarly corrupts Israeli academia. In 2007, a Hebrew University anthropology graduate student, Tal Nitzan, claimed, in the words of Haifa University Economics Prof. Steven Plaut, that "the absence of any history of rapes of Arab women by Israeli Jewish soldiers proves that the Jews are racists and oppressors, people who do not even regard Arab women as sexually desirable." Her 206-page thesis, "largely a collection of tiresome feminist rhetoric and postmodernist gibberish, not all of it related to rape," in Plaut's criticism, was awarded an honors prize by Nitzan's university advisers.[3] Negative publicity caused Hebrew University administrators to dissemble and spin. Meanwhile, Plaut noted, "this past spring a gang of Arabs terrorized the Galilee by raping Jewish women for political motives and was apprehended. Some of their victims were children. Nitzan and her professors have nothing to say about THAT wave of politically-motivated rapes." In all, a minor "damned-if-you-do, damned-if-you-don't" preview of Puar's anti-Zionist, anti-Jewish "research."

In 2013, more than 1,600 Pakistani women were murdered by family members and others in "honor killings." A reported 217 were raped first, then killed; 193 were burned to death. The official with a national helpline who released the figures estimated that they represented only 10 percent of such cases.[4] The number of conferences held, papers read and books published by universities, prestigious or otherwise, exposing the extent of and reasons for "honor killings" in Muslim-majority cultures, including Palestinian, remains *de minimis*. Such cultures are

3 "Guilty by Reason of Innocence: New Insanity From Israel's Academic Leftists," *New York Jewish Press*, Jan. 3, 2008 and long version, "SCOPUSGATE," www.americandigest.org/mt-archive, Jan. 3, 2008.

4 "1600 Pakistani women murdered, 370 raped in 2013," *The Nation* [Pakistan], March 7, 2014.

protected from delegitimization by a double standard.

Seeking easy, even fantastical self-justifying answers—let alone pretexts for satisfying primal urges to robbery and bloodshed—is how humanity justifies a chronic need for scapegoats. At its height nearly 2,000 years ago, the Roman Empire encircled the Mediterranean basin. It stretched outward from there, bounded on the east by the desert trading city of Palmyra—in headlines in 2015 due to its bloody occupation during Syria's civil wars by Islamic State primitives and their partial destruction of its ancient ruins—to Hadrian's Wall in the northwest, separating Roman England from wild Scotland. Historians have estimated that this empire comprised 55 million people, of whom five million, nine percent, were Jews. The population of that region today is approximately 600 million people. Extrapolating, its Jewish component ought to be roughly 54 million. Instead, Jews are estimated to number around 14 million worldwide, or about as many people as in Ecuador or Zimbabwe. Such is the price paid by the ultimate scapegoat.

The need for sacrificial lambs grows acute in periods of deep uncertainty, such as the present. Western civilization, strongest in its English-speaking core after World War II, momentarily triumphant after the disintegration of the Soviet communist empire in 1989 – 1991, today faces not only Middle East turmoil, Russian aggression, Chinese expansionism, North Korean nuclear threats and a nuclearizing, millenarian Iran. Mislead by a secular fundamentalist intelligentsia, it also suffers a crisis of confidence exacerbated among what should be its intellectual elite. A collapse of reason or at least the willingness to reason accompanies disparagement of the very Enlightenment values that underlay the West's long dominance. So in their anxiety many in the West's intelligentsia look for an offering. They find it in the ram of Israel, the horns of the Jewish state snared in a thicket of ideological thorns. These are composed of leftist, Islamist and neo-Nazi Jew hatred.

The secular fundamentalism common if not predominant among Western elites ill-prepares them to recognize, let alone confront Islamic fundamentalism. Lacking positive belief, especially a "fighting belief" in anything transcendent, they are morally self-disarmed. Economic fragility and demographic shifts in many countries also cause uncertainty. Anxious individuals and societies search for plausible explanations. In doing so, many have rediscovered a certain people. Once again, for growing numbers—not only in Arab-Islamic states but also from Greece to Great Britain, Sweden to Spain—Israel, if not the Jews, is their misfortune. Fashionable people, including "women's and gender studies" professors speaking at once-fashionable places like Vassar provide toxic rationales. Their audiences include Jewish studies faculty who, demoralized by a secular liberal universalism they realized too late was not reciprocated, not universal when it came to them, to Jews as Jews, sit trapped in silence.

Related, Not Relative

Palestinian Arab leadership once knew better than Mahmoud Abbas and UNESCO about Jerusalem's Jewish connection. In 1924 the Supreme Muslim Council in the city published an English-language pamphlet for visitors to Temple Mount, "A Brief Guide to al-Haram al-Sharif." It stated that "the site is one of the oldest in the world. Its sanctity dates from the earliest times. Its identity with the site of Solomon's Temple [the First Temple] is beyond dispute. This, too, is the spot, according to universal belief, on which [Israelite King] David built there an altar unto the Lord and offered burnt offerings and peace offerings."

Barbarians come in several forms. Like the Islamic State in Syria and Iraq's destruction of pre-Islamic historical sites, UNESCO and Abbas sought to erase the Temple Mount's centrality to Jews and Judaism. UNESCO did so while simultaneously slamming Israel for—among other alleged illegalities—security measures taken in response to Palestinian terrorist attacks. So rhetorically UNESCO behaved as ISIS while accusing Israelis of unjustified violence—another anti-Jewish, anti-Zionist U.N. "two-fer."

Meanwhile, in 2017 archaeologists Assaf Avraham and Peretz Reuven found an Arabic inscription over an eighth century C.E. mosque in a Palestinian village that mentions the Jewish Temple in Jerusalem. Islamic coins and other vessels from the period featured the Jewish menorah.[5] Not that such confirmation is allowed to matter.

In scrubbing the Jews from their own geography, history and religion the U.N. agency acted in the spirit of the European Union's former foreign affairs chief, Catherine Lady Ashton (United Kingdom, Labor Party). In a short statement marking International Day of Commemoration in Memory of the Victims of the Holocaust in 2014, Lady Ashton never mentioned the words "Jews" or "Jewish." Canadian Prime Minister Justin Trudeau did the same thing shortly after his election in 2016. He issued a seven-sentence official statement on International Holo-

---

5 "Arabic Inscription," Ashernet Photo cutline, *Intermountain* [Denver] *Jewish News*, Dec. 15, 2017.

caust Commemoration Day that referred to "millions of victims," "the Holocaust" and "Nazis" but not to Jews. In 2017 U.S. President Donald Trump—father of a Jewish daughter, grandfather of Jewish grandchildren—likewise omitted Jews from the White House's Holocaust Commemoration Day announcement. A spokeswoman explained the administration wanted to be "inclusive," alluding to all Nazi victims. As if the Holocaust could be universalized into a great example of man's inhumanity to man rather than left unrevised, undiluted in its primary form, the epitome of man's inhumanity to the Jews. Post-liberal news media across the United States, including *The Washington Post*—which had not taken note of Ashton or Trudeau's lapses—criticized Trump's omission editorially.

Another serious UNESCO attempt to erase the Jews from their land, history, and country, potentially preparatory to their physical erasure, came in July, 2017—a declaration falsely describing Hebron and the Tomb of the Patriarchs there exclusively as a "Palestinian heritage site." In October, Trudeau was back at it. He dedicated Canada's National Holocaust Monument in Ottawa. Though in the form of a Star of David, the monument made no mention of antisemitism or the six million Jews murdered in the Holocaust. The omission provoked an outcry leading to a more accurate replacement plaque, but whence came the omission in the first place? One senses a growing uneasiness with Jewish history and the Jews' survival, an uneasiness in some fostered by a compulsion in others to erase Jewish history, the Jewish state and—logically, imperatively extended—ultimately the Jews themselves. So it is more accurate to say the Holocaust did not end but rather was interrupted. The ultimate goal of the denigration of Jews and demonization of Israel is, for purists, genocide's completion. Hence the functional position of Iranian leaders bent on nuclear weapons and speaking as revisionists if not deniers in regard to the Shoah: "The Holocaust never happened. If it did happen, it wasn't particularly unique. Either way, we intend to finish it."

For the expedient, the goal is the return of the Jews to their proper, pre-Emancipation status as an oppressible if not actually oppressed minority, one that may enjoy certain privileges but not rights, not equality or statehood. *Dhimmi*, in essence. The Jews, deprived of the Jewish state, are to be returned virtually if not physically to the ghetto and their pre-Napoleonic status—the perpetual "other," the eternally rootless and definitely non-sovereign Jew. The cosmic order—rent by the ahistorical and threatening return of an indigenous people to their ancient land, speaking their revived "dead" mother tongue and ruling themselves, the properly subservient if not despised Jews no less—would be restored.

Assimilation and/or Annihilation—But not Normalization

The above claim may seem alarmist if not ridiculous. In free countries of the West, historically high rates of intermarriage—more often out-marriage between Jews and non-Jews leading to non-Jewish children—suggest the real danger to collective Jewish identity is being loved too much, to paraphrase Irving Kristol. In America, Jews as individuals and as a group have enjoyed life in the diaspora's most free, prosperous and tolerated, even accepted community. But public opinion surveys suggest the moral-cultural basis of that diaspora, of that America, may be fragmenting. Widespread support for "traditional values"—that is, Judeo-Christian standards in a rule-of-law oriented Anglo-Protestant framework—has declined. The slippage from libertarian right to libertine left trends consistently toward radical personal autonomy. Such an idolized self is incompatible with civic community and national continuity, with a citizenship assuming mutual rights and responsibilities. Whether such laissez-faire cultures will have the spine to resist passionate, hate-filled movements ("If they're so passionate, they must be authentic, and if authentic, they must be tolerated, even welcomed" runs the pop psychology response) seems questionable.

This is especially so given Western European and North American multi-cultural confusion about what makes tolerant communities—diverse in origin yet sustainable on the basis of common beliefs and traditions—and unites countries. It clouds thinking about why terrorists with Islamist backgrounds periodically attack people in nightclubs, at concerts and on mass transit. To what degree can a nation successfully absorb and assimilate disparate populations before its social bonds, Lincoln's necessary "mystic chords of memory," snap? Faced simultaneously with large-scale migration from Arab and Islamic lands and demographic decline among native majority groups, many among European elites dare not ask the question. This leaves an opening for rightist nationalists and old prejudices made new, especially anti-Zionist antisemitism.

The Israeli historian Haim Hillel Ben Sasson asserted that the building blocks of nationhood include a self-identifying people, on its own soil, speaking its own language and worshipping its particular religion. The United States, and Canada—the latter though bedeviled by French Quebec—were for generations uniquely successful in transcending "blood-and-soil" nationalism in favor of a unifying though not homogenizing "civic religion." The American creed rested on individual freedom, property rights and economic opportunity, minority religious tolerance by a Protestant majority itself fragmented among sects, and a common language, English. Today's demographic and cultural shifts may weaken Western democracies' ability to recognize, let alone resist non-Western imperial and genocidal impulses.

After World War II, many thought "Never again!" echoed. How could it not, following the Nuremberg war crimes trials and mountains of evidence, the records kept by Nazis and their collaborators, photographs and films, concentration camp ruins, corpses stacked like logs, and survivor testimonies? But those who thought they heard the echo appear to have been mistaken. Those surprised by Ambassador Bernard's dinner party declaration about "those people" and their "shitty little country" had not been paying attention.

"Never again!" notwithstanding, the post-Holocaust era has witnessed "Again!" repeatedly. Auto-genocide in Cambodia, genocide or its attempts in Biafra, Rwanda, East Timor, Bosnia, Darfur and, in slow motion, Tibet resulted in millions of deaths and do not exhaust the list. And witness is the proper description. The United Nations violated its basic purpose by ineffectual or complete non-involvement in all these cases. Culpability extends to leading individual powers, including the United States, as former President Bill Clinton, for example, belatedly acknowledged regarding Rwanda.

Raphael Lempkin, an expert on international law and himself a Jewish refugee of the Nazi years, coined the term genocide. His attention to and recognition of the problem was drawn first by the 1915-1917 Ottoman Turkish mass murder of Armenians. Lempkin hoped the word itself would make the threat and commission of genocide more instantly recognizable and thereby induce nations to make it criminal. But Hitler's attention too was caught by the Armenian genocide. What aroused Lempkin to extend international law to prevent a recurrence suggested to Hitler the possibilities when realpolitik trumped conscience.

Efforts to pre-empt genocide by stigmatizing it have been disappointed persistently. Jews in particular should not have been surprised, nor now be taken unaware or fall into denial about the transformation of "Never again!" into a passive cliché, let alone a slogan like "Not in my name!" invoked on behalf of Palestinian Arabs against Israeli Jews.

In the spring of 1948, the armies of five Arab countries plus Palestinian Arab "irregulars" invaded the new state of Israel. Their leaders publicly proclaimed a new "extermination" of the Jews, rejecting the

U.N.'s 1947 partition plan that recommended two new statelets, one Arab, one Jewish in the remainder of Mandatory Palestine, in addition to already existing Transjordan (today's Jordan). Extermination, as if, following Nazi parlance, Jews amounted to a pestilential infestation the elimination of which human hygiene required. For Israel's Jews, "Again!" also loomed in late May, 1967 and early October, 1973.

But post-Rwanda, post-Bosnia, the specialists, experts and diplomats take genocidal threats more seriously, so they say. In 2009, the congressionally-funded U.S. Institute of Peace, in conjunction with the U.S. Holocaust Memorial Museum and the American Academy of Diplomacy, issued a 174-page report, *Preventing Genocide: A Blueprint for U.S. Policymakers.* The study, conducted by a foreign policy Who's-Who, recalled the Nazi genocide of European Jewry and invoked the post-Holocaust assertion "never again!" It referred to mass murders in Kosovo, Rwanda, Darfur and elsewhere. But it did not mention Iran's menacing of Israel.

"Preventing Genocide was not meant to be comprehensive," USIP Executive Vice President Tara Sonenshine told this writer at the time. Rather, it was intended to guide the Obama administration "regarding organization of the National Security Council and intelligence agencies ... [about] how to recognize the danger of genocide" before it is committed. Not being comprehensive allowed all concerned to evade the most foreboding insinuation of renewed genocide: Iranian threats against "the cancer" of Israel, which loudly echoed Nazi warnings against the Jewish "bacillus," recalling as they did the Arabs' 1948 and 1967 forecasts of Israel's "extermination" and paralleled by Palestinian execrations of Israel and Jews.

So in its implicit revival, the Jewish question reemerges by often explicitly avoiding mention of Jews. Responses, like that of the U.S. Institute of Peace and U.S. Holocaust Memorial Museum, to threats of genocide sequester the Jewish state. Instead, one hears alarms about Zionism and Israel. George Orwell, whose early insights into modern tyranny and ideologically-driven hatred will be cited more than once below, saw the dangerous technique coming when he wrote of Big Brother's ruling party in the 20th Century's foremost dystopian novel, *1984*: "He who controls the past controls the future. He who controls the present controls the past." The novel appeared in 1948, coincidentally the year of Israel's rebirth. Today the Palestine lie epitomizes historical revisionism and denial—as highlighted, for example, by UNESCO—in its attempt to control the past and thereby foreclose the Jewish future.

The lie fuels a compulsion to answer the Jewish question with revisionist-enabled erasure. This happens because when it comes to the Jews, that chosen or choosing people in their promised land or land they made one of great promise, Eliot's humankind cannot bear too much truth. Certainly it cannot bear too much about Jewish exceptionalism. Like its larger and more obvious twin, American exceptionalism, the Jews' influential and often beneficial particularities infuriate many, including many who've profited thereby. Curiously, U.S. and Jewish national exceptionalism have similar ideological roots. Rabbi Lord Jonathan Sacks, former chief rabbi of the United Kingdom, philosopher and widely-selling author explained the connection in receiving the American Enterprise Institute's 2017 Irving Kristol Award. Referring to "a key moment in political history in biblical Israel," when a little before 1,000 B.C.E. the people demanded that the Prophet Samuel appoint a king over them, Sacks said:

> What happened … is precisely a social contract, exactly on the lines set out by Thomas Hobbes in *The Leviathan*. People are willing to give up certain of their rights, transfer them to a central power, king, a government, who undertakes to ensure the rule of law internally and the defense of the realm externally. In fact, One Samuel, Chapter Eight is the first recorded instance in all of history of a social contract.

> But what makes the Hebrew Bible unique and … completely different from Hobbes and Locke and Jean-Jacques Rousseau is that this wasn't the first founding moment of Israel as a nation, as a political entity. It was in fact the second because the first took place centuries earlier in the days of Moses at Mount Sinai when the people made with God not a contract but a covenant. And those two things are often confused, but actually they're quite different.

> In a contract, two or more people come together to make an exchange. … A covenant isn't like that. It's more like a marriage than an exchange. In a covenant, two or more parties each respecting the dignity and integrity of the other come together in a bond of loyalty and trust to do together what neither can do alone. A covenant isn't about me. It's about us. … Or in that lovely key phrase of American politics, it's

about 'we, the people.' ... [T]o put it as simply as I can, the social contract creates a state but the social covenant creates a society. ...

Biblical Israel had a society long before it had a state, before it even crossed the Jordan and entered the land, which explains why Jews were able to keep their identity for 2,000 years in exile and dispersion because although they'd lost their state, they still had their society. Although they'd lost their contract, they still had their covenant. And there is only one nation known to me that had the same dual founding as biblical Israel, and that is the United States of America which had its social covenant in the Declaration of Independence in 1776 and its social contract in the Constitution in 1787.

And the reason it did so is because the founders of this country had the Hebrew Bible engraved on their hearts. Covenant is central to the Mayflower Compact of 1620. It is central to the speech of John Winthrop aboard the *Arbela* in 1630. It is presupposed in the most famous line of the Declaration of Independence.

Listen to the sentence. See how odd it might sound to anyone but an American. 'We hold these truths to be self-evident, that all men are created equal and endowed by their Creator with certain inalienable rights.' Those truths are anything but self-evident. They would have been unintelligible to Plato, to Aristotle, or to every hierarchical society the world has ever known. They are self-evident only to people, to Jews and Christians, who have internalized the Hebrew Bible. And that is what made G. K. Chesterton call America 'a nation with the soul of a church.'

Sacks then asserted that "the Hebrew Bible and America have the same story," what Lincoln called a new birth of freedom, or, in the Bible, the Exodus. "That is why Jefferson drew as his design for the great seal of America the Israelites following a pillar of cloud through the wilderness. It is why Lincoln called Americans the 'almost chosen people.' It is what led Martin Luther King [Jr.] on the last night of his life to see himself as Moses and to say, 'I've been to the mountaintop and I have seen the

Promised Land.'"

Deniers of positive American exceptionalism cannot explain the centuries-long migration, legal and illegal, of millions of people decade after decade from virtually all other countries and cultures to a United States the deniers deem deeply if not fundamentally flawed. Deniers of a similar Israeli exceptionalism face a related difficulty. So for many, if not most of them, both exceptionalisms must be rejected. George Gilder, author of *The Israel Test,* put it this way:

> Do you admire and emulate excellence and accomplishment, even if it excels your own? Or do you envy and resent it? And try to tear it down?

> That's the Israel Test and it is administered by cosmic law— the law of capitalist success: The good fortune of others is also one's own. The people who admire and emulate excellence thrive. Those who resent and envy it gnash their teeth and tear their hair and never accomplish anything worthwhile. ...

> Israel, per capita, is the most creative and innovative country on the face of the earth.

> Since 1991, venture capital in Israel has increased sixtyfold. Israel has become an extension of Silicon Valley that is excelling its source. It is a paragon of defense-technology innovation. In 2008, a study by Deloitte and Touche showed that Israel has become the world's chief fount of innovation outside the U.S. in such fields as microchips, telecom, software, biotech, medical devices, and cleantech. Only Germany is close, and they are ten times larger.

> Israel epitomizes the excellence and accomplishment of Jewish culture. It is hated by antisemites not because of any flaws or legal infractions but because of its unique virtues, which show up and shame the forces of mediocrity everywhere.

Asked "can Israel save Western civilization? The way you write about technology and medicine, among other things, I am beginning to wonder," Gilder replies, "Western civilization, in part, originated in

Israel. Now Israel is a crucial source of invention, military intelligence, and entrepreneurial creativity that may yet save the West."[6]

Those who hated the West, especially as led by the United States after World War II—whether the Soviet bloc and Chinese Communists in particular or the Marxist left and its numerous descendants in general, whether pan-Arab nationalists of the 1960s and '70s, contemporary pan-Islamic supremacists or the post-modern intelligentsia—frequently targeted Israel as well, if not first. Rather than recognizing it as an example to follow or neighbor to welcome, they made it a beleaguered Western outpost. "First the Saturday people, then the Sunday people," as an old Islamic triumphalist slogan put it. First "the little Satan," then "the Great Satan," as the Iranian mullahs pray.

But Israel turned out to be too strong to destroy in conventional warfare. So its enemies emphasized both a ceaseless psychological war—pivoting on the "Zionism-is-racism" smear and thereby "justifying" terrorism—and sought non-conventional means of mass destruction of the Jewish state. Equating Zionism with racism is a psychological warfare tactic that grew out the 19th century European left's hostility to nationality groups, especially small ones, and to religious communities. All were to disappear in the mandatory universalism of a triumphant proletarian paradise. Or else. This psych-war device was employed by Russian Bolsheviks and Soviet communist and passed on by the latter to the Arab League. It amounts to the meta-libel driving anti-Zionist antisemitism.

Along the way, the order of Middle Eastern battle flipped, becoming "first the Sunday people, then the Saturday people." Accelerating with the 1975-1990 Lebanese civil wars, ancient Christian communities were pressured, sometimes attacked and in places driven in large measure from Christianity's early homelands in the Middle East. Not only in Lebanon, but also in Jordan, the West Bank and Gaza Strip, Iraq, Syria and Egypt, pre-Islamic Christian populations have been abraded. Since the 19th century, in fact, tens of thousands of Christian Arabs have been killed by Muslim Arabs and millions have emigrated. This, not Israel's treatment of Israeli Arabs, Christian or Muslim and together comprising the freest Arab communities in the Middle East, or of Palestinian Arabs, was real Middle East religious and ethnic cleansing. Beginning in the later 19th century and intensifying in the late 20th and early 21st centuries, such persecution enjoyed the advantages of being incompat-

---

6 George Gilder, interviewed by Kathryn Jean Lopez, *National Review online*, July 30, 2009.

ible with the Palestinian narrative and of possessing diminishing reso-
nance in increasingly secular cultures of the formerly Christian-influ-
enced West. As a result, it passed largely unremarked. Meanwhile, a sort
of obsessive-compulsive disorder triggered by falsehoods about Israel's
treatment of its Christian and Muslim minorities spread virally.

Western and Israeli attempts to show themselves as friends and
benefactors not only fell flat, they proved infuriating, confirming the ax-
iom that "to make an enemy, do a person a favor." As Gilder explained,
"… [F]acing the most critical Israel Test are my fellow evangelicals, who
are inclined to support Israel as the heart of their religion but who also
can be gullible about the so-called oppression of the Palestinian Arabs.
This is just stupid, because the Palestinian Arabs have benefited more
from Israel than any other people—by far. … The key period was between 1967 and 1987 [the start of the first intifada] when the Israelis administered the territories after Arabs refused all negotiations with their
famous three 'nos.' The Arabs were adamant against trading 'land for
peace' following their defeat in the '67 war, so Israel inherited the territories. [Here Gilder updates Churchill's 1921 observation about Zionist
development enriching Arabs in Mandatory Palestine.]

> During this 20-year period under Israeli rule, some 250,000
> Israelis settled in the Territories. These were the supposedly
> predatory settlers. They supplied the infrastructure of power,
> water, education, and medical care that attracted nearly ten
> Arab settlers [not so much attracted Arab settlers but helped
> increase, if not by intent then by proximity and connection,
> the Palestinian Arab population of the Gaza Strip and West
> Bank] for every one Israeli. During this period, the economy
> in the territories grew some 25 percent per year, nearly the
> fastest in the world, and far faster than that of Israel itself,
> which was still bogged down in socialism. Arab life expec-
> tancy rose from 40 to around 70. Their incomes tripled while
> their population soared. Seven universities and 2,500 facto-
> ries were established. It was the golden age for Palestinian
> Arabs.

> Then, in the early 1990s, the U.N. and the West sold out the
> country to Yasser Arafat and his terrorist forces. The Pales-
> tine Liberation Organization became the world's leading per
> capita recipients of foreign aid as international organizations

squandered billions on them and thus transformed the Palestinians from entrepreneurs and workers into terrorists, welfare queens, and political poseurs of victimization and violence.

Hearing Gilder's essentially economic-political critique, Lopez asked "is [fighting] antisemitism enough of a reason itself to defend Israel?" to which he replied, "Perhaps it is. Antisemitism is essentially hatred of capitalism and excellence. It epitomizes all the most reactionary and destructive forces in the world economy and culture. It should be opposed wherever it arises, from U.S. campuses to Middle Eastern regimes. But it is the achievements of Israel, not the animus of its enemies, that make its defense both possible and imperative."[7]

In denying Jewish/Israeli exceptionalism, the Palestine lie unspools a narrative of interwoven allegations. The fanatical staying power of anti-Zionist antisemitism insulates these widely disseminated, tenaciously held falsehoods. They include:

- Zionists expelled an indigenous Palestinian Arab people from its homeland;
- Israel seized the majority of Palestinian land in its 1948 War of Independence, leaving Palestinian Arabs stateless;
- Israel has denied Palestinian Arabs their internationally recognized "right to return" to what became Israel;
- Jewish settlements on land conquered in the 1967 Six-Day War are illegal according to international law;
- Jews of today have little or no direct connection to biblical Jews so claims on their behalf as members of an ancient people returning to its historical homeland are mistaken; and
- Israel established an apartheid state, proving that "Zionism-is-racism."

These, like lesser charges that Israelis steal Palestinian water; tried to subvert Egypt by flooding it with aphrodisiac chewing gum; sent guided animals to attack Arabs and used radiation to assassinate Palestinian leader Yasser Arafat not only rewrite but also simply fabricate history to re-Satanize the Jews.

Lord Acton's assertion that only truth gives worth to history raises the question: What is truth? What the party, Nazi, Communist or oth-

---

7 Ibid.

erwise that controls the present insists about the past? The philosopher's question, beloved by college sophomores, asks If a tree falls in the forest and there's no one there to hear it, did it make a sound? That is the wrong question. More to the point: If a tree falls and there's no one to hear it, is it still down? If it falls on you and there's no one to help, are you still pinned? Does objective reality exist regardless of your particular perception or feelings, let alone the ideology in the name of which your particular Big Brother tosses it down the Memory Hole? If you cross the street listening to music through ear buds while engrossed in your cell phone screen and don't see the oncoming bus, will you still be crushed, your self-perception as an untroubled pedestrian notwithstanding?

Post-modernists and critical theorists to the contrary, reality exists outside our willing or unwilling admission. And it does so unforgivingly beyond our denial of facts.

Journalists, at least most American ones before post-modernism's corrosive subjectivity and relativism set in on campus, aspired to convey truth. Melville Stone, the Associated Press' renowned general manager, put it this way a century ago: "I have no thought of saying The Associated Press is perfect. The frailties of human nature attach to it." But, "the thing it is striving for is a truthful, unbiased report of the world's happenings ... ethical in the highest degree." AP's "Statement of News Values and Principles" noted as recently as 2006 that Stone "wrote those words in 1914. They are true today."

Maybe yes, probably no. In one example of many, the Associated Press decreed in 2013 it no longer would use the word "illegal" to describe migrants—legally speaking, alien persons—in the United States in violation of U.S. law. In such conformism it was merely catching up to those who'd previously insisted on "undocumented immigrants" as, if not truthful, at least exhibiting "sensitivity." It first would become unspeakable to report that they had entered the United States illegally—not to mention "jumped the line" ahead of legal applicants. Once unspeakable, it eventually would be unthinkable. At least that sort of thought control was the goal, and is of all similar revisionism and falsification, including that mobilized on behalf of the Palestinianism narrative. Ah, but as Galileo might have muttered if he had worked for AP when the 2013 speech-and-thought-control directive came down instead of contended with the Renaissance Church's insistence on an Earth-centric universe, not "yet it does move" but rather "yet they are illegal."

By the time of the second intifada (2000 – 2005), Associated Press reporting of Arab-Israeli violence and its causes had become routinely unreliable, its Jerusalem bureau chronically resistant to correcting factual errors or chronological (cause-and-effect) inversions, not to mention supplying necessary context. In a seminal essay, Matti Friedman, a reporter and editor in AP's Jerusalem bureau from 2006 – 2011, highlighted the problem:

> In one seven-week period, from Nov. 8 to Dec. 16, 2011, I decided to count the stories coming out of our bureau on the various moral failings of Israeli society—proposed legislation meant to suppress the media, the rising influence of Orthodox Jews, unauthorized settlement outposts, gender segregation and so forth. I counted 27 separate articles, an average of a story every two days. In a very conservative estimate, this seven-week tally was higher than the total number of significantly critical stories about Palestinian government and society, including the totalitarian Islamists of Hamas, that our bureau had published in the preceding three years.

Why such skewing? According to Friedman, "a reporter working in the international press corps here understands quickly that what is important in the Israel-Palestinian story is Israel. If you follow mainstream coverage, you will find nearly no real analysis of Palestinian society or ideologies, profiles of armed Palestinian groups, or investigation of Palestinian government. Palestinians are not taken seriously as agents of their own fate. The West has decided that Palestinians should want a state alongside Israel, so that opinion is attributed to them as fact, though anyone who has spent time with actual Palestinians understands that things are (understandably, in my opinion) more complicated. [But] Who they are and what they want is not important: The story [that is, the Palestinian narrative] mandates that they exist as passive victims of the party that matters."[8]

Because the party that matters, the villain of the piece, is Israel. And that can and must be so because the Jewish state makes the best demon. What was wrong with AP's Israeli-Palestinian coverage was wrong with that of *The New York Times, Washington Post, National Public Radio, the BBC, The Guardian, The Independent* and their new media reflections and rivals like the *Huffington Post, BuzzFeed* and *Vox*. So long

8 "An Insider's Guide to the Most Important Story on Earth; A former AP correspondent explains how and why reporters get Israel so wrong, and why it matters," by Matti Friedman, *Tablet* online magazine, Aug. 26, 2014.

before revelations of AP's late 1930s and World War II accommodations with the Nazi propaganda ministry broke in 2017—and which the wire service initially attempted to minimize—that last "mainstream" journalism idol had revealed its feet of clay.

It continues to be vital, as Samuel Johnson instructed James Boswell in 18th century London, that we free our minds of cant, by which the great lexicographer meant sanctimonious or virtually meaningless speech used mainly from convention or habit. Defining terms is essential to begin any intelligent discussion, and a more apposite definition of cant—especially regarding the Palestinian narrative—comes courtesy of Webster's: "The special words and phrases used by those in a certain sect, occupation, etc: jargon."[9]

Jargon, in particular that of the post-modern, secular left prayer book, rather than Melville Stone's "truthful, unbiased" reports, comprises much of today's journalism. And applied to coverage of the Arab-Israeli conflict, it informs a specific sect, the old/new Jew-haters. AP's major worldwide competitor, Reuters News Service, in and after the second intifada, avoided the words terrorist and terrorism, even though accurate, in favor of more "neutral" terms. It did so in part to protect Reuters' staff from retaliation by the very terrorists staffers neutrally white-washed.[10] This exemplified the practice of news media large and small, for more than three decades, to substitute "militant" for terrorist when describing Palestinian Arab killers of Israeli Jews. Reuters' enforced exculpation of extremist Muslim mayhem but permitted the terrorist identification of violent white racists. This should remind readers: What starts with the Jews does not end with them.

Post-modern is often post-factual and anti-objective. It asks, and answers, "Who's to say what the facts are? We each have our own narratives." It demands, in prejudged dismissal: "Who are you to tell me what's accurate and inaccurate, what's right and wrong?"

Albert Einstein's theory of relativity helped usher in the 20th century, broadening scientific vistas and, through mistaken popularization, undermining that category of wisdom once known as common sense. Einstein said that as one approached the speed of light, time, space and matter became relative. That was, cosmologically speaking, a new truth, or rather newly recognized eternal truth.

---

9 *Webster's New World Dictionary of the American Language* (Second College Edition, 1978).

10 "The Case of Reuters; A news agency that will not call a terrorist a terrorist," by Tom Gross, *National Review,* July 26, 2004.

He did not say that therefore our perceptions of fact and fiction, right and wrong, moral categories of good and evil were relative or outmoded. But the social "sciences" in general, creative arts and journalism in particular—took the seductive and elastically self-justifying bit of moral relativity in their mouths and ran with it. They have yet to recover. Illustrating the law of unintended consequences, Einstein's scientific break-through, as incorrectly popularized, damaged discriminating thinking and informed debate in fields apart from the hard sciences.

Much the same happened, as Paul Johnson also discusses in his history of the first eight decades of the twentieth century, *Modern Times*, with Sigmund Freud's insights, however subjective or flawed, into the subconscious and emotional repression. Freud, like Einstein, was an old school European Jewish intellectual who had to flee as the continent, previously the center of Western civilization, yielded in the 1930s to fascism and Nazism's anti-civilization. Freud never said that because repressing emotions can lead to psychological problems people should not keep their feelings in check. One assumes he would have rejected out of hand the distortion of his ideas in the 1960s and beyond as "if it feels good, do it," "let it all hang out" and subsequent commercialization by Nike footwear as "just do it."

But through such erroneous dissemination the insights of Einstein and Freud inadvertently opened a new age of radical personal autonomy and of the self as both shaman and idol. Each person simultaneously could act as his or her own witch doctor and icon of adoration. This possibility facilitated the spread of secular fundamentalism. This replacement for Judeo-Christian belief was fundamentally amoral and therefore poorly placed to resist a new age of anti-factual, anti-objective superstition, including renewed antisemitism. If the Palestinian Arabs hate the Israelis that much, the process goes, they must really have a reason. If they're so driven to violence—throat-slashing, skull crushing, even suicidal bombing violence—then their feelings must be authentic and their cause therefore genuine. So one person's terrorist becomes another person's freedom fighter, and, in fact, the victim morphs into the murderer, or in the case of Israeli children, women and elderly, murderers-to-be or their collaborators. Hence, the killer becomes the hero, a "martyr" if he or she dies in the act.

This is false. Martyrdom, like much else at the core of the three major monotheisms—Judaism, Christianity and Islam—and the cultures derived from them, is of Jewish origin. A Jewish martyr was someone killed for his or her faith, someone willing to die rather than renounce

Judaism. The concept did not, could not mean a Jew ready to die while killing non-Jews for the presumed sin of not being Jewish.

Halachically, that is, according to Jewish law, Jews are required to live by the commandments, not just the Ten Commandments but all 613 *mitzvot*. This word is often mistranslated as "good deeds." While having that sense, *mitzvot* carry the force of requirements. Jews may, in fact are obligated to violate the commandments if necessary to save a life. Biblically, this is in the spirit of Moses' instructions, conveying the word of God to the Israelites:

"I have set before you this day the blessings and the curse, life and death, good and evil. Therefore, chose life, that you may live." The rabbis interpreted this as meaning "chose to live life in the fullest, for good." When Muslim fanatics like those of Hamas or Hezbollah taunt Jews, taunt the West by proclaiming "we love death more than you love life!" they perversely and unwittingly testify to their own evil.

But there are three instances in which a Jew must chose to die: If one is compelled on pain of death to commit rape, to murder, or to convert. Early on a prayer was written—because it was too frequently needed—to be recited by Jews on the point of martyrdom. It recognized the difference between martyrdom, required in those three cases, and suicide, which was forbidden. Impermissible because body and soul, created by God and therefore sacred, are not man's to dispose of, but rather to maintain and uplift, in ways small and large, and sometimes difficult, each day.

So what Islamic fundamentalists praise and Western media mindlessly quote as "martyrdom operations"— terrorist attacks in which the perpetrator perishes, as intended, along with those murdered—are oxymoronic. They contradict the original inspiration for and meaning of religious martyrdom. A martyr may die for his or her faith but not kill "unbelievers" for it. One person's bank robber is not another's non-authorized withdrawal specialist and a terrorist is never a freedom fighter, let alone a martyr. That is true even if, as currently understood, genuine and therefore fashionable, he's murdering a Jew.

As for Galileo, at many of today's universities, he would have been guilty of "hate speech" likely so disturbing as to have sent undergraduates marinated in multi-culturalism (in reality often "anti-Western-culturism") scurrying for "safe spaces," beating heretical free thinkers and free speakers along the way. Such spaces contradict the legacy medieval universities bequeathed—after sometimes deadly struggles with Church authorities—to their modern successors. This legacy was the universality of free inquiry and open debate. The academic left's jujitsu-like re-branding of inquiry and debate as aggression, but violent intolerance —when it comes to opinion proscribed by the left—as "resistance" necessitates such spaces. The West's once vibrant, now often reactionary institutions of higher learning strive in too many cases for anything but "truthful, unbiased accounts, ethical in the highest degree."

An oft-cited editorial in the Wellesley College student newspaper epitomized the retreat of liberal arts institutions into the mental equivalents of medieval cloisters. "We have all said problematic claims," the editorial awkwardly reads. "Luckily most of us have been taught by our peers and mentors at Wellesley in a productive way." If that doesn't sound like it was cut-and-pasted from a dystopian novel, what comes next is truly Orwellian:

"'If people are given the resources to learn and either continue to speak hate speech or refuse to adapt their beliefs, then hostility may be warranted.' In other words, if you say things some people find offensive, then there will be physical consequences."[11] Jews and non-Jews with historical memory get the message: If you don't convert, then the Inquisition will break your body on the rack.

Back at Wellesley (room, board and tuition to close one's mind in 2017 estimated at $63,000 annually), six professors that year asked the administration to cancel invitations to controversial speakers because "'there is no doubt that the speakers in question impose on the liberty of students, staff and faculty at Wellesley.' This weird interpretation of free speech—that saying offensive or politically incorrect things deprives others of rights—is not exclusive to the faculty. Here's how the student editorial staff describes the objective of free speech: 'The spirit of free speech is to protect the suppressed, not a free-for-all where anything is acceptable, no matter how hateful or damaging.'"[12]

Campus hostility long has been warranted and practiced against defenders of the Jewish state. But in reality they, not their enemies, are the suppressed. Books have not been burned. Not yet. Individuals have not been "disappeared." Not so far. But as the ancient orthodoxy of Jew-as-scapegoat reestablishes itself, books reportedly have been hidden or gone unstocked in libraries and bookstores, scoured from college reading lists. Philo-Semites, pro-Israel heretics have not yet been pilloried in monastery courtyards, but they have been denied tenure track ad-

11 "Wellesley College Students: 'Hostility' Is Warranted Against People who Say Anything Offensive," *The Federalist* online, Apr. 14, 2017.
12 Ibid.

vancement or even fired and their disciples, their students, ostracized in classrooms and occasionally assaulted on campus.[13] Public arguments in favor of those scapegoated, let alone opposing delegitimizing the Jewish state, have been stigmatized as "controversial" and even hate speech. Minds close, tempers flare, violence looms.

In the 1980s and '90s, university Middle East studies programs, sometimes suborned by funding from Saudi Arabia and other Arab oil kingdoms, turned increasingly anti-Israel. As an earlier age had it, they took the king's shilling and did the king's bidding. Such subsidies might no longer be necessary, the previously indoctrinated now themselves sometimes tenured indoctrinators. Undergraduates behaving as fascists scream "Fascist!" at speakers from the right and pro-Israel lecturers. They themselves resemble nothing so much as out of uniform Hitler Youth or Soviet-era Young Communist League members. There's little difference, politics being "U"-shaped rather than linear so the extremes at the open ends of the "U," more or less equidistant from liberal democracy at the closed loop, closely reflect each other.

Undocumented immigrants instead of illegal aliens. U.S. imperialism in place of anti-communism. Conservative clerics substituted for Islamic extremists. So liberal democratic societies slowly commit suicide by euphemism. Except when it comes to Israel, its Jews and their supporters. Then euphemism invokes anti-Zionism in place of antisemitism and points, like a weather vane, not toward suicide, but rather homicide.

In this particular case perhaps no other politically correct identity group has manipulated language, the press, politics and academia so successfully as to claim privileged victimhood and justify bloodshed of their alleged victimizers as the Palestinian Arabs in their war against Jews and Israel. Kurds, Tibetans, Baluchis and countless other larger and more deeply-rooted ethnic-national groups can only long for such attention. In the West, the Palestinian narrative has become the equivalent of Islam's *shahada*, a profession of faith for devotees of the cult-like religious substitute embraced by secular fundamentalist "progressives." It's a substitute some critics have dubbed "Palestinianism." It belongs under the classification the great 20th century cultural historian Jacques Barzun termed "thought-cliché."

---

13 "Was a University of Maryland Professor Fired for Being Pro-Israel?" by Ben Sales, Jewish Telegraphic Agency in *The Forward*, Sept. 24, 2017.

CHAPTER FOUR

The Post-Modern Escape from Judgment

THE REV. JIM JONES in 1978 led and/or forced 900 followers of his Peoples Temple Christian Church Full Gospel to drink the literally poisoned Kool-Aid of culthood in Guyana. Speaking of full gospel cults, Jones was himself a former communist and student of Stalin, Mao and Hitler. He should have paid closer attention to Arafat. A Peoples Temple version of the latter's 1974 U.N. speech and analog to the assembly's passage the following year of the "Zionism-is-racism" resolution might have legitimized for Jones and his followers their murder of investigating Congressman Leo Ryan (D-Calif.). It might have elevated Jones, as such a narrative did Arafat, from small-time religio-nationalist racketeer (who ordered the 1973 murder of U.S. Ambassador Cleo Noel), to ersatz tribune of the dispossessed. If not obviating the slaughter, it could have provided a justification for the Jonestown massacre of his own followers. As the Palestinian narrative turned terrorist murders of dissenting Arabs as well as Jews into acts of resistance and liberation, such a halo could have cast Jones as a spiritual leader rather than megalomaniacal killer.

If Jones lacked what Hollywood calls "a backstory," one propping up the main scenario, that of the Palestinian Arabs has proven invaluable. Old antisemites, including those of the reactionary right, glom onto it. Anti-Zionists, especially those of the post-liberal left, exhibit the Palestinian narrative as incontestable. An acquaintance, a major donor to several American pro-Israel organizations, explained in 2016 that a progressive friend of his insisted "'in general, truth is a relative thing and if you state something which is factually untrue, it may, nevertheless, in fact, be considered to be true if it ought to be true.' However, she warned me that this rule only applies to 'progressive' objective lies. If what is said is unhelpful to the progressive agenda then it is a lie and factual relativism does not apply." The Palestinian narrative, the lie of Palestine, is a key element in the progressive agenda. Factual relativism definitely applies.

Fact-based empiricism led to the scientific and industrial revolutions underpinning today's often overfed, technically interconnected, medically advanced, but—due in no small part to its growing denial of objective truth—culturally decaying West. Such rejectionism is why as a political/social adjective today "progressive" requires quotation marks and often is best understood as regressive or, in fact, reactionary.[1]

Former California State University (Fresno) professor emeritus and Stanford University Hoover Institution senior fellow Victor Davis Hanson has summarized the intellectual and ideological shell game that turns lies into narratives and uses "discourse"—another academic weasel-word—about narratives to displace reasoned debate meant to get at facts and truth. Touching upon its World War II-era roots in ex post facto self-justification of cowardice and defeatism, Hanson observes:

Lying in America has become not lying when 'good' liars advance alternative narratives for noble purposes—part of our long slide into situational ethics and moral relativism.

Every new bad idea in America today can ultimately be traced to the university. And it seems to take only about 30 years for academia's nihilism to filter through the elite institutions and make its way into popular culture. So it is with our present idea of truth as a mere construct.

In the 1980s and 1990s professors in the liberal arts became enamored of the French-speaking postmodern nihilists — among them notably Paul de Man, Michel Foucault, Jacques Derrida, and Jacques Lacan. They refashioned an old philosophical strain of relativism found as far back as the Greek sophists and Plato's discussion of the noble lie. They were influenced by Friedrich Nietzsche's attacks on absolute morality, and their youth was lived during the age of Joseph Goebbels and *Pravda*. The utter collapse of France in six weeks

1 "Understanding America's Disturbed Politics: Progressive Means Reactionary," by Eric Rozenman, *New English Review*, January, 2015.

in May and June 1940 and the later shame that most of the nation either was passive or actively collaborated with the Nazi occupiers rather than proving brave resistance fighters made the idea of empiricism and truth an especially hard pill to swallow for the postwar French postmodernists."[2]

In fact, Vichy France was a collaborationist state, its officials and countless supporters direct or indirect collaborators.

De Man was, as much as any one individual, the father of post-World War II "deconstructionism" in the United States. This theory seeped into humanities departments across the country, in many cases eventually making their very names oxymorons. De Man, an immigrant who did well for himself, died in 1983 after teaching at Bard College, Johns Hopkins and Cornell universities (Ph.D. Harvard, 1960).

But four years after de Man's death, Belgian scholar Ortwin de Graef revealed that between 1940 and 1942, between the ages of 20 and 22, De Man had contributed approximately 170 articles to the Belgian dailies *Le Soir* and *Het Vlaamsche Land*, both propaganda outlets of the Nazi occupation.[3] He also was a bigamist. In 2014, Prof. Evelyn Barish of the City University of New York published *The Double Life of Paul de Man*. Turns out that the still small voice in the back of one's head that used to be recognized as conscience could be trumped. If it reminded one of moral crimes like Nazi collaboration or ignoring a distant wife and children to take on another family, why not then, devise a louder voice insisting on the "indeterminacy" of texts and personalized—often highly retouched—"narratives" instead of history. So troubled psyches provide balm for themselves. So hatred of the Jewish state preemptively soothes any otherwise embarrassing mental inflammation caused by hatred of the Jews. Again, Eliot was correct; humankind cannot bear too much reality. Certainly not individuals about their own shortcomings. Regarding the post-modernists, Victor Davis Hanson continued:

> While this group comprised quite different thinkers, they mostly agreed that reality was socially constructed and arbitrarily defined by the language of those in power.
>
> In fact, 'truth' for a postmodernist is supposedly what those

---

2 "Why Hillary Is Never Held Accountable for Her Lies," by Victor Davis Hanson, *National Review*, Aug. 30, 2016.

3 "Acts of Undermining," by Ian Tuttle, *National Review*, May 15, 2017.

who control us say it is, largely in efforts to perpetuate their own race, class, and gender privilege. You can see how thoroughly popular culture has picked up this mostly banal relativist observation and transformed it into 'the Truth'—and why today we assume that lying is simply a narrative, not a window into one's character.

Relativist slogans abound (e.g., 'One person's terrorist is another's freedom fighter'). 'Hands up, don't shoot' was never uttered by Michael Brown, who was not an innocent 'gentle giant' but a strong-armed robber who sought to take a policeman's gun and then charged at the cop. But since his fictitious last utterances should be true, therefore they are and, presto! became the slogan of Black Lives Matter.

In the opposite fashion, there is to be no such thing as Black Lives Matter protesters calling for frying police or killing cops, since negation of the truth serves a far more noble purpose than would confirmation.[4]

The early fabrication of a "documentary" entitled *Palestinian Lives Matter* was utterly predictable. Its creator-promoters' linked the incessantly asserted "plight of the oppressed Palestinians" with the Black Lives Matter campaign. Black Lives Matter presented itself as a protest movement against unjustified killing of black men by police, often but not always white, at a time when whites were almost twice as likely as blacks and three times as likely as Hispanics to be victims of police shootings. Police shootings of blacks has been twice the African America share of the U.S. population, but in the 75 largest counties, comprising most of the population, blacks appear to commit disproportionately high percentages of robberies and murders, according to Heather Mac Donald, author of *The War on Cops* and Thomas W. Smith Fellow at the Manhattan Institute.[5] In any case, African Americans seem more likely to be killed by other African Americans than by police.

Nevertheless, BLM issued a manifesto of more than 70 pages that included the de rigueur, progressive anti-Israeli indictments. This document alleged Israeli responsibility for "the genocide taking place against

4 Victor Davis Hanson, *National Review*, Aug. 30, 2016.

5 "Police shootings and race," by Heather Mac Donald, posted on the *Volokh Conspiracy* website, *The Washington Post*, July 18, 2016.

the Palestinian people" and asserted "Israel is an apartheid state" encouraging "discrimination against the Palestinian people."[6] BLM was supported through other progressive organizations that had received $33 million from non- if not anti-Zionist, left-wing political financier George Soros. Soros as a Jewish child had escaped the Holocaust; as an adult he fingered Israel and the United States as the main obstacles to Middle East peace and called for ending American foreign aid to Israel. Hence his originally covert, and denied, major funding to help launch J Street. J Street, popular with more than a few left-leaning American Jews, is the anti-AIPAC (American Israel Public Affairs Committee) self-described as "pro-peace, pro-Israel." In fact it focuses less on peace or Israel than on emphasizing Palestinian grievances and supporting, through its related political action committee, politicians with dubious records on U.S.-Israel ties. Jointly with the National Iranian American Council—the mullahs' de facto voice in Washington—it celebrated the Obama administration's 2015 Iranian nuclear deal.

Veteran journalist and *Washington Times* Editor Emeritus Wesley Pruden reacted this way: Black Lives Matter "was a positive thing, but the movement now is trying to turn the rage against injustice to destructive rage against Israel. It's an old phenomenon. Blame the Jews. ... Until now the Jew-baiters tried to camouflage their game, being careful to say they weren't talking about the Jews, just the Zionists, the Jews who wanted to build and protect a Jewish homeland.[7] When a black student at Harvard tried this line on Martin Luther King Jr., he was having none of it. 'When people criticize Zionists,' he told him, 'they mean Jews. You're talking antisemitism.'"[8]

Israel's imagined genocide against the Palestinian Arabs has been, as noted, curiously unsuccessful. Gazans and West Bankers fared better in terms of infant mortality, educational attainment, electrification, water and sewer provision and so on under Israeli control than they had under Egyptian and Jordanian occupation (1948 – 1967). They also

6 "Black Lives Matter blindsides Jewish supporters with anti-Israel platform," *The Washington Times*, Aug. 15, 2016.

7 "Black Lives Matter and the endless war against the Jews," Pruden on Politics, *The Washington Times*, Aug. 25, 2016.

8 "The Socialism of Fools: The Left, the Jews and Israel," by Seymour Martin Lipset, *Encounter magazine*, December, 1969. This account of King's remark has been questioned, but support for King's view also appears in "'I have a dream' for peace in the Middle East/King's special bond with Israel," by John Lewis, www.SFGATE.com/opinion/openforum/article/I-have-a-dream-for-peace-in-the-Middle-East-2880295.pl, Jan. 21, 2002.

enjoyed higher living standards in the subsequent decades—including even during the violence of the second intifada (2000 – 2005)—than Arabs in Algeria, Egypt, Morocco, Syria and Yemen, according to the 2005 U.N. Report on Human Development. Of 177 countries and territories rated, Arabs of the West Bank and Gaza Strip placed 106. Israel ranked 23, Qatar—oil and natural gas rich, population poor—placed highest of Arab countries at 40.

Israel's alleged racist ethnic cleansing has been even less effective against its own Arab population, who comprise approximately 21 percent of the country's total. "The health of the Arab Israeli population is improving, along with that of Israel's Jewish population. In terms of life expectancy and infant mortality rates, the Arab Israeli population ranks highest in the Arab and Muslim world," a 2017 study reported. Life expectancy of an Arab Israeli born in 2015 was 79—the same as an American in 2017 after two years of decline, attributed in part to fatalities related to the U.S. epidemic of opioid abuse.[9]

The U.N. Human Development reports in 2002, 2003, 2004 and 2005 for the Arab countries highlighted numerous "freedom deficits." These studies, largely by Arab specialists, found shortfalls in individual and political freedom, education, women and minority rights, religious tolerance, economic growth, research, knowledge, artistic output and so on. One reason given was religious, that is Islamic, fundamentalism. Others were political corruption and oppression. Not mentioned was the social, cultural and intellectual—not to say moral—costs of insisting on conflict with Israel, in denial of Jewish, not to mention Christian equality. What no objective measure found was an Israeli genocide of Arabs, Palestinian or otherwise.

In Western terms, the Arab-Islamic war of intolerance against Israel and Jewish equality has been a distraction from and excuse for political, economic and social shortcomings and dictatorial rule in Arab countries. But in Arab-Islamic terms, or at least pan-Arab/Islamist ones, it continues as an existential necessity, a religious touchstone.

King, who fought for civil rights for all, embraced the Jewish state of Israel. Black Lives Matter, which imagines it fights for civil rights for blacks, would erase the Zionist project. How did the latter's anti-Zionist antisemitism—representative of such bias on the reactionary left—originate?

---

9 "The Health of the Arab Israeli Population," by Dov Chernichovsky, Bishara Bisharat, Liora Bowers, Aviv Brill and Chen Sharony, A chapter from *The State of the Nation Report 2017*, Taub Center for Social Policy Studies in Israel.

Philip Carl Salzman, McGill University professor of anthropology and author of *Culture and Conflict in the Middle East*, among other books, offered an explanation: "These [BLM's manifesto] statements are antisemitic not only because they are false and modern versions of traditional antisemitic blood libels, but also because BLM selectively chooses the Jewish state out of all the states in the world to demonize. What has inspired BLM to engage in this counter-factual, antisemitic rant?" According to Salzman, it "has been guided to antisemitism by the concept of 'intersectionality.'"[10]

"Intersectionality," sourced to a 1989 article by legal scholar Kimberle Crenshaw, is a one-size-suffocates-all assertion that "all oppressed peoples and categories of people share a position, and by virtue of that fact are potential allies in the struggle against their oppressors." But, Salzman adds, only in recent years has it "escaped academia and swarmed into the streets." It also has been "extended beyond individuals to types of oppression. … Thus, women can never be treated equally or fairly, if blacks face racial prejudice, and the disabled are not given sufficient support to be equal to the abled, and unless the Palestinians are liberated from the Israelis, and the Israelis are liberated from their country, their lives and their homes. To make the point, the Israelis are accused of having had a hand, direct or indirect, in the oppression of blacks, women, and the disabled everywhere."

That is, extending the hoary tropes of Jew-hatred. The Jews killed Christ, drained the blood of Christian children, poisoned medieval wells, started the French Revolution, World Wars I and II and control the banks and news media. For the most effective, eternal demons it could not be otherwise. Now, thanks to "intersectionality," the Jews have moved on to blacks, women and the disabled. On the post-liberal left, as it drifts further from what used to be democratic liberalism, the anti-Zionism of the late 19th and early 20th century European Marxist left blends ever more seamlessly with the old antisemitism of the reactionary right and Islamic supremacists.

Salzman cites journalist James Kirchick's critique that "intersectionality compels one to adopt agendas that have nothing to do with his or her own. Worse, in the name of 'solidarity' with other supposedly 'oppressed' groups, it leads to alliances with those actively hostile to one's cause. This is how a gay rights organization led by well-meaning pro-

---

10 "Where Does Black Lives Matter's Antisemitism Come From?" by Philip Carl Salzman, *Gatestone Institute*, Sept. 21, 2016 (www.gatestoneinstitute.org/8956black-lives-matter-antisemitism).

gressives can be duped into disinviting private citizens of the one country in the Middle East respecting the humanity of gays [Israel], all at the behest of people who use cultural relativism to excuse Muslim societies that throw homosexuals from the tops of buildings." Here Kirchick refers to a trend exemplified by that of three women booted from the 2017 "Chicago Dyke March" for carrying Jewish pride flags. One of the trio, Laurie Grauer, said she and her friends "were told they were unwelcome at the 1,500-person march because their flags were offensive and threatening. ... In a statement, march organizers say they are not antisemitic, but they are anti-Zionist. They support the liberation of Palestine and all oppressed people everywhere. But Grauer says she wasn't carrying an Israeli flag [but a gay pride flag with a Jewish star], and she wasn't even talking about Israel until she was cornered by other marchers."[11] Jews frequently assume their history as the epitome of an oppressed people and Israel as the liberation from and renaissance in the face of that oppression is generally recognized. So they often remain oblivious to the fact this has rarely if ever been the general case, even immediately after the Holocaust, and in an era of anti-Zionist antisemitism is less so.

Salzman identifies other flaws of "intersectionality." "If we look at the 'hot spots' of the world, who are the oppressors and who the oppressed, in Afghanistan, in Iraq, in Syria, in Nigeria? If only simple-minded ideas such as 'intersectionality' could help us clarify the destructive disasters and human tragedies—drought, corruption, intolerance, civil war—but unfortunately they are useless.

> Further, 'intersectionality' focuses on people's victimhood. People are 'oppressed' and disadvantaged, and that becomes the most important thing about them. Reducing people to victims takes away their ability to understand, their ability to act, their motivation, tenacity, resourcefulness, force of character, and everything that enables people to engage the world. ...

> In addition 'intersectionality,' in identifying all the oppressed as one, united and with common interests, is incoherent and oblivious to the facts (often, it seems, unpopular in radical social movements). The idea, for example, that victims of Islamophobia and homophobia are natural allies flies in

---

11 "Chicago woman kicked out of march over Jewish pride flag," WGN-TV, June 26, 2017.

the face of the fact that Islamic law and many Muslims are strongly opposed to homosexuals, and that Iran, for instance, executes homosexuals (even teenagers) by hanging them from cranes in public squares. The Islamic State [the 2014 – 2017 "caliphate" in much of Iraq and Syria] does not require large machinery; it throws homosexuals off buildings.

There is also a lack of affinity between victims of Islamophobia and victims of racial prejudice. The Arab world—the heart of Islam—has for many centuries, up to today, carried on an extensive black slave trade in Africa, sending Arab expeditions to capture slaves. There has been much observation in recent decades of slaves taken from the south by the Arabs of northern Sudan.

Salzman adds that "intersectionality" advocates, including Canada's Green Party and the left-wing, antisemitic Podemos Party in Spain "and racial groups such as Black Lives Matter, often seem not to identify oppressors and oppressed." Among those so ignored are the Chinese occupiers of Mongolia, Tibet and Turkestan; Sunni Muslim killers of Yazidis and Christian Arabs; and Turkish, Iranian and Arab oppressors of the Kurds. Instead, "intersectionalists" "turn to the historical sacrificial victim, the Jews, selectively demonize Israel and celebrate the Jews' terrorist enemies, the Palestinians, as poor, suffering victims. ... So we should not be surprised to see Quebec nationalists marching with Hezbollah flags and 'anti-racists' in European demonstrations chanting 'Hamas, Hamas, Jews to the gas.' Supporters of 'intersectionality' cheer terrorists when they murder Jews. To them, that is just 'social justice' at work."

Einstein is credited with having observed that "everything should be made as simple as possible, but not simpler." That being so, the "intersectionality" that purports to connect Black Lives Matter and anti-Israel Palestinian Arabs does not rise even to the level of over-simplification. Delusions that American Jewish organizations conspire with Israeli police to teach U.S. law enforcement how to suppress blacks (organizations like the Jewish Institute for National Security Affairs have conducted counter-terrorism exchanges between American police chiefs and sheriffs and Israeli security officials) agitate the susceptible. So BLM's manifesto, reiterating threadbare anti-Israel charges—apartheid, oppression, genocide—was banal. Suffused, however unconsciously, with post-modern categorizations, it could hardly have been otherwise. However, given the toxicity of those categories and charges, not laughable.

If victimhood can be powerful, at least in negative and propagandistic senses, false victimhood strenuously asserted can be more so. Hitler's propaganda incessantly insisted that the noble German people had been and was being victimized by the Jews. The Jews, conspiring phantom-like and oxymoronically with Bolsheviks and capitalists and manipulating Great Britain and the United States, threatened Germany with annihilation. So Germans had to destroy the Jews before they were themselves destroyed.

In a speech secret at the time, S.S. Reichsfuhrer Heinrich Himmler reiterated with brutal clarity Hitler's view of Germany's struggle against the Jews. To his senior officers, gathered in Poznan, Poland on Oct. 4, 1943 Himmler easily referred—as if they were facts rather than fantasies—to the medieval German view of Jews as "swine," the 19th century "scientific" description of them as a bacillus infecting Germany and the 20th century, Protocols-derived image of Jews as "saboteurs" of nations:

> I also want to speak to you here, in complete frankness, of a really grave chapter. ... I am referring here to the evacuation of the Jews, the extermination of the Jewish people. This is one of the things that is easily said: 'The Jewish people are going to be exterminated,' that's what every Party member says, 'sure, it's in our program, elimination of the Jews, extermination—it'll be done.'

> And then they all come along, the 80 million worthy Germans, and each one has his one decent Jew. Of course, the others are swine, but this one, he is a first-rate Jew. Of all those who talk like that, not one has seen it happen, not one has had to go through with it. Most of you men know what it is like to see 100 corpses side-by-side, or 500, or 1,000. To have stood fast through this—and except for cases of human weakness—to have stayed decent, that has made us hard. This is an unwritten and never-to-be-written page of glory in our history, for we know how difficult it would be for us if today—under bombing raids and the hardships and deprivations of war—if we were still to have Jews in every city as secret saboteurs, agitators and inciters. If the Jews were still lodged in the body of the German nation, we would probably

by now have reached the stage of 1916-1917 [when Germany was stalemated in World War I, facing mounting losses and declining public morale].

> The wealth they possessed we took from them. I gave a strict order … that this wealth will of course be turned over to the Reich in its entirety. We have taken none of it for ourselves. Individuals who have erred will be punished in accordance with the order given by me at the start, threatening that any-one who takes as much as a single Mark of this money is a dead man. … We had the moral right, we had the duty to-wards our people, to destroy this people that wanted to de-stroy us. But we do not have the right to enrich ourselves by so much as a fur, as a watch, by one Mark or a cigarette or anything else. We do not want, in the end, because we de-stroyed a bacillus, to be infected by this bacillus and to die. … All in all, however, we can say that we have carried out this most difficult of tasks in a spirit of love for our people. And we have suffered no harm to our inner being, our soul, our character. …"[12]

In fact, the Holocaust, in addition to being history's biggest mass murder, also was its greatest robbery. Germans and Germany, whether by the number two Nazi leader, Hermann Goering with his collection of art looted from Jews, by the Reich enriched with stolen jewelry and other valuables or ordinary Germans who acquired Jewish-owned businesses at fire-sale prices or simply moved into dwellings vacated by deported Jews (as did Poles and other nationalities in areas made Judenfrei), dra-matically profited at the expense of their former fellow citizens. Where ideology and theology lead to mass murder, mass robbery—down to wholesale ripping of gold fillings from the teeth of victims—follows.

Echoes Then and Now

Himmler had a colleague. Haj Amin al-Husseini, avatar of Pal-estinian Arab nationalism and early and influential proponent of Isla-mism, repeatedly broadcast from wartime Berlin messages that rein-forced in the Middle East Hitler and Himmler's world view. Essentially,

---

12 "From a Speech by Himmler Before Senior SS Officers in Poznan, October, 4, 1943, 'Evacuation of the Jews,'" Yad Vashem SHOAH Resource Center, www.yadvashem.org .

al-Husseini substituted Arabs and Muslims for Germans and the "Aryan people" but retained the call to annihilate the perpetually threatening, eternally irredeemable Jews. And not just the call: Nazi leaders, with al-Husseini's encouragement, prepared for S.S. Einsatzgruppen to follow Gen. Erwin Rommel's Panzerarmee Afrika, had it been victorious, into Egypt and British Mandatory Palestine. Once there, they would have rounded up and murdered Egyptian and Palestinian Jews as such S.S. groups were doing to the Jews of eastern Europe and German occupiers had made a start on in Morocco and Tunisia. This is not to taint Palestinian nationalism through unfair guilt by association. Rather, it describes a compatible collaboration to bring the oldest hatred to its ultimate conclusion.

In late 1941, al-Husseini reached Germany from Iraq after the British regained control in Baghdad from a pro-Nazi regime that had been backed by and was sheltering him. In Berlin, the Palestinian Arab leader met with Hitler. Al-Husseini later testified he found in *der Fuehrer* a far-sighted leader ready, once he triumphed over the Jews and their allies in Europe, to support the Arabs under the mufti in annihilating the Jews of the Middle East. "A few hours after seeing the grand mufti, Hitler ordered invitations sent for a conference to be held at a villa on Lake Wannsee. The meeting's purpose was to plan the comprehensive extermination of all Europe's Jews."[13] In response, 15 Nazi leaders, with S.S. Obergruppenfueher Reinhard Heydrich presiding, agreed at the Wannsee Conference on Jan. 20, 1942 to the administrative cooperation necessary for the "total solution of the Jewish question." Of the 15, eight held doctorates. Formal education hardly inoculates against antisemitism. Resistance to Jew-hatred relates instead, as we shall see, to an ethical choice. Credentials, academic or otherwise, say nothing about ethics.

During the war al-Husseini worked directly with Himmler. Rather than tarnish his standing after the Axis defeat and exposure of the Holocaust, the mufti's war-time activities made him something of a hero in Egypt, British Mandatory Palestine and beyond. Later, Yasser Arafat would claim him as both a relative and inspiration. To this day the Palestinian Authority honors his memory.

Al-Husseini was appointed Grand Mufti (religious judge) of Jerusalem by British authorities in Mandatory Palestine in 1924. He had been inciting the murder of Palestinian Jews, as in the massacres of 1920, 1921 and 1929, even before Hitler's National Socialist German

---

13 *Nazis, Islamists, and the Making of the Modern Middle East*, Barry Rubin and Wolfgang G. Schwanitz, Yale University Press, 2014, page 8.

Workers' Party (Nazi for short) won a plurality in the 1933 elections. What makes the lie of Palestine important not only for Arabs and Jews but all those threatened by Islamic extremism are two trends fed and exemplified by al-Husseini. These are Islamist ideology and contemporary terrorism that reflects Arab and Islamic, particularly Palestinian, roots. These pre-existing roots were irrigated first by imperial German, then by Nazi German ideology. The dry academic term Islamist, for a politicized Islam, in this case actually describes Islamo-fascism. The phrase Islamo-fascism was briefly and accurately in use in the United States after al-Qaeda's Sept. 11, 2001 attacks, but subsequently dismissed as an alleged oversimplification or anti-Muslim slur.

However, a fairly straight ideological line begins with the puritanical Wahhabi school of Islamic thought and practice, founded in the 18th century in what is today Saudi Arabia and runs through the early 20th century Muslim Brotherhood to—with German assistance—the Palestinian supremacism of Hamas and Fatah. Muhammad ibn Abd al-Wahhab's beliefs were intolerantly supremacist. Today they underlie anti-Christian, anti-Jewish and anti-Western anger and aggression seen everywhere from Jerusalem and Tel Aviv to Paris and London to New York and San Bernardino. The Saudi royal family, dependent on the country's Wahhabi-inclined clergy for religious legitimacy, for decades pumped hundreds of millions of Western petro-dollars into Islamic schools (madrassas) and mosques influenced by Wahhabism worldwide.

In some respects, al-Wahhab mirrored Martin Luther. Both meant to purify or reform the practice of their existing religions, Islam and Roman Catholicism, respectively, when they made their initial critiques. But whereas Luther's revolutionary reformation would change Christendom and help lead, however unintentionally, to Protestantism, the growth of nationalism, the Enlightenment and Industrial Revolution, al-Wahhab's had quite another effect.

The Turkish Ottoman Empire had failed in Islam's latest crusade into Europe, its army defeated at the gates of Vienna in 1683. But Islam's political-social "structure and traditions ... were totally inimical to the parliamentary and absolutist state forms in the rest of Europe." Instead of "centralization, secularization and—at least in the West—ever-greater participation" in politics and government, "Ottoman defeats sparked a deep yearning for moral and spiritual renewal. Many Muslims rejected any technical or political explanation for Muslim weakness in the modern world. ... The answer, these critics argued, was more Islam. For this reason the eighteenth-century central Arabian preacher Muhammad ibn Abdul Wahhab (1703 – 92) called for an Islamic reformation, a return to [what he conceived of as] the uncorrupted principles of medieval Islam. He joined forces with local tribal chief Muhammed ibn Saud, and later with his son Abd al-Aziz. Between them they eventually gained control of much of the Arabian peninsula. The religious radicalization of the Arab world, in other words, began in central Europe, before the walls of Vienna."[14]

That is, what the West awoke to after Sept. 11, 2001 and called "Islamic fundamentalism" began long before "infidel" U.S. forces landed in Saudi Arabia as part of Operation Desert Shield in 1990 after Iraq under Saddam Hussein conquered Kuwait. It long had preceded British and French colonialism, Herzl and the first Zionist settlements in Palestine, the arrival of American oil companies or the development of U.S.-Israel military-diplomatic ties. The Germany states of Kaiser Wilhelm II and of Adolf Hitler, both fighting the British Empire and, of course, in their minds the Jews, found it useful.

Max von Oppenheim was born in 1860 to a German Jewish family that had converted to Catholicism. He studied Arabic and wrote of his travels through Muslim lands. His articles came to the attention of the German foreign ministry, which was concerned about the spread of Islam in its African colonies. In 1896, von Oppenheim was appointed attaché to the German consulate in Cairo and there he became convinced Berlin could use pan-Islamic movements against the British. His dispatches advised the Kaiser to back Islamists.[15]

The Kaiser sided with the Ottoman sultan against Theodore Herzl and his Zionist movement. Competing with the British, Germany established the German Orient Bank and invested in the Berlin-to-Baghdad railroad. By 1914, Ottoman religious leaders issued a *fatwa* calling on all Muslims to participate in a *jihad* against the British, French and Russian allies. Many Muslims ignored the decree and tried to avoid conscription. But one who did enlist, from an influential Jerusalem family, was Haj Amin al-Husseini. Though he would change sides mid-way through the conflict—al-Husseini's tactical maneuvering was a constant feature of his long life—he never wavered in his strategic obsession with *jihad* against the Jews.

The Germans opened World War I "propaganda bases" throughout the Middle East. These distributed polemical pamphlets with titles

14 *Europe; The Struggle for Supremacy, From 1453 to the Present,* by Brendan Simms, Basic Books, 2013, page 92.

15 "Max of Arabia," by Sean Durns, *The Jerusalem Post*, Aug. 8, 2017.

like "They Cheat God and the Infidels" and "England and the Caliphate." Captured Allied troops from North Africa and India were indoctrinated in two Berlin camps complete with mosques and a weekly handout entitled *al-Jihad*. So Imperial Germany attempted to leverage suppressed Islamic imperialism against British and French imperialists.

The ideological trail continued, with variations on the theme necessary to time and place, through al-Husseini and one of his admirers, Hassan al-Banna. As founder of Egypt's Muslim Brotherhood in 1928, al-Banna's own prominence extended beyond the Arab world's most populous country and beyond British Mandatory Palestine. So did al-Husseini's. Their influence promoted al-Banna's view that "Islam is superior and nothing must be made superior to it."

Soon after came Brotherhood chief ideologist Sayyid Qutb, who reinforced al-Husseini and al-Banna's Islamic supremacism—and their rabid anti-Jewish, anti-Zionist views—for Egyptians, Palestinian Arabs and many others. Five years after the Holocaust, Qutb explained that in the early days of Islam, "the Jews did indeed return to evil-doing, so Allah gave to the Muslims power over them. The Muslims then expelled them from the whole of the Arabian Peninsula. ... Then the Jews again returned to evil-doing and consequently Allah sent against them others of his servants, until the modern period. Then Allah brought Hitler to rule over them. And once again today the Jews have returned to evil-doing, in the form of 'Israel' which made the Arabs, the owners of the land, taste of sorrows and woe."[16]

Egypt's Nasser—a pan-Arabist, not a pan-Islamist—had the troublesome Qutb hanged in 1966. But as is often the case, the death of the man did not lead to the death of his beliefs.

Al-Husseini's rejection of Jews as equals and transformation of them into anti-Arab, anti-Muslim demons melded with Nazi typology to promote genocide. This toxic religious-political brew would provide continuing pretexts for Palestinian anti-Jewish, anti-Israeli terrorism. Often minimized if not indulged by Western governments, Palestinian Arab terrorism would function as "the gateway drug" for much Cold War and post-Cold War terrorism—that is, the intentional intimidation or murder of non-combatants to influence larger audiences and achieve political, religious or other goals—and for the revived Islamic triumphalism called Islamism today. University of Maryland Prof. Jeffrey Herf notes in his 2009 work, *Nazi Propaganda for the Arab World* (Yale University Press) that among the many listeners mesmerized by al-Hus-

---

16 Rubin and Schwanitz, page 251.

seini's war-time broadcasts with their hostility to the Allies and the Jews was a young Iranian. The world later would know him as the Shiite Muslim Ayatollah Ruhollah Khomeini, founder of the Islamic Revolutionary Republic of Iran.

The DNA of contemporary anti-Zionist antisemitism, its European and Middle Eastern strands nourished during both world wars, persists little changed in Islamist Jew-hatred, Sunni or Shi'a. However, it is amplified by Western secular fundamentalism. Like Marxism, anti-liberal secular fundamentalism amounts to a replacement cult for traditional religious belief. And it reiterates the original leftist hostility to Jews and Judaism highlighted by Dennis Prager and Joseph Telushkin in their best-seller, *Why the Jews? The Reason for Antisemitism.*

They note that "Marxism and Socialism, like Christianity, Islam, nationalism and the Enlightenment, were born with Jew-hatred. Their two main ideological sources, Marx and the early French socialists, developed anti-Semitic ideas which have characterized much of the Left to this day."[17] Unlike Islamist Jew-hatred, the secular fundamentalist version—its anti-democratic left roots cosmetically updated by the jargon of post-modernism—can be made to sound progressive.

That hatred became explicit, and its effectiveness was reinvigorated, as historian Robert Wistrich stressed, with U.N. General Assembly passage in 1975 of the Zionism-is-racism resolution. Prager and Telushkin put it this way: "Whereas almost the only countries opposing the resolution were democracies, every Leftist government in the world" with the exception of Romania, which did not vote, "declared the Jews' national movement racist and therefore illegitimate."[18] And, as racist and illegitimate, it could and must be destroyed, its original League of Nations and United Nations' endorsements notwithstanding.

Palestinian terrorism was made legitimate, especially for and by its Western apologists, through the narrative. Palestinian terrorists, for example, weaponized airliner hijacking in the 1970s. Osama bin Laden and al-Qaeda learned from the PLO, then exceeded their teachers. The PLO had found that terrorism pays; hijacked airliners, their crews and passengers could be traded for concessions from the Western governments affected and for pressure on Israel. Al-Qaeda members, more committed than PLO hijackers to the Muslim Brotherhood's credo of

---

17 *Why the Jews? The Reason for Antisemitism*, by Dennis Prager and Joseph Telushkin, Simon and Schuster, 1983, page 137 (Touchstone/Simon and Schuster paperback, 1985).

18 Ibid., page 147.

"dying in the path of Allah," upgraded hijacked airliners, their crews and passengers from bargaining chips to guided munitions, making sure thousands of others also "died in the path of Allah."

Al-Qaeda was a spin-off from the Egyptian al-Jama'a al-Islami-yya, which had assassinated Egypt's President Anwar as-Sadat in 1981. Al-Jama'a itself had splintered from the Brotherhood. In turn, Al-Qaeda spawned, among others, the Islamic State in Iraq and Syria. As a result of this fundamentalism's spread, American airline passengers stood in line for X-rays that rendered them naked to security personnel while in the Middle East millions of Arab and Muslim refugees attempted to flee their homelands.

As for bin Laden, one of his most important teachers and mentors was Abdullah Yusuf Azzam. Azzam was born in British Mandatory Palestine in 1941. After living in Jordan and Saudi Arabia, he was residing in Pakistan when the Soviets invaded Afghanistan in 1979. Orator, religious leader and military strategist, Azzam established the Office of Services of the Holy Warriors in Pakistan and, more than any other individual, reignited "the Islamic power rage against those non-Islamic powers that had conspired against Islam since before the Crusades."[19]

According to Steven Emerson, head of the Washington, D.C.-based Investigative Project on Terrorism, Azzam and Palestinian Sheikh Tamim al-Adnani "visited dozens of American cities between 1985 and 1989," recruiting thousands of anti-Soviet mujahideen and raising funds. In a 1988 speech in Kansas, Azzam declared that "humanity is being ruled by Jews and Christians. [By t]he Americans, the British and others. And behind them, the fingers of world Jewry, with their wealth, their women and their media.'" Hallucinating further along the rutted path of anti-Jewish conspiracy theories laid down by *The Protocols of the Learned Elders of Zion* and renewed by the Nazis, he fantasized that "the Israelis have produced a coin on which it is written 'We shall never allow Islam to be established in the world.'" In a 1988 speech, Azzam also invoked the blood libel itself, talking about how Jews "mix the blood of a Christian or Muslim into dough."

The Protocols of the Learned Elders of Zion, often referred to as *The Protocols of the Elders of Zion* or simply *The Protocols*, is another strand, along with the other interwoven charges of blood libel, deicide and "Palestinian genocide" in the perpetually recombining DNA of Jew-hatred.

---

19 "Osama Bin Laden: The Past; Abdullah Assam: The Man Before Osama Bin Laden," by Steve Emerson, International Association for Counterterrorism & Security Professionals, www.iacsp.com.

Devotion to the Palestinian narrative is a contemporary *Protocols*-like incarnation. The work's reach, like that of the original blood libel, extended and extends far beyond its initial and immediate audiences. *The Protocols'* tale of an international Jewish conspiracy to rule the world reflects and engraves the nation/race-killer template. It perpetuates hatred of Jews as individuals and a collective animus against Jews as a people.

The Times of London exposed *The Protocols* in 1921 as a turn-of-the-century Russian forgery that plagiarized earlier French fiction. It had appeared, in various and varying pamphlet versions, in the first years of the 20th century and well served Russia's pro-monarchist, anti-modernizing, antisemitic Black Hundreds. The work contributed to incitement that led to pogroms like the Kishinev massacre, immortalized by the Hebrew poet Chaim Nachman Bialik in "On the Slaughter" (1903). Based on eye-witness testimony, the poem includes the lines:

> Executioner, here's my neck:
> Slaughter! You've got the ax and the arm.
> The world to me is a butcher-block—
> we, whose numbers are small
> it's open season on our blood:
> Crack a skull—let the blood
> of infant and elder spurt on your chest,
> and let it remain there forever, and ever.

Open season on the Jews was yet to come in a way neither Bialik nor most of his readers could imagine. Intrigued by *The Protocols'* lurid if vague account of an international Jewish conspiracy to dominate the world, Czar Nicholas II ordered an inquiry into the work's origins. He concluded, with disappointment, that it was false and cautioned that the reputation of a good cause [antisemitism] should not be soiled by a lie.

He needn't have worried. *The Protocols'* lie of a world-wide Jewish conspiracy has become—and throughout the Arab-Islamic world remains—perhaps history's second most influential fabrication, trailing only the blood libel itself. Henry Ford, for example, printed 500,000 copies of an English translation of *The Protocols* and distributed them across the United States in the 1920s. In the 1950s, Egyptian leader Nasser endorsed its explanation of 300 Zionists attempting to control the world. In the 1970s, Saudi King Faisal regularly gave visitors copies as gifts.

> When [U.S. Secretary of State] Henry Kissinger attended a state dinner in his honor hosted by Saudi King Faisal in 1975, the plot asserted by *The Protocols* set the tone. Kissinger recounts how the king informed him that "Jews and Communists [Hitler's "Jewish Bolsheviks"] were working now in parallel, now together, to undermine the civilized world as we knew it. Oblivious to my [Jewish] ancestry—or delicately putting me into a special category—Faisal insisted that an end be put once and for all to the dual conspiracy of Jews and Communists. The Middle East outpost of that plot was the State of Israel, put there by Bolshevism for the principal purpose of dividing America from the Arabs."[20]

The Hamas Charter of 1988 owed much to the conspiracy theories enshrined in and spawned by *The Protocols*. Relapsing to the early medieval European obsession with the Jew as anti-Christ, responsible for all the world's calamities, it alleged of the Jews that "with their money, they took control of the world media. … They were behind the French Revolution, the Communist revolution, and most of the revolutions we heard and hear about, here and there. … With their money they were able to control imperialistic countries and instigate them to colonize many countries in order to enable them to exploit their resources and spread corruption there.

"They were behind World War I, when they were able to destroy the Islamic Caliphate [nominally continued until then by the sultan of Ottoman Turkey]. … They were behind World War II, through which they made huge financial gains by trading in armaments, and paved the way for the establishment of their state … to enable them to rule the world."[21]

Iran's supreme leader, Ayatollah Ali Khamenei, also embraced while attempting to update the old line of the hidden Jewish-Zionist hand behind every ill. His book *Palestine*, is an obsessive-compulsive's farrago of hate-filled clichés. In method and tone it parallels Unibomber Ted Kaczynski's anti-establishment manifesto, the ayatollah substituting Jews for Kaczynski's demonical government and business. Early in 2017, Khamenei—who on International Holocaust Remembrance Day 2016 released a video denying the Holocaust—claimed that "the West's degra-

---

20 "The Scandal of U.S.-Saudi Relations," by Daniel Pipes, *National Interest*, Winter 2002-2003.

21 Rubin and Schwanitz, pages 251-252.

dation 'is most likely among Zionist plots aiming to destroy the society.'

"He elaborated, saying that gender equality takes away from a woman's main responsibility of being a housewife and mother. One week before the ayatollah's words were published, Palestinian-American activist Linda Sarsour, who helped organize the January, 2017 Women's March on Washington, got into the act. She claimed—with no sense of irony, let alone accuracy—that Zionism and feminism were incompatible," an incompatibility exemplified, no doubt, by among others Prime Minister Golda Meir and Esther Hayut, who in 2017 became the Israeli Supreme Court's third female president. In Sarsour's fevered version, "'rightwing Zionists' were keeping Palestinian women from being visible in social justice circles."[22] "Social justice," in the mouths of anti-Zionist antisemites, is another confiscated God-word, like accusations of racism, deployed to camouflage and justify their own bigotry.

Illustrating the growing acceptance of anti-Zionist antisemitism, *Glamour* fashion magazine named Sarsour one if its 2017 "Women of the Year." Never mind that she supported the anti-Jewish BDS campaign and terrorist bomber Rasmea Odeh, who killed Edward Joffee and Leon Kanner in Jerusalem in 1969 and later lied on immigration documents to become an American citizen. Illustrating the abandonment of intellectual honesty in academia, Sarsour also was selected that year to a New York University panel inquiring into antisemitism. In other words, what pro-Jewish, pro-Israel Jews have to say about anti-Zionism and antisemitism is biased; what defenders of murderers of Jews have to say about it is commendable.

The Palestinian mainstream was still making use of the *Protocols* in 2017. Palestinian Media Watch (PMW), a non-profit monitoring organization based in Israel, reported that Fatah spokesman Osama Al-Qawasmi invoked it on Palestinian Authority TV. Appearing on the "Topic of the Day" program April 16, Al-Qawasmi claimed the *Protocols* instructed "the Zionists"—not the Jews, a difference here and so often without a distinction—to create "extremist" Islamic "religious streams" that would undermine Arab regimes by causing "internal disputes."

Of course. In czarist times those clever, manipulative Zionist/Jews had the foresight and power to prepare to weaken the Arabs/Muslims of the 21st century, plotting even then to trick them into debilitating divisions. According to Internet videos and posts from 2014 and after, ISIS—the Islamic State in Iraq and Syria, a Muslim Brotherhood deriv-

---

22 "The Offbeat: Same Idiocy, Different Century; Today's most bizarre Zionist conspiracy theories," *The Jerusalem Post*, July 6, 2017.

ative several times removed—in actuality was the Israeli Secret Intelligence Service. It stirred upheaval in the Arab world and flooded Europe with Middle Eastern immigrants to destroy its white, Christian societies. ISIS leader Omar al-Baghdadi in fact was a Mossad agent named Simon Elliot. Indictments of Osama bin Laden as a secret Jew cannot be far behind. They will echo Islamic fundamentalists' propaganda against Mustafa Kemal Ataturk, founder of modern, secular Turkey and destroyer of the Ottoman caliphate, as a covert Jew.

"Corroboration" for the Islamic State in Iraq and Syria as Israeli Secret Intelligence Service fantasy could be found on Web sites like www.arabnyheter.info, along with claims that both the Ukrainian government and pro-Russian secessionists fighting it were led by Jews. This was another example, according to one poster, that "there are Jewish fingerprints all over everything bad that is happening in our world!" Exactly as *The Protocols* warned and as Hamas indoctrinates.

As for Al-Qawasmi, 2017 was not the first time he had cited *The Protocols* as legitimate. According to Palestinian Media Watch, he did so in 2015, alleging that it instructed Jews *not* to live in the Gaza Strip. Such ruthless Zionist forebearance.

In any case, members of the Palestinian public apparently did not need Al-Qawasmi to vouch for the forgery. PMW also noted that Norwegian NRK-TV's "Sunday Evening News" broadcast a segment on Feb. 10, 2013 examining Palestinian Authority "hate incitement" against Israel. At a café in Ramallah, where the NRK crew planned to ask patrons about *The Protocols*, it found them already discussing the work as genuine and as a guide to Israeli aims. One of the segment's conclusions was that "the most antisemitic text in the world is alive and well" among Palestinian Arabs.[23]

Anti-Jewish clichés are confirmed by their mere persistence. Without them Ayatollah Khamenei's book; the hundreds of anti-Israeli, antisemitic callers chronically indulged by C-SPAN's *Washington Journal* television program; and the countless anti-Israeli, anti-Jewish trolls populating the "talk back" or comment sections of Western newspapers from *The Guardian* (U.K.) to *The Washington Post* could not exist. For the anti-Israeli, anti-Jewish obsessive-compulsive, every factual support of Zionism and Israel instantaneously becomes proof of Jewish manipulation and subterfuge. It is not that Jews ever were the anti-Christ; it is rather that anti-Israel serves as the anti-Jew.

---

23 "Fatah spokesman presents *The Protocols of the Elders of Zion* as authentic document," Palestinian Media Watch, June 8, 2017.

The Necessity of Disbelief

Azzam taught bin Laden, and bid Laden financed Azzam. Together they co-founded al-Qaeda. Once more, what begins with the Jews does not end with the Jews.

This is too tiresomely factual to be relevant in the post-modern, deconstructionist sense. Regarding the anti-democratic left's "true lies" and its dogmatic belief in the right's "lying truths," Victor Davis Hanson added that "Orwell was onto the game far earlier than the French postmodernists. He rightly saw it as a postwar pathway of the Left to assuming and keeping power: What was written [in *Animal Farm*] on the barn wall on Monday as an absolute commandment was crossed out and replaced on Tuesday, in the fashion that the Soviet Union used to airbrush out sudden enemies of the people from all past pictorial records. Who knew what the party line would be by Wednesday? What frightened Orwell was not so much lying British industrialists or celebrities, but officers of the state who sought to dismiss the idea of the truth itself and justify the dismissal on ideological grounds."[24]

To lying industrialists, celebrities and officers of the state, victims of post-modernism must also add a variety of de facto clerics in this introverted belief system. Lying celebrities, demented by anti-Zionism antisemitism, were epitomized early by actress Vanessa Redgrave and more recently by Roger Waters, the robotically anti-Israel and increasingly antisemitic former member of the 1970s rock group Pink Floyd. Redgrave and Waters among others exhumed and rehabilitated the old, "genteel" British antisemitism as hatred of the Jewish state.

Subversion of contemporary education by the post-liberal left's multicultural conceit helps account for the prevalence of Redgrave, Waters et. al. Today education must not be understood as synonymous with learning. More accurately—especially in humanities or social sciences—it often simply means years spent in school, in what are assumed to be educational institutions. Data, information, facts, knowledge and wisdom are not synonyms. Repeated surveys suggest college graduates know less history than do entering freshmen. Time in school itself attests neither to knowledge nor wisdom.

The disjunction between education and learning can be seen in the career of Edward Said. Said epitomized the academic intersection of de Man, Foucault, Derrida and Lacan's post-modern nihilism and moral relativism with the Palestinian narrative. A Palestinian American

---

24 . Hanson, *National Review*, Aug. 30, 2016.

and Parr Professor of English and Comparative Literature at Columbia University, Said exemplified the "academic scribbler" of whom John
Maynard Keynes had warned. His influence in the late 20th and early
21st century captivated, if not enslaved, diplomats, other intellectuals
and journalists and excused madmen in arms if not authority. An Ivy
League faculty member, he also served as a member of the PLO's Palestine National Council. Said dealt not in knowledge or wisdom but rather
sophisticated polemics. In doing so, he provided the holy grail of anti-Israel "Palestinianism" with his enduringly influential, ultimately distorting 1978 work of Middle East revisionism, *Orientalism*. Here layered
in academic jargon was the big lie technique of Bolsheviks and Communists, of Nazis and conspiracy theorists from both the anti-democratic
left and right, as well as of anti-Western fundamentalists both secular
and religious.

The journalist and Middle East specialist Lee Smith, a former student of Said's, noted in his invaluable inquiry, *The Strong Horse: Power,
Politics, and The Clash of Arab Civilizations* that Said had been "one of
the early Anglophone advocates of French post-structuralism." Positing
an iron-clad, stereotypical view of Arabs as "the Other," Said asserted
that "every European, in what he what he could say about the Orient
[the Middle East for Westerners in the 19th Century] was consequently
a racist, an imperialist and almost total ethnocentric."[25] Of course, such
a sweeping generalization is itself almost totally ethnocentric. In addition, it opens the door to unacknowledged racism and deflects examination of "Oriental," that is, Islamic, imperialism, which over centuries
conquered and held great swaths of territory.

Orientalism, Smith wrote, "was not a book about the contemporary Middle East. ... But Said's conclusion—that the work of these [19th
century European] writers and scholars had served as a handmaiden of
the Western imperial endeavor to subjugate the Middle East—resonated
with modern Arab concerns. The book was very much of its time, keyed
to the self-image of a confident post-Algeria, post-Vietnam intellectual left for whom the Palestinian cause, with the paramilitary [terrorist]
élan of Yasser Arafat and the youthfully glamorous violence of his Soviet-backed cadre, *represented the revolutionary work that remained to be
done* [emphasis added]."[26]

Exactly what work was that for a post-Vietnam left in newly-em-

---

25 *The Strong Horse: Power, Politics, and the Clash of Arab Civilizations*, by Lee Smith,
Anchor Books, 2007 (2010 edition), page 35.
26 Ibid.

phasized sympathy with anti-Zionist "liberation" movements? Stimulated in part by sympathy and support for Arabs recently defeated by Israel in the 1967 Six-Day War, the work in general amounted to overturning the "hegemony" of the U.S.-led West. This would be accomplished in no small measure at home by negating the traditional American Anglo-Protestant civic culture of individual rights, responsibilities and equality resting on the sanctity of human life and other such oppressive bourgeois poses. It would be advanced overseas by, in particular, "liberating Palestine." That is, destroying the Jewish state, not coincidentally the only working Middle Eastern country based on individual rights, responsibilities and equality and increasingly a U.S. ally and recipient of American military aid.

Once more Smith: "Said was the transitional figure between the academy and the world of mainstream Arab politics. And thus it was no accident that American academics came to sound like Arab nationalist and Islamist ideologues claiming that the 9/11 attacks were justified due to America's bad policies in the Middle East. ... If you were not working to expose the racist lies fabricated for the purpose of destroying Third World peoples, then, willingly or not, you were collaborating with the state." So "if ideas or policies are not shaped in response to changing realities or interests, but determined by immutable qualities, like anti-Muslim and anti-Arab racism, then information is irrelevant and debates are a waste of time, for the central issue is always the same—whatever is wrong with the Middle East is the fault of the West."[27] And especially of the Jews and their state.

By 1967 the "New Left"—sounding, if with its beads, granny glasses and long hair not looking like the old left—was using the Vietnam and Six-Day wars to indict, respectively, the United States and Israel as militarist and imperialist. Uncle Sam was the greater imperialist, Israel the lesser. A generation later Islamism's "great Satan" and "little Satan" for America and the Jewish state hardly would amount to a variation on a theme.

How the New Left, despite its failure in North America and Europe to produce successful political parties, came to dominate the liberal arts disciplines of academia and thereby "shaped the sensibilities of a generation" and transform the West's intellectual atmosphere is the subject of Joshua Muravchik's *Making David into Goliath: How the World Turned Against Israel*. Here Said rates an entire chapter, "Edward Said Conquers Academia for Palestine." Muravchik explains that "for half a century fol-

---

27 Ibid., page 37.

lowing the Bolshevik seizure of power in Russia, the global Left divided into two main camps, communism and social democracy. ... Except for a brief moment in the late 1940s, communist regimes and movements were hostile to Israel, whereas Social Democrats supported the Jewish state overwhelmingly, until [Austria's Jewish premier] Bruno Kreisky and the Arab oil weapon appeared on the scene" in the 1970s.

"But in the 1960s, the New Left became dominant among the postwar generation .... In time it was to lend great weight to anti-Israel sentiment in the Western world including the United States, where the New Left achieved cultural power far greater than older leftist currents had exerted. In contrast to the Communists and Social Democrats who focused on the working class, the New Left appealed to students and the college-educated."[28] As the movement's "amorphous" ideology radicalized, "the books and ideas that for generations were regarded as the backbone of Western civilization were now systematically 'deconstructed.' Moses and Jesus, Plato and Aristotle, Augustine and Aquinas, Shakespeare and Tolstoy, Locke and Burke, Hamilton and Jefferson were exposed as but so many 'dead white males' .... At long last, their victims' day had come, and the study of their oppression and resistance replaced the traditional 'canon' on the front stage of higher education.

"The young professoriate was steered by new stars, and one of the brightest in their firmament was an American of Palestinian origin, Edward W. Said." His influence "ranged across literary criticism, politics, anthropology, Middle East studies and other disciplines including post-colonial studies, a field widely credited with having grown out of Said's work that examines the ongoing effects of colonialism. ... According to the Social Sciences Citation Index, he remains one of the most cited authors in the humanities."[29]

Said's "springboard," Muravchik writes, was *Orientalism*. "It expressed perfectly the temper of the intellectual times. Said's objective was to expose the evil worm at the core of Western civilization, namely, its inability to define itself except against an imagined 'other.' That 'other' was the Oriental, a figure 'to be feared ... or to be controlled.'" This two-dimensional construct, which ignores the bulk of Western religious, cultural and historical development over millennia, "echoed a theme of 1960s radicalism which was forged in the movements against Jim Crow and against America's war in Vietnam, namely, that the Cau-

---

28 *Making David Into Goliath; How The World Turned Against Israel*, by Joshua Muravchik, Encounter Books, 2014, page 98.

29 Ibid, page 99.

casian race was the scourge of humanity [and Israel would be reimagined as the spearhead of the Caucasian scourge]. Rather than shout this accusation from a soap box, as the activists had done, Said delivered it with an erudition that awed readers in admiring assent. The names of abstruse contemporary theoreticians and obscure long-ago academicians rolled off pages strewn with words that sent readers scurrying to their dictionaries."[30]

Said, polished "deconstructionist" and "post-modernist" that he appeared, "was more than just an intellectual on the make. He was also a man with a cause. A year after the appearance of *Orientalism*, Said published *The Question of Palestine*." Ah, the question of Palestine. Of Israel. Of the Jews. Edward Said as Farouk Qaddumi with a deconstructionist thesaurus.

"Fifteen years earlier, the Palestine Liberation Organization had been founded in the effort to crystallize a distinctive Palestinian identity." In other words, as late as 1964, the Palestinian Arabs, a people supposedly "from time immemorial," had yet to coalesce. To PLO terrorism that largely fashioned such an identity, Said added the "dramatically different face" of a prestigious Western academic. "Upon Said's death [in 2003], Alexander Cockburn lamented that 'the Palestinians will never know a greater polemical champion.'" Exactly. Penetrating Said's vocabulary, one found a polemicist, not a scholar.

"In the Leftist worldview, politics was at its core a contest between the forces of good and evil or of progress and reaction." This supports the understanding of the post-democratic left as a secular fundamentalist religious movement, a replacement, or supersession, for the three major monotheisms. Such institutional architecture was implicit in both the old left and New Left, with the Kremlin as a new Vatican, the Soviet *nomenklatura* acting as a replacement clerical hierarchy for the former. In the West, humanities departments and law schools often functioned as revived monasteries and faculty like Said as bishops in a new Holy See.

"To the Old Left this meant the struggle of the proletariat against the bourgeoisie. But to the New Left, of which Said was an avatar, the lines of conflict were demographic, young against old, female against male, and above all black against white. The Marxist notion of class struggle had never resonated in America, which lacked Europe's history of hereditary social position. Race was a different matter. For Europe, colonialism and imperialism were the original sins. But in America the

---

30 Ibid, page 100.

victimization of blacks through slavery and segregation was the running sore. ... Said rolled American racism and European colonialism into one ball of wax: white oppression of darker-skinner peoples."

His unique contribution to this pre-existing formula was "in portraying 'Orientals' as the epitome of the dark-skinned; Muslims as the representative Orientals; Arabs as the essential Muslims; and finally, Palestinians as the ultimate Arabs. Abracadabra! Israel, in conflict with the Palestinians, was transformed from a redemptive refuge from 2,000 years of persecution to the very embodiment of white supremacy."[31] And more; the Jews, who for a generation after the Holocaust epitomized the oppressed Other, would be ousted from that role by Palestinian Arabs, oppressed by Nazi-like Zionists of the Jewish state.

Said worked in soil already fertilized by disciples of the post-war, largely French deconstructionists. These were the "New Philosophers" of the late 1960s. They embraced, according to author Paul Berman, "'Third Worldism.' This was a leftism of a slightly new kind—the doctrine that looked for a new and superior revolutionary society to emerge not from the industrialized Western countries, who constituted the 'First World,' and not from the Soviet Bloc, who constituted the 'Second World,' but instead from anticolonial movements in the poorest regions of Africa, Asia and Latin America." These New Leftists "gazed with veneration at leaders like Mao Zedong, Ho Chi Minh and Fidel Castro .... But Third Worldists venerated the communist leaders because those people were anti-imperialists from the formerly colonized zones, and not because of their communism."[32]

Berman draws on Pascal Bruckner's dismemberment of the "Third Worldist" pose, *The Tears of the White Man: Compassion as Contempt*. It "lays out for critical examination a lengthy catalog of left-wing European clichés about the poor and oppressed in other parts of the world," highlighting how "under a Third Worldist influence, even the most brilliant of Western intellects had proved to be absurdly incapable of recognizing everyday people in faraway places as everyday people." This was, in short, the sin of Said's Orientalists in reverse. Instead of allegedly racist descriptions of Arabs and Muslims by 19th century Europeans, one found romanticization of these same Arabs and Muslims as functional equivalents of Rousseau's non-existent noble savages. "Fantasies, in short," Berman states. And the noblest of them all—by virtue of their

31 Ibid, page 102.

32 *The Flight of the Intellectuals; The Controversy Over Islamism and the Press*, Paul Berman, Melville House Publishing, 2010, 2011, page 268.

ceaseless war against the colonialist, imperialist, racist Jews—would come to be the perfectly fantasized Other, the Palestinian Arabs.

"The intellectual class, in Bruckner's portrait, has come to resemble the medieval clergy, a 'penitential caste,' which communicates its dogma of remorse by expounding multicultural theories of inexpiable Western guilt, and looks for ever newer ways to display its own humility," Berman says.[33] And the secular intelligentsia served in the mid- to late-20th century as the medieval Roman Catholic clergy had in its day—displaying its own humility in the oldest of ways: sacrificing on superficially updated grounds the primal Westerner and most ancient of Others, the Jew.

The September, 1999 issue of *Commentary* magazine published an exposé, "'My Beautiful Old House' and Other Fabrications," written by Israeli legal researcher Justus Reid Weiner. It showed that Said largely had falsified his background, including his bona fides as a persecuted "Palestinian." Said then rushed out an autobiography confirming Weiner's findings "without acknowledging or making any attempt to explain the earlier contrary claims ....In reaction to the exposé, Said and several of his supporters unleashed a ferocious assault on Weiner."[34] Shoot the messenger. This tactic amounted to a strategy, metaphorically and actually, for anti-Zionist antisemitism.

Muravchik goes on to note how scholars including Robert Irwin, a historian of Orientalism and author of *Dangerous Knowledge*, refuted Said and how Columbia University's professor of English and Comparative Literature had discounted "almost entirely Ignaz Goldziher, who was arguably the most important Orientalist of them all." Said's intellectual dishonesty was such that he ignored "countless cases" in which the work of actual Orientalists contradicted his sweeping generalizations.

No matter. In coming up with the equivalent of a slot machine's three cherries, Said's *Orientalism* hit the academic jackpot: In a time "when it was widely asserted that all white people were inherently bigoted .... Nowhere was the evidence laid out in greater depth and seeming sophistication than in Said's pages." Among other malign effects, his disciples in the United States took over the Middle East Studies Association, which they still occupy. So, Zionism, which once saw itself as a "workers' movement" and part of the Old Left, "became redefined against its will as a movement of white people competing for land with people of color. This transformation meant that from then on the Left

33 Ibid, 272.
34 *Making David Into Goliath*, Muravchik, page 103.

would be aligned overwhelmingly and ardently against Israel." And this had been Said's goal all along, as he confessed decades later. Muravchik quotes him as saying "I don't think I would have written that book had I not been politically associated with a struggle. The struggle of Arab and Palestinian nationalism is very important to that book."[35]

∽

Christian supersessionism for centuries had assigned Jews a theological and social inferiority confirmed by their satanic associations. Those imagined associations, asserted as proven, routinely flared in popular passion and mystery plays throughout medieval and into Renaissance times. Pope Pius V justified his expulsion of the Jews from the Papal States in 1569, for example, because "they seduce a great many imprudent and weak persons with their satanic illusions, their fortune-telling, their charms and magic tricks and witcheries, and make them believe the future can be foretold, that stolen goods and lost treasures can be recovered and much else can be revealed."[36] Not until 1962 – 1965 and Pope John XXIII's Vatican II Council would the doctrine of supersessionism be rejected.

But "Palestinian supersessionism," finding a welcome among Western leftists, trumped the old traditional Christian variety (itself making a comeback among anti-Zionists). In *1984*, George Orwell introduced the "two-minute hate," the object of which today is not the novel's Trotsky-like character Emmanuel Goldstein, supposed enemy of the Stalinist "Big Brother," but Israel. In keeping with its classical antisemitic roots, the daily anti-Zionist hate lasts not just for two minutes but runs like the obsessive-compulsive disorder it is, around the clock.

In the American Anglo-Protestant civic culture—especially as expanded over time, often under political pressure, by assimilation and integration—a wide variety of non-Anglo-Protestants, including Jews, thrived. In the latter 20th century, the god of communism had failed. So the "progressive" overturning of liberal, democratic-capitalist America based on this Anglo-Protestant ("Judeo-Christian") civic culture would be accomplished partially through multi-culturalism. With its neo-Marxist charges—colonialist, imperialist, racist and so

---

35 Ibid, page 119.

36 *The Devil and the Jews, The Medieval Conception of the Jew and Its Relation to Modern Antisemitism*, by Joshua Trachtenberg, Yale University Press, 1943; Meridian Books, World Publishing Co. and The Jewish Publication Society, 1961, page 76.

on—multi-culturalism in deconstructionist terms "privileged" Said's "the Other." In partnership with "diversity" (misunderstood as if the U.S. motto was, as Vice President Al Gore Jr. once erroneously put it, *e unum pluribus* instead of *e pluribus unum*), multi-culturalism undermined civic bonds in favor of social-cultural balkanization. The resultant aggrieved identity groups increasingly outflanked the democratic process. That process required establishing common ground, building consensus, winning elections, passing legislation and accepting that half a loaf was better than none and socially more sustainable than the whole loaf and everyone else be damned. In other words, it required cooperation and compromise with those not like oneself, one's group or class. Ironically, cooperation with a multitude of different individuals instead of Balkan balancing of Others. How bourgeois, how boring, how functionally cross-cultural and utterly non-telegenic. For post- and anti-democratic groups to get their way, to outflank the old liberal order, they would need and find bogeymen.

In the case of "the Palestinian cause," the revolutionary work that remained to be done was answering "the question of Palestine" by scapegoating and eliminating Israel. Hence the replacement of the pre-World War II, pre-Holocaust "red-black" (communist-fascist) alliance of convenience. Highlighted by the Molotov-Ribbentrop pact, that temporary, anti-democratic expedient has been echoed by the post-colonial "red-green" (far-left/Islamic fundamentalist) anti-democratic cabal. One such early and high-level connection joined Fidel Castro with Muammar Qaddafi in the 1970s. The Cuban dictator accepted the Libyan tyrant's proposal to join forces in regard to the "Non-Aligned Movement." Qaddafi and Castro hoped to move NAM, previously led by Indian Prime Minister Jawaharlal Nehru, in a more clearly anti-Western direction. Qaddafi's condition for Castro's participation, which the latter met, was new Cuban hostility to Israel.

Castro's original political hero had been Benito Mussolini, creator of Italian fascism, to which Mussolini moved from his earlier socialism, from one extreme to its fraternal twin without pausing in the antithetical center at liberal democracy. With his hours'-long harangues, the Cuban leader emulated his early idol's operatic speeches. But Castro's "Viva la revolucion!" could not disguise the fact that by the 1980s more than one million Cubans—10 percent of the population—had risked their lives to flee his proletariat paradise. Via Qaddafi, anti-Zionism would add to the reactionary nature of the regime in Havana.

Arafat, notwithstanding his slogan asserting "It is a revolution until victory!" also was functionally a counter-revolutionary. He did not fight to win freedom and prosperity for Arabs any more than Castro ruled his island to bring such conditions to Cubans. In Jordan's 1970-1971 "Black September" rebellion against King Hussein and in Lebanon's post-1975 civil wars and elsewhere, Arafat killed more Arabs than he did Israelis. His revolution strategically sought one thing only, regardless of countless tactical shifts. That was the undoing of the Zionist revolution, the negation of the successful national liberation of the Jewish people. This no matter how many innocent Arab lives—Muslims and Christians—would be sacrificed.

Arafat, his successor Mahmoud Abbas and their PLO worked ceaselessly to deny to Jews sovereignty and equality on any portion of their ancestral homeland. They rejected "two-state solution" offers of national independence—if that required peaceful coexistence with Israel as a Jewish state—in 2000 at Camp David, 2001 at Taba, Egypt, in 2008 after the Annapolis conference and in 2014 and 2016 when U.S. Secretary of State John Kerry and Vice President Joseph Biden, respectively, proposed "frameworks" in which to renew talks to that end. Arafat and Abbas refused, just as their predecessors had rejected territorially more favorable offers from the British in the 1930s and the United Nations in 1947 even before Israel's 1948-1949 War of Independence.

Arafat's counter-revolution envisioned not so much a new, 22nd Arab country, but rather denial of statehood for the Jews. That's why building institutions of a state-in-waiting—as Palestinian Jews of the *yishuv* did in the half-century before Israel's independence—was chronically sporadic and half-hearted under the PLO. There was one notable exception: The multiplication of security and intelligence agencies (whose members often committed acts of anti-Israel terrorism) with which to appease various Palestinian clans and factions and suppress the Palestinian public as necessary.

Arafat intended to return the Jews to their historic status as one more inferior non-Arab/non-Sunni Muslim minority. Such Middle East minorities include the Kurds of Iraq, Iran, Syria and Turkey; Copts of Egypt and various other Christian sects, among them Lebanon's Roman Catholic Maronites, Lebanese and Syrian Greek Orthodox and Iraqi Chaldeans; Berbers (Imazighen) of the North African states; Druze; Yazidis; Circassians and others, even Shi'ite Muslims under Sunni Muslim rulers. Ending the Jews' temporarily renewed ability to defend themselves as a nation would help restore the "natural order" and enable Arabs, particularly Palestinians, to regain their "dignity" and "rights." The struggle was not for equality with the Jews. Rather, it was a zero-sum game that required someone—non-Sunni Muslim minorities in general, the Jews in particular—to lose.

Until that loss, the Jews' humiliating sovereign equality would fire pan-Arab, pan-Islamic Sunni supremacism like no other cause since the collapse of the Ottoman caliphate in the aftermath of World War I. And intentionally or not, answering the question of Palestine by erasing the existence of Israel would revive an earlier, related query, the one that as Jonathan Rosen noted so agitated 19th and early 20th century European intellectuals, ideologues and dictators. That would be the Jewish question.

The rock group "The Who" had it right in the last lines of its 1971 hit, "Won't Get Fooled Again": "Meet the new boss/Same as the old boss." Arafat's anti-Zionist, anti-Jewish revolution was actually a counter-revolution. It combined Arab Sunni supremacism and fascist methods, with antisemitism as connective tissue. It brought nothing new. At its heart, its propaganda reached back through late medieval times to classical antiquity, with Imperial Germany and the Third Reich and associated Nazi propaganda for the Arab world as way stations. But to be successful, the lies at its core had to confiscate Jewish truths.

CHAPTER FIVE

'Palestine is a Term the Zionists Invented!'

I T IS SAID that all people have a name for their native country in their native language. Not quite all. For example, those Arabs who claim to be Palestinians do not. Palestine is an English word, derived through the Latin *Syria-Palestina* and that from the Hebrew, *pleshet*, which referred to the Philistines. These were the people who settled on the Mediterranean coast southwest of Judea and Samaria around 1,200 B.C.E. The Israelites understood them to have come from *Caphtor*, the Mediterranean island of Crete specifically, Mediterranean locales generally. The Arabic "Filistin" derives from the English "Palestine," not the other way around.

In Washington, it's often said, a *faux pas* is telling the truth prematurely. Or, sometimes more to the point, when conventional wisdom has made truth appear false, truth-telling *ex post facto*. As when former House Speaker Newt Gingrich observed during his 2012 Republican presidential primary bid that the Palestinians were an "invented" people, "historically part of the Arab community.

"They had a chance to go many places, and for a variety of political reasons we have sustained this war against Israel now since the 1940s, and it's tragic." "Sustained" meaning that the West—led by the United States—helped foster and perpetuate the Palestinian Arab "refugee" issue and identity. It did so primarily by funding but not supervising, decade after decade, the United Nations Relief and Works Agency and the anti-Israel campaign rooted in UNRWA.

UNRWA became a key support first of the Palestine Liberation Organization and later Hamas. Its refugee schools spewed antisemitic, anti-Zionist propaganda. Its PLO and Hamas personnel prevented—

murderously when they deemed necessary—UNRWA from implement-
ing its original, temporary, mission. This was to have been the "rehabilitation" of Arab refugees from Israel's 1948-'49 War of Independence and
resettling them outside the camps in the Gaza Strip, West Bank, Jordan,
Syria and Lebanon. Instead, the temporary camps were perpetuated as
permanent slums (though some, three generations later, have come to
resemble working class neighborhoods throughout the Middle East, including south Tel Aviv). Festering, they provided generations of terrorist
recruits, and by their presentation of immiserated Arab refugees, influenced opponents of the Jewish state from Christian relief organizations
and journalists to academics and diplomats. They did so thanks primarily to American and European largesse, followed by that of the Israelis.
Arab states, so taken with the Palestinian issue emotionally, were less
so financially. Regardless of recurrent sizeable pledges, they contributed
little to UNRWA.

The usual suspects, including members of the U.S. news media,
academics and Palestinian spokesmen, erupted at Gingrich's *"faux pas."*
In doing so they shed more heat than light. The obvious question, who
were the Arabs of British Mandatory Palestine, the parents, grandparents and great-grandparents of today's "Palestinians," went largely unasked. More accurately, avoided when not furiously repressed.

Israeli Prime Minister Golda Meir supposedly had said that "there
is no such thing as a Palestinian people." This, allegedly, was "racist."
Google cites the statement more than 18,000 times. But as the Elder of
Ziyon Website has noted, it's false:

"Here is what Meir said, referring to when the bulk of Zionists
returned to their land in the first half of the 20th century, quoted in the
June 15, 1969 *Sunday Times* [U.K.]:

'There were no such thing as Palestinians. When was there
an independent Palestinian people with a Palestinian state?
It was either southern Syria before the First World War, and
then it was a Palestine including Jordan. It was not as though
there was a Palestinian people in Palestine considering itself
as a Palestinian people and we came and threw them out and
took their country away from them. They did not exist.'

Notice that she stated it in the past tense, and given the time-
frame she was referring to, her statement is indisputable....
There is another interesting thing about the timing of her

statement. The first time that Palestinian Arabs were recognized as a 'people' by the United Nations was not in the 1940s or '50s. It was in December, 1969, six months after Meir spoke on the topic. In General Assembly Resolution 2628, it refers to the 'people of Palestine'—the first time that this term was used by the United Nations to refer exclusively to Palestinian Arabs.[1]

Before 1948 and the proclamation of a Jewish state called "Israel" with citizens then by definition "Israelis," "Palestinian" often meant Jew, in particular Zionists settling British Mandatory Palestine. Hence Jewish institutions such as the Palestine Land Development Company, *The Palestine Post* (today's *Jerusalem Post*), Palestine National Fund (now the Jewish National Fund) and Palestine Philharmonic Orchestra (Israel Philharmonic Orchestra). All manifested, in differing degrees and ways, the Zionist effort to renew—not newly-establish—the Jewish people in *eretz Yisrael.*

"And the first time that the term 'Palestinians' was used by the United Nations in reference to Palestinian Arabs," Elder of Ziyon noted, "was a year later, in A/Res/2628 in November, 1970.

"Isn't it interesting that for more than 20 years after the Palestinian Arab exodus, the United Nations never referred to them as a people? Only after the [1967] Six-Day War, when the Arab world changed its tactics from bragging about 'throwing the Jews into the sea' and into 'Jews as tyrants, Arabs as victims' did the United Nations pick up on this new construct of recognizing a people and a state whose existence were denied even by Arabs only a few years beforehand."[2]

Meir's observation had faded by the time Gingrich provided his potentially teachable moment—had journalists and politicians been teachable on this point—in December, 2011. Gingrich then told an interviewer from U.S. cable television's Jewish Channel, "Remember, there was no Palestine as a state. It was part of the Ottoman Empire. And I think we've had an invented Palestinian people, who are in fact Arabs, and were historically part of the Arab community."[3]

"Palestinian Arab leaders quickly branded the statements 'ri-

1 "Golda Meir, the U.N., and 'Palestinians,' June 30, 2010, www.elderofziyon.com, http://elderofziyon.blogspot.com/2010/06/golda-meir-un-and-palestinians.html.
2 Ibid.
3 "Touching a Nerve—Palestinian Origins," by Andrea Levin, CAMERA, Dec. 22, 2011, http://www.camera.org/article/touching-a-nerve-palestinian-origins/ .

diculous,' 'racist,' 'vulgar,' 'ignorant,' and a threat to 'peace and stability." Andrea Levin, president and executive director of CAMERA—the 65,000-member, Boston-based Committee for Accuracy in Middle East Reporting in America—commented that the news media "largely covered the controversy as a political *faux pas*, an indicator of pandering to Jewish voters and an attempted detour away from creating a Palestinian state. Indeed, many journalists inferred and reported that the Gingrich statements primarily indicated opposition to modern day statehood" for Palestinian Arabs.

As a result, the day after the December 9 interview aired, Gingrich's office "issued a statement ... explicitly saying he 'supports a negotiated peace agreement between Israel and the Palestinians, which will necessarily include agreement between Israel and the Palestinians over the borders of a Palestinian state."[4] But when a teachable moment must be quashed, outrage—real and feigned—must be unleashed. So Palestinian Prime Minister Salam Fayyad [a rare actual moderate and uncorrupted Palestinian Authority leader, later to be pushed out by PA President Mahmoud Abbas' ruling clique] urged Gingrich to apologize. He claimed "our people has been on this land from the beginning. And it is determined to stay until the end."

Really?

PA chief negotiator and later PLO secretary general Saeb Erekat, a serial fabricator granted unlimited credibility by Western journalists and politicians, said: "Mark my words ... these statements of Gingrich's will be the ammunitions [sic] and weapons of the bin Ladens and the extremists for a long, long time."[5]

In 2002, Erekat told CNN, frequently credulous when receiving anti-Israel propaganda, of the graves of 500 Palestinian Arabs massacred by Israel troops in Jenin on the West Bank. The charge circled the globe before being contradicted by the reality of 56 Palestinian deaths, nearly all combatants, in house-to-house fighting in Jenin during which 23 Israeli troops also died, partly because Israel foreswore bombing in the built-up neighborhood. In 2005, Erekat claimed in an *International Herald Tribune* commentary that Israel fielded the world's "fifth largest" military when, according to the International Institute for Strategic Studies, the correct ranking was 18. In that same year he asserted to Agence France Presse that the 2003 diplomatic "road map" for Israeli-Palestinian peace promoted by the United States, Russia, United

---

4 Ibid.
5 Ibid.

Nations and European Union committed Israel to releasing Palestinian prisoners. The "road map" did not mention Palestinian prisoners. No matter, when Saeb Erekat—later secretary general of the PLO—spoke, Western news media transcribed.

Palestinian activist and PLO member Hanan Ashrawi—a Christian Arab woman lacking any significant political base of her own but nevertheless a frequent news media "Palestinian spokesperson"—labeled candidate Gingrich's observation "very racist," betraying "an unforgivable bias. ... It is unbelievable that Mr. Gingrich, who studied history at two outstanding American universities and even taught history, could make such a misguided comment, solely for the sake of political pandering."

Ashrawi, in the 1970s a graduate student girl-friend of ABC TV's Beirut correspondent—and later network anchor—Peter Jennings, has been, like Erekat, a Palestinian English-speaker long in unconditional possession of a Western media platform. Jennings himself was a chronic on-air critic of Israel and Palestinian apologist. For example, during the 1972 Munich Olympics massacre of Israeli athletes, as *The New Republic's* editor, Martin Peretz, later observed, Jennings implicitly excused the Palestinian terrorists as "helpless and desperate."[6] Chronically, with such unreliable sources, conflicts of interest and false "framing," news media abetted construction and maintenance of the Palestinian narrative.

A spokesman for the Arab League echoed Ashrawi. Even former U.S. Senator John Sununu (R-N.H.), who had served as President George H. W. Bush's chief of staff, felt compelled to jump in: "When bigots speak, their words have purpose. They intentionally choose phrases that inflame, denigrate, and marginalize other races, religions, or nationalities."

Yes, that is the purpose of bigots who intentionally inflame, denigrate, and marginalize other races, religions, or nationalities, including bigots specializing in the anti-Jewish lie of Palestine. Unfortunately for Erekat, Ashrawi and the others, the history they fumed Gingrich was rewriting was all on the former speaker's side. The author and scholar Marie Syrkin (a Labor Zionist and sometime endorser of Peace Now positions) wrote in a 1970's essay:

> The characterization of Palestinian nationalism as 'artificial' does not come from Zionist adversaries but from classic Arab sources. In the period before and after the issuance of

---

6 "Peter Jennings, The ABC's of Bias," *Honest Reporting*, Feb. 6, 2003, http://honestreporting.com/peter-jennings-the-abcs-of-bias/ .

the Balfour Declaration, Arab nationalists consistently protested the use of the name 'Palestine' or the adjective 'Palestinian' to demark them from other Arabs in the region. All
the declarations for the nascent Arab nationalist movement
from 1880 on concentrated on 'the unity of Syria' with no
references to Palestine as other than 'south Syria.' Nothing
could be more explicit than the statement of the General Syrian Congress in 1919: 'We ask that there should be no separation of the southern part of Syria, known as Palestine, nor
of the littoral western zone which includes Lebanon, from
the Syrian country. We desire that the unity of the country
should be guaranteed against partition [by the victorious
World War I allies] under whatever circumstances....

George Antonius, the noted Arab historian, wrote in his 1939
work *The Arab Awakening*: 'Except where otherwise specified the term Syria will be used to denote the whole of the
country of that name which is now split up into mandated
territories of [French] Syria and the Lebanon, and [British]
Palestine and Transjordan [today's Jordan].'[7]

The Palestinian Arab leader Haj Amin al-Husseini originally opposed the Palestine Mandate on the grounds that it separated Palestine
from Syria. In his early days he emphasized that there was no difference between Palestinian and Syrian Arabs in national characteristics
or group life.[8]

Arab-American historian and Princeton University professor
Philip Hitti testified against partition before the Anglo-American Committee in 1946: "There is no such thing as 'Palestine' in history, absolutely not...[It is but] a very small tiny spot there on the southern part of the
eastern shore of the Mediterranean Sea, surrounded by a vast territory
of Arab Muslim lands, beginning with Morocco, continuing through
Tunis, Tripoli and Egypt, and going down to Arabia proper, then going
up to Transjordan, Syria, Lebanon, and Iraq — one solid Arab-speak-
ing bloc — 50,000,000 people."[9] The "solidity" of that "Arab bloc" would

---

7 *The Palestinians: People, History, Politics,* edited by Michael Curtis, Josephy Neyer,
Chaim L. Waxman and Allen Pollack, Transaction Books, 1975, page 200, in chapter
on "Palestinian Nationalism: Its Development and Goal," by Marie Syrkin.
8 Ibid.
9 *Palestine Betrayed*, Efraim Karsh, Yale University Press, 2010, pages 39-40, citing Abu

be exposed in the post-2011 Arab Spring blood-letting, though by then "Palestine" and "the Palestinians" had far outrun Hitti's assertion of their non-existence.

His "vast territory of Arab Muslim lands" also included minority groups large and small, non-Arab, non-Muslim or both. Among them, as noted, were and are Kurds, Berbers, Copts, Maronites, Druze, Greek Orthodox, Circassians, Yazidis, and, of course, Jews. Even among Sunni Arabs, for example, Egyptians sometimes disparaged inhabitants of the Arabian peninsula as simply "Arabs," people of lower status than Egyptians themselves (for example during World War I, as related in Michael Korda's *Hero: The Life and Legend of Lawrence of Arabia*). They were still doing so regarding oil-rich parvenus like the Saudis in the first years of the 21st century, according to Lee Smith in *The Strong Horse*. But Hitti's description reflected the supremacism or arrogance, conscious or unconscious, of pan-Arab (predominantly Sunni Muslim) nationalism. It had little or no room to recognize "the Other," let alone accord such groups equality, Edward Said's prestidigitations notwithstanding.

According to Syrkin, Ahmed Shukeiry also rejected the idealization of a historically-rooted Palestinian Arab national identity. "Later founding head of the PLO [Palestine Liberation Organization], he told the [U.N.] General Assembly in 1956: 'It is common knowledge that Palestine is nothing but Southern Syria.'"[10]

It is argued, including by many Israelis, that a specific Palestinian Arab people has been forged in the crucible of the 20th and 21st century Arab-Israeli conflicts, its lack of deeper historical roots notwithstanding. This is said to be particularly so as that conflict centered—or at least purportedly centered—on the Palestinian-Israeli struggle. But not in the view of Azmi Bishara, for one. Bishara, a former Israeli Arab Knesset [parliament] member, fled the country in 2007. He was being questioned about passing information to the enemy, the Iranian-backed Lebanese Shi'ite Hezbollah (Party of God), in war time. In a televised interview in 2009 he stated:

> Well, I don't think there is a Palestinian nation at all. I think there is an Arab nation, I always thought so and I didn't

---

Khaldun Sati al-Husri, al-Uruba Awalan (Beirut: Dar al-Ilm li-l-Malain, 1955, pages 11-13; Hearing before the Anglo-American Committee of Inquiry, Washington, D.C., State Department, Jan. 11, 1946, Central Zionist Archives (CZA), V/9960/g, pages 10-11.

10 *The Palestinians*, Curtis, Neyer, Waxman and Pollack, pages 200-201.

change my mind. I don't think there is a Palestinian nation, I think it's a colonial invention, Palestinian nation. When were there any Palestinians? Where did it come from? What I think—there is an Arab nation. I never turned to be a Palestinian nationalist, despite my decisive struggle against the occupation [against Israel]. I think that until the end of the 19th century, Palestine was the South of Great Syria.[11]

Neither Gingrich nor Bishara were ahead of the curve.

Zahir Muhsein, a member of the Palestine Liberation Organization executive committee, told the Dutch newspaper *Trouw* on March 31, 1977 that "The Palestinian people does not exist. ... The creation of a Palestinian state is only a means for continuing our struggle against the state of Israel for our Arab unity.

"In reality today there is no difference between Jordanians, Palestinians, Syrians and Lebanese. Only for political and tactical reasons do we speak today about the existence of a Palestinian people, since Arab national interests demand that we posit the existence of a distinct 'Palestinian people' to oppose Zionism. Yes, the existence of a separate Palestinian identity exists only for tactical reasons. Jordan, which is a sovereign state with defined borders, cannot raise claims to Haifa and Jaffa, while as a Palestinian, I can undoubtedly demand Haifa, Jaffa, Beersheva and Jerusalem. However, the moment we reclaim our right to all of Palestine, we will not wait even a minute to unite Palestine and Jordan."[12]

Muhsein's point was not new among Palestinian Arab representatives, not even with Shukeiry in 1956. The First Congress of Muslim-Christian Associations in Jerusalem in 1919 was called to choose delegates to the Paris Peace Conference. In Paris the victorious World War I Allies—in particular Great Britain and France—would divide the Middle Eastern remnants of the defeated and crumbling Ottoman Turkish Empire. Muslim and Christian Arab delegates chosen in Jerusalem wanted the diplomats to get something straight: "We consider Palestine as part of Arab Syria, as it has never been separated from it at any time. We are connected with it by national, religious, linguistic, natural, economic and geographic bonds."

After World War II, a new generation of Arab representatives reiterated that position. In 1947, the United Nations was considering the

---

11 Interview, Israel Channel 2 Television, Jan. 8, 2009.
12 Interview, *Trouw*, March 31, 1977.

second partition of British Mandatory Palestine. The first, in 1921, had separated Transjordan from remaining mandatory lands. Transjordan—now Jordan—constituted more than three-fourths of the area originally intended for the mandate in which the Jewish national home was to be reestablished. A key element of the lie of Palestine claims that Israel, with its territorial gains in the 1948-1949 War of Independence added to the U.N.'s 1947's proposed allotment, holds "78 percent of historic Palestine" and the Arabs only 22 percent. This is not only a convenient historical revision, it is also necessary to the lie.

Colonial Secretary Winston Churchill awarded Transjordan (originally a British protectorate) to King Abdullah I as a consolation prize for Abdullah's Hashemite dynasty since it had just lost Arabia to ibn Saud and to Abdullah himself for ceding the new Iraqi throne to his brother. The Hashemites had the support of T. E. Lawrence ("Lawrence of Arabia") and others attached to the British administration in Cairo; Ibn Saud, who became the founder of Saudi Arabia, had been backed by rival British imperial officials in India. Korda, in his biography of Lawrence puts it this way:

> [Lawrence] was one of the political architects, if not the chief political architect, of the Hashemite Kingdom of Jordan. Already in 1921 there were considerable misgivings about Lawrence's solution to the problem of how to reward Abdullah [who helped lead the Lawrence-organized, British-funded Arab revolt against the Turks during World War I] for giving up any claim he had to the Iraqi throne in favor of his brother Feisal. The Balfour Declaration had prudently not attempted to define the exact frontiers of Palestine, but both historically and biblically it had always included the area to the east of the Jordan [River], as well as the west bank. Approximately three-quarters of the territory to which the Zionists aspired was now a separate country, under the rule of an emir and sharif of Mecca, with Jewish settlement forbidden there—an area moreover which potentially could have sufficient water and could be ideal for settlement and modern farming, but which would remain a sandy wasteland.[13]

One of the rare pro-Zionists in the British colonial administration

---

13 *Hero: The Life and Legend of Lawrence of Arabia*, by Michael Korda, HarperCollins, Harper Perennial, 2010, pages 519-520.

was Col. Richard Meinertzhagen, a flamboyant, sometimes violent mirror-image of Lawrence. Korda continues:

> The reaction of Lawrence's fellow political adviser ... Meinertzhagen was apoplectic and immediate, and echoed the feelings of the Zionist leadership: 'The atmosphere in the Colonial Office is definitely hebraphobe... Hubert Young and little Lawrence do their best to conceal their dislike and mistrust of Jews but both support the official pro-Arab policy of Whitehall and frown on the equally official policy based on the Balfour Declaration; the latter is the only policy I recognize. I exploded on hearing Churchill had severed the Transjordan from Palestine.... Lawrence was of course with Churchill and influenced him.... This reduces the Jewish National Home to one-third of Biblical Palestine.

Meinertzhagen's "foaming at the mouth" self-description of his reaction to the separation of Transjordan from what shortly would become the League of Nations' British Mandate for Palestine was "mild compared with those of the Zionists themselves, in Palestine and in the United States. The Israelis' belief that Jordan is, or ought to be, the Palestinian [Arab] state, and that the West Bank and the Gaza Strip were always intended to be part of the Jewish state, thus goes back to 1921." West of the Jordan River, the disturbed inhabitants of Palestine "suddenly found themselves living in a much smaller country than either the Jews or the Arabs had expected."[14]

Soon after, Churchill, Sir Herbert Samuel—new civilian high commissioner for British-controlled Palestine—and Lawrence made an inspection tour. "At one point, as Churchill, Samuel and Lawrence stood surrounded by a crowd of chanting, shouting Arabs, Churchill took off his hat to thank them for their prolonged cheers. 'What are they saying?' he asked Lawrence. 'Death to the Jews,'" quietly explained Lawrence, who prudently carried a pistol.[15]

Rather than Israel taking 78 percent of "historic Palestine," the actual division when the fighting stopped in 1949 was: Jordan, 77.5 percent; Israel, 17.5 percent; the Jordanian-occupied West Bank and Egyptian-occupied Gaza Strip the remaining five percent of the lands originally envisioned for the Palestine Mandate. No matter, the allega-

---

14 Ibid, page 520.
15 Ibid., page 520.

tion that Israel occupied more than three-fourths of "historic Palestine," a central element in the Palestinian narrative, persists.

Twenty-six years after the British created Transjordan, the U.N. General Assembly heard from the Arab Higher Committee in 1947 that "Palestine was part of the province of Syria" and "politically, the Arabs of Palestine were not independent in the sense of forming a separate political identity."[16]

But the Palestinian narrative, the interwoven lies of Palestine, is sacrosanct. In post-modern jargon, it is "privileged." An idol of two fundamentalisms, leftist secular and Islamic, it commonly exists beyond examination, debate and truth. So the uproar over Gingrich's *"faux pas"* led to virtually no worthwhile journalistic follow-up. Perhaps because to expose Palestinian national identity as a 20th century construct, like Soviet, Yugoslav, Rhodesian, North Korean and others largely imposed and maintained by force, would be to unravel it. At the least, doing so might minimize its claims. It would reveal that Palestinian nationalism has been—in contrast to Zionism, Jewish nationalism—destructive rather than constructive. Its primary objective was not to build a second Palestinian Arab state after Jordan, but rather to destroy Israel.

What was Israel to Palestinian Arab leaders? It was not just the world's only Jewish state, a blasphemous infliction on Arab-Islamic land. It also proved an identity-shaking reproach: The planet's most conspicuous example of successful post-colonial nation-building was a tiny, besieged territory populated initially mostly by Holocaust survivors and dispossessed Jewish refugees expelled from Arab lands. These latter refugees in the Jewish *nakba* numbered 840,000, of whom nearly 600,000 settled in Israel—compared to between 472,000 and 650,000 Arab refugees from what became Israel (more on the figures below).

The Arabic term *al-nakba* refers to the "catastrophe" and humiliation caused by Arab failure to destroy Israel in the 1948 war and resultant Arab self-dispossession. *Al-nakba* carries with it the sense of lost dignity imposed by having to live alongside victorious Jews behaving as equals, free and sovereign. In the Jews' *nakba*, refugees from Arab states lost land and other possessions worth as much as four times that left by Arabs fleeing Israel, according to figures circulated in the 1980s by the World Organization of Jews from Arab Countries. Yet almost from the beginning, the Jewish refugees built, the Arab refugees sought to destroy. From dozens of countries, speaking scores of languages, this apparent Jewish debris—degraded Holocaust survivors and dispossessed

---

16 Curtis, Neyer, Waxman and Pollack, page 200.

refugees from Arab lands—in two generations constructed a diverse democracy, a world leader in arts, technology and, of necessity, warfare. Former Israeli prime minister Ehud Barak echoed George Gilder by describing his country—in a commentary criticizing one of his successors, Benjamin Netanyahu—as "the most successful nation-building project of the 20the century: powerful scientifically, economically and militarily, with a vibrant culture."[17] On Israel as a success, at least there the two political opponents, former members of the same commando unit—Barak and Netanyahu—agreed. And they were correct.

The United Nations grew from 51 member states in 1945 to 192 in 2016. Additional countries included new states, old nations like Israel reborn and others newly freed. None achieved as much in their first seven decades in as many fields, let alone under such constant pressure as had the Jewish state. But rather than win for itself and its Jews the "normality" anticipated by the founder of modern political Zionism, Theodore Herzl, rather than deflate what he and his followers imagined was the primary cause of antisemitism—the Jews' abnormal statelessness—Israel's very successes, the jealousy and sense of inferiority they engendered in many other lands, among many other people, helped reignite the ancient hatred. Like a super virus, antisemitism is holistically self-contained, mutating to counter remedies and virtually always self-protecting. Therefore, Jewish statelessness and Jewish statehood both are cause for suspicion and hatred.

So when it came to competing Palestinian nationalism, Saeb Erekat—like a poker player with a bad hand—bluffed and raised, hoping others would fold their cards. In this he acted, though with a more avuncular mien, as had previous generations of Palestinian Arab spokesmen. He sought to put beyond challenge the fiction of an ancient, indigenous Palestinian Arab people existing "from time immemorial" and possessing claims superior to any the Jews, the Israelis advanced. In Munich on Jan. 31, 2014 Erekat reportedly asserted that Palestinian Arabs "cannot accept Israel as the Jewish state because they lived in the region long before the Jews." In the context of debate over the Jordan Valley [and Israel's insistence on retaining its own forces in the area as part of any agreement with the Palestinian Authority], Erekat claimed that his ancestors were the real descendants of the biblical Canaanites and lived in the region "5,500 years before Joshua bin-Nun, [according to the Torah, Moses' successor who led the Israelites into the Promised Land]."[18]

17 "Netanyahu has undermined Israel's security," *Washington Post*, Sept. 15, 2016.
18 "The fabricated Palestinian history," Feb. 7, 2014, by Nadav Shragai, *Israel HaYom*.

Erekat was not exaggerating, he was inventing. The "Palestinian narrative" of millennia-deep roots in *eretz Yisrael*/Palestine is neither solid, liquid nor gas. It's a vacuum. In a magazine-length follow-up, Nadav Shragai of the Jerusalem Center for Public Affairs investigated Erekat's fantasy, checking it against scholars of national movements, historians, Palestinian sources and the Quran. The conclusion? As Prof. Raphael Israeli, a Hebrew University Middle East scholar and expert on Islam put it, the Palestinian-Canaanite link Erekat asserts is "absurd. ... The Palestinians don't really have roots here. They know this very well, so they are trying to invent origins for themselves."

After quoting Prof. Israeli, Shragai cited two methods of constructing a national identity. The first is determining a grouping "on the basis of a shared culture and history. The second method is used by nations who do not have such a common history and thus need to invent it all from scratch."

Jewish culture and history, first rooted in and later focused on the land of Israel, goes back more than 3,000 years. Biblical and extra-biblical documents, supported by countless archeological finds, confirm it.

On the other hand, as Daniel Pipes has written, the notion of Palestinian Arab national identity extends not three millennia and more but barely one century, specifically from 1920.[19] In 1937, a Palestinian Arab leader named Auni Bey Abdul-Hadi told Britain's Peel Commission that "there is no such country [as Palestine]! 'Palestine' is a term the Zionists invented! There is no Palestine in the Bible. Our country was for centuries part of Syria."

From 1516 to 1917 when it was conquered by Great Britain during World War I, the area that became British Mandatory Palestine had been part of the Turkish Ottoman Empire. No district in it was called by its Muslim rulers "Palestine" and the inhabitants of the region, including Arabs, did not refer to themselves as "Palestinians."

Nevertheless, as typified by Erekat's claims, "the core of Arab propaganda has been based for years on the claim that the Palestinian people have been settling in present-day Israel for thousands of years, well before the Jews arrived as 'occupiers,'" Shragai wrote. "As the argument goes, the Palestinians, by virtue of their being descendants of the Canaanites, or the Philistines, or the Jebusites, are the real indigenous nation that sprung organically from this land. Then, as now, so the argu-

---

19 . "The Year the Arabs Discovered Palestine," by Daniel Pipes, *Middle East Review*, Summer, 1989.

ment goes, they are being occupied by the Jews."[20]

This claim gained force—perhaps became necessary—among Palestinian Arab nationalists after Israel's establishment in 1948 and its victorious War of Independence. It acquired additional currency after Israel captured the West Bank and Gaza Strip from Jordan and Egypt, respectively, in the 1967 Six-Day War. (Transjordan, following its conquest in 1948, had renamed Judea and Samaria "the West Bank" and itself Jordan. Only Great Britain and Pakistan recognized Amman's expanded claim to sovereignty.)

Inconveniently for Erekat's historical revisionism, about 1,000 B.C.E. the Israelites under King David defeated the non-Arab, non-Muslim Jebusites and turned the latter's main city into their own capital, Jerusalem. The Philistines, Mediterranean "sea people," landed around two or three centuries earlier on territory centered in the Gaza-Ashdod corridor, not the hill country of Judea and Samaria or the Galilee. Archaeological finds, including pottery styles, support the Hebrew Bible's identification of Philistine with Cretan or broader Mycenaean Greek culture. With more advanced Iron Age weapons and better military organization, the Philistines bedeviled the Israelites to the northeast off-and-on for centuries, even after temporary defeat at the hands of King David.

The Philistines' obliteration as a distinct people came at the hands of Babylonian armies under King Nebuchadnezzar II just before 600 B.C.E. The same forces would go on to besiege Jerusalem, capturing it and destroying the First Temple (Solomon's, built in the first half of the tenth century) in 586 B.C.E. Although Israelite leadership would be carried into Babylonian captivity, the Jews—in Babylon they would be referred to by that name for the first time—maintained their national identity. On the banks of the Euphrates River they longed and prayed for return to their holy city on Mt. Zion:

> By the rivers of Babylon/ There we sat down, yea, we wept/ when we remembered Zion./ Upon the willows in the midst thereof/We hanged up our harps./ For there they that led us captive asked of us words of song,/ And our tormentors asked of us mirth:/ Saying, 'Sing us one of the songs of Zion.'/ How shall we sing the Lord's song/In a foreign land?/ If I forget you, O Jerusalem/ Let my right hand forget its cunning./ Let my tongue cleave to the roof of my mouth,/ If I do re-

---

20 "Fabricated Palestinian History," Shragai, Israel Hayom.

member you not;/ If I set not Jerusalem/ Above my chiefest joy…(Psalm 137:1-6).

The Jews remembered. Forty-seven years later, in 539 B.C.E., Persian King Cyrus the Great conquered Babylonia and extended an empire that would cover much of the Middle East for the next two centuries, until Alexander the Great. One of Cyrus' acts after taking Babylon, as related on The Cyrus Cylinder in the British Museum, was to free subject peoples, including the Jews. The Prophet Isaiah conveyed the royal decree this way:

'I am the Lord, who makes all things/ Who stretches out the heavens all alone/ Who spreads abroad the earth by Myself/ Who frustrates the signs of the babblers, and drives diviners mad, who turns wise men backward, and makes their knowledge foolishness/ Who confirms the word of His servant, and performs the counsel of His messengers, Who says to Jerusalem, 'You shall be inhabited,' to the cities of Judah, 'You shall be built,' and will raise up her waste places/ Who says to the deep, 'Be dry!' and will dry up your rivers/ Who says of Cyrus, 'He is My shepherd, And he shall perform all My pleasure, saying to Jerusalem, 'You shall be built,' and to the temple, 'Your foundation shall be laid'" (Isaiah 44: 25-28).

Many of the Jews not only remembered but also returned from Babylonian captivity, to rebuild Jerusalem and lay the foundation for the Second Temple. One of their leaders, Ezra, described Cyrus' role as follows, echoing what the Persian declared of himself:

'This is what Cyrus king of Persia says: The Lord, the God of Heaven, has given me all the kingdoms of the earth and has appointed me to build a temple for him at Jerusalem in Judah./ Anyone of his people among you—may his God be with him, and let him go up to Jerusalem in Judah and build the temple of the Lord, the God of Israel, the God who is in Jerusalem./ And the people of any place where they may still be living are to provide them with silver and gold, with goods and livestock, and with freewill offerings for the temple of God in Jerusalem.'/
"Then the family heads of Judah and Benjamin, and the

priests [Cohanim] and Levites—everyone whose heart God had moved—prepared to go up and build the house of the Lord in Jerusalem/.... Moreover, King Cyrus brought out the articles belonging to the temple of the Lord, which Nebuchadnezzar had carried away from Jerusalem and had placed in the temple of his god [i.e. Marduk]/ Cyrus, King of Persia, had them brought by Mithradates the treasurer, who counted them out to Sheshbazzar the prince of Judah." (Ezra 1:2-5, 1:7-8).

As for claims like that of Erekat to "Canaanite," "Philistine" or other ancient identities, Shragai noted, "not only do the Palestinians deny, erase, and distort Jewish history—sometimes going to absurd lengths—but they also invent thousands of years of a new history of their own. All of sudden, the biblical Canaanites are Arabs, Jesus is a Palestinian who preached the virtues of Islam and not Christianity, and Moses? Well, Moses was a Muslim, after all."

Jesus-was-a-Palestinian is a favorite confiscation by Palestinian spokespersons, including Hanan Ashrawi, and target of transparent historical and theological revisionism advanced by anti-Jewish Christians. The Rev. Dr. Naim Ateek and his Sabeel Ecumenical Liberation Theology Center in Jerusalem epitomize this religio-historical jujitsu. They blatantly attempt to revive and promote the anti-Jewish charge of deicide, making not just Jesus, a Jew from Judea under Roman rule, a Palestinian Arab under Israeli oppression, but transforming Jesus-the-Palestinian into the Palestinian Arabs en mass. Eager to retrieve theological supersessionism discarded by Popes John XXIII and John Paul II, Sabeel traffics in reactionary "the Jews-killed-Christ" deicide claims. That is, in a slice of the original blood libel.

Decrying a "Palestinian Via Dolorosa," Sabeel has worked with the Global Ministry of the United Church of Christ and Disciples of Christ. According to Dexter Van Zile, a Christian media specialist and another former colleague of this author, the "overall effect is to portray Israel as a Christ-killing nation, and the Palestinians as innocent lambs of God who suffer for the sins of both Israel and for the failings of the international community." This "crucifixion imagery" attempts "to portray the Palestinians as innocent, Christ-like victims of a crucifixion perpetrated by Israel, the Jewish State."[21]

---

21 "Sabeel's Demonizing Liturgy," Dexter Van Zile, CAMERA, Dec. 7, 2007, www. camera.org.

Historically, Rome killed the Jewish Jesus, and the people he preached to in Judea were predominantly Jews and pagan gentiles. What they were not were Palestinian Arabs. Today's "Romans"—from the salons of Europe and faculty senates of North America to the Shi'ite holy cities of Qom and Karbala, to Sunni preachers and polemicists in Gaza and Nablus—wish to crucify the Jewish state. If Jews die in the process, individually or *en mass*, well, to update one of Josef Stalin's leading apologists, *New York Times*' Moscow correspondent Walter Duranty, one has to deconstruct some eggs to privilege a narrative omelet.

As for those ancient Palestinians, as Shragai reported, a Hamas' interior minister in the Gaza Strip, Fathi Hamad, has declared, "every Palestinian in Gaza and all over Palestine can prove their Arab roots, whether they be in Saudi Arabia and Yemen, or anywhere else. ... Speaking personally, half of my family is Egyptian."[22] Hence, the common "Palestinian" last name, al-Masri, the Egyptian.

Azmi Bishara, the expatriate former Knesset member wanted for espionage, wrote that Palestinian nationalism, "acting out of a need to compete with Zionism ... has anchored its origins with those of the Canaanites." Walid Shoebat, a former Fatah member who immigrated to the United States, converted to Christianity and spoke on behalf of his new religion and Israel, said, "We knew full well that our origin was not Canaanite. ... My grandfather would often remind us that our village, Beit Sahour, near Bethlehem, was empty when his father arrived there with six other families. Today there are over 30,000 residents" in Beit Sahour.

The Palestine Exploration Fund's Survey of Western Palestine described Beit Sahour as the "ruins of a village" in 1883. In 1922, the British Mandate census put its population at 1,519. In 2007, the Palestinian Central Bureau of Statistics said the population was 12,367. In any case, the residents' historically recent background was Arab but not Palestinian.

Contrary to Erekat's Canaanites-as-Arabs fantasy—taught in Palestinian Authority schools as history—the ancestors of the small population of Arabs resident in the land, mostly the 141,000 Muslims in 1878, generally did not possess roots going back to "time immemorial." Instead, their ancestors arrived beginning in the late 1400s and after from the Arabian Peninsula, Transjordan, Syria and Egypt, according to Prof. Shaul Bartal. Shragai quotes Bartal, a Middle Eastern scholar

---

22 "Another Tack: A Delegitimization Called Nakba," by Sarah Honig, *Jerusalem Post*, May 14, 2015.

at Bar-Ilan University, as asserting that today's Palestinian Arabs "are not the 'farmers who have lived in Palestine for generations,' but rather immigrants who only arrived recently.

"It was only toward the latter stages of the 19th century that the country began to blossom thanks to the emergence of a new presence— Zionism—and the amazing results" of a growing economy that required more labor, provided more opportunity and comparatively more health-ful living conditions. Shragai adds that "in 1939, then-U.S. President Franklin D. Roosevelt said that the immigration of Arabs to Palestine since 1921 was outpacing immigration of the Jews during that same pe-riod."[23] That was so in no small measure due to British interference. Au-thorities in Mandatory Palestine yielded in the face of Arab complaints and violence against Palestinian Jews in the 1930s and restricted Jewish, but not Arab, immigration just as European Jews most required a refuge.

If one wants to investigate "ethnic cleansing" and "displacement" or "dispossession," here is a good place to start. And Arieh L. Avneri's *The Claim of Dispossession: Jewish Land Settlement and the Arabs, 1878 – 1948* is an indispensable guide. (English edition, 1982, Hide-kel Press, Tel Aviv; Hebrew edition, 1980, Yad Tabenkin Institute for Kibbutz Research, Efal, Israel, Herzl Press, New York City; Hakibbutz Hameuchad Publishing House.) Examining countless land purchases by individual Jews and Zionist organizations throughout this 70-year period, scouring the records of Turkish and British land offices and court cases, Avneri documented repeatedly the extent to which Jewish resettlement led to reclamation of wastelands including sand dunes and malarial swamps. The founding Zionist "myth" of draining swamps and irrigating dunes has deep roots. Avneri shows over and over how Zion-ist reclamation sparked sudden interest in or renewed attraction to the (newly-more-valuable) land by Arabs. These included numerous absen-tee owners, resident tenant farmers, migratory Bedouin tribes, settled clans and others. And Avneri found cases of both cooperation as well as conflict between resettling Jews and Arab owners or migrants.

Some of the "Arab" arrivals transformed into "Palestinians" had not been Arabs at all, but Greeks, Bosnians and others from the Balkans and other parts of Europe. They included also Turks, Armenians, Kurds, Sudanese, Circassians, even Persians and Afghans, as Joan Peters noted in her best-seller, *From Time Immemorial; The Origins of the Arab-Jewish Conflict Over Palestine* (Harper & Row, 1984). The vehement campaign to discredit *From Time Immemorial*, despite Peters' extensive research,

---

23 "Fabricated Palestinian History," Shragai, *Israel Hayom.*

indicated the extent to which "Palestinianism" even then demanded a "shoot-the-messenger" cult-like adherence.

Vehement though the denunciations were, the facts—if often ignored—remained. As Fred M. Gottheil pointed out, affirming Avneri's population tallies, when Zionist development of British Mandatory Palestine accelerated, the area's Arab population grew much faster than rates of natural increase alone would have supported. And rates of natural increase were themselves rising in part due to improved sanitation and health care resulting from Zionist settlement. Essentially, wrote Gottheil, an economics professor at the University of Illinois, Jewish settlement and attendant economic opportunities attracted large numbers of Arab migrants.[24] This while al-Husseini's massacres and rebellion led to British curtailing of Jewish but not Arab immigration.

As for Arab refugees from what became Israel in 1948, Joan Peters made a discovery that returned attention, however briefly, to another double standard invoked uniquely to create and sustain a Palestinian Arab identity, in particular the "refugee problem." She "came across a 'seemingly casual' discrepancy between the standard definition of a refugee and the definition used for the Palestinian Arabs. In other cases, a refugee is someone forced to leave a permanent or habitual home. In this case, however, it is someone who had lived in Palestine for just two years before the flight that began in 1948 ...."[25]

Further, "Miss Peters came across a statement by Winston Churchill that she says opened her eyes to the situation in Palestine. In 1939 Churchill challenged the common notion that Jewish immigration into Palestine had uprooted its Arab residents. To the contrary, according to him, 'So far from being persecuted, the Arabs have crowded into the country and multiplied till their population has increased more than even all world Jewry could lift up the Jewish population' ... Arabs crowded into Palestine? As Miss Peters pursued this angle she found a fund of obscure information that confirmed Churchill's observation. Drawing on census statistics and a great number of contemporary accounts, she pieced together the dimensions of Arab immigration into Palestine before 1948 ... Miss Peters concludes that 'the Arab population appears to have increased in direct proportion to the Jewish presence ... Although the Jews alone moved to Palestine for ideological reasons, they were not

24 "The Smoking Gun: Arab Immigration into Palestine, 1922 – 1931," by Fred Gottheil, *Middle East Quarterly*, Winter, 2003.

25 "From Time Immemorial: The Origins of the Arab-Jewish Conflict Over Palestine," Reviewed by Daniel Pipes, *Commentary*, July, 1984.

alone in emigrating there. Arabs joined them in large numbers...

> ...Non-Jewish immigrants came from all parts of the Middle
> East, including Turkey, Syria, Iraq, Lebanon, Transjordan (as
> Jordan was once known), Saudi Arabia, the Yemens, Egypt,
> Sudan, and Libya. Thanks to British unconcern, Arab immi-
> grants were generally left alone and allowed to settle in Man-
> datory Palestine. So many Arabs came, Miss Peters estimates,
> that 'if all those Jews and all those Arabs who arrived in ...
> Palestine between 1893 and 1948 had remained, and if they
> were forced to leave now, a dual exodus of at least equal pro-
> portion would in all probability take place. Palestine would
> be depopulated once again.'

> ...What took hundreds of thousands of Arabs to Palestine?
> Economic opportunity. The Zionists brought the skills and
> resources of Europe. Like other Europeans settling scarcely
> populated areas in recent times—in Australia, Southern Af-
> rica, or the American West—the Jews in Palestine initiated
> economic activities that created jobs and wealth on a level
> far beyond that of the indigenous peoples. In response, large
> numbers of Arabs moved toward the settlers to find employ-
> ment.

> The conventional picture has it that Jewish immigrants
> bought up Arab properties, forcing the former owners into
> unemployment. Miss Peters argues exactly the contrary,
> that the Jews created new opportunities, which attracted
> emigrants from distant places. To the extent that there was
> unemployment among the Arabs, it was mostly among the
> recent arrivals.

> This reversal of the usual interpretation implies a wholly
> different way of seeing the Arab position in Mandatory Pal-
> estine. As C. S. Jarvis, governor of the Sinai in 1923-1936,
> observed, 'It is very difficult to make a case out for the mis-
> ery of the Arabs if at the same time their compatriots from
> adjoining states could not be kept from going in to share that
> misery.' The data unearthed by Joan Peters indicate that Ar-
> abs benefited economically so much by the presence of Jew-

ish settlers from Europe that they traveled hundreds of miles to get closer to them."[26]

Peters was making—at greater length and to much greater, hostile attention—points highlighted by Avneri four years earlier.

> In turn, this explains why the definition of a refugee from Palestine in 1948 is a person who lived there for just two years: because many Arab residents in 1948 had immigrated so recently. The usual definition would have cut out a substantial portion of the persons who later claimed to U.N. representatives be refugees from Palestine and thereby eligible for housing, food and other subsidies.

> Thus, the 'Palestinian problem' lacks firm grounding. Many of those who now consider themselves Palestinian refugees were either immigrants themselves before 1948 or the children of immigrants. This historical fact reduces their claim to the land of Israel; it also reinforces the point that the real problem in the Middle East has little to do with Palestinian-Arab rights.[27]

Erekat's "I am a Canaanite, therefore this land is my land" claim doesn't get much help from the Quran either. Nadav Shragai quoted Prof. Nissim Dana, author of *To Whom Does This Land Belong?—A Re-examination of the Quran* [translation of the Hebrew title]: "In the Quran ... there are 10 passages which state that Allah bequeathed the land to the Jewish people. ... It is written that there is not only the right but the obligation placed on the Sons of Israel to inherit the land. On the other hand, there is no mention in the Quran of bequeathing the land to Muslims, Arabs, Palestinians, or any other nation not called the Jewish people." For example, Sura 10, verses 90 – 93 says "We prepared for the children of Israe'il a safe abode" a *mubasa'a sidqeen*—a phrase apparently so special that it appears just once in the Quran. Sura 21, verses 71 and 81—echoes Genesis in which God instructs Abraham to leave Ur of the Chaldees and go to a land He will show the first monotheist. The Quranic phrases say Allah commanded Ibrahim to abandon Mesopotamia for "the blessed land" Allah has promised Ibrahim and his offspring,

---

26 Ibid.
27 Ibid.

"the land we have blessed for the sake of the entire world."[28]

Can a fabrication be left in ruins? If so, that is where history of the sort Lord Acton recognized leaves Saeb Erekat's invention of millennia of Palestinian Arab history in "Palestine." In *eretz Yisrael* archaeological ruins are inescapable. They attest to Canaanite, Israelite, Philistine, Jewish, Roman, Byzantine, Muslim, Mameluke, and Ottoman civilizations and rule. But not Palestinian Arab. There are no physical traces of something that never was. John Hayes Holmes was a Unitarian pastor, a liberal leaning activist—he co-founded the American Civil Liberties Union—and author of *Palestine Today and Tomorrow—A Gentile's Survey of Zionism* (McMillan, 1929). British Mandatory Palestine, he wrote, "is the country to which the Jews have come to rebuild their ancient homeland. ... On all the surface of this earth there is no home for the Jew save in the mountains and the well-springs of his ancient kingdom. ... Everywhere else the Jew is in exile. ... But, Palestine is his. .... Scratch Palestine anywhere and you'll find Israel [by which Holmes meant *b'nai Israel*, the children of Israel, the House of Jacob]."

Much of what passes for news coverage seems either oblivious or in denial of this. For example, the Associated Press (in the pages of *The New York Times*), *The Washington Post* and *USA Today*, among others, provided generally respectful if not celebratory treatment to the opening of a $24 million, 43,000 square feet Palestinian Museum of Art, History and Culture in May, 2016. The reporting was a classic of ignorance or bias influenced by the Palestinian narrative.

USA Today reported that the facility (the Palestinian Authority's biggest single construction project to that date), in the West Bank town of Bir Zeit, about 13 miles north of Jerusalem, "showcases a beautiful building with sweeping views. All that's missing are the exhibits." As this author noted shortly thereafter, "promised future exhibits sound contemporary and political, not historical." It could hardly be otherwise since Palestinian Arab history began around the turn of the 20th century, "not in renewal of deeply-rooted trends but in reaction to and rejection of Zionism and Jewish national development of British-created Palestine."[29]

Perhaps reporting more than it realized, *USA Today* called the museum "an unfortunate metaphor for *a people long in search of a national identity* [emphasis added] and homeland." Nevertheless, as "The Palestinian History Hoax" observed, Palestinian Authority President

---

28 "Fabricated Palestinian History," Shragai, *Israel Hayom*.
29 "The Palestinian History Hoax," by Eric Rozenman, *The Algemeiner*, June 1, 2016.

Mahmoud Abbas cut the ribbon to open the facility and declared, "'We have been planted here since the dawn of history.' Then where were the ancient artifacts? The trick—hardly new—was that the museum's opening was less about history than polemics. Press accounts noted the debut was 'timed to coincide with *Nakba* week—"catastrophe" in Arabic, a reference to the 1948 creation of Israel that led to the displacement of hundreds of thousands of Palestinians.'"

Actually, "what led to the Arab 'catastrophe'" was unanimous rejection by Arab countries at the United Nations and by Palestinian Arab leadership, of the U.N.'s 1947 plan to partition British Mandatory Palestine into two statelets, one Arab, one Jewish. As this writer noted, "the Jews, disappointed at the sliver of the original mandatory lands allotted to them, nevertheless accepted. The catastrophe, for the other side, was the failure of armies from five Arab countries and Palestinian Arab 'irregulars' to destroy Israel the next year. No Arab war against Israel, no displacement. The English translation of *nakba* ought to be 'consequences.'"

Where, *The Washington Post* asked in covering the museum's debut, were missing "Palestinian" exhibits like "the Roman-era glass"? Where? "In Jerusalem's world-renowned Israel Museum and in collections of the Israel Antiquities Authority, among countless other elements documenting a people's 3,000-year-plus connection to its homeland. Why would *The Post* ask? Maybe because it fell for the museum at Bir Zeit, in spite of the facility being what one Israeli cabinet member called an 'attempt to take away the Jewish identity of this contested place.'"[30] How could the press not fall for an empty museum during *Nakba* Week? It is hard to keep one's balance under the sway of the lie of Palestine.

The Palestinian Arabs' "what's yours is mine and what I now claim as mine was never yours" mentality regarding Jews and their history also was on display three years before Mahmoud Abbas cut the ribbon on an empty Palestinian Museum of Art, History and Culture. In February 2013 the director-general of the Palestinian Authority's "Department of Antiquities and Cultural Heritage" protested the Israel Museum's display of artifacts from Herodium. Herod the Great built Herodium, a palace-fortress, in the Judean Desert about eight miles southeast of Jerusalem, three miles from Bethlehem, 2,000 years earlier. At the time he was the Roman-backed King of Judea. Nevertheless, the PA official complained that removal by the Jewish state of artifacts from a site constructed by a long-ago monarch of a previous Jewish state violated in-

---

30 Ibid.

ternational law and appropriated cultural property that should remain in the West Bank.

Of course, Palestinian officials have made of international law the statutory equivalent of bubble gum, purportedly popped by the most mundane Israeli actions. But whose cultural property? Even if Herodium were to be encompassed by the geography of some future Palestinian Arab country, that hardly would change the underlying archaeological strata. Those strata show no Palestinian Arab antiquity. Whether left *in situ* or exhibited in the Israel Museum, they do demonstrate, however, a long and rich Jewish one. If Palestine is a lie Zionists invented, then its embrace by Palestinian Arabs, anti-Zionists and antisemites is one of history's bigger double-or-nothing bluffs.

CHAPTER SIX

Privileged Imperialism, Roman and Arab

I F THE PEOPLE TODAY called Palestinians have no tie to the ancient Philistines, and modern Israel did not displace a state called Palestine but rather refreshed Jewish settlement and sovereignty in part of *eretz Yisrael*, why are the terms Palestinian and Palestine still with us? These misleading words, invoked by the Romans as anti-Jewish propaganda, continue to career through history primarily as a polemic portmanteau, though often by users unconscious of that effect. Elliot A. Green dissected the origin and use of the word "Palestine" in history and politics a generation ago in a small Jewish and Zionist journal. He later posted another version online. To summarize:

"... [N]either Palestine nor Syria is an indigenous name for the country either is nowadays supposed to represent. These were originally names given by outsiders, sailors and merchants coming from the west, to loosely defined regions along the eastern Mediterranean coast and their hinterlands. Syria was the more inclusive."[1] As used by Greeks and Romans "it included the notion of Palestine, as we see from Herodotus, who wrote of 'Palestinian Syria' (using the word as an adjective, not a noun.) Hence for him it was merely a section of Syria" which for ancient classical writers loosely "included the Syria of today plus Israel, Lebanon, the settled western part of Jordan and much of southeastern Turkey."[2] For the Greeks, "Syria" was "mainly a broad geographic term" and not "the land of one nation or people.

"The natives called the coastal strip of Lebanon and Syria 'Canaan'

---

1 "What did Rome Call the Land of Israel—and Where Were Its Borders?" by Elliot A. Green, *Midstream*, November, 1995.

2 Ibid.

(Greeks called it Phoenicia); inland Syria was called Aram; Israel (on both sides of the Jordan River) was divided into two kingdoms, Israel and Judah. Also in place were the smaller states of Ammon, Moab and Edom, northeast, east and south of the Dead Sea. Pleshet in the Hebrew Bible (Philistia) occupied the coastal strip south of Jaffa. ... However, since 'Palestine' has come down to the modern West through Rome (*and to the modern Arabs through the West* [emphasis added]), the circumstances of its adoption as a Roman official name need to be considered. On the same grounds, the Roman name for the Land of Israel when Rome had its closest contact with the Jews and their land seems most significant for political discussion today."[3]

As Green details, "Judea (Iudaea) was the Roman name for the Land of Israel during the heyday of the Roman Empire. This meant not only the area called Judea in Israel today [the southern West Bank in much current usage]; it included the whole area ruled and/or chiefly inhabited by Jews. Consider Pliny, Suetonius and Tacitus in Latin, and Plutarch as well as the geographers Strabo and Ptolemy in Greek. [Pliny the Elder's great work, *Natural History*, Green notes elsewhere in the article, "aspired to present universal knowledge [and] wrote admiringly of Judea's capital and religious center: 'Jerusalem, by far the most illustrious city of the East, not merely of Judea'.]. ... Therefore, Lord Robert Cecil, acting British foreign secretary, was right to use the name Judea for the whole land in his famous remark: 'Our wish is that Arabian countries shall be for the Arabs, Armenia for the Armenians, and Judea for the Jews' (Dec. 2, 1917)."

In Jewish usage at the time, Green notes, "Judea" often meant the kingdom of Judah (Yehuda), with its capital of Jerusalem and covering some of the central and most of the southern West Bank. The Jews recognized the much larger Greco-Roman "Judea" as *eretz Yisrael*, the land of Israel. The Christian New Testament would contribute to modern confusion by using "Judea" both ways. The New Testament also twice refers to "the land of Israel" (Matthew 2:21-22) but never uses the noun "Palestine" or adjective "Palestinian." If the Jew named Yeshua—Jesus in Greek—"was a Palestinian," neither he nor his contemporaries knew it.

As for Rome, not until Hadrian after 135 C.E. did "Palestine" come into official use. It did so as an element of anti-Jewish psychological warfare and propaganda, ultimately with success. Writes Green:

Palestine obviously derives from Philistia (Pleshet in He-

---

3 Ibid.

brew), the southern coastal area of the country. ... By the time the Romans conquered the country, in 63 B.C.E., the kingdom of Judea, ruled by the Hasmonean dynasty [descendants of the Maccabees, whose overthrow of Seleucid Greek rule 80 years before is commemorated by the holiday of Chanukah], stretched along both sides of the Jordan and controlled, besides Judea proper, most of the coastal plain, Samaria, most of the Galilee and the Golan Heights. ... Roman hegemony meant several political reorganizations of the country after Herod's death. The first great Jewish revolt (66 – 73 C.E.) ended in Roman victory in the course of which the [Second] Temple was destroyed (70 C.E.). The Romans now again reorganized the country, which was already designated the province of Judea (Provincia Iudaea). ... However, in the year 135 C.E., when the Emperor Hadrian's forces had suppressed the [second] Jewish revolt led by Bar-Kochba, the emperor renamed the province Provincia Syria Palaestina. The name change had obvious political implications. This becomes even clearer when we bear in mind that at the same time Hadrian forbade Jews to live in a large zone in the heart of Judea around Jerusalem. Furthermore, Rome planted colonists in the zone who belonged to various foreign peoples, chiefly Syrians and Arabs [and] veterans of the Roman legions, no doubt including many Europeans. The Arabs surely deserved a reward from the [manpower-stretched] Romans since the Province of Arabia had 'provided the Romans important military support in the suppression of the Bar-Kochba Revolt.'[4]

After their conquest in 635-640 C.E., Arab terminology was "paradoxical," according to Green. "However, the Arabs later on did not see this land as a separate country. They typically considered the country merely an undifferentiated part of *Bilad ash-Sham* (usually translated as Syria or Greater Syria). This view lasted until the end of the British mandate period [1948]. ... Before the Crusades the Arabs did use the name Filastin. However, this name referred only to the southern region of the country, what the Romans had called Palaestina Prima. After the Crusades the name was not used by the Muslim Mamluk [non-Arab] rulers. The Crusaders had typically called the country the Holy Land

---

4 *Jews, Idumaeans, and Ancient Arabs*, Aryeh Kasher, Tubingen, 1988.

(Terra Sancta), sometimes using the Land of Israel (Terra Israel) or other names.

"Holy Land was still the usual Western name for the country in the nineteenth century, although it alternated with Palestine, Judea, Zion, the Land of Israel, Land of the Bible etc. ...."[5] To the extent "Palestine" prevailed over the others by early in the 20th century, it did so, says Green, apparently "out of the 'scientific' motive to avoid the religious connotations of Holy Land. Thus Palestine was again a Western name as it had been in ancient times. 'Palestine' was first officially applied to the country in modern times in 1920 when the peace negotiators at the San Remo Conference juridically established the country as the Jewish National Home. Before World War I it was an administratively indistinct area of the Ottoman Empire and was shared among various Ottoman administrative departments," none of them called Palestine and very few of whose inhabitants, and those few usually Christians, not Muslims, considered themselves "Palestinians."

Does this leave us in Palestine or Israel, the West Bank or Judea and Samaria? Once more, Green: "The Roman change of name was part of a complex of related oppressive measures of national despoliation, punishment, and oppression. From the start the name was laden with connotations of Roman hatred for rebels (and for Jews in particular), the slaughter of hundreds of thousands in the war and through the legionnaires' vengeful acts, the ruin of hundreds of villages and towns, the enslavement of survivors, expulsion of a people from its homes and lands (nowadays called 'ethnic cleansing') etc.

"The name 'Palestine' cannot be divested of the negative overtones of its history, from the circumstances of its Roman official origin. It cannot be considered a 'neutral, value free,' purely 'scientific' term, as some would have it regardless of its use even by some Zionists. This is not only because of its current use as an anti-Israel slogan, but because of the context of its origin as a Roman official name. Felix Abel, the noted Catholic historian of the country, frankly states that the name change was 'another indication of the anti-Jewish orientation of imperial policy.'"[6]

Leap ahead to 1950. Having seized Judea and Samaria (Yehuda and Shomron in the original Hebrew, Samaria the name of a district in British Mandatory Palestine) in the 1948-1949 Arab-Israeli war, Transjordan renamed the territories the West Bank. This implied they

---

5 "What Did Rome Call the Land of Israel?" Green, *Midstream*.
6 Ibid.

complemented and formed one unit with the East Bank. The Hashemite Kingdom of Transjordan (literally "across the Jordan River" but now in possession of both banks) renamed itself Jordan. Over time this substitution of West Bank for Judea and Samaria took hold. Hence by the 1990s news media reflexively referred to the area as "the West Bank" and cast Israeli use of Judea and Samaria—common regardless of political outlook—as "biblical names" used by Jewish settlers and their supporters on the right. As if Jerusalem, Beersheva, Galilee and so on also were not "biblical names" in common, but unremarked, contemporary use. As Rome tried to erase the Jewish connection by changing Judea to Palestine, so too—consciously or not—was the effect of the latter 20th century replacement of Judea and Samaria with West Bank.

Occupiers in Palestine or Jews in Eretz Yisrael?

But what has this history, ancient and more recent, with its anthropology and semantics, have to do with the present? Does it matter given Israel occupation of "Palestine" and rejection of the Palestinians' right of return?

Just this: There is no Palestinian Arab "right of return" to that minority of Mandatory Palestine that became Israel. Contemporaneous U.N. resolutions recognized the fact. That was one reason the Arab states rejected them.

As for the contentious post-1967 Six-Day War Jewish settlements on the West Bank, they are not illegal, assertions by former U.N. Secretary General Ban Ki-moon, United States ex-President Barack Obama or subscribers to the Palestinian narrative notwithstanding. International law not only permits but actually encourages Jewish communities west of the Jordan River, including the West Bank (and Gaza Strip). The League of Nations' Palestine Mandate, Article 6 (1922), and succeeding U.N. Charter, Chapter 12, Article 80 (1945), as well as the Balfour Declaration (1917), San Remo Treaty (1920) and Anglo-American Convention (1924) either recognize or assume such Jewish rights.

Neither are Israelis required to withdraw from all the territory gained in the 1967 Six-Day War and retained in the 1973 Yom Kippur War. The two key U.N. Security Council resolutions dealing with those conflicts, 242 and 338—and the explanations by their authors—make that plain.

Nevertheless, visiting Lebanon in 2012, U.N. Secretary-General Ban alleged that Jewish "settlements, new and old, are illegal." In 2011, he told a U.N. committee that "settlements in the occupied Palestinian territories are illegal under international law." The year before that, visiting Israel and the West Bank, Ban declaimed "the world has condemned Israel's expansion plans in East Jerusalem. Let us be clear: All settlement activity is illegal anywhere in the occupied territory and must stop."

Let us be clear, indeed. Ban didn't know what he was talking about. Either he was stubbornly ignorant, or he was a useful, even willing dupe of the secretariat staff. Ambassador Richard Schifter, a former U.S. assistant secretary of state for human rights and humanitarian affairs under Presidents Ronald Reagan and George H.W. Bush and a member of President Bill Clinton's National Security Council, told this writer it was the later. Ban's staff, some members of which functioned as supporters of the world body's permanent pro-Palestinian advocacy agencies, wrote the anti-Israel script and the secretary-general read the lines, Schifter contended.[7] And why not? There was little cost, Israel serving as full-time U.N. whipping boy.

But there was a not-so-hidden cost. Every time Ban misspoke on the subject, he undermined international law and the U.N.'s own legitimacy. As this writer pointed out in *Los Angeles Times* and *Washington Times*' commentaries,[8] the relevant law—much of it rooted in the United Nations and its predecessor, the League of Nations—in outline runs like this:

The San Remo Treaty of 1920 saw the victorious World War I Allies deal with the remnants of the defeated Ottoman Turkish Empire. Among other things, the Allies at San Remo created an entity called "Palestine" on both sides of the Jordan River. The powers meant Palestine to be the land on which Great Britain would turn its 1917 Balfour Declaration—now part of international law—into reality, assisting the Zionist movement in re-establishing the Jewish national home.

Also in 1920, the Franco-British Boundary Convention demarcated the French mandate for what would become Syria and Lebanon from that of the British in Palestine. This too was done in part to prepare for the Jewish national home.

Article 6 of the League of Nations' 1922 Palestine Mandate en-

---

7 Conversation with the author and Gil Kapen, associated with Schifter in the American Jewish International Relations Institute, at the ambassador' Bethesda, Maryland home, Aug. 19, 2016.

8 . "Israeli settlements are more than legitimate," by Eric Rozenman, *Los Angeles Times*, Dec. 11, 2009 and "Ban Ki-moon wrong about Israeli settlements," by Eric Rozenman, *Washington Times*, March 15, 2013.

couraged "close Jewish settlement" on the land west of the Jordan River, so long as non-Jewish residents were not disadvantaged. West of the river, because Great Britain the year before had severed Transjordan (today's Jordan) from mandatory Palestine, creating, also as noted, a new Arab country and banning Jewish settlement there "until practicable." But Arabs in the areas of Jewish land acquisition and development in that part of Palestine left open to Zionist expansion rarely were disadvantaged. Based on his research in Jewish, Ottoman Turkish and British Mandatory archives, referred to previously, Aryeh Avneri concluded that the Jews typically paid above-market prices for often marginal lands—dunes, malarial swamps and other "waste places"—then rehabilitated them, creating new economic opportunities that attracted an ever increasing Arab population. As Britain's secretary of state for the colonies would tell the House of Commons in 1938, "the Arabs cannot say that the Jews are driving them out of the country. If not a single Jew had come to Palestine after 1918, I believe the Arab population of Palestine would still have been around 600,000 at which it had been stable under Turkish rule. ... It is not only the Jews who have benefited from the Balfour Declaration. They can deny it as much as they like, but materially the Arabs have benefited very greatly from the Balfour Declaration."[9]

Avneri refers to earlier calculations putting the population of Palestine at 205,000 Muslims, Christians and Jews in 1553-1554. In 1800, the figure had increased to only 275,000, with 246,300 Muslims. "The sparseness of the population ... was an indication of the neglected state of the countryside. Ever since the Roman conquest the country was not ruled by its inhabitants. Foreign conquerors came one after another and each left destruction in his wake. The Crusades and conquests by the Arabs, Mamelukes and Mongols turned the land into a desolate waste."[10]

Turkish rule beginning in 1516 brought some respite, but in addition to invasions by Napoleon and Ibrahim Pasha, earthquakes, locusts, epidemics and drought recurred. So by the start of Jewish colonization in 1880—after conquest by Egypt's Mohammed Ali and settlement of many Egyptians—the Muslim population stood at 425,000 to 440,000, total population including Christians and Jews between 465,000 and

---

9 *The Palestinians: People, History, Politics*, edited by Michael Curtis, Joseph Neyer, Chaim L. Waxman and Allen Pollack, Transaction Books, 1975, "Palestinian Nationalism: Its Development and Goal," by Marie Syrkin, page 202.

10 *The Claim of Dispossession, Jewish Land-Settlement and the Arabs, 1878 – 1948*, by Arieh L. Avneri, Yad Tabenkin, 1982, page 37.

480,000.[11]

"Despite the massive increase through immigration, the total Arab population in the nineteenth century increased only slightly. One of the chief causes for this slow growth lay in the incessant internal wars between the 'Qais' villages and the 'Yaman' villages, wars that extended over hundreds of years."[12] And emigration helped offset immigration. At the beginning of the 20th century, what would become Mandatory Palestine was still "a backwater" of the Ottoman Empire, sunk in "torpor." "The first real stimulus to economic development came from Zionist settlement. The land purchases, the melioration of the land (despite the limitations imposed by the Turkish authorities), the building boom, the planting of vineyards and citrus groves, the increase in commercial and transportation ties with the outside world—all contributed to the creation of new opportunities for employment and subsistence." In addition, Turkish administrators built railroads, registered land, extended telegraph lines, paved roads and built ports. This "helped indirectly in the Jewish settlement effort and in the strengthening of the economy. Palestine attracted not only Jews who came because of national motivation, but also Arab immigrants from neighboring countries, who hoped to find easier ways to earn a living than prevailed in their native lands."[13]

Avneri's conclusion that Zionist settlement and reclamation after 1880 attracted not only Jews but Arabs to what became Israel—and as many or more Arabs than Jews—is well-documented even though incessantly denied. The Palestinian Exploration Fund conducted between 1871 and 1878 the most scholarly survey at the time of the land west of the Jordan River. Among other things, it found the size of Haifa at "no more than 440 x 190 meters." Jerusalem "was relatively large"— one square kilometer. "Photos from the period also demonstrate just how accurate the survey was in portraying the relative emptiness of the country."[14]

Avneri describes an inspection tour of the Haifa area by a group of Russian Lovers of Zion in 1891. One of the prospective buyers, Menahem Ussishkin, recalled "'... We observed everything carefully and all we saw was centuries-old desolation. Hardly anyone lives in this whole wide valley. Here and there we came upon some Bedouin tents. All

---

11 Ibid., pages 12-13, 39.

12 Ibid., page 19.

13 Ibid., pages 24-25.

14 *Industry of Lies: Media, Academia, and the Israeli-Arab Conflict*, Ben-Dror Yemini, Institute for the Global Study of Antisemitism and Policy, 2017, page 323.

around were marshes and sands, covered by desert bushes, thorns and thistles. In our mind's eye we saw a brilliant future, but the present was bleak indeed.' When the land was purchased for Jewish settlement 34 years later, its appearance was unchanged."[15] From Lebanon to the Negev Desert, the Mediterranean Sea to the Jordan River, similar examples abounded.

After World War I, settlement by Arabs—often illegal—and Jews accelerated in the territory now under British rule. The 1924 Anglo-American Convention extended international law stemming from the Balfour Declaration, the San Remo Treaty and Palestine Mandate. In the convention the United States endorsed Great Britain's administration of the remaining mandatory lands so long as London helped bring a Jewish state into being.

Near the end of World War II, the United Nations succeeded the League of Nations. The 1945 U.N. Charter, Chapter XII, Article 80, continues Jewish rights recognized under the League's Palestine Mandate. That is, it upholds Article 6's encouragement of "close Jewish settlement" on the land west of the Jordan River. The language holds that the charter protects "the rights whatsoever of any states or any peoples or the terms of existing international instruments." Article 80 was sometimes known as "the Palestine article."

So Ban was mistaken, "world condemnation" misbegotten. Obama's clenched-teeth insistence on the "illegitimacy" of Jewish settlement activity on the West Bank (by which he included new Jewish neighborhoods in eastern Jerusalem) charitably could be described as historically and legally misinformed. More accurately, as hostile.

But Israel's adversaries also chronically charged that Jewish communities in Judea and Samaria violated Article 49 of the Fourth Geneva Convention Relative to the Protection of Civilian Persons in Time of War (1949). The Convention states that "individual or mass forcible transfers, as well as deportations of protected persons from occupied territory to the territory of the occupying power or to that of any other country ... are prohibited." Its sixth paragraph stresses that "the Occupying Power shall not deport or transfer parts of its own civilian population into the territory it occupies."

Rebutting the tendentious Prof. Juan Cole (University of Michigan, modern Middle East and South Asian history) Tamar Sternthal, also a former colleague of this author, wrote that critics of the Jewish state "interpret this to be applicable to Israel's settlement of the West

---

15 Avneri, pages 48-49.

Bank and Gaza [Strip], understanding Israel to have become a 'belliger-ent occupant' of this territory through entry by its armed forces." How-ever, "those who argue that the settlements are legal point out that the Geneva Convention does not apply to the West Bank or Gaza for, under its Article 2, the Convention pertains only to 'cases of ... occupation of the territory of a High Contracting Party' by another such party. The West Bank and Gaza were never the territory of a High Contracting Par-ty; their occupations after 1948 by Jordan and Egypt, respectively, were illegal and neither country ever had lawful or recognized sovereignty. The last legal sovereignty over the territories was that of the League of Nations Palestine Mandate, which stipulated the right of the Jewish peo-ple to settle in the whole of the Mandated territory, a right preserved by Article 80 of the U.N. Charter."[16]

Suppose, for the sake of debate—not that Islamists or the left in-telligentsia tolerate debate about anything having to do with Israel, or much else, for that matter—that the Geneva Convention did apply to the West Bank and Gaza Strip. It still "would not outlaw Israeli settlements, since the relevant Article 49 was intended to outlaw the Nazi practice of forcibly transporting populations into or out of occupied territories to death and work camps. ... Israel simply did not transfer Palestinian Arab populations out of the West Bank and Gaza."[17] Further, Article 49 did not apply to Israel because Israelis were not forcibly transferred into the territories.

No matter. Since according to the Palestinian narrative Zionism is racism and Israelis are new Nazis, Jewish communities in the disputed territories of Judea and Samaria must, by their very existence, violate the Geneva Conventions. The equation runs Jew-Zionist-Nazi, there-fore colonialist-racist-criminal. *Ipso facto*. First the verdict, as the Red Queen bellowed to Alice in Wonderland, then the trial—recurrently in session in faculty senates and student governments on campuses all across occupied Native American Indian territory.

The New York Times Apologizes. And Apologizes. And Apologizes

But even if the League of Nations in 1922 recognized and the Unit-ed Nations in 1945 reaffirmed Jews' historic, religious and legal rights to settle west of the Jordan River, nevertheless U. N. Security Council Res-olution 242—adopted in 1967 and perhaps the most important council

16 "The Unscholarly Scholar," CAMERA, by Tamar Sternthal, Aug. 30, 2004.
17 Ibid.

measure dealing with the Arab-Israeli conflict—surely requires Israel to withdraw from all the territories it conquered in the Six-Day War. It certainly does according to the Palestinian narrative's invocation of "the 1967 borders." But it does not do so in fact, as even *The New York Times* eventually was forced to admit. And between Israel and the West Bank, Israel and the Gaza Strip, there are no such borders, only temporary truce lines.

To deal with the outcome of the Six-Day War, the U.N. Security Council adopted Resolution 242 on Nov. 22, 1967. In the next decade the measure became, thanks to U.S. Secretary of State Henry Kissinger's shuttle trips and Egyptian President Anwar as-Sadat's surprise 1977 visit to Jerusalem, the basis of successful Arab-Israeli diplomacy. This included the 1974 Israeli-Syrian disengagement agreement, 1979 Egyptian-Israeli peace treaty, 1993 letter from Yasser Arafat to Israeli Prime Minister Yitzhak Rabin in which the Palestine Liberation Organization said—out of one corner of its mouth—it recognized Israel's right to live in peace and security, and the 1994 Jordanian-Israeli treaty.

Resolution 242 emphasizes somewhat contradictorily "the inadmissibility of the acquisition of territory by war and the need to work for a just and lasting peace...." Such a peace should include, the Security Council declared, "withdrawal of Israeli armed forces from territories occupied in the recent conflict ... termination of all states of belligerency and ... [the right of every state in the area] to live in peace within secure and recognized boundaries free from threats or acts of force." The resolution's authoritative English version notably did not say "withdrawal from the territories" or from "all territories."

One of 242's co-authors, U.S. Undersecretary of State Eugene Rostow, explained why: "Five and a-half months of vehement public diplomacy in 1967 made it perfectly clear what the missing definite article in Resolution 242 means. Ingeniously drafted resolutions calling for withdrawals from 'all' the territories were defeated in the Security Council and the General Assembly. Speaker after speaker made it explicit that Israel was not to be forced back to the 'fragile' and 'vulnerable' Armistice Demarcation Lines, but should retire *once peace was made* [emphasis added] to what Resolution 242 called 'secure and recognized' boundaries, agreed to by the parties. In negotiating such agreements, the parties should take into account, among other factors, security considerations, access to the international waterways of the region, and, of course, their respective legal claims."[18]

18 "Bricks and Stones: Settling for Leverage; Palestinian Autonomy," *The New Republic,*

Another of the resolution's co-authors, Lord (Hugh) Caradon, British ambassador to the United Nations, explained in 1974 what 242's drafters thought of Israel's pre-Six Day War boundaries with the West Bank (the 1949 Israeli-Jordanian armistice line or "green line") and around the Gaza Strip (the 1950 Israeli-Egyptian armistice line): "It would have been wrong to demand that Israel return to its positions of June 4, 1967 [when the Six-Day War erupted], because those positions were undesirable and artificial. After all, they were just the places where the soldiers of each side happened to be on the day the fighting stopped in 1948. They were just armistice lines. That's why we didn't demand that the Israelis return to them."[19]

For Israel those lines were neither secure nor recognized. This strongly implied that different, expanded boundaries would become part of the "just and lasting peace" for all parties to the 1967 conflict that Resolution 242 envisioned. Expanded by how much and to where remains a matter for the final negotiations called for by 242 and companion Security Council Resolution 338. Resolution 338, adopted after the 1973 Yom Kippur War Egypt and Syria waged against Israel, basically calls for the parties to begin the diplomatic process envisioned by Resolution 242.

Resolution 242 was moot on Israeli civilian as opposed to military withdrawal. No Israelis had settled—or no Jews had resettled—in Sinai, Gaza, the Golan or West Bank as of November, 1967. But they could—certainly in the West Bank (Judea and Samaria) and the Gaza Strip—under the provisions of the League of Nations/U.N. Palestine Mandate. By implication, if 242 did not require complete Israeli military withdrawal from the territories, then eventually Israeli civilians would be able to live there. So could Palestinian Arabs. Rostow, a legal scholar, stressed that "the Jewish right of settlement in the area is equivalent in every way to the right of the existing Palestinian population to live there." So both parties had the right to claim portions of the territories.

Meanwhile, the status of the West Bank and Gaza Strip was not "illegally occupied Palestinian land." It remained disputed territory over which sovereignty had not been determined, somewhat akin to Kashmir, parts of which have been long occupied by India and Pakistan respectively, all of which is claimed by both and commonly referred to diplomatically and journalistically as "disputed." In small print on maps accompanying its sections on the West Bank and Gaza Strip, the CIA's

---

April 23, 1990.

19 Lord Hugh Caradon, in the *Beirut Daily Star*, June 12, 1974.

World Fact Book in 2018 affirmed those territories' disputed nature, noting their dispensation "is a final status issue to be resolved through negotiations."

Nevertheless, in the years after the Six-Day and Yom Kippur Wars, the PLO, its Arab supporters and Soviet bloc spoke incessantly of "Israeli occupied Palestinian territory," or simply "Palestine." They insisted 242 required total Israeli withdrawal and as a condition for peace talks, not partial evacuation as a result of successful conclusion of negotiations. Hence the upside down slogan of "[all-the-] land-for-peace" rather than the accurate "[some] land-after-peace." By dint of repetition, the large and well-documented "complete withdrawal" lie took hold in academia and journalism, perhaps nowhere more tightly than in the foreign bureaus and Manhattan newsroom of *The New York Times*. In its July 11, 2000 edition *The Times* erroneously reported that 242 "calls for an end to the Israeli occupation of the entire West Bank and Gaza Strip ...." Prompted by the Committee for Accuracy in Middle East Reporting in America, *The Times* corrected the mistake.

But it the made a similar error in an August 19, 2000 report. The newspaper printed a second correction on August 24. Regardless, such is the grip on assumptions of the narrative of righteous Palestinian grievances against expansionist Israel that on September 6 *The Times* referred to 242 as "the United Nations resolution that calls for Israeli withdrawal from all territory occupied in the 1967 war, which includes East Jerusalem." After a third reminder from CAMERA, the paper's third correction in two months on the same issue read:

> An article on Wednesday about the Middle East peace talks referred incorrectly to United Nations resolutions on the Arab-Israeli conflict. While Security Council Resolution 242, passed after the 1967 Middle East War, calls for Israel's armed forces to withdraw 'from territories occupied in the recent conflict,' no resolution calls for Israeli withdrawal from all territory, including East Jerusalem, occupied in the war.

At that point, *Times'* Executive Editor, Joseph Lelyveld, "convened his staff and said: 'Three times in recent months we've had to run corrections on the actual provisions of U.N. Resolution 242, providing great cheer and sustenance to those readers who are convinced we are opinionated and not well-informed on Middle East issues.'"[20] If by "opin-

20 "Introduction: Correcting the Record on 242," by Amb. Dore Gold, Jerusalem Cen-

ionated" he meant biased against Israel and by "not well-informed" he meant in thrall to the Palestinian narrative, then yes, those convinced readers were onto something, as countless *Times'* errors, substantive omissions, repeated reliance on biased sources and related journalistic malpractice regarding its Arab-Israeli reporting testified then and since.

To its credit, *The New York Times* newsroom would not err again on 242. But two years later its double Pulitzer Prize-winning columnist Thomas Friedman, impervious to his own paper's corrections, committed the same mistake. The Associated Press and even *The Jerusalem Post* also have been among numerous news outlets getting 242 wrong over the years. That the mistakes always tilt in favor of the *ex post facto* Palestinian misinterpretation indicates how, like a creeper vine choking a host tree, the Palestinian narrative squeezes truth.

Former U.S. President Jimmy Carter, in his error-ridden 2006 best-seller, *Palestine: Peace Not Apartheid*, claimed the resolution specified Israeli "withdrawal to the 1967 border [sic.]." His 242 inversion was one of more than three dozen substantive mistakes in the anti-Zionist, antisemitic book. Challenged, Carter adamantly refused to correct and his publisher, Simon and Schuster, denied responsibility, saying it relied on its authors for accuracy. Apparently being an ex-president, at least in Carter's case, means never having to admit you are fallible. Not, anyway, when it comes to anti-Israel dicta. Not even when senior staff and 14 advisory border members of the Carter Center in Atlanta resigned in exasperation and disgust. These included Emory University professor of Middle Eastern history Kenneth W. Stein. In leaving the center Stein, a former senior Carter White House staffer and later center director, targeted *Palestine: Peace Not Apartheid's* "gross inventions, intentional falsehoods and irresponsible remarks."[21]

Even if Israel is not required to withdraw all troops completely from territory seized in the 1967 war, might Jewish villages and towns built there since then themselves be illegal? The Carter administration, relying on a 1978 opinion by State Department legal advisor Herbert J. Hansell, decided they were. But Hansell had misapplied key sources.

In bolstering State's belief in the settlements' illegality, Hansell cited international legal scholar Prof. Julius Stone's 1959 analysis "Legal Controls of International Conflict." But Stone himself would later maintain that assertions of settlement illegality amounted to "subver-

---

ter for Public Affairs, http://www.jcpa.org/text/resolution242-gold.pdf.

21 "Former aide criticizes Carter; In L.A., Kenneth Stein says 'falsehoods' in book on Mideast prompted his resignation," *Los Angeles Times*, Jan. 13, 2007.

sion … of basic international law principles." In fact, referring to the U.N. General Assembly's adoption of its Palestine partition plan in 1947, Stone pointed out that Israel's Declaration of Independence the following year noted the world body's irrevocable recognition of the Jewish people's right to reestablish its own state.[22] Arab rejection diplomatically and militarily of that right and the partition plan did not limit Jewish rights in what had been British Mandatory Palestine. Stone's work is an important examination of the legal aspects of the Arab-Israeli conflict. Among other things, he noted the inapplicability of the Fourth Geneva Convention, Article 49(6) (discussed above) to Israeli settlement. Stone cited earlier analyses by Prof. Stephen Schwebel, who would serve as a judge on the U.N.'s International Court of Justice from 1981 to 2000.

Schwebel had distinguished between territory taken in "aggressive conquest" (Japan in China in the 1930s, Germany during World War II, for example) and that gained in self-defense (including Israel's capture of the Syrian Golan Heights, Egyptian Sinai Peninsula, and non-sovereign West Bank and Gaza Strip in 1967). "Where the prior holder of territory had seized that territory unlawfully, the state which subsequently takes that territory in the lawful exercise of self-defense has, against that prior holder, better title."[23] So Hansell contradicted Schwebel, and would be contradicted later by Stone. In any case, Jimmy Carter had vacated the White House less than a month when President Ronald Reagan said, "As to the West Bank, I believe the settlements there—I disagreed when the previous administration referred to them as illegal, they're not illegal."[24]

What they are, like eventual sovereignty over Arab villages and towns on the West Bank, is subject to negotiations called for by U.N. Security Council Resolutions 242 and 338 and presumed by the 1993 Israeli-Palestinian Liberation Organization Oslo process and 2003 United States, United Nations, Russia and European Union-backed "road map." That fact is one reason Palestinian Arab leaders have long resisted or sabotaged direct negotiations with Israel according to those resolutions and the compromise outcome they imply. Palestinian officials have preferred instead, with cynical support from many countries, to "internationalize" their Israel problem, their Jewish state question. Using a sort of fun house mirror leveraging, they have done so since al-Qaeda's Sept.

22 *Israel and Palestine: An Assault on the Law of Nations,* by Julius Stone, Johns Hopkins University Press, 1981, page 62.

23 "What Weight to Conquest," Prof. Stephen Schwebel *American Journal of International Law,* 64, 1970.

24 *New York Times,* Feb. 3, 1981.

11, 2001 attacks by applying for and sometimes gaining "statehood" status at U.N. agencies, threatening a "unilateral declaration of statehood" (redundant since Arafat made such a non-functional declaration in 1988) and being allowed by the Vatican, Interpol—if Jews are the underlying obsession, then an a terrorism-celebrating entity can join the police—and others to take on some trappings of an actual country.

Such maneuvers themselves attempt to contravene international law. The 1934 Montevideo Convention on the Rights and Duties of States sets forth basic attributes of national status. These include, among other things, a permanent population, defined territory and a government and ability to enter into relations with other states. "Palestine" has been divided between the West Bank and Gaza Strip; between the Fatah movement's Palestinian Authority administering the former, a Hamas regime ruling the latter. Its territory has yet to be allocated in negotiations according to Resolutions 242 and 338 and the 1995 Israeli-Palestinian Interim Accords. Counts of its permanent population by the Palestinian Central Bureau of Statistics and Palestinian Authority appear contradictory, the latter's number based on non-standard methodology and inflated. So it does not qualify as a country.

PA President Mahmoud Abbas, in a speech to an emergency meeting of the Organization of Islamic Cooperation called to deal with the Trump administration's recognition of Jerusalem as Israel's capital, tried diplomatic jujitsu as well as sheer *chutzpah*, urging countries to reconsider recognition of the Jewish state since it had undefined borders.[25] Abbas was silent on the fact that lack of definition persisted due to his own refusal to negotiate a compromise and applied more precisely to "Palestine."

Neither would a Palestine propped up absent negotiations according to 242 and 338 qualify for statehood under the U.N. Charter, Articles 3 and 4. These say membership is open to "peace-loving states." Again, Palestine, whether the Gaza Strip under Hamas, the West Bank overseen by Fatah, or both—their official outlets weekly if not daily inciting violence against Israelis—hardly has affirmed its peace-loving bona fides. Neither have a number of other pre-existing U.N. states, but they apparently are considered "grandfathered" into membership.

Nevertheless, the premature endorsement by many of the notional state of Palestine provides another unintended teachable moment. The lesson is that international law—whether embedded in the League of

---

25 "While U.S. Jewish Groups Including J Street Fume, Israel Mum: Israel's leaders atypically quiet after Abbas asserts their state is invalid," *Times of Israel*, Dec. 15, 2017.

Nations' Palestine Mandate, Article 6; the U.N. Charter, Chapter 12, Article 80; the Fourth Geneva Conventions; U.N. Security Council Resolution 242; or as in the case of the U.N.'s anti-genocide convention and Iran's threats to annihilate Israel—will not be upheld to protect the Jews and their state. Rather, it either will be disregarded or, as with allegations of war crimes against Israeli leaders for their country's acts of self-defense, will be invoked to construe intangible walls of a virtual ghetto.

Some refugees are more equal than all other refugees

Periodically, but not often, an American newspaper report about Israeli-Arab contention will put the Palestinian-claimed "right-of-return" in quotation marks or refer to the "so-called" right-of-return. When doing so, it accurately signals readers that there is more, or perhaps less, to the phrase than it would otherwise appear. Much less, it turns out.

The key document cited by supporters of a Palestinian right of return is Resolution 194 (1949), passed in the wake of the first Arab-initiated war against Israel. The supporters cite the resolution despite the fact that the Arab states continually violated its central provision, which called for the creation of a Conciliation Commission and 'establishment of contact between the parties themselves and the Commission at the earliest possible date ... to seek agreement by negotiations [and thereby reach] a final settlement of all questions between them.'

Through many years and multiple wars, the Arab states refused even to meet with Israel, much less try to reach a peaceful settlement. The only clause the Arab side ever acknowledged was paragraph 11, which suggested (it could not "require," since it was a General Assembly rather than a Security Council resolution) [General Assembly resolutions are non-binding, unlike some Security Council resolutions] that 'refugees wishing to return to their homes and live at peace with their neighbors should be permitted to do so at the earliest practicable date ... [R]epatriation, resettlement and economic and social rehabilitation of refugees and payment of compensation [should be facilitated].'[26]

Because this only recommends that refugees be permitted to return, it can hardly be characterized as creating a 'right.' Moreover, the requirement that returnees first accept living 'at peace with their neighbors' meant that Palestinian returnees would have to accept Israel's right to exist, something that very few of them, even today, seem truly willing to do. Further, it did not even hint at any return rights for descendants of refugees.

It should also be noted that (1) the resolution applies equally to Palestinian refugees from Israel and to the *similar number of Jewish refugees from Arab countries* who came to Israel after 1948 [emphasis added, see below], and (2) that it placed repatriation, resettlement, and payment of compensation on an equal footing. This equal footing was also included in other GA resolutions of that era, such as Resolution 393 of December 2, 1950, which stated that '...without prejudice to the provisions of paragraph 11 of General Assembly resolution 194 ... the reintegration of the refugees into the economic life of the Near East, either by repatriation or resettlement is essential ... for the realization of conditions of peace and stability in the area.'[27]

Two more U.N. General Assembly resolutions on the subject, 394 (1950) and 513 (1952), attempted to deal with this particular refugee issue. Resolution 394 called on "the governments concerned" to see that refugees, "whether repatriated or resettled" in the lands in which they now resided, "will be treated without any discrimination in either law or in fact." In law and in fact Arab countries did discriminate against Arab refugees from what had become Israel in a variety of ways, commonly confining them to camps originally meant to be temporary and limiting their ability to become naturalized citizens and in some cases restricting their educational and occupational opportunities.

Resolution 513 spoke of "reintegration either by repatriation or resettlement." The General Assembly did not try to establish a binding

---

26 "BACKGROUNDER: The Palestinian Claim to a 'Right of Return,'" by Alex Safian, Ph.D., CAMERA, Sept. 1, 2000, www.camera.org
27 Ibid.

right of return. This is evident since all Arab states then members of the United Nations voted against the original General Assembly resolution dealing with the matter, 194, when the question was called in 1949. They did so also because it implicitly recognized Israel. Arab leaders were determined not to recognize Israel, not to resettle and integrate brethren they had made homeless by launching and losing a war to destroy the new Jewish state. A U.N. former director of aid to Palestinian refugees in Jordan, Ralph Galloway, declared, "The Arab states do not want to solve the refugee problem. They want to keep it as an open sore, as an affront to the United Nations and as a weapon against Israel. Arab leaders don't give a damn whether the refugees live or die."[28]

How many Arab refugees were there? The U.N. Mediator for Palestine on the scene just after the 1948-'49 war estimated 472,000. The difference in the Arab population of the territory that became Israel between the last British Mandatory and first Israeli censuses (1945 and 1948) respectively was 650,000. Around 150,000 Arabs remained, becoming Israeli citizens. But instead of being dealt with like all other refugee groups by the U.N. High Commissioner on Refugees, Palestinian Arabs were placed under a newly-created organization, initially intended to be temporary. This was the U.N. Relief and Works Agency or UNRWA.

But UNRWA did not work to resettle refugees and integrate them into the Arab countries from which many had come—hence the "refugee" designation to any Arab who had resided for a minimum of just two years in what became Israel. It did not seek to bring the envisioned Conciliation Commission into operation. Instead UNRWA became an ever-expanding welfare program and permanent job bureaucracy for Palestinian Arabs, a custodian perpetuating Palestinian displacement and resentment against Israel. Through indoctrination via its schools and other institutions it also served as a fever swamp of anti-Zionist, antisemitic incitement. Thanks to UNRWA's unique regulations, Palestinian Arabs became the only post-World War II refugee group to, by definition, inherit refugee status from generation to generation. Though less than 50,000 of the 1948-'49 Arab refugees were estimated to have survived by the second decade of the 21st century, the United Nations, news media, academics, diplomats and others continued to speak of "6.5 million Palestinian refugees (and descendants)."

As noted, of the 840,000 Jewish refugees from Arab countries,

---

28 *The Palestinians; People, History, Politics*, edited by Curtis, et. al., 1975, Terence Prittie, page 71.

where their ancestors had resided in many cases for centuries and in some cases millennia—even before the Muslim conquest—nearly 600,000 immigrated to Israel. They were housed initially in tent and tin shack refugee camps (*mabarot*) by a country then rationing food. These Sephardi (North African and Middle Eastern) Jews were integrated—often with difficulty—into the Ashkenazi (European) dominated Jewish state. Today roughly half of Israel's 6.5 million-plus Jewish citizens are immigrants or descendants of immigrants from Arab countries. But none are refugees.

A post-World War II Germany lying in rubble absorbed approximately 10 million German-speakers expelled by Poland and Czechoslovakia. At least five million Hindus fled to India during the 1948 partition of the subcontinent from what became Pakistan, and a roughly equal number of Moslems ran from India to Pakistan. Neither the children of the Germans ethnically cleansed from Poland nor those booted out of what was Czechoslovakia remain refugees. Nor are the populations exchanged in the subcontinent and their offspring. Turkey expelled nearly five million Greeks, Armenians and Kurds in the first third of the 20th century, more than half of them dying en route. None of their descendants are refugees today.[29] But for some reason the world has maintained a much multiplied population of Palestinian refugees. That reason is the Palestinian narrative, the lie of Palestine, an intoxicating cocktail of old ambitions and renewed hopes. It raises once more the Jewish question and fuels what should be understood as the post- post-Holocaust era. That is, "Never Again!" was then. This—including glib misappropriations of "never again!" by a variety of grievance and identity groups—is now.

---

29 *Industry of Lies; Media, Academia, and the Israeli-Arab Conflict*, Ben-Dror Yemini, ISGAP, 2017, page 77.

CHAPTER SEVEN

Blood Libel—From William of Norwich to Muhammad al-Dura

T HE BLOOD LIBEL'S first recorded appearance in Christian culture—beyond, that is, the essential indictment for deicide—came with the fable of 11th century "child martyr" William of Norwich. He allegedly was kidnapped and slaughtered by Jews who required Christian blood for ritual purposes. Similar episodes based on missing Christian children culminated in the 12th century legend of Little Saint Hugh of Lincoln and were recounted by Geoffrey Chaucer as "The Prioress' Tale" in the first great work of modern English literature, his *Canterbury Tales.*

The sacrosanct stature of the Palestine lie in many quarters enables it to function as a post-modern incarnation of the medieval blood libel, which as noted at the outset, channels an anti-Jewish accusation older than Christianity. The new blood libel does for leftist secular fundamentalists and devout politico-religious Islamic fundamentalists what its earlier incarnation did for European Christendom. It makes Jew-hatred holy.

The libel is rooted, as mentioned, in a second century B.C.E. Hellenistic charge mocked by Flavius Josephus in his *Against Apion.* The accusation insisted that Jews captured, fattened and killed Greeks to use their flesh and blood in religious rites. In classic form it reiterates some version of the charge that "Jews use the blood of Christian children in Passover matzohs." This nightmarish indictment merged with the "Christ-killer" allegation to become, on its own and in later variations, a warrant perpetually outstanding against the Jewish people.

137

The blood libel was "a complex of deliberate lies, trumped-up accusations, and popular beliefs about the murder-lust of the Jews and their bloodthirstiness, based on the conception that Jews hate Christianity and mankind in general."[1] It links to "the delusion that Jews are in some way not human and must have recourse to special remedies and subterfuges to appear, at least outwardly, like other men."

Ancient history? Made literary by Chaucer, it reappeared nearly a millennia later in comic book form—Germany between World Wars I and II featured, among other entertainments, comic books combining science fiction, *untermenschen* (subhumans), Jews and vampires. The blood libel reemerged from its timeless cocoon barely updated in widespread accusations that the Israel Defense Forces' field hospital dispatched to Haiti as humanitarian relief after the devastating 2010 earthquake was a cover for the theft and black market sale of human organs. That the hospital was the first and perhaps most efficient such relief effort, as several news outlets reported, mattered little. The charge appeared again in Palestinian allegations that Israelis "harvest" organs from the bodies of "martyrs" killed attempting or carrying out terrorist attacks.

In 2016, CNN flashed an onscreen banner that read "The Trump Transition: Alt-Right Founder Questions If Jews Are People."[2] The network apologized the next day, saying airing the banner, known in television as a chyron, "was poor judgment and we very much regret it and apologize."[3] According to JTA, the CNN segment "concerned statements made over the weekend by Richard Spencer at an event of the white supremacist think tank the National Policy Institute. Spencer suggested that the news media had been critical of presidential candidate Donald Trump in order to protect Jewish interests. 'One wonders if these people are people at all, or instead soulless golem,'" Spencer said. Clever verbal jujitsu: the *golem*, in medieval Jewish fables, is an inanimate strongman brought to life in threatening times to protect Jews.

The American "alt-right"—typically neo-Nazis out of uniform—though a fringe movement, gained considerable news media attention in 2016. Spencer and other spokesmen often aligned their anti-immigrant, "white nationalist" positions with Trump's presidential campaign. That Trump's daughter Ivanka had converted to Judaism; her husband,

---

1 "Encyclopedia Judaica: Blood Libel," *Encyclopedia Judaica*, 2008, The Gale Group, at Jewish Virtual Library, http://www.jewishvirtuallibrary.org/blood-libel .

2 CNN (Cable News Network), "The Lead," Nov. 21, 2016.

3 Jewish Telegraphic Agency, Nov. 22, 2016.

the candidate's son-in-law Jared Kushner, was one of his closest advisors; and the couple were raising Trump's Jewish grandchildren did not inhibit Spencer's revival of a form of the "Jews-versus-humanity" innuendo. The longest lasting lies often are the most useful, their internal contradictions easily homogenized by true believers.

"The blood libel led to trials and massacres of Jews in the Middle Ages and early modern times; it was revived by the Nazis. Its origin is rooted in ancient, almost primordial concepts concerning the potency and energies of 'blood.'"[4] Take your pick: the Jew as medieval vampire or as 20th century "bloodsucker," in the shouts of demonstrators outside Freddy's Fashion Mart, a store in a building owned by Jews in New York City's Harlem. Morris Powell and the Rev. Al Sharpton led recurring protests there in 1995, until one man took their words seriously and shot up the store, then set it alight. Eight people died. Sharpton, already notorious for his anti-police, anti-prosecutor incitement in the fictitious 1987 Tawana Brawley rape case, would go on to be a high-profile player in the Democratic Party, host a program on the MSNBC cable television channel and frequent White House guest and, according to news reports, civil rights advisor during the Obama administration. As the Holocaust receded into history, antisemitism—at least in the right circles—became more deniable and less an obstacle.

The blood libel charge against Jews, of which "blood sucker" is one variant, whether meant figuratively or literally, is particularly obscene since "blood sacrifices, practiced by many pagan religions, are expressly forbidden by the Torah. The [Jewish religious] law of meat-salting (*melichah*) is designed to prevent the least drop of avoidable blood remaining in food. Yet pagan incomprehension of the Jewish monotheist cult, lacking the customary images and statues, led to charges of ritual killing."[5]

"Incomprehension" is a polite way to put it. In any case, in the Middle Ages, "as Christianity spread in Western Europe and penetrated the popular consciousness, using the emotions and imagination even more than thought and dogma in order to gain influence, various story elements began to evolve around the alleged inhumanity and sadism of the Jews."[6] With variations, the libel appeared across Europe over centuries, leading to massacres like that in Munich in 1286. At times, heads of state and the church opposed circulation of the blood libel. Emperor Frederick II of Hohenstaufen did in 1243 and Pope Innocent IV in

4 Jewish Virtual Library, "Blood Libel."
5 Ibid.
6 Ibid.

1247. But the charge proved stronger than their condemnations. It filled a need, like the often-imposed Jewish role as ultimate sacrifice that it supported. So from the 1600's on the blood libel expanded into Eastern Europe as well. In 1759, after his own investigation, Cardinal Lorenzo Ganganelli, later Pope Clement XIV, recommended the Vatican act against the blood libel in Poland and Lithuania as had Pope Innocent IV for Jews in Germany and France 500 years earlier. Again, to little avail.

Blood libel accusations proliferated in Russia during the 19th century and first two decades of the 20th alongside and as part of rising antisemitism in general. Perhaps the most renowned case was that of Mendel Beilis, 1911 – 1913, fictionalized in Bernard Malamud's Pulitzer Prize-winning 1967 novel, *The Fixer*. Inquiries repeatedly exonerated Jews, but officials as senior as Czar Nicholas II did not disavow the possibility such accusations could be true in other cases. They were always useful to those who wanted to expropriate, demonize or delegitimize Jews, landowners, monks and nobles among them. Although the blood libel, promoted by a French diplomat, had returned to the Middle East in 1840 in the form of the "Damascus Affair" and spread decades later in Russia, it remained for the Nazis to revive the accusation as state policy. They conducted blood libel investigations and trials at Memel in 1936, Bamberg in 1937 and Bohemia in 1940. People believe what they want to believe, and, when it comes to Jews, or today to Israelis, often the more outlandish, the more impossible, the better.

The defeat of the Third Reich did not end the blood libel any more than it uprooted antisemitism or made permanent the prohibition demanded by "Never again!" Blood libels were "repeated in the Arab countries … in a number of ways in various books, as in Egypt in the 1960s, the titles referring to 'Talmudic human sacrifices' or 'the secrets of Zionism.' …

"Mustafa Tlass, a key political figure in Syria for decades [defense minister for dictator Hafez al-Assad, ostentatious fan of movie star Sophia Loren], first published his book on the 1840 Damascus blood libel in 1983. The work, called *Matzah of Zion* and reprinted in a number of editions and translated into many languages, became an influential and frequently quoted source."[7] Tlass supposedly confirmed "how Jews and Zionists constantly perpetrate ritual murders. Newspapers as well joined in, with Egypt's government-sponsored *Al-Ahram* publishing in October 2000 a full-page article called 'Jewish Matzah Made from Arab Blood.'

---

7 Ibid.

"TV series and discussions also evoke the blood libel, as on the Al-Jazeera network and in the Al-Manar (Hezbollah television channel) series *The Exile* in 2003. The image of the Zionist in these visual depictions, watched by millions all over the world, is that of the *Der Strummer* Jew, bloodthirsty and frighteningly ferocious," noted Jewish Virtual Library. *Der Strummer* was Nazi propagandist Julius Streicher's weekly tabloid, published from 1923 to the end of World War II. Its anti-Jewish caricatures epitomized Adolf Hitler's Jew, at once sub-human and diabolically clever.

The blood libel and related tales repeatedly led to the torture, murder, or expulsion of countless Jews. The libel never died, periodically re-emerging in its original form but rebranded. Ahad Ha-Am's observation that the blood libel showed the whole world could be wrong, the Jews right, since it was "based on an absolute lie" brings us to the Palestine Liberation Organization's Covenant, Article 22. It recycles Christ-killer, nation-killer themes via Marxist-Leninist jargon:

"Zionism is a political movement organically linked to world *imperialism* and hostile to all movements of liberation and progress in the world. It is a *racist* and *fanatical* movement in its formation, *aggressive, expansionist* and *colonialist* in its aims, and *fascist* and *Nazi* in its methods. … Israel is a *constant threat* to peace in the Middle East and the *entire world.* … [T]he people of Palestine looks to the support of all liberal men of the world and all the forces of good, progress and peace ….[emphases added]." Zionism as a "constant threat" to world peace, the Jew as enemy of the human race. The latest iteration of the Jews being right and much of the rest of the world wrong is the lie of Palestine, neatly summarized in the PLO "covenant."

Those who believe in an imperialist, racist, fanatical Israel, a Jewish state colonialist, fascist and Nazi in its methods, nothing less than a threat to world peace, can be brought to believe that Israelis have committed and are committing genocide against Palestinian Arabs, in the process slaughtering hundreds of thousands if not millions of them. College students across Europe and North America so believe. The fact there has been no such genocide—but rather that Israelis have defended themselves against genocidal attempts—means nothing. Neither did, nor does, the fact Jews never use blood, human or otherwise, in religious worship. Ahad Ha'am was on to something, but something bigger than even he realized.

Only two races

Having survived the Holocaust, Viktor Frankl, a psychiatrist and liberated inmate of the concentration camps, asserted in his memoir/ psychological exploration *Man's Search for Meaning* that "from all this [genocide occasionally interrupted by individual acts of righteousness, sometimes even by a camp guard] we may learn that there are two races of men in this world, but only these two—the 'race' of the decent man and the 'race' of the indecent man. Both are found everywhere, they penetrate into all groups of society. No group consists entirely of decent or indecent people."[8] Some groups are led by the decent, others suppress them.

Talmudic sages teach that decency—doing the right thing in matters small and large—is not a static condition but an active, daily choice. A key part of that continuous choice is how one relates to one's fellow human being, regardless of his or her race, religion, national origin, creed or sex. Is one a *mensch*—an empathetic, just fellow human being—or not? In the Torah the ancient Israelites are instructed to appoint judges who will respect neither rich nor poor but judge fairly regardless of the status of those in court. Contrary to identity politics and grievance-mongering essential to early 21st century leftist and populist agitation, human beings are required to judge each other as individuals, not as representatives of any class, confession, tribe, country, ethnicity or gender. Anything else is bias, and bias supplants rights with privilege.

To Frankl's race of "decent men," the two-dimensionality of the lies of Palestine is plain. For example, Israel is the Middle East's only multi-ethnic, multi-cultural democracy in which minorities—including Arab Muslim and Christian minorities—exercise the same civil rights as the majority (in this case Jewish). Decency requires it be recognized and treated as such. Instead, an indecent, increasingly vociferous worldwide movement ceaselessly denounces it as a "racist, apartheid" regime.

As with the original blood libel, in this case too much of the world is wrong and the Jews and friends of the Jewish state are right. The medieval blood libel's rejection by popes and an emperor mattered little. The charge was simply too good, too useful not to use. Perversely intact after millennia, it is refueled by "Palestinianism," a fetish not just of "Palestinianized Islamism" but also of contemporary secular fundamentalism. So of course Israel—in which an Arab sits on the Supreme Court, Arabs

---

8 *Man's Search for Meaning*, by Viktor Frankl, 1959, page 86 (in Beacon Press paperback, 2006 edition).

have commanded army units and headed departments of major hospitals and one represented the country as "Miss Israel" (Rana Raslan, 1999)—illustrates the worst of racism and apartheid. As the Jewish state, it cannot be otherwise. It must not be otherwise.

In one example of many in which the old blood libel flows through contemporary Palestinianism, Sheik Khalid al-Mughrabi, a preacher and instructor at al-Aqsa mosque on Temple Mount in Jerusalem's Old City, reasserted it in a 2015 sermon. According to Palestinian Media Watch, a private Israeli organization that monitors, translates and publicizes Palestinian communications and educational media, al-Mughrabi wrapped a number of anti-Jewish, anti-Israeli conspiracy theories into one talk. He told worshippers that the Nazis slaughtered European Jews in the Holocaust because Jews had been kidnapping children to use their blood in Passover bread. The sheik also claimed that Jews worshipped Satan, plotted the Sept. 11, 2001 destruction of New York City's World Trade Center and attack on the Pentagon in Washington, D.C., and controlled the Freemasons, who sacrifice their wives and children in secret ceremonies.[9]

Al-Mughrabi perched at and preached from Al-Aqsa mosque. It is often cited, by non-Muslims, as Islam's third holiest place, after Mecca and Medina. It is not clear than many Muslims would make the claim, which might be inferred to lessen the importance of demands for Temple Mount and Jerusalem. In his old-new anti-Jewish lunacy the sheik was hardly alone. Else how, for one example among countless others, could Penny Gross have been recommended to serve in 2016 as the U.N.'s Human Rights Council's special rapporteur on human rights violations in the Gaza Strip?

Gross, a professor of law and globalization at Queen Mary College, London, had called for a "total boycott" of Israel, parroted the "apartheid" and "ethnic cleansing" canards against the Jewish state, compared Israeli treatment of Palestinian Arabs to that meted out by the Islamic State in Iraq and Syria to those unlucky enough to have fallen under its control, and lamented the fact that the United Kingdom and United States had not started bombing Israel in response to such "massacres." In other words, she was totally—therefore perhaps respectably—unhinged on the matter of Israel. As the non-profit U.N. Watch organization noted, the special rapporteur's mandate implies that the individual monitors "the situation of human rights in the Palestinian territories,'" but

9 "Jews make matzah break from blood, sacrifice humans to Satan—in Al-Aqsa lesson," Palestinian Media Watch, June 2, 2015.

"this is false. In fact, the text of the mandate... makes clear that the rapporteur is charged with investigating only 'Israel's violations.' Not only does the rapporteur's jurisdiction not cover Palestinian actions against Israelis, it also ignores rights violations by the Palestinian Authority and Hamas against other Palestinians."[10]

Gross didn't get the job. It went to a candidate with similar beliefs in the crimes of the Jewish state but who did not yet call for its bombing by Anglo-American forces. This was S. Michael Lynk, a law professor at Western Ontario University. Lynk was another academic obsessed by Israel, but not just by it alone. Three days after al-Qaeda terrorists destroyed the World Trade Center and attacked the Pentagon, he blamed the West for provoking the mass murders. When his selection was announced in spring, 2016 Canada's foreign ministry urged that someone else be chosen, someone "professional, neutral and credible."

But credibility and the United Nations rarely overlap, particularly regarding Israel. Canadian Jewish organizations noted Lynk's pre-U.N. activities included calling for the Jewish state to be prosecuted for war crimes, accusing it of ethnic cleansing and comparing it to Nazi Germany. Of course Lynk promoted the boycott, divestment and sanction (BDS) movement on university campuses across North America, a movement aimed, as detailed below, at Israel's delegitimization and destruction.[11]

So when Lynk submitted his first report as special rapporteur at the end of October, 2016 it unsurprisingly charged that Israel's occupation of the West Bank "is dripping in human rights violations" that severely hamper Palestinian economic and societal development. As to the double standard by which anti-Zionism merges with antisemitism, reports from U.N. special rapporteurs on the situation of human rights in Russia, China, Cuba, Syria or any other actual, large-scale human rights violator did not make news. That's because while violations in such places periodically make headlines, no such special rapporteurs exist. The special rapporteur on human rights in Iran sometimes highlights serious violations, not that they much trouble the United Nations or Iran, let alone rate serious news coverage. Only the Jewish state suffers complete double standard obsession. By such targeting, inhibitions are diminished against violent answers to the Jewish state question and

---

10 "Candidate for U.N.'s Palestine observer compares Israel to Islamic State," *Times of Israel*, March 11, 2016.

11 "Expected U.N. appointee has history of anti-Israel bias, Canadian Jewish groups say," Jewish Telegraphic Agency, March 24, 2016.

resumption of the Holocaust in contemporary fashion.

Professors Gross and Lynk's Israel-as-ISIS, Israelis-as-Nazis derangement can be understood as a secular version of al-Mughrabi's religious instruction. Resolutions of the United Nations' oxymoronically named Human Rights Council and much output from similarly contradictorily-titled Middle East studies departments confirm that the post-World War II era of anti-antisemitism is well and truly over.

Anti-Israel canards—pieties of the anti-Israel left, slogans of the neo-Nazi right—rest on factual and ethical inversions essential to the lie of Palestine. The word for such selective moral indignation is hypocrisy. As noted, the lie of Palestine means to return Jews to their pre-1948 status as a stateless, defenseless, persecuted minority. Its centrality to the ideological-theological creeds of the secular fundamentalist left and Islamic triumphalists—and usefulness to the reactionary right—demonstrates its broad appeal. Nothing has proved handier in advancing reghettoization of the Jews in the court of public opinion. Sheik Khalid al-Mughrabi's warning of the Jews' bloody compulsions followed that from a former Jordanian legislator. Reporting on Palestinian Media Watch's account of al-Mughrabi's sermon, an Israeli news outlet added that "in September 2014 Sheikh Abd Al-Mun'im Abu Zant, a former Jordanian member of parliament, revived the blood libel in an interview with [the Palestinian Authority's] al-Aqsa TV."[12] "On their religious holidays, if they cannot find a Muslim to slaughter, and use drops of his blood to knead the matzos they eat, they slaughter a Christian in order to take drops of his blood, and mix it into the matzos that they eat on that holiday," Abu Zant said.

In July 2014, Daoud Shihad, a spokesman for the Iranian-subsidized Palestinian Islamic Jihad terrorist group, asserted "'Israel is targeting the Palestinians. … I would just like to remind you of the ruling by the Israeli rabbis, who have instructed the soldiers to knead the [dough for] bread that the Jews eat with the blood of Arab and Palestinian children'" (reported by the Washington-based Middle East Media Research Institute. MEMRI translates Middle Eastern communications media from Arabic, Farsi and other languages into English in real-time for use by journalists, scholars and the general public).

"A year earlier, in May 2013, Egyptian politician Khaled Zaafrani during an interview on al-Hafez TV, a Salafist [Sunni Islamic fundamentalist] Egyptian station, also brought up the blood libel. 'It is well-known

12 "Temple Mount preacher: Jews make Passover matzohs with children's blood," *Times of Israel*, June 3, 2015.

that during Passover they make matzos called the "Blood of Zion." They take a Christian child, slit his throat, and slaughter him … they never forgo this rite."[13] Such repetition no doubt contributed to the ADL's 2014 "Global 100" survey finding that the Arab- and Muslim-majority countries of North Africa and the Middle East harbored the highest average rate of people holding antisemitic stereotypes: 74 percent.

Epitomizing the resurrected libel, helping produce the same effects, was the case of "the Palestinian William of Norwich," 12-year-old Mohammad al-Dura. He allegedly was killed by Israeli soldiers on Sept. 30, 2000 at the start of the deadly second intifada (2000 – 2005). A videotape shot by Palestinian cameraman Talal Abu-Rahma, with a voice-over done in Israel by France 2 Television's Charles Enderlin, himself Jewish, aired the same day. France 2 gave the edited video free to other media and the story spread world-wide. The 55-second tape shows the boy cowering against his father, both seeking cover behind a large concrete barrel. The two, Enderlin intoned, are "the target of fire coming from the Israeli position. The child signals, but … there's a new burst of gunfire. … The child is dead and the father is wounded."

In Arab countries Muhammad al-Dura quickly became a symbol of Israeli cruelty. Streets, parks and newborns were named for him. New videos called on young people to seek "martyrdom" and join al-Dura in paradise. But France 2's video does not show any Israeli soldiers—neither the 55 seconds aired nor another 27 minutes filmed by Abu-Rahma. The tape pictures the boy collapsing, then ends. A further frame, omitted by Enderlin, shows al-Dura raising his head and arm. The reporter claimed he cut the "agony of the child." But when other French journalists compelled France 2 to let them view the entire 27 minutes of tape, they found no excruciating scenes of a suffering al-Dura.

Israel initially conceded the boy might have been shot by its troops in the Gaza Strip. But a later re-enactment suggested that the soldiers on the scene, barricaded inside a building at Netzarim across an intersection from the boy and his father, could not have hit them where they took cover. Writer James Fallows concluded "whatever happened to him, he was not shot by the Israeli soldiers. …"[14] A Jan. 25, 2005 column in the French newspaper *Le Figaro* echoed Fallows and reiterated what others had said: A review of the terrain suggested that—if the boy was

---

13 "Islamic Jihad: IDF soldiers told to bake Palestinian blood into bread," *Times of Israel*, July 27, 2014.

14 "Who Shot Muhammad al-Dura?" by James Fallows, *The Atlantic Monthly*, June, 2003.

hit at all and the scene was not another "Pallywood" production like others staged at Netzarim and seen in footage of crowds there on Sept. 30, 2000—then Palestinian bullets struck him.[15]

German filmmaker Esther Shapira also reached this conclusion in a documentary broadcast by Germany's ARD network in March 2002. A second investigation by Shapira and Georg M. Hafner, aired on ARD in March 2009, raised further questions about the alleged al-Dura shooting. They said biometric analysis of faces indicated the boy shown at autopsy and al-Dura were not the same.

One of the more prominent of numerous critics of France 2 Television's al-Dura coverage and the channel's persistent protestations of its accuracy was Phillipe Karsenty. Karsenty headed a watchdog called Media Ratings. He examined Abu Rahma's raw footage and pronounced Enderlin's report a hoax. In 2006 a French court found Karsenty guilty of defaming France 2 and Enderlin. Karsenty appealed. The following year the appeals court requested France 2 turn over the raw footage from its al-Dura report.

During the appeals process, the Israeli Government Press Office called the 2000 story "the creation of the myth of Muhammad al-Dura." The Press Office said the invention "has caused great damage to the State of Israel" and amounted to "an explicit blood libel" that "caused damage and dozens of dead." The GPO letter concluded that the incident was staged since Israeli troops could not have shot the boy from the angle at which they were positioned, that key parts had been cut from the video France 2 provided to other outlets, and cameraman Abu Rahma had arranged other "action scenes" in Gaza at the start of the second intifada.

In France, though the appeals court ordered France 2 to submit all 27 minutes of footage for review, Enderlin delivered just 18. Boston University Prof. Richard Landes, who previously had viewed more than 20 minutes of the raw video, testified that two clearly staged scenes were missing. Of the footage Enderlin provided, little showed Muhammad al-Dura and that which did indicated he was still alive at its end. In 2008 the appeals court reversed the lower court's judgement that found Karsenty guilty of defaming France 2. The appeals court said Karsenty "exercised his right of free criticism in good faith" and noted "contradictory answers" given by Enderlin to questions about editing of the video and by Abu Rahma about the sequence of the scenes and conditions under which they were filmed.

The next month, hundreds of French journalists posted a petition

---

15 "The Al-Dura Cover-up," Andrea Levin, CAMERA, Feb. 22, 2005.

in support of Enderlin on the Web site of the magazine *Nouvel Obser-vateur*. They described him as the victim of an "obstinate and hateful campaign to tarnish [his] professional dignity." *Mai oui*, those obstinate, stiff-necked Jews again. Such was the insular nature of many journalists and their self-assumed infallibility that they were shocked to find the court would "grant the same credibility" to press critics as to journalists themselves.

Claims and counter-claims continued. Among them was the 2007 revelation—by David Yehuda, the Israeli doctor who treated him—that Jamal al-Dura's scars, which the father had cited as proof of injuries caused by gunfire from Israel's troops when his son was killed, resulted from earlier surgery. They were, Yehuda said, the result of a 1994 tendon transplant repair he had performed after doctors at Shifa Hospital in the Gaza Strip could not heal injures caused when Palestinian thugs had attacked Jamal al-Dura with an axe in 1992.

In 2013, the wheels of the Israeli government grinding almost too slowly to matter, a review committee released its report on the al-Dura affair. It concluded there was no evidence Muhammad al-Dura was killed as alleged in France 2 Television's report. However, the committee added, the claim was used to foment hatred and terrorism against Israel and contributed to the delegitimization of the Jewish state. It stressed "the need for [news] media outlets to implement the highest professional and ethical standards when covering asymmetric conflicts" and "critically evaluate information provided by local stringers, especially in arenas in which repeated attempts to stage or fabricate media items have been documented."[16] Unlikely. Asymmetric conflicts, to the post-democratic left, Islamist apologists and old-new right are by definition "unfair" conflicts in which the technologically superior West has an undeserved advantage over morally justified, oppressed people of color in the third world. Conflicts of Others versus imperialists. So William of Norwich and Little Saint Hugh of Lincoln reverberate through the centuries to the present, if in new masks. They confirm, for all who want and need to believe in it, some kind of blood libel against the Jews. So Muhammad al-Dura endures metaphorically if not factually as the Palestinian William of Norwich.

---

16 "Backgrounder: Mohammad Al-Dura," by Ricki Hollander and Gilead Ini, CAMERA, May 20, 2013. This detailed examination is an invaluable source for understanding the media and ideological manipulation exemplified by the al-Dura affair.

Repeal, but No Remedy

In 1991, prodded by the administration of President George H. W. Bush, with Assistant Secretary of State for International Organizations, John R. Bolton (in 2018, President Donald J. Trump's national security adviser) as point man, the United Nations' repealed its 1975 "Zionism-is-racism" resolution. But the measure's toxic waste spill—as psychological warfare—went largely untreated by the United States, Israel, pro-Israel groups and academics. So its poison continued to spread. Likewise, al-Dura's image, his myth, which fits so comfortably into the Palestinian narrative, performs the same function as have William of Norwich, Little St. Hugh of Lincoln and their alleged cohorts for all those who must believe in the intolerable blood lust of the Jewish state and its supporters.

The image of Muhammad al-Dura and accusation of his killing by Israel helped inflame—or justify preexisting—anti-Jewish, anti-American and anti-Western opinion in the months before al-Qaeda's destruction of the World Trade Center and attack on the Pentagon. Throngs bearing al-Dura's picture would march in European cities and chant "Death to Israel!" "Death to the Jews!" Al-Qaeda later released a video that linked the boy's image with those of the burning Twin Towers and of *Wall Street Journal* reporter Daniel Pearl uttering his last words before being beheaded in Pakistan: "My name is Daniel Pearl. My father is Jewish. My mother is Jewish, I am Jewish. Back in the town of B'nei Brak, there is a street named after my great-grandfather, Chaim Pearl, who was one of the founders of the town." Twentieth century Jews reestablished B'nei B'rak, a place frequented by rabbinic sages and mentioned in the Passover Haggadah. "I am Jewish," Pearl concluded. What more could be needed to justify decapitation?

Al-Qaeda's murder of Pearl in 2002, though widely covered, was little examined as part of the campaign of anti-Zionist antisemitism. Literally and symbolically, Jew haters, Israel haters, murdered a Jew in part as human sacrifice to expiate what they invented as the sins of Pearl's people. But at the border of conscious and subconscious, these disturbing sins—inhumane blood-lust, self-justifying hatred of mankind, or at least a large portion of it—they perhaps recognized as their own. Such sins still apparently required human sacrifice to cleanse the sinners. Yet the sacrifices would not be those of the sinners themselves. Rather, the scapegoated and sinned-against would be offered, as they had been before.

Joshua Trachtenberg wrote *The Devil and the Jews; The Medieval Conception of the Jew and Its Relation to Modern Antisemitism* at the depth of the Holocaust. He implicitly connected medieval antisemitic superstition with modern Nazi madness. Three quarters of a century later some still spread the superstition. In the process, they persist in invoking the image of the satanic Jew. Hence the demonization of Israel, the Jewish state.

So the new blood libel, the lie of Palestine, functions as did the old, a negative psychological projection en masse. The Jew and/or his state serve, when not as Satan incarnate, then as scapegoat. So not by accident, nor only by happy propaganda stroke, have Iranian leaders insisted since their Islamic revolution of 1979, that the United States is "the Great Satan," Israel "the Little Satan." When it comes to behaving satanically, toward their own peoples and others, the guilt to be borne is that of the anti-Zionist antisemites. But if the tale of William of Norwich/Mohammad al-Dura of Palestine fails to move them sufficiently, to justify them to themselves, an equally potent fable lies to hand. Revived repeatedly, it relates how the Jews supposedly threaten "Islam's third holiest shrine," Jerusalem's al-Aqsa mosque.

CHAPTER EIGHT

'Al-Aqsa's in Danger!'
Al-Husseini's Holy Incitement

WHAT THE MUHAMMAD AL-DURA tale exemplifies in micro, the "al-Aqsa is in danger!" charge does in macro. Whether manipulating the image of a 12-year-old boy or the status of what is called Islam's third holiest shrine, the incendiary potential of the Palestine lie remains the same. Journalist and novelist Nidra Poller termed the al-Dura charge a "long-range ballistic myth." If so, then "Al-Aqsa is in danger" has for nearly a century been gasoline on the fire of Jew-hatred among Palestinian Arabs and an accelerant for anti-Zionism and antisemitism throughout Arab and Islamic lands, justification for warheads rhetorical and, if need be, actual. It has reverberated quite recently, as in the July, 2017 Temple Mount killings of Israeli Jews by Palestinian Arabs in the name of holy al-Aqsa.

Like the al-Dura example, it's been another lie central to continuation of the anti-Israel conflict that Western journalists, academics and diplomats have been reluctant if not frightened to examine. To see UNESCO, the United Nations Educational, Scientific and Cultural Organization back-handedly endorse the fabrication, as the agency did in 2016 and 2017, is to be reminded of the oft-cited lines in W. H. Auden's poem "September 1, 1939:" "As the clever hopes expire/Of a low dishonest decade... The unmentionable odor of death/Offends the September night."

Auden wrote of the day World War II, long in the making and enabled by moral exhaustion of Western leaders and their people, particularly in France and to a marked extent in England—erupted. Near the end of that conflagration, in which 55 million people died, six million enslaved Jews among them, the Allied victors formed the United Nations. They established the world body largely as an instrument to prevent future wars and genocides. Yet the United Nations, which initially welcomed Israel as a member state in 1949, ultimately would become perhaps the most influential purveyor and certifier of anti-Zionist antisemitism.

U.N. agencies, including U.N.E.S.C.O., the General Assembly, at times even the Security Council and virtually always the U.N. Human Rights Commission—and when that body became too noxious, its barely remodeled successor, the U.N. Human Rights Council—produced innumerable resolutions condemning Israel for all sorts of non-existent crimes. This has been widely noted. So too the fact the commission and council did so while their membership—sometimes chairmanships—included actual chronic and major human rights violators such as Libya, Saudi Arabia, Iran, Russia, China and Cuba, countries the two bodies rarely scolded.

As for the General Assembly, Northwestern University international law professor Eugene Kontorovich and researcher Penny Grunseid noted, "Israel is referred to as the 'occupying power' 530 times in U.N. General Assembly (UNGA) resolutions. Yet, in seven major instances of past or present prolonged military occupation—Indonesia in East Timor, Turkey in northern Cyprus, Russia in areas of Georgia, Morocco in western Sahara, Vietnam in Cambodia, Armenia in Azerbaijan, and Russia in Ukraine's Crimea—the number is zero. The UNGA has not called any of these countries an 'occupying power.' Not even once."[1]

That imbalance would be striking if the tilt undermined any other country. But Israel, the Jewish state, functions in the revival of open, widespread antisemitism as the individual Jew did in pre-Holocaust Jew-hatred. So at the United Nations it is old business renewed as usual. This provides another illustration of the double standard by which anti-Zionism sanitizes antisemitism. As for the United Nations, Abba Eban, an Israeli ambassador and foreign minister, once observed, "If Algeria introduced a resolution declaring the world was flat and Israel flattened it, it would pass by a vote of 164 to 13, with 26 abstentions."

U.N. arithmetic starts with one Jewish state but 57 member countries of the Organization of Islamic Cooperation (why no Organization of the Christian Conference?), among them the 21 actual countries of

---

1 "At the U.N., Only Israel is an 'Occupying Power,'" *Wall Street Journal*, Sept. 13, 2016. http://www.wsj.com/articles/at-the-u-n-only-israel-is-an-occupying-power-1473808544 .

the Arab League (why no League of Spanish-speaking Countries?) plus the Palestine Liberation Organization as "Palestine." U.N. math adds dozens of other countries, including many members of the European Union, desirous both of oil from and their own exports to the Middle East and of hoping to placate, at someone else's expense, their own often large and growing but poorly assimilated Muslim minorities. The U.N.'s anti-Israel bias would be self-parody but for its ultimately annihilationist object.

As we have seen, in one six-week period in late 2016, the General Assembly tarred Israel and Israel only as an "occupying power," the U.N. "special rapporteur for human rights in the occupied Palestinian territories" indicted Israel's control of the West Bank, and the United Nations Educational, Scientific and Cultural Organization (UNESCO) attempted via resolution to erase 3,000 years of Jewish history and religion by declaring Jerusalem's Temple Mount an Islamic-only shrine. One could almost be forgiven for imaging that the PLO "Covenant" must be correct: Israel threatens world peace, so the United Nations responds to that danger.

The "occupying power" and, in some formulations, "the illegal Israeli occupation" is another easily unraveled thread in the Palestinian narrative. Nonetheless, many mistakenly—or disingenuously—cling to it. In 2003, early in my tenure as Washington director of the Boston-based Committee for Accuracy in Middle East Reporting in America, CAMERA President and Executive Director Andrea Levin and I met with *Washington Post* Foreign Editor David Hoffman. We wanted to discuss several recent examples of what we considered anti-Israel bias in the *Post's* coverage. Hoffman himself had served as the newspaper's Jerusalem bureau chief and gained respect as its Moscow correspondent. He later would win a Pulitzer Prize for his book *The Dead Hand: The Untold Story of the Cold War Arms Race and its Dangerous Legacy.* But this day, Levin and I were barely seated when Hoffman demanded, with some vehemence, "Do you believe the West Bank and Gaza Strip are occupied?"

Apparently, representatives of a pro-Israel organization previously had tried to tell him that was not the case. "Yes," I replied, having answered this question more than once. "Similar to the United States, Great Britain, France and the Soviet Union's occupation of Germany after World War II—a result of defeating an aggressor in war. The difference is that, unlike the Allies, Israel has historical claims to the territories." For whatever reason, perhaps surprise, Hoffman did not pursue that and we turned to our agenda items. But Levin and I were struck by the fact this, of all other possibilities, was his opening, and challenging, question, a default defense mechanism when meeting critics of his staff's Israel reporting.

Israel conquered the West Bank, Gaza Strip, eastern Jerusalem, the Sinai Peninsula and the Golan Heights in self-defense in the 1967 Six-Day War; it had been immediately threatened and previously attacked from them. It retained those areas similarly in the 1973 Yom Kippur War. It returned the Sinai—geographically by far the largest, and with its Israeli-developed oil fields at least temporarily the most lucrative portion of the occupied territories—to Egypt under the 1979 Egyptian-Israeli peace treaty. It leveled an attractive, sea-front Israeli-built town, Yamit, and abandoned several surrounding post-'67 agricultural communities in the process.

Negotiations with Syria (spurned by Damascus before eruptions of the Syrian civil wars in 2011) are yet required to resolve the status of the Golan. They await either the restoration of, or successors to, a unitary Syrian state with leaders willing to talk and able to uphold an agreement.

Israel reunified Jerusalem as its capital shortly after the Six-Day War. Though Jerusalem was the capital of Jewish states long before London, Paris or Berlin were capitals of the United Kingdom, France or Germany, respectively—not to mention Jerusalem's prominence as the 3,000-year-old center of Judaism—this renewed reality has been denied internationally except, in 2017, by the United States, followed by Guatemala. Israel unilaterally evacuated the Gaza Strip, including 8,000 civilians in more than 20 settlements, in 2005. Soon afterward, Hamas ousted Palestinian Authority President Mahmoud Abbas' administration from the Gaza Strip in 2007's "five-day war."

The PA of Abbas and his Fatah movement remained in daily supervision of nearly all Palestinian populated areas of the West Bank, as it had since the 1993 Oslo accords. But the Israeli military continued as the legitimate occupational authority in the West Bank pending successful negotiations according to terms of U.N. Security Council resolutions 242 and 338, Israeli-Palestinian pacts including the 1995 Israeli-Palestinian Interim Agreement and related initiatives. If Israel was guilty of violating international law regard "the occupation," it may not have been for stationing forces in the West Bank 50 years after the Six-Day War but rather for quitting the Gaza Strip absent an agreement negotiated according to resolutions 242 and 338.

In any case, no power since the Ottoman Empire in 1917 has ex-

ercised sovereignty over the West Bank and Gaza Strip. Great Britain
was in military occupation from 1917 to 1922, then as League of Na-
tions/United Nations mandatory power from 1922 to 1948. Jordan illegally occupied the West Bank from 1948 to 1967 as a result of aggression
in the 1948-1949 Israeli War of Independence. Egypt likewise illegally
occupied the Gaza Strip during the 1948 – '67 period. There was virtually no discussion in those 19 years of Arab occupation of the need for a
second Palestinian Arab state in the West Bank and Gaza, in addition to
Jordan on the East Bank. As noted, the Hashemite Kingdom comprises
three-quarters of the land originally intended for the League of Nations'
Palestine Mandate and includes a majority Palestinian Arab population.
Hence, that part of their narrative that insists Palestinian Arabs have
been stateless and "ethnically cleansed" from Palestine has, in the first
instance, been false since 1922 and in the second erroneous even after
1948, with most Palestinian Arabs at the time remaining in either Jordan, the West Bank, Gaza or Israel as Israeli citizens.

Believers in the Palestine lie can dismiss Israel's current, obligatory
occupation of disputed territories as a legal fiction. They might deny
exposure of the Muhammad al-Dura myth as Zionist obfuscation. But
even if forced to abandon these key strands of the narrative, they would
have a more emotive, more inflammatory charge ready. It combines the
classical-medieval blood-libel, the early Christian "Christ-killer" accusation and the Jewish plot for world control fervidly related in *The
Protocols of the Learned Elders of Zion*, the 19th century fraud still alive
and well in some quarters in the 21st century. It is the "Al-Aqsa is in
danger!" grotesquerie, a Rosetta Stone in deconstructing the Palestinian
narrative.

"Whether printed in cartoons, preached in mosques or taught in
schools," the lie that Al-Aqsa mosque is in danger of collapse and the
Jews at fault "is accepted as common knowledge across the Arab world.
Millions of Muslims accept it as truth. The message is clear: Jews seek
to expel the Arabs from Jerusalem," Nadav Shragai has written.[2] Shragai
charges that "Al-Aqsa is in danger" functions as a "modern blood libel
… directed at the state of Israel, the Zionist movement, and the Jewish
people. It has become integral to the Muslim, Arab, and Palestinian discourse, accepted by very large numbers as the absolute truth."

"Discourse," though used uncritically by Shragai, should be recognized as a brother to "narrative." Both are tools in the post-modernist

---

2 *The 'Al-Aksa is in Danger' Libel: The History of a Lie*, by Nadav Shragai, Jerusalem
Center for Public Affairs, 2011.

rhetorical kit by which facts, debate and truth are first obscured, then denied and finally inverted to support otherwise dubious if not spurious ideological arguments. The "al-Aqsa is in danger!" rumor is not "discourse" but rather a representation of familiar fantasy: Like the original blood libel, like *The Protocols of Zion's* undying portrayal of a Jewish cabal—in the otherwise fabulist manner of a mad villain and his associates from a James Bond script, seeking world control through instruments as divergent as the Free Masons, the Rothschilds and the Bolsheviks—it features evil Jews furthering their apocalyptic aims by means both audacious and blasphemous. In this version the diabolical object is destruction of the Temple Mount mosque and its replacement by the biblically prophesized Third Temple. In some manifestations the al-Aqsa libel directly appropriates these antisemitic motifs.

Like the classical/medieval blood libel, the al-Aqsa charge is not only false but also completely inverted. As Jews are commanded never to use blood in food, ritual or otherwise, Temple Mount and Al-Aqsa mosque represent, as Shragai says, "the greatest concession ever made by one religion to another…." After Israel took east Jerusalem, including the Old City with its Temple Mount, from Jordan in the 1967 Six-Day War, it attempted to convince the predominantly Muslim Arab population in that part of the city of its good faith. It imagined it would thereby win goodwill throughout the Muslim world. Immediately after his troops raised their flag over the mount in 1967, Defense Minister Moshe Dayan ordered it removed.

"To our Arab neighbors we extend the hand of peace," Dayan said. "To members of the other religions, Christians and Muslims, I hereby promise faithfully that their full freedom and all their religious rights will be preserved. We did not come to Jerusalem to conquer the Holy Places of others."[3]

Israel established a self-denying "status quo." It would retain overall authority in Jerusalem but Dayan relinquished management of Temple Mount, with al-Aqsa and the Dome of the Rock shrines, to officials of Jerusalem's *wakf* (Muslim religious endowment), then still under Jordanian control. Muslims would be permitted to continue worshipping in al-Aqsa, but Jews were forbidden from praying on Temple Mount, their most sacred place. This remarkable gesture—in retrospect a national-religious abnegation by Dayan—nevertheless did nothing to severe the roots of the already 45-year-old al-Aqsa libel.

Historically, the libel made a certain sense. Conquering Romans,

---

3 Ibid.

Byzantine Christians and Muslims in turn had denied Jews access to Temple Mount. Making their belief in religious supersessionism physical, Christians had built churches over Jewish synagogues. Muslims conquerors likewise erected mosques over churches. Al-Aqsa became a mosque when, after the Muslim conquest of Jerusalem, the remains of the Byzantine church St. Mary's of Justinian were converted to Islamic worship in 711 C.E. So the possibility that conquering Jews might replace al-Aqsa with the Third Temple could seem logical to those themselves inclined to supersessionism. Never mind that Jewishly—despite the fantasies of marginal millenarians—the Third Temple is unlikely to be built by human beings. A strong, even predominant strain among observant and mystical Jews, who pray daily for the event, is that the Third Temple rather will descend intact from heaven after the days of the Messiah, no human assembly required.

Jerusalem and Temple Mount, neither mentioned in the Quran, did not always loom large among Islamic concerns. Caliph Abd al-Malik, seeking to consolidate his authority versus the rebel Ibn al-Zubayr in Mecca and provide an alternate and lucrative pilgrimage destination, built the Dome of the Rock (Shrine of Omar) in 688-691 C.E. on the site of the First and Second Temples. In 715 the Umayyad dynasty constructed a second mosque on Temple Mount and called it al-Aqsa ("the furthest mosque"). This was an allusion to what until than had been a figurative name, the otherwise unspecified place from which Mohammad was said to have ascended to heaven on his night journey.

Subsequently, several Quranic verses were construed to refer obliquely to Jerusalem rather than the furthest mosque in Mecca or Arabia. Temple Mount was renamed by Muslims as al-Haram al-Sharif, the Noble Sanctuary.[4] Early in this century, the PLO issued an "advisory" to journalists instructing them to replace "Temple Mount" with "al-Aqsa compound." From terrorist to militant, from Judea and Samaria to West Bank, similarly now from Temple Mount to "al-Aqsa compound." It was a revisionist practice many media, including *The Washington Post* and *New York Times*, often adopted.

From the end of Ummayyad rule in 750 to the Crusader conquest of Jerusalem in the 1100s, Muslim interest in Jerusalem, Temple Mount and the physical al-Aqsa faded. But when under Christian control, Jerusalem's status as Islam's third holiest city, after Mecca and Medina, took hold in Muslim minds. Depending on which Islamic dynasty ruled and

---

4 "The Battle Over Jerusalem and the Temple Mount," by Ricki Hollander, CAMERA, Nov. 6, 2014.

on outside intrusions such as the Crusader conquest, Muslim interest in Jerusalem would wax and wane. It intensified when its political significance grew but declined along with lessened non-Muslim associations.[5]

Haj Amin al-Husseini introduced the "al-Aqsa's in danger!" libel (sometimes more broadly "Defend Muslim Holy Sites!"). Shragai recounts that after World War I, al-Husseini was active in a pro-Syrian, Christian-Muslim organization fiercely opposed to Zionism and Jewish immigration to Palestine. In 1920, that seminal year for pan-Arab attention to Palestine, he incited a crowd of several thousand Muslims in a religious procession to Jerusalem. The procession turned violent and five Jews were murdered, more than 200 injured. British authorities sought to arrest al-Husseini, who fled to Jordan and then Syria. He was sentenced in absentia to 10 years in prison, but pardoned five months later by Sir Herbert Samuels. Samuels, a Jew determined to demonstrate his "even-handedness," was the new British governor-general of Mandatory Palestine.

Back in Jerusalem as an Arab hero who had rebelled against the British and fought the Jews, al-Husseini nevertheless won appointment by the British as mufti (religious judge) in 1922. In 1924 he was elected head of the new Supreme Muslim Council. Then just 28 years old, Al-Husseini would incite hatred of Jews and an Islamist supremacism in the Middle East and Europe for decades to come.

As mufti and council head he planned to renovate both the Dome of the Rock and al-Aqsa. They "had indeed fallen into neglect and disrepair" under the late Ottomans and British, Shragai notes. But al-Husseini made sure the needed improvements "would attract plenty of publicity," exalt his personal status in the Muslim world, harness Muslim countries "to the national struggle of the Palestinians" and focus attention of Muslims worldwide on the Islamic holy places in Jerusalem.[6]

To boost fund-raising for renovation, the mufti's emissaries began warning of a Jewish threat. Al-Husseini exploited the Jews' struggle to regain their right to pray at the Western Wall (part of the retaining wall of Temple Mount) endorsed centuries earlier as a privilege granted by an Ottoman sultan. The mufti did so "to whip up animosity against them and accuse them of much more ambitious aims: the destruction of the mosques" and building of the Third Temple in their place.

In 1928, the National Committee of the Jews of the Land of Israel

---

5 "The Muslim Claim to Jerusalem," by Daniel Pipes, *Middle East Quarterly*, September, 2000.

6 "Al-Aksa is in Danger!" Shragai, JCPA.

published an open letter contradicting the Supreme Muslim Council's charge that Jews aimed "to take over the holy places of Islam." In it the committee denied any desire on the part of Jews to infringe "the rights of Muslims to the places that are holy to them. However, our Arab brothers must also recognize the rights that Israel has in this land, to our own places," rights recognized implicitly four years earlier in the Supreme Muslim Council's "A Brief Guide to al-Haram al-Sharif." The attempt to describe efforts to pray at the Western Wall as the base "for an attack on the mosques [not to mention al-Husseini's new identification with the Wall as yet another Islamic shrine, the place at which Mohammed was said to have tethered his steed, al-Buraq, before the night journey to Heaven] ... is nothing but the fruit of a fevered imagination or malicious libel," stressed the Jewish committee's letter. Exactly; imagination and libel.

It would be quite a successful libel, in no small measure just because it was fevered and malicious. Muslims soon would begin to disrupt attempts by Jews to pray at the Western Wall and early in August, 1929 they attacked Jews who came to pray there.

In response, on August 15, tens of thousands of Jews marched to the wall on the holiday of Tisha B'av, which commemorates the destruction of the two biblical temples, the first in 586 B.C.E. by the Babylonians, the second by Romans under Titus in 70 C.E. Regarding Tisha B'av, still told in synagogues is the story of Napoleon Bonaparte, who, hearing Jews on that day lament the loss of their Temple and their land, asked how long they had been doing so. When told for millennia, the French emperor supposedly replied that a people who so remembered its homeland and temple one day would be rewarded with restoration.

Al-Husseini was obsessed with ensuring that restoration never occurred and, at first, that Jews be "ethnically cleansed" from the Middle East. Later, as a Berlin-based colleague of Adolf Hitler, he would plan the elimination of Jews everywhere. The Arabs' anti-Jewish campaign, including al-Husseini's incitement, intensified during the third week of August, 1929. Then "the signal came from al-Aqsa. Masses of *fellahin* [Arab peasants] from the surrounding villages assembled, bearing clubs and knives." They attacked Jewish neighborhoods in Jerusalem "and from there the pogroms spread. ..." British police—often Arabs themselves—not being inclined to intervene, "the mayhem went on for a week. One hundred and thirty-three Jews, mostly in Safed and Hebron, were butchered. Three hundred and thirty-nine Jews were injured. Eight Jewish settlements had to be abandoned, and the events came to be etched as a terrible calamity in the collective memory of the Jews of Israel."[7]

Al-Husseini's al-Aqsa libel concoction was now established. It would grow from falsely alleging a Jewish threat to the mosque to the breath-taking revisionism of Yasser Arafat and the Palestinian side during the Camp David negotiations in 2000 and Taba talks in 2001, at both of which the United States and Israel offered a West Bank and Gaza Strip Palestinian country, with eastern Jerusalem as its capital, in exchange for the Arabs agreeing to an end to the conflict and to coexisting with the Jewish state. Instead, Arafat denied Jewish temples ever stood on Temple Mount. He rejected the two-state proposal if it meant Palestinian Arab refugees and their much-multiplied descendants had to "return" to West Bank and Gaza "Palestine" instead of to Israel. And— to change the subject from Western and Arab criticism he received for spurning the two-state deal—he soon launched the second intifada (2000 - 2005) in which more than 1,100 Israelis and visitors and more than 3,000 Palestinians would perish.

Incredibly, at Taba, Israeli negotiators agreed to full Palestinian sovereignty over east Jerusalem, including Temple Mount—provided the Palestinian side acknowledge the site's sacred status in Judaism. The Palestinian representatives refused. Israel's dovish foreign minister, Prof. Shlomo Ben-Ami, a Labor Party member, said, "What particularly outraged me on that occasion wasn't only the fact that they refused, but the way in which they refused: Out of a kind of total contempt, an attitude of dismissiveness and arrogance. At that moment I grasped they are really not [Egyptian President Anwar] Sadat [who made peace with Israel in 1979]. That they were not willing to move toward our position even at the emotional and symbolic level. At the deepest level, they are not ready to recognize that we have any kind of title here," let alone overriding title.[8]

In other words, from the 1920s into the 21st century, from fabricating an incendiary charge that the Jews threatened al-Aqsa mosque to falsely denying the reality and location of the First and Second Temples on the same platform later partially occupied by the mosque, a location central to Jewish religion and history, the lies of Palestine congealed. They combined, strengthening each other as twisted strands make a rope, so a blasphemous peace with Jews as equals could be avoided.

Al-Husseini's restoration of the two mosques on Temple Mount

7 Ibid.
8 Interview with Shlomo Ben-Ami, *Ha'aretz*, Nov. 25, 2001.

had provided stirring symbols of early Palestinian Arab nationalism. His dire warning of a Zionist-Jewish threat to these renewed pan-Arab, pan-Islamic sanctities would help propel "the Great Arab Revolt" of 1936 – 1939. This anti-Jewish, anti-British uprising, supported by Italy and Germany, strongly induced London to virtually close mandatory Palestine to further Jewish immigration. To placate Arabs, Great Britain barred access by Jews to their national home the British had been charged with helping reestablish. The British acted just as Nazism in Germany and the associated rise of similar antisemitic, fascist movements elsewhere in Europe heightened the necessity of mandatory Palestine as the Jewish refuge.

The denial by Western countries of asylum for any significant number of Jewish refugees increased the urgency of Palestine as Jewish sanctuary. The refusal of Cuba, Canada and the United States to accept 908 Jews crowding the *S. S. St. Louis* on their "voyage of the damned" in 1939 provided a well-known example of the general trend. So one effect of this particular key element of the Palestine lie, the Jewish threat to al-Aqsa, would be solidifying the entrapment of European Jewry on the eve of Nazi conquest. So Arab, particularly Palestinian Arab, action and British reaction intensified and broadened the Holocaust.

In 1937, al-Husseini escaped Jerusalem and British authorities and continued directing the Palestinian Arab Revolt from French-controlled Lebanon. In 1939, he bribed his way out of Lebanon and landed in British-administered Iraq. There he labored mightily against Jews and Zionists in general and against that country's large and ancient Jewish minority in particular. His efforts, under the short-lived pro-Nazi government of Rachid Ali al-Gaylani—who like al-Husseini would spend World War II working for the Third Reich in Berlin—culminated in the *Farhud* (Arabic for "violent dispossession"). This was the pogrom against Baghdad's Jewish community on June 1 – 2, 1941. During the Farhud, Arab rioters murdered more than 150 Jews, wounded 600 and looted 1,500 houses and stores. "The Farhud marked the beginning of the end for Iraq's 2,500-year-old Jewish community of 125,000 that began with the Babylonian Captivity under Nebuchadnezzar in 586 B.C.E. and culminated in total expulsion in 1951. By the mid-1950s the fate of Iraq's ancient Jewish community was replicated in every Arab country."[9] In this *nakba*, this real "ethnic cleansing," the total Jewish population in Arab lands plummeted from approximately 856,000 to 7,600.

9 *Jihad and Genocide*, by Richard L. Rubenstein, Rowman and Littlefield, 2010, page 77.

While in Baghdad, al-Husseini tirelessly propagandized for anti-Allied, pro-Nazi Arab factions like Rachid Ali's. He wrote to Hitler from Iraq several times in the first half of the year, declaring "that the 'Palestine problem united all of the Arab states in a mutual hatred of England and the Jews'" and "the warm sympathy felt by the Arab peoples toward Germany and the Axis is an established fact."[10] After the British restored a pro-Allied Iraqi government, al-Husseini fled, first to Mussolini's Italy, then to Germany.

When Israel Prime Minister Benjamin Netanyahu erroneously asserted in 2015 that al-Husseini gave Hitler the idea for the Holocaust, his critics—political and journalistic, Israeli and American—pounced. But going after Netanyahu for allegedly smearing the Palestinian cause through guilt by association, they obscured the historical record, whether unintentionally or not. The Palestinian Arab "George Washington," still revered today, was an enthusiastic collaborator with fascist Italy and especially Nazi leaders in Berlin in the Final Solution and planned to expand it to the Middle East.

Late in 1941, "Hitler made known his binding decision to exterminate all of Europe's Jews," Rubenstein writes, citing historians Christopher Browning and Christian Gerlach. Hermann Goering, Hitler's number two, "instructed *SS Gruppenfuhrer* Reinhard Heydrich …. To draw up 'an overall plan covering the organizational, technical and material measures necessary for the accomplishment of *the total solution of the Jewish problem* [emphasis added] of which we desire." During this period al-Husseini met with Hitler. "Hitler told the Mufti that he would 'carry on the battle to the total destruction of the Judeo-Communist empire in Europe," would invade the southern Caucasus and "give the Arab world 'the assurance that its hour of liberation had arrived." After that, he would then treat the mufti as the Arab world's "most authoritative spokesman."[11]

During World War II, al-Husseini planned the destruction of North African and Palestinian Jewry—his intentions thwarted by the Allied defeat of German occupation forces in Tunisia and of Gen. Erwin Rommel's *Afrika Korps* at the Second Battle of El Alamein, both late in 1942. During the war the mufti collaborated with important Nazi officials including Heinrich Himmler and Adolf Eichmann. The mufti, in Eichmann's words, "made a powerful impression" on both men and "had an acknowledged influence in Arab-Jewish affairs," according to

---

10 Ibid., page 75.
11 Ibid., page 79.

a deposition to the 1946 Nuremberg war crimes tribunal by Eichmann aide Dieter Wisliceny. With Hitler's approval, al-Husseini helped recruit for the *Waffen SS* a division of Bosnian Muslims who fought for the Axis in the Balkans. He also disseminated propaganda in support of the Nazi cause. Even before finding refuge in wartime Berlin, al-Husseini had issued a *fatwa* (Islamic religious ruling) proclaiming *jihad* (holy war) against Great Britain. One item in his bill of indictment, according to Rubinstein: "unheard of barbarisms" including profanation of al-Aqsa mosque.

Al-Husseini was principal speaker at a protest rally in Luftwaffe Hall in the German capital on Nov. 2, 1943, anniversary of the 1917 Balfour Declaration that had affirmed British support for restoration of the Jewish national home in Palestine. Senior Nazi officials and pro-Nazi Muslims from the Arab Middle East, Iran and other parts of Asia attended. Himmler and Nazi Foreign Minister Joachim von Ribbentrop sent messages of support, affirming "their commitment to 'the obliteration of the Jewish National Home' [in Palestine]" and "the fight against world Jewry."[12]

In this address Al-Husseini claimed Jews inflicted a great calamity on the Arabs, referred to their "depraved belief" they are the Chosen People of God and accused Jews of being the most important force behind destruction the Ottoman "Empire of the Islamic Caliphate." Rubinstein notes that today's Islamists make a similar charge, accusing the founder of secular 20th century Turkey, Kemal Mustafa Ataturk, of being "a false Muslim and a real crypto-Jew who aimed at the destruction of Islam. The Mufti's accusation was similar to the Nazi charge that the Jews conspired to bring about Germany's defeat in World War I and in its own way was equally poisonous." Al-Husseini "also included ... the accusation, long a staple of Islamist anti-Jewish propaganda, that the Jews wanted to destroy the al-Aqsa mosque and restore the ancient Jerusalem sanctuary."

Not finished, the Mufti asserted that Jews wanted to erect their kingdom in Palestine, endangering all humanity but especially the Arab and Muslim world, for it would be a "partition wall" separating Asian and African Muslims. "It is a bloody dagger in the heart of the Arab fatherlands," he declared. In their lust for power, al-Husseini's demonic Jews would continue until they controlled "Syria, Transjordan, Iraq, a part of Saudi Arabia and a part of Egypt." And, according to biographer Moshe Perlman, the Mufti also stated in his Luftwaffe Hall address that

---

12 Ibid., 83.

"the Treaty of Versailles was a disaster for the Germans as well as for the Arabs. But the Germans know how to get rid of the Jews. That which bring us close to the Germans and sets us in their camp is that up to today the Germans have never harmed any Muslim, and they are again fighting our common enemy who persecuted Arabs and Muslims. But most of all they have definitely solved the Jewish problem."[13]

Al-Husseini "employed the same kind of inflammatory rhetoric in dozens of other speeches and writings … in the service of Nazi Germany," Rubinstein notes. Close to Eichmann, one of the key officials in wartime deportation of European Jews to the death camps, the Mufti reportedly visited Auschwitz incognito and was on good terms with the commandant there, Rudolf Hoess, and the commandants of Mauthausen, Bergen-Belsen and Theresienstadt. He intervened repeatedly to prevent Jews, including groups of children, from being transferred to British Palestine.

For example, in 1943 when London was negotiating with Bucharest on the possibility of admitting to the Mandate 4,000 Bulgarian Jewish children and 500 adult chaperones, "he sent the foreign minister of Bulgaria a strongly worded letter that began with a comment: 'The Jewish danger for the entire world, and particularly for those lands that Jews inhabit, has for most nations become an objective fact and causes them to take measures of self-defense. The Axis powers and their allies [including Bulgaria at the time] count among the first to have recognized that one must as a vital national necessity take active measures so that this hostile element and her ideas and paralysis of economic life be brought to a halt." Instead of Palestine, the Mufti suggested that the Jews be sent to Nazi-occupied Poland "where they can be placed under stronger control."[14] He made similar interventions regarding Romanian and Hungarian Jews, accusing the Jews "of promoting emigration from Europe and the Near East in order to set up a 'strategic center' in Palestine for 'the domination of the world.'"

Harvard University Prof. Emeritus Alan Dershowitz also helped illuminate the mufti's portrait. Dershowitz wrote that "the official leader of the Palestinian Muslims, Haj Amin al-Husseini, the grand mufti of Jerusalem, collaborated in the Nazi genocide, declaring that he sought to 'solve the problems of the Jewish element in Palestine and other Arab countries' by employing 'the same method' being used 'in the Axis coun-

13 Ibid, page 87.
14 Ibid., page 91.

tries."'[15] Husseini, who was declared a Nazi war criminal at Nuremberg, wrote the following in his memoirs:

"'Our fundamental condition for cooperating with Germany was a free hand to eradicate every last Jew from Palestine and the Arab world. I asked Hitler for an explicit undertaking to allow us to solve the Jewish problem in a manner befitting our national and racial aspirations and according to the scientific methods innovated by Germany in the handling of its Jews. The answer I got was: 'The Jews are yours.'

"Husseini planned a death camp for [Palestinian] Jews modeled on Auschwitz, to be located in Nablus. He broadcast on Nazi Radio, calling for genocide against all the world's Jews: 'Kill the Jews wherever you find them—this pleases God, history and religion.'"[16] Professor Edward Said, Dershowitz continues, citing the author of *Orientalism* and a founding proponent of the Palestinian narrative, "has acknowledged that this Nazi collaborator and genocidal anti-Semite 'represented the Palestinian Arab consensus' and was 'the voice of the Palestinian people.' Yasser Arafat referred to Husseini as 'our hero.'" In fact, while virtually all surviving Nazi officials and collaborators after World War II either denied or tried to hide their support of and work with the Third Reich, al-Husseini, safely back in Cairo thanks to connivance of the French and others, was widely celebrated as a hero. Hassan al-Banna, founder of Egypt's Muslim Brotherhood, mothership of late 20th century Sunni Islamic terrorist groups including al-Qaeda and Hamas, publicly proclaimed al-Husseini to be a man above men, a virtual demi-god.

Two of the Palestinian Arabs' top commanders in the 1948 war against the new state of Israel were Abdul Qhader al-Husseini, a nephew of the mufti, and Hasan Salameh, one of Haj Amin al-Husseini's key aides. As early as 1933 Abdul Qhader al-Husseini had founded a group of Palestinian Arab "irregulars" called the Organization for Holy Struggle. Salameh headed "The Mediterranean Irregulars" and joined with al-Husseini in the 1936-1939 Arab Revolt as co-leaders of the Army of Holy War against British authorities and Palestinian Jews. They also led their terrorist militia in the struggle against Israeli independence. Revered by Palestinian Arabs as nationalist fighters, both repeatedly planned and led terrorist attacks against Jewish noncombatants as well as against British forces and armed Jewish groups.

In November, 1947 Arab assaults and Jewish retaliation intensified.

15 "Hezbollah's Goal: 'Going After [the Jews] Worldwide," by Alan Dershowitz, *The Huffington Post*, Aug. 10, 2006.

16 Ibid.

This followed the U.N. General Assembly vote that month to partition the remainder of the Palestine Mandate between tiny Jewish and Arab states when Great Britain withdrew in May, 1948. The Jewish Agency under David Ben-Gurion (who would become Israel's first prime minister) accepted—by necessity—this second partition (after creation of Transjordan) of Mandatory lands. The Arab states and Palestinian Arab leadership rejected it. They pledged to go to war to prevent Jewish independence in any boundaries whatsoever.

In February, 1948 three British truck bombs, driven by Arab irregulars and British deserters, exploded on Ben Yehuda Street in Jerusalem, killing approximately 50 civilians and injuring roughly three times that many. In Cairo, Abdul Qhader al-Husseini claimed credit for the blasts. In Palestine, the Army of the Holy War did the same, even though Hussein al-Khalidi, secretary of the Arab Higher Committee, denounced the attack as "depravity unfit for the Arab spirit."

Two months later, Salameh parachuted into Palestine as part of a five-man team led by a German Nazi native to the Mandate. Salameh had been among a group of Arabs the Mufti arranged to be trained in Germany as fighters, in Salameh's case as a paratrooper. The team's objective was mass murder of Jews. However, the operation began unraveling as soon as the men jumped. British forces captured the German leader; Salameh escaped.

Both Abdul Qhader al-Husseini and Hasan Salameh died in the 1948 war. But Salameh had a son who would carry on his father's mission of killing Jews to destroy Israel. Ali Hasan Salameh was the "Red Prince" of Fatah and a key aide to Fatah and Palestine Liberation Organization leader Yasser Arafat. Arafat's bid to overthrow Jordan's King Hussein failed in "Black September," 1970-1971. After days of PLO insurrection in the Palestinian-majority kingdom, the monarch's Bedouin-led army responded, killing between 2,000 and 4,000 Palestinian Arabs, combatants and non-combatants alike. Thousands of PLO members were arrested, and even more Palestinian Arabs were exiled. Salameh was at Arafat's side when the pair, disguised as members of an inter-Arab team sent to mediate the conflict, flew out of Jordan.

Salameh became a key source—though apparently not a paid agent—and personal friend of Robert Ames, the CIA's Beirut station chief.[17] As operations chief for the PLO's "Black September" unit, he planned numerous anti-Israeli attacks, though apparently not the mas-

---

17 *The Good Spy; The Life and Death of Robert Ames*, by Kai Bird, 2014, Crown/Random House.

sacre of 11 Israeli athletes at the 1972 Munich Olympics, for which the Israelis held him responsible. This terrorist kidnapping, the stand-off with German police televised worldwide, and murder of the Israelis, is still a source of Palestinian pride. It's considered perhaps the principle event that forced their cause into the international spotlight.

For Jews it is a reminder: the Olympics continued as if nothing important, nothing contradictory to "the Olympic spirit" of international harmony through sport, was taking place. International Olympics Committee Chairman Avery Brundage and officials from the other participating countries thereby conveyed a message to Israelis, to Jews: You don't count, again, at least not enough for us to actually inconvenience ourselves on your behalf. As U.S. Olympic Committee chairman in 1936, Brundage successfully had fought efforts to boycott the games in response to Germany's antisemitic, racist exclusionary policies. In 1972, as IOC head, he had unsuccessfully striven for inclusion of a team from white minority-ruled Rhodesia (today Zimbabwe). Until the 2016 Games, officials resisted Israeli and Jewish demands for a formal memorial to the Israeli Olympians slain by the PLO in 1972. Perhaps the participation by a team from "Palestine" in the opening parade of the 2016 games, some members with *kefiyeh*s draped about their shoulders, others waving the flag of "Palestine," amounted to a perverse Olympian offset.

In any case, Salameh also founded the PLO's Force 17, which functioned both as the PLO/Palestinian Authority's presidential security force and another of the movement's terrorist arms. He was killed in Beirut in 1979 by the Mossad, Israel's external intelligence-security service, when a parked Volkswagen exploded as Salameh drove past.[18] Ames, his CIA contact and friend, also would die in Beirut, one of 63 people—including 17 Americans—killed in the 1983 truck bombing of the U.S. embassy by the Islamic Jihad Organization. By then Ames was the agency's top Middle East analyst and Near East director. And Lebanon's Islamic Jihad Organization morphed into Hezbollah, the Iranian-founded, funded and trained Shi'ite "Party of God."

From the Kaiser's "Max of Arabia"—Max von Oppenheim—to Hitler's Haj Amin al-Husseini and on through Abdul Qhader al-Husseini and Hasan Salameh to Yasser Arafat and Ali Hassan Salameh, there is a thread that runs so true. Churchill recognized it as "fanaticism and a

---

18 *The Quest for the Red Prince*, by Michael Bar-Zohar and Eitan Haber, William Morrow & Co., 1983; *The Hit Team*, by David B. Tinnin and Dag Christensen, Little Brown Co., 1976.

sort of envy." This anti-Zionist antisemitism is multi-faceted. It is rooted in religious and ethnic-national denial of Jewish rights, Jewish history and equality. It leads—in a patriarchal shame-and-honor culture faced with and implicitly rebuked by an Israel that succeeded in many fields and against all odds—to thwarted supremacism, hatred and rage.

'Al-Aqsa is Still in Danger!'

The mufti's al-Aqsa libel would endure, periodically revived after 1967 to great effect. In August, 2015 Palestinian Authority President Mahmoud Abbas renewed the charge and called on his people to defend the shrine against Jewish plots. Less than two months later the "stabbing intifada" (sometimes referred to as the "al-Aqsa intifada") broke out. More than 30 Israelis and foreign visitors would be murdered, more than 300 wounded, in knife, gun, vehicular and other attacks. And more than 200 Arabs would be killed, most attempting or committing assaults, during the next year.

Abbas exhorted Palestinian Arabs to "martyrdom" in defense of al-Aqsa in a televised speech that was posted on his Web site. The Palestinian president—then illegitimately in the 11th year of a four-year term—declared "the al-Aqsa [mosque] is ours ... and they [Jews] have no right to defile it with their filthy feet. We will not allow them to, and [including the Old City's Church of the Holy Sepulcher] we will do everything in our power to protect Jerusalem." Abbas asserted that "we bless every drop of blood that has been spilled for Jerusalem, which is clean and pure blood, blood spilled for Allah, Allah willing. Every Martyr (*Shahid*) will reach Paradise, and everyone wounded will be rewarded by Allah."[19]

Palestinian Media Watch noted that this speech echoed another by Abbas from the preceding October, "when he said that Palestinians have to 'prevent' Jews from entering the Temple Mount." That address "PA TV chose to broadcast 19 times in three days," sparking anti-Jewish violence. In the official Palestinian view, the Jews still, allegedly, endangered al-Aqsa. Via official Palestinian media, the always potent charge was amplified enough to cause bloodshed.

However, sometimes alleging the imminent destruction of al-Aqsa by Jews would not be necessary. An Israeli/Jewish presence on Temple Mount would be sufficient. During widespread brush fires in late

19 Palestinian Media Watch, "Abbas: We won't allow Jews' 'filthy feet," Sept. 17, 2015, Palestinian Authority Television, Sept. 16, 2015.

2016—some set by Arab arsonists—that destroyed hundreds of homes and forced tens of thousands of Israelis to evacuate, Saudi Imam Mohamad al-Arefe, tweeted the popular hashtag "Israel is burning" to his 1.6 million social media followers. He said, "The fire is still burning in the Zionist entity!" adding he hoped Allah would "liberate the al Aqsa [mosque] from [Israel's] filth." Echoing Churchill's observation about causes of Arab hostility, Israeli Prime Minister Benjamin Netanyahu's Arabic-language spokesman, Ofir Gendelman, "slammed the celebrations on Arabic social media as 'despicable fanatic hatred.'"[20]

In July, 2016 Omar al-Abed entered the home of the Salomon family in the Jewish community of Neve Tzuf-Halamish in Samaria as they celebrated Shabbat, and the birth of a baby boy. Al-Abed, 19, carrying a Quran and armed with a butcher knife, stabbed to death Yosef Salomon, 70, and his children Chaya, 46 and Elad, 36. Tovah Salomon, 68, Yosef's wife and mother of the two other victims, also was stabbed and seriously wounded. Elad's wife, Michal, ran upstairs with the couple's five children, locked them in a bedroom and called security. A soldier on leave shot al-Abed through a window and wounded him.[21] Prior to the attack, al-Abed posted his "last testament" on Facebook, reportedly saying life was not worth living without al-Aqsa. "Without" apparently referred to the fact that after three Israeli Arabs killed two police at the holy site, Israel briefly installed metal detectors at entrances to the shrine.

People and nations may not always get the leaders they deserve, but they can be judged by the leadership they celebrate. Haj Amin al-Husseini is still praised by Palestinian Arabs. He was by Arafat, who claimed to be his nephew; by Arafat's successor, Mahmoud Abbas; by the PLO and its Fatah faction, both of which Abbas headed; and by Arabs and Muslims further afield. When President George W. Bush in 2003 first publicly pledged U.S. support for a West Bank and Gaza Strip Palestinian state, side-by-side and at peace with Israel, he laid down an essential condition: Its leaders would have to be free from the stain of terrorism.

This requirement, like the Palestinians' 1993 Oslo peace process pledge to end anti-Israel terror, remains unmet. To comply would mean treating Israelis, treating Jews, as sovereign equals, as human beings, brothers in Frankl's "decent race."

---

20 "As Israel burns, many on Arabic social media cheer; Hashtag 'Israel is burning'— used primarily to rejoice in the flames—soars to third most popular worldwide," *Times of Israel*, Nov. 24, 2016.

21 "Palestinian man found guilty of murdering three Israelis at their Shabbat table," JTA, Dec. 27, 2017.

Haj Amin al-Husseini's "al-Aqsa is in danger!" myth has, for nearly a century, incited anti-Jewish, anti-Israeli terrorism. Its recurrent invocation has proven irresistible and effective. A leading early 21st century Israeli Arab Islamist, Sheik Raed Salah, three time mayor of Umm al-Fahm and firebrand preacher, has managed to combine the al-Aqsa charge with its brother, the blood libel.

Umm al-Fahm would become a hotbed of anti-Israeli, anti-Jewish extremism. From it Salah led the Northern Branch of Israel's Islamic Movement. Jeremy Corbyn, then a parliamentary back-bencher, later head of the United Kingdom's Labor Party, invited Salah to tea at Parliament in 2012. According to Corbyn, Salah was a "a very honored citizen … who represents his people well." Salah had represented his people in part by reasserting the blood libel. In a 2007 speech during Friday prayer services near Temple Mount, Salah alleged the Israeli "conquest" caused disturbances and obstruction. He prayed this "conquest" would be temporary like previous non-Muslim takeovers. He praised fallen terrorists as "martyrs."

Then, "Salah said that he and other Muslims never made their Ramadan bread with the blood of children, adding, 'Whoever wants a more comprehensive explanation, should ask what happened to some of the European children whose blood was mixed with flour for use in holy bread.'"[22] Properly inflamed, the crowd "erupted," attacking and injuring three police officers.

Israel banned the Islamic Movement's Northern Branch in 2015, charging it with aiding Hamas and the Muslim Brotherhood. On July 14, 2017 three Israeli Arabs from Umm al-Fahm, cousins all named Muhammad Jabarin, using two submachine guns, a pistol and a knife killed two Israeli Druze Border Police guarding Temple Mount before themselves being shot to death. Ideological offspring of al-Husseini, Salah and others of their ilk, the trio reportedly hoped to spark a Muslim-Jew religious conflagration.

If President George W. Bush's vision of Israel and Palestine, side-by-side, democratic and at peace, is to be realized, then a "denazification" of the Palestinian national movement and its narrative, of which the al-Aqsa libel is an always emotive component, remains to be accomplished. Instead of Nuremberg-style war crimes trials and executions of senior leaders, Israelis have released literally thousands of terrorists, including those who have committed murders, as "confidence-building

---

22 "Islamic Movement Leader Salah Convicted of Racist Incitement on Appeal," *The Jerusalem Post*, Nov. 10, 2014.

measures" to induce Palestinian leadership to resume what often have been called peace talks.

A "confidence-building measure" for Israelis would see the Palestinian public carry out the necessary purge of its own leadership, past and present. Past, by means of a historical "truth commission"; present, by electing leaders committed to democracy for their own people, as well as for Israeli Jews. Until then, the Palestinian public could begin simply by following the path to wisdom attributed to philosophers as varied as Confucius and Spinoza: Calling things by their proper names, starting with recognizing the libels of al-Aqsa and blood as lies central to anti-Jewish bigotry.

CHAPTER NINE

'Never Again!' Again

MEMBERS OF VIKTOR FRANKL's decent race are always present but often scarce. Perhaps epitomizing them were World War II Albanians. They were Muslims both secular and observant and Christians who, at the risk of their own lives, saved their Jewish neighbors and newly-arrived, desperate Jewish "guests." Their stories are less well known than that of Danes who ferried Denmark's Jewish community from Nazi occupation across the Baltic Sea to safety in Sweden. Try to imagine Denmark rescuing or Sweden welcoming endangered Jews today. But the examples of wartime Albanians, based on their unassuming physical and moral courage, were literally heart-warming in their person-to-person, family-to-family, friend-to-friend and even host-to-stranger humanity.

In acts of dangerous decency extending sometimes for months and even years, living a traditional Albanian moral code of *besa*—which connects personal honor to respect for others—Albanians protected all the country's 200 Jews plus several thousand more seeking refuge. Meanwhile, in purportedly cultured Germany and France, the Jews were rounded up. In the birthplace of modern democracy and in its greater extension, the United Kingdom and the United States, respectively, Jews seeking refuge were largely turned away. Civilizations speak for themselves. Decent is as decent does.

Among the characteristics of Frankl's "decent race"—those guided, even if unconsciously by John Adams and Winston Churchill's ethical Ur-text of Western civilization, the Hebrew Bible—is adherence to the Ninth of the Ten Commandments. Carried physically or metaphysically down Mt. Sinai from God by Moses, it orders: "You shall not bear false witness against your neighbor." But there appears to be an anti-empir-ical exemption: Bearing false witness against the Jews and their state.

"In *Mein Kampf*, Adolf Hitler discussed the use of a lie so 'colossal' that no one would believe that someone 'could have the impudence to distort the truth so infamously.' He said such a 'Big Lie' was often more effective than a small one."[1]

The quote appeared two days after the death of U.S. Supreme Court Justice Antonin Scalia. Scalia, among many other things, had warned against the "smug certainties" of one age that are discarded by the next. The devoutly Catholic Scalia also had no tolerance for Jew-hatred. One of today's smug certainties is that useful variant of anti-Jewish big lies, the lie of Palestine. It bears false witness, asserting as noted above that the Jews committed "ethnic cleansing" and established an "apartheid" regime. With the frisson of enjoying a previously forbidden pleasure, it indicts Jews/Zionists as new Nazis to the Palestinian Arabs' new Jews. Hence the graffiti in Paris subways in the summer of 1982—the year of Israel's war against the Palestine Liberation Organization in Lebanon—featuring on opposite sides of an equal sign the Star of David and a swas-tika. Hence the mock Israeli flags after the start of the second intifada in 2000 as placards on American college campuses, in which the cen-tral blue Star of David is replaced by a swastika. Likewise the insistence in 2018 by Polish Prime Minister Mateusz Morawiecki that Jews were among the "perpetrators" of the Holocaust. Such intended transference is hardly original, but monotonously insistent.

Recep Tayyip Erdogan was a determined Islamist who on his elec-tion as Turkish prime minister in 2003 began disassembling the secu-lar, Western orientation imposed on his country by modern Turkey's founder, Kemal Mustafa Ataturk, in the 1920s and '30s. This resurrected a question that panics many Western political scientists: Are Islam, or better Muslim-majority polities—and democracy compatible? Turkey in the Ataturk mold was long held out as a positive, even definitive answer to that question. The query became impolitic to ask the more Islamists influenced countries like Pakistan and Indonesia, and growing Muslim minorities in Europe proved difficult to assimilate. As part of his reori-entation, Erdogan as prime minister and later president undermined previously good Turkish-Israeli military and commercial relations and relentlessly demonized the Jewish state. Even though he accepted a par-tial restoration of bi-lateral security cooperation in 2016 to help offset

1 John Fund review of *Speer: Hitler's Architect*, by Martin Kitchen, *National Review*, Feb. 15, 2016.

threats from the Islamic State and Syrian, Kurdish and Iranian challenges, Erdogan's anti-Zionism and antisemitism complemented his Islamist politics.

An opposition member of parliament, Aykan Erdemir, acknowledged in 2014 "that 12 years of Erdogan rule have significantly fostered antisemitism in Turkey."[2] The authors of the newspaper commentary quoting Erdemir, Gunther Jikeli and Kemal Silay, were, respectively, a fellow at the Moses Mendelssohn Center for European-Jewish Studies, Potsdam University, and professor of Turkish studies at Indiana University. They noted that after protesters had surrounded Erdogan at the site of the Soma coal mine disaster in which 300 died, he shouted at one, "Why are you running away, spawn of Israel?" an anti-Jewish slur.

"Openly antisemitic hate propaganda is frequently published in the Turkish media…. Instead of condemning their Holocaust denial and incitement to hatred of Jews, the Turkish PM [prime minister, later president] has become known for his own antisemitism," they wrote.[3] Among other things, Erdogan claimed Israel was behind the Egyptian military's ouster in 2012 of Muslim Brotherhood-affiliated President Mohammed Morsi. Erdogan also told a CNN interviewer in 2011 "we know that hundreds of thousands of Palestinians were killed" by Israel and accused "the Israeli people" of genocide.

In reality, as if reality mattered, not even close. In 2007, Gunnar Heinsohn and Daniel Pipes compiled statistics for all 67 conflicts since 1950 with more than 10,000 deaths. The Arab-Israeli struggle ranked 49th, with 51,000 killed, most of these being soldiers in national armies, not Palestinian Arabs.[4] Placing first were the upheavals of Communist China, 40 million dead; second, Soviet bloc repression, late Stalinist and post-Stalinist, 10 million; fifth, the Korean War, 1950 – 1953, 2.8 million; eighth, the Vietnam War, 1954 – 1975, 1.8 million. A 2013 update cited an analysis by Prof. Murtaza Haider of Toronto's Ryerson University, "Islam at War—With Itself." It said more than 90 percent of the 11 million Muslims who perished in conflicts between 1950 and 2007 "were killed by fellow Muslims." That, of course, excluded continuing slaughter in Afghanistan, Iraq and the Syrian civil wars. The latter killed

---

2 "'Spawn of Israel': Erdogan's Antisemitic Obsessions; The pro-Erdogan Islamist newspaper blaming the Jews for Turkey's mining disaster is just the tip of the iceberg: The Turkish PM's antisemitism is deeply rooted and is now spreading more widely in Turkey," by Gunther Jikeli and Kemal Silay, *Ha'aretz*, May 22, 2014.

3 Ibid.

4 "Arab-Israeli Fatalities Rank 49th," *FrontPageMagazine.com*, Oct. 8, 2007.

an estimated 500,000—mostly non-combatants, mostly Muslims—between 2011 and early 2018. It's not just that Islam has bloody borders with the non-Islamic world, as Samuel Huntington pointed out in *The Clash of Civilizations and the Remaking of World Order* (Simon & Schuster, 1996). So too with its internal divisions.

But when it comes to the Jews and their state, facts are not just fungible, they're fleeting. So *The Protocols of the Elders of Zion* and Adolf Hitler's *Mein Kampf* "are popular and easily available" in Turkey (the former published 114 times in Turkish between 1946 and 2012, the latter selling more than 100,000 copies in two months in 2005. Of course, Erdogan has labeled Israel a "terror state" and accused political rivals of working with the Mossad, Israel's external intelligence agency. His antipathy for Jews resonated widely in Turkey, Jikeli and Silay wrote.[5] They noted a 2014 ADL poll that indicated 69 percent of the Turkish public held a "very unfavorable opinion of Jews." The Anti-Defamation League questioned 53,000 adults in 102 countries attempting to establish, for the first time, a research survey baseline for the level of antisemitism worldwide. Among its findings, 26 percent of respondents were "deeply infected with antisemitic attitudes," and two-thirds either had never heard of the Holocaust or did not believe historical accounts of it to be accurate.[6]

"Erdogan's 'criticism' of Israel is, in fact, demonization," Jikeli and Silay asserted. "He accuses Israel of what British philosopher Bernard Harrison terms 'utterly exceptional crimes'—that is, hyperbolized criticism of Israel whose exaggerated content does not reflect reality and is fed by antisemitism." Here clearly are Sharansky's 3-Ds, the double standards, demonization and delegitimation by which hatred of Israel reveals itself as hatred of Jews.

How convenient for all those eager, even compelled, to reassert their hostility to Jews—especially to Jews as a people, a tiny tribal nation—without being required to acknowledge themselves as the Nazis' heirs. After all, the Jews are eternally annoying. They always have insisted on their universal prophetic message of one God, and not just any god but the One of ethical monotheism, the One who insists on individual responsibility to Him and to one's fellow humans. It's the Jews who drummed up all those damned "thou shall" and "thou shall nots" standing between man and the pleasure principle, including the pleasure of suppressing one's fellow man, of raping his women and ultimately of

5 "'Spawn of Israel,'" Jikeli and Silay, op. cit.
6 "The ADL Global 100: An Index of Antisemitism," Anti-Defamation League, 2014.

shedding his blood and thereby feeling the life-or-death power of a god or at least a demi-god. This is especially so when the victim, the sacrifice, belongs to a comparatively weak, socially certified unassimilable and safely tortured minority. Hence the still recurrent rape-and-murder policy of marauding gangs, militia and armies. To have insisted such behavior was not only wrong but also sinful, who the hell did those Jews think they were, anyway?

A Malaysian prime minister, Mahathir Mohamad, thought he knew. Opening a meeting of the 57-country Organization of the Islamic Conference in 2003, Mahathir explained, Protocols-like, that the Jews "invented socialism, communism, human rights and democracy, so that persecuting them would appear to be wrong, so that they can enjoy equal rights with others. With these, they have gained control of the most powerful countries and they, this tiny community, have become a world power."

Mahathir "highlighted the growing gap between the West and the Muslim world" and "called on Muslims to emulate the Jewish response to oppression, arguing the Jewish people had 'survived 2,000 years of pogroms not by hitting back, but by thinking.'" His back-handed compliment presaged a more direct version by famed American investor Warren Buffet. In 2016, Buffet, the "Oracle of Omaha"—whose first foreign acquisition for his Berkshire Hathaway firm was Israel's Iscar Ltd., a builder of robot-like machines that build other machines—told a group of visiting Israel Bonds investors that "the United States and Israel have a common destiny." He stressed that "if you are looking for brains, energy and dynamism in the Middle East, Israel is the only place you need to go."

As for the Malaysian leader, he charged that the devilishly clever Jews got "others to fight and die for them." But according to Mahathir, the Jews and Israel could not defeat the world's 1.3 billion Muslims once the latter reformed theological interpretations that shunned science and development but rather asked "our young people to blow themselves up and kill people and invite the massacre of more of our own people." He added that religious views that rejected technology and progress, along with accusations that Islam promoted terrorism "were the major reasons all Muslim people were suffering 'oppression and humiliation. … It cannot be that there is no other way. … We must not antagonize everyone. We must win their hearts and minds." Meanwhile, he said, highlighting science and technology would help Muslim countries to build their own advanced weapons.[7]

The United States, Australia and Israel criticized Mahathir's charges. U.N. Secretary-General Kofi Annan—after making the pro forma diplomatic critique of alleged "disproportionate Israeli force" and "illegal settlements"—"said he understood 'feelings of humiliation, anger and fear' among Muslims but condemned suicide bombings as detrimental to the Islamic cause." According to Annan, "'these acts of terrorism, abhorred and rejected by all of you, defile and damage even the most legitimate cause."[8] Annan was not a Muslim political leader, let alone religious spokesman, but rather a Protestant from Ghana who served as the U.N.'s top executive. He evaded the question of the cause and legitimacy of those feelings of "humiliation, fear and anger."

Jews invented human rights and democracy so persecuting them would appear to be wrong, so they can enjoy equal human rights with others. Makes one angry, doesn't it? *Israelis defend themselves against suicide bombings and other acts of terrorism. They establish communities on land where the League of Nations' and United Nations' Palestine Mandate encouraged Jewish settlement.* Humiliating. *They don't hit back, they think.* (Or at least think before hitting back.) How unfair.

In superficial Freudian terms, the Hebrew Bible's ethical monotheism, elaborated in the Talmud—the encyclopedic rabbinical commentaries on the Bible—promotes "unhealthy" repression of one's "genuine" emotions and desires. More positively, it calls on each human being to behave as Frankl's moral person, the race of the decent versus the race of the indecent. Exasperation at the Jews for their "legalism"—a derogatory code word, advanced by the early Church and sustained by some evangelical preachers to this day, for the Jewish framework of ethical monotheism—is at times relatively dormant, at others enraging. Today it particularly enrages fundamentalists, both secular and Islamic. The former's ideological religion makes an idol of man as the measure of all things, imagines radical personal autonomy can maintain societies both free and orderly and reopens the Jewish question, implicitly if not explicitly. That question is how can we tolerate such an imperious people claiming to bear an eternal message from a non-existent, judgmental God? And why should we, when they are so few?

Some have made a related argument: Antisemites hate Jews because the Hebrew Bible gives them the lead role in the human drama. The New Testament relates stories about the life of one man, Jesus Christ.

---

7 "Mahathir attack on Jews condemned," CNN, Oct. 16, 2003.
8 Ibid.

The Quran gives the biography of another individual, Mohammad. But the Hebrew Bible puts the spotlight on the Jews as a people for roughly 1500 years or 60 generations. And without that Bible and its people, Christianity and Islam lack their specific foundations, their adherents an undisputed claim to top billing in the drama of humanity's intimate relationship with its Creator.

Under cover of righteous indignation and moral superiority, both confiscated by proponents of the Palestine lie, Jews early in the 21st century have been attacked and sometimes murdered in Israel, Belgium, Bulgaria, Canada, France, India, Sweden, the United States and elsewhere. These assaults echo preliminary anti-Jewish crimes in the late 19th and early 20th centuries. Such a process culminated in the destruction of European Jewry, after which it was declared, following the defeat of Germany and its allies in World War II, "Never again!"

This assertion turned out to be premature. As noted, since "Never again!" there have been many other such crimes, many other "agains." And, little-acknowledged, the possibility of "Again!" hung over the largely abandoned Jews of Israel not only in 1948 but also in May of 1967 and early October, 1973. The quote from Primo Levi, author of *Survival in Auschwitz* among other related works, highlighted at the outset of this book—"It happened, and therefore it can happen again. This is the core of what we have to say"—is not only about Jews. It rarely is.

In the aftermath of the Nazis and the Holocaust, "Again!" had to be repackaged, for a generation or two. The swastika became a *kefiyeh*. Rebranding meant that Levi's insight simultaneously could be embraced operationally while denied rhetorically and psychologically by legions of supporters of the anti-Israel crusade. Rejection of "Again!" could be upheld ceremoniously while ignored in practice by right-thinking people from Kofi Annan and Bill Clinton when it came to Rwanda to Barack Obama and every other Western leader in response to the horrors of Syria's civil wars.

As for "Again!" regarding the Jews and Israel, spokesmen for the boycott, divestment and sanctions (BDS) movement periodically deny their campaign is antisemitic. Yet among the "Palestinian civil society" groups that gave birth to BDS were Hamas, the al-Aqsa Martyrs' Brigades of Fatah and stand-ins for the Popular Front for the Liberation of Palestine, all three designated as terrorist organizations by the U.S. government.[9] These BDS founders have incited, committed and celebrated

---

9 "Unmasking BDS: Radical Roots, Extremist Ends," by Dan Diker, Jerusalem Center for Public Affairs, 2014.

the murder of Israeli non-combatants—crimes under international law. Hamas, as noted, envisions the genocide of the Jewish people. Further, BDS says nothing against Palestinian violation of Palestinian human rights, does not insist on creation of a pluralistic Palestinian democracy or support a two-state solution and peace. Rather, with its public focus on "the occupation" merely a smokescreen disavowed at times even by BDS activists, it seeks the destruction of the world's one Jewish state— which happens to be democratic and pluralistic, in which Israeli Arabs enjoy equal rights.

Israeli Arabs, who comprise 20 percent of the population, face much higher unemployment rates and lower average pay than Israeli Jews. Yet in 2016, for example, 16 percent of all students in Israeli higher education were Arabs, 23 percent of all Israeli doctors were Arabs and 46 percent of pharmacists. Seventy-three percent of the Jewish state's Arab minority saw "Israeli" as part of their identity and 77 percent wanted their community fully integrated into Israeli society, according to figures from The Center for a Shared Society.[10] That is, life for Arabs—never mind for Jews—in the Israel the BDS movement seeks to destroy is better than that for other Arabs in most Arab countries. But destroying Israel is not about improving Arab life; it's about destroying the Jews' state, no matter what. And once their state is destroyed, then the further, interrupted destruction might resume.

Reghettoizing the Jews

The Palestine lie has reopened the Jewish question. The reghettoization of the Jews, in particular by Israeli Jews of themselves, indicates its effectiveness. As antisemitism drove Jews into ghettos, anti-Zionism drives Israel to wall itself in.

"Netanyahu unveils plan to 'surround entire state with a fence; Threat from 'carnivorous animals' in neighboring countries necessitates sophisticated barriers," an Israeli online newspaper headlined.[11] It's one thing for first world nations to fence in parts of their borders to stem waves of uncontrolled migration from failed states and third world countries; European nations were doing it while Israeli Prime Minister Benjamin Netanyahu spoke. Likewise, countries fortify portions of their

---

10 "The truth about Israeli Arabs; We cannot allow extremist leaders to dictate our future," Op-Ed by Dov Lipman, *The Jerusalem Post*, Jan. 15, 2016.

11 "Netanyahu unveils plan to 'surround entire state with a fence,'" *Times of Israel*, Feb. 9, 2016.

frontiers against conventional or unconventional military threats; Saudi Arabia did along part of its boundary with Yemen shortly before the Israeli leader announced his plan. But it's something else again to want or need to surround an entire nation-state with a physical barrier. For Jews to be contained inside one in some respects repeats something ominous, something old.

A vulnerable people can be forced into a ghetto, a gated quarter like that first decreed for the Jews of Venice in 1516 and those enforced in Lodz, Vilna (Vilnius), Warsaw and many other European cities by the Nazis in World War II. Or a threatened people can partially protect itself with a functional equivalent of ghetto walls when "the world community" ignores any responsibility for helping maintain its frontiers as open and peaceful. In 2015 and 2016, European countries tied themselves in knots simultaneously attempting to welcome and hinder masses of Syrian and other Middle Eastern refugees culturally and socially unassimilable, at least in such numbers in the short- to mid-term. The United States divided bitterly over how extensively to wall off its border with Mexico against millions of illegal Hispanic migrants. But no one and no chronic, widespread compulsion threatens all Libyans, all Mexicans or even all Syrians with genocide. That distinction is reserved for the Jews.

Israel delayed building a West Bank security barrier for nearly the first two years of the second intifada. Call it denial by a tiny, besieged Middle Eastern country whose citizens internally insist on feeling like borderless Western Europeans. Finally, with suicide bombers walking across the largely unmarked 1949 Israeli-Jordan armistice line to detonate themselves in malls, pizza parlors and Passover seders, the Jewish state began in 2002 construction on parts of a planned 400-mile line of fence, electronic monitors, ditches and, in some built-up areas, walls. After an appeal by West Bank Arabs—not by Israeli Arabs or Jews, not by citizens of the Jewish state—to the Israeli Supreme Court, Israel's military was ordered to reroute the fence so it encompassed not 12 to 14 percent of the West Bank but only seven to eight. Combined with Israel Defense Forces' reoccupation of Palestinian population centers on the West Bank and raids and arrests of terrorism suspects, the security barrier contributed to a dramatic drop in lethal terrorist attacks inside Israel.

Never mind. Western news media, including *The Washington Post* and *New York Times*, coyly echoing the "apartheid Israel" mantra, regularly referred to the barrier as a "separation" wall. Despite the fact it saved Jewish lives, or perhaps in part because it did, the International Court of Justice, an arm of the United Nations based in The Hague, opined in 2004 that the barrier was illegal. This was another example of international law as bubble gum when it came to Jewish and Israeli rights and claims. Denying the evidence of hundreds of terrorist attacks that had murdered nearly 1,000 Israelis—Jews and Arabs—and foreign visitors in the previous four years, and wounded, often grievously, even more, the court declared that military exigencies did not justify the security fence. Further, the judges ruled, Israel should have constructed it on its side of the green line, not in the West Bank.

In rebuttal, the United States, many European countries and Israel noted the ICJ lacked jurisdiction. The Palestinian complaint, a matter of negotiation under the 1993 Arafat-Rabin letter and resultant Oslo "peace process," was political, not legal. In any case, the court's opinion was advisory, without force of law. The barrier was intended to be a temporary counter-terrorism measure, not a final border, pending a negotiated Israeli-Palestinian settlement. Meanwhile, private Arab landowners separated from their property were offered both financial compensation and access through numerous gates.

Not that one would know this from much of the resultant news reporting and commentary. When it comes to Israel, what anti-Zionists and antisemites invoke as international law more often is "lawfare," a facsimile meant to supplant the real thing and always to Israel's disadvantage. If, as Clauswitz observed, war is the continuation of politics by other means, then lawfare is too, a perversion of international statutes by willful misinterpretation and unwarranted application. Like the U.N. General Assembly's 1975 "Zionism-is-racism" resolution itself, the ICJ's 2004 opinion against the security barrier came wrapped in the language of legalisms and moralizing but served as a psychological warfare cudgel against the Jewish state in the court of public opinion. Such measures, like countless other anti-Israel U.N. resolutions issued by the General Assembly or sub-agencies such as the U.N. Human Rights Council, lack a Security Council measure's force of law. So while not actually international law, by repetition they get treated as such and become "customary law," a category of imposed prejudice employed against sovereign democratic governments carrying out the will of their own voters. These measures prove enduringly useful in popular delegitimization of the Jewish state. They are—keeping in mind the "three 'D's" of contemporary Jew hatred—functionally antisemitic.

So 2016 found Netanyahu announcing "his intention to 'surround the entire State of Israel with a fence,' including sealing off [remaining] openings in the West Bank security barrier." The prime minister "said the extensive project would also address the potential threat of cross-border tunnels into Israeli territory. ... In its 2014 conflict with Israel, the Gaza-based terrorist group Hamas, as well as firing thousands of rockets and mortar shells into Israel, used a network of subterranean passages to infiltrate Israeli territory, launch attacks and in one case, during fighting inside Gaza, kidnap the body of an IDF soldier."[12] If history does repeat itself as Marx said, first as tragedy, then as farce, perhaps Act III is as obscenity: In 1943, desperate Jews sought to escape being murdered by Nazis in the Warsaw Ghetto by means of "tunnels," the city's sewers; in 2014, having blended Nazi ideology with Islamic extremism, fanatical Hamas members sought to murder Jews by tunneling into Israel and turning historical repetition from farce to gleeful homicide.

"'In our neighborhood, we need to protect ourselves from the carnivorous animals,' Netanyahu said in an apparent reference to extremist Islamist movements. ... 'At the end of the day, in the State of Israel as I see it, there will be a fence like this one [the border fence with Jordan then under construction] surrounding its entirety.' The multi-year project would cost "many billions," the prime minister said.[13]

A sophisticated fence-and-sensor system long has separated Israel from Lebanon and parts of Jordan. In 2013, Israel completed a roughly 18-feet high, 120-mile long barbed wire and sensor fence on its border with Egypt's Sinai Peninsula "to prevent terror groups, drug smugglers and African migrants from infiltrating," the *Times of Israel* added.

If and when all the work is completed, the Jewish state—established to "normalize" Jewish life at long last but responding to actual continuing dangers—will have ghettoized itself physically as its neighbors and many others have done to it psychologically.

Obsession with "the Israeli occupation" ill-becomes faculty and students squatting on occupied Native American lands in the United States and Canada or similarly inclined European clergy, union leaders and journalists living with untroubled consciences on the territories of earlier indigenous peoples. Many if not most current countries rest on lands that once belonged to others, others often conquered, submerged, driven out or slaughtered in wars of aggression. Their very names—Hungary, Romania, Argentina, England, Mexico among others—testify to the fact. When New Zealand's 21-year-old Lorde, an international singing phenomenon, crumbled before BDS demands and cancelled a

---

12 Op. Cit., "Netanyahu Unveils Plan," *Times of Israel*.
13 Ibid.

2017 performance in Tel Aviv, writers noted that if her anti-occupation principles were serious, she would immediately vacate her homeland, established as it was by English colonists extirpating the native Maoris. Only one contemporary country embodies a returned indigenous people that has held on through wars of defense. But that unsettling singularity too counts as an Israeli sin.

Even without "occupation" Israel's enemies would still play their most potent charge. That is the "racism" indictment. It is potent despite its transparent falseness. As Israel was rescuing Ethiopian Jews, long ostracized by their non-Jewish neighbors, columnist William Safire wrote that "for the first time in history, thousands of black people are being brought to a country not in chains but in dignity, not as slaves but as citizens.[14] Because it was apt, Safire's comment drew repeated criticism from Israel's enemies. They pointed to discrimination these black Israeli Jews faced from white ones, as if that invalidated the rescue of more than 60,000 people long considered inferior by other blacks in Ethiopia. A generation later, some discrimination persists, but success stories abound, especially among Ethiopian Jews who arrived in Israel as children.

Still, BDS spokesman Omar Barghouti decries Israel's "racism" against its Arab citizens. Barghouti received his master's degree from Tel Aviv University but dismisses this example of Israeli non-racism as "personal," not illustrative. He calls for, among other things, the non-existent (see above) Palestinian Arab "right of return" to what became Israel in 1948. He assumes this would end the country's existence as a Jewish state. Forecasting "the rapid demise of Zionism," Barghouti has declared, "I, for one, support euthanasia."[15] Rendering the Jews again a non-sovereign, easily oppressable minority is a goal of BDS, in common with anti-Zionist antisemitism generally. It is a goal that looks and smells close enough to the original to be recognized as racist.

Supporting BDS from its early days and preceding it in the same work has been the United Nations' Committee on the Inalienable Rights of the Palestinian People. According to Ambassador Schifter, the committee resulted from the joint effort by Libya's Qaddafi and Cuba's Castro noted above. Separately funded and with a staff insulated from direct oversight by the U.N. secretary-general's office, the Committee for

---

14 *New York Times*, Jan. 7, 1985.

15 "What is the Real BDS Endgame? The Elimination of Israel," by Ehud Rosen, Jerusalem Center for Public Affaris, Feb. 12, 2014.
http://jacp.org/article/what-is-the-real-bds-endgame/#sthash.SYmWP6U1.dpuf

the Protection of the Inalienable Rights of the Palestinian People has worked relentlessly for decades to reopen "the question of Palestine" and provide it with a final solution. That would be a reversal of the U.N.'s 1947-1948 role in supporting the founding of Israel in fulfillment of its responsibility, inherited intact from its predecessor, the League of Nations, to help reestablish the Jewish national home in Palestine. Hence the campaign the Palestinian Authority planned for 2017 to generate international rejection of the 1917 Balfour Declaration. The effort failed, in part due to Britain's Conservative Party and Prime Minister Theresa May, who issued a centennial endorsement of the declaration. The League of Nations enshrined Balfour's 1917 commitment five years later in its Palestine Mandate. BDS, a Western European and North American megaphone for Palestinian rejectionism, incontrovertibly meets the "3-D" test.

Twenty-first century anti-Zionist, antisemitic assaults, whether promoted on secular leftist, Islamic fundamentalist or old far-right grounds mirror religiously-based attacks against Jews by Christians centuries earlier. The all-purpose indictment of "racist" substitutes perfectly for the medieval condemnation of "heretic," as others have noted in different controversies. But the newer outrages have the advantages of being repackaged ideologically and culturally via post-modern relativism (which flows in only one direction, from traditional Western individual or "bourgeois" liberalism toward leftist totalitarianism). They are sanitized intellectually and morally via theories of De Man, Said, Frantz Fanon and other polemicists of liberation of the oppressed Other that somehow never results in their actual liberty. Academic indulgences such as critical theory and oxymoronic "Marxist humanism"—Marxist-Leninism in practice having resulted in the deaths of approximately 100 million human beings—ultimately help to annihilate morality.

When a Palestinian Arab drives an axe into the brain of a rabbi at prayer, as at Kehilat Yaakov synagogue in Jerusalem's Har Nof neighborhood on Nov. 18, 2014, in a two-man attack that literally butchered five worshippers and wounded six others, the deed is "authentic," self-actualized. When Israeli police kill such terrorists, they are committing "crimes." Self-defense is a universal human right, except for Jews (and other "enemies of the people," other contemporary kulaks useful to the ostentatiously anti-imperialist, anti-racist but in fact anti-democratic left). The post-democratic left's class enemies are the anti-democratic right's "bacilli," "aliens" and "traitors." Yet always first and foremost, the legitimate target, currently an "oppressor" of "people of color" is the Jew.

Obscenely ironic, since the Jew was the original and for anti-Zionist antisemites remains the perpetual Other.

The roots of such modern/old ideas began to reveal themselves in writings like as those of Friedrich Engels. Engels desired the annihilation of "reactionary" minority peoples. BDS' Barghouti desires the "euthanasia" of the Jewish state. No people but the Jews—the oldest, deadest white males of Western civilization, Abraham and Moses being their exemplars, their actual skin color utterly and properly irrelevant—could be caricatured as more reactionary. Damned by contemporary progressives are the original progressives, the radically civilizing Jews.

Annihilating Israeli Jews and their supporters elsewhere because they supposedly embody racist reaction concludes an ideological argument. Further, doing it to satisfy psychological urges is a bonus, providing an old entertainment, relished periodically for centuries. From the First Crusades' devastation of European Jewish communities as its 11th century participants moved toward the Holy Land; the mass murders of Jews in 1348-1349 for allegedly poisoning wells to spread the Black Death that killed at least a third of Europe's population; through the Chmielnicki massacres in 17th century Ukraine—three years of depraved torture-murders of tens of thousands of Jews; to pogroms like that in Kishinev, Russia in 1903; Mandatory Palestine in 1920, 1921, 1929, 1936-1939 and, perhaps epitomizing the Holocaust in micro, in the Polish town of Jedwabne in 1941 the entertainment has recurred. In Jedwabne, several dozen Poles, in cooperation with German paramilitary, rounded up 340 of their Jewish neighbors—men, women and children—locked them in a barn and set it ablaze. This, like the tortures and mutilations of numberless Jewish men and women lined up for the gas chambers, was serial brutality and mass murder as sport, with Jews in their proper and recurrent role as object.

After the U.S.-led coalition ousted its Taliban rulers in 2002, Afghanistan revived the national sport of *buzkashi*. An ancient Central Asian analogue of polo, *buzkashi* features not a ball but a goat carcass. Antisemitism substitutes Jews for goats and in many times and places has been more popular.

In 1995, Pope John Paul II observed that "terrorism attacks the very foundations of civilization and threatens to erase them altogether by killing man's sense of sin." His perspective evaporates in the stifling intellectual hothouse of post-traditional, secular fundamentalism and its strange, ultimately omnivorous bedfellow, Islamic triumphalism. Most, if not all, schools of Islamic thought still take the concept of sin

186 Є *Jews Make the Best Demons*

seriously. Secular fundamentalism exists in no small measure to shed internalized restraints of sin and guilt. But both dismiss Western, that is Judeo-Christian, civilization's insistence on the inherent, God-given dignity of the individual above his or her tribal, religious or racial membership. That dignity—which transcends group or "identitarian" politics, including politics based on victimhood whether actual or contrived—made murder, as Cain's of Abel, a sin before it was a crime.

Impatience with individual rights that require dealing with each person as a singular and equally human being carrying a spark of the divine, as Jewish mystics asserted early, characterized pre-World War II fascism. Today it still marks neo-Nazi movements and is a hallmark of the much larger wave of Islamic fundamentalism and of the "anti-fascist" fascism of the hard left exemplified in campus and street riots against conservative or traditionally-minded speakers. It characterized "liberation theology" of both the Christian secular far left, *pace* Fanon's scriptural *The Wretched of the Earth*, which decrees that "the last can be the first only after a murderous and decisive confrontation between the two protagonists. This determination to have the last move up to the front ... can only succeed by resorting to every means, including, of course, violence."[16] Of course, depending on who gets to define "the last" and "the first." Every means, we understand, moves through silencing and shunning to kidnaping, brain-washing, rape, torture, assassination, suicide bombings and concentration camps. Why not? There are no innocents when entire classes, defined by reactionaries or progressives, it never matters, are condemned as guilty. For anti-democrats, it's who's in charge of the Inquisition that counts, not whether or not there will be an Inquisition. And the Jew is always, to such temperaments, a proper subject of inquisitors.

Antipathy to individual rights, including to property and privacy, is intrinsic to fascism, Marxism, Islamo-fascism and the post-liberal, that is, illiberal left. Dismissive of, when not hostile to, Christianity and Judaism, adherents of anti-democratic illiberalism ultimately must reject the U.S. Declaration of Independence. In perhaps world politics' most revolutionary assertion, both quintessentially American and simultaneously universal, it proclaimed in 1776 that "we hold these Truths to be self-evident, that all Men are created equal and endowed by their Creator with certain unalienable Rights, that among these are Life, Liberty and the Pursuit of Happiness." (By happiness the Founders

---

16 *The Wretched of the Earth*, by Frantz Fanon, English translation, New York, Grove Press, 2004, pages 2-3.

meant the results of a life of virtue, which they identified with good character, not late 20th century assumptions about good times. Earlier state constitutions, following John Locke that an individual's right to property inhered in his right to life, sometimes included the substantive "property" for the generalized "happiness.")

Thomas Cahill spotlighted the connection between Judaism and the Declaration. In his best-seller, *The Gifts of the Jews; How a Tribe of Desert Nomads Changed the Way Everyone Thinks and Feels*, Cahill asserted that the wandering, rag-taggle tribe that become the Jews broke with the ancient world's vision of life as an endless cycle, time a spinning wheel. For the Jews, time was chronological—beginning, middle, and triumphant end. It was about something, and that meant that individuals possessed unique destinies.

Cahill himself concluded it would be impossible to "imagine the great liberation movements of modern history without reference to the Bible," from the abolitionist and prison-reform movements of the 19th century to the anti-communist and human rights campaigns of the 20th century. Such movements often were clergy-led and claimed religious authority. Democracy itself, Cahill claims, could not have arisen without the Hebrew Bible. It "grows directly out of the Israelite vision of individuals, subjects of value because they are images of God, each with a unique and personal destiny. There is no way that it could ever have been 'self-evident that all men are created equal' without the intervention of the Jews."[17]

But the radical or hard left, like the far right, prefers the old conception of men and women as undifferentiated masses—with the stark exception of members of ruling cliques, to which activists and apparatchiks assume they will belong. Call one's chosen humanity, one's idealized and idolized class the workers, the proletariat, the volk, the white race, black people, the women, the Palestinians, anything but individuals free to think and act on their own. These masses are to be mobilized by political party, secular elites or identity group grievance mongers. They are not to freely choose leaders who, an election or two down the road, will be replaced by others of differing opinions. Instead, they are to follow, to worship the Dear Leader, Brother Leader, Supreme Leader, Der Fuhrer. In parallel, Islamists prefer the *ummah*, the global community of believers, to individuals who concur or dissent as conscience moves them. Impatience with individualism and individual dignity underlies

---

17 *The Gifts of the Jews: How a Tribe of Desert Nomads Changed the Way Everyone Thinks and Feels*, Thomas Cahill, Random House, 1999, pages 248-249.

hostility in America to constitutional limitations on government. Internationally, it objects periodically and particularly to Jewish individuality and dignity.

On campus and in the street, hostility to individual liberty as opposed to group uniformity contributes to outright hatred not only toward Israel and its advocates but also toward politically conservative and culturally traditional speakers. It spreads malignantly to include whites as a race due to their "inherent" racism and "white privilege" and reduces blacks to cyphers in a tally of the inherently oppressed and therefore perpetually exonerated, undifferentiated Other. Such groupthink also fuels the disdain Islamic triumphalists—presuming themselves exemplars of the *ummah*—feel for Western ideas of free choice.

The 1648 Peace of Westphalia rejected the marauding depredations European armies committed during the devastating Thirty Years' War. Among other things, it drew a distinction between soldiers and civilians and established laws of armed conflicts. After millennia of human slaughter, it became, at least in the West, a crime for combatants to kill noncombatants. Individuals did have inherent rights, including to their own lives. At long last, soldiers slaying civilians no longer was just killing but rather murder. Even if subsequently violated, it grew to be more than an aspiration. A perverse achievement of fascism, communism and Islamism—of the romanticization of violence on behalf of the oppressed Other—has been to supersede and reverse Westphalia. When "one person's terrorist is another's freedom fighter," when "by any means necessary" is legitimate, the distinction between combatant and non-combatant is erased and civilization retreats, the decent race declines.

The Declaration of Independence's assertions of unalienable rights to life, liberty and the pursuit of happiness meant that unjust deprivation of these natural rights—not man-granted privileges—was therefore not only a crime against individuals but also a crime against humanity. Such deprivation sinned not only against individuals and mankind in general but also against the Creator of nature, against God. Absent such a foundation, institutions like the U.N.'s International Court Justice may still claim legality but—as in its 2004 advisory opinion against Israel's anti-terrorist security barrier—have abandoned the moral foundation from which law derives.

Laws of war, unalienable rights including life and liberty? Crimes, sins, morality? To post-structuralists, post-modern relativists and the like, and certainly to believers in the lie of Palestine, such sentiments—in defense of Zionists, to protect the Jewish state—are bourgeois nonsense when not tools of the oppressor. "Critical theorists" deny a Creator, seeing instead a man-made god whose ethical instructions white men of privilege tried to channel, to their advantage, into law. Such progressive self-justifications are as welcomed as old bigotries when one wishes to yield to primordial blood-lust; when one exalts the murder of children and torture of the elderly not of one's own identity group, one's own tribe; when aiming for totalitarian power rather than accepting democratic compromise.

Blood-lust is a human motive as deeply rooted as artistic creativity, if not more evident. Aimed at the few, the different or the weak it is as old as recorded history and, no doubt, older. Against the Jews it has been, like plagues and stock bubbles, one of Western civilization's recurrent, even base-line norms. Homicidal as directed against Jews, it becomes suicidal as it reveals civilizational self-loathing. Well-schooled (not to be confused with well-educated) non- or anti-religious Western Europeans or North Americans not infrequently accept and sometimes approve anti-Israeli terrorism. They imagine it illustrates the weak defending themselves against the strong. But such acceptance or endorsement echoes fascist celebration of violence by the strong against the weak.

No criticism of the romanticized Other, today's re-run of Rousseau's noble savage—will be tolerated. And in the first rank of such immaculately conceived, guilt-free groups, regardless of their failings and depredations, stand today's Palestinian Arabs. When the victims are Israelis, are Jews, justifications of power thirst and brutality are made to sound plausible by the lie of Palestine.

This leaves us with Frankl's race of the indecent calling the shots, and shoot they do in some places, and where they have not yet, soon might. George Orwell not only warned in *1984* that the anti-democratic future might be "a boot, smashing a human face, forever" but also that it would be justified as well as enforced. He foresaw as much in 1939 in *Coming Up for Air*, warning of "streamlined men who think in slogans and talk in bullets." Orwell had forecast—after Stalin's purges, show trials and man-made famines but before Hitler's genocide—that decent people sometimes would not be able to recognize, let alone resist such streamlined men and women. Today such types are seen not merely chanting but rather screaming in rage at protests in countless Western cities, on American university campuses where some students excuse antisemitism because Jewish classmates are "Zionist baby-killers."

Look at the face of the intruders pictured breaking up a pro-Israel talk at University College London in the fall of 2016, or any such mini-riot. Study the countenance of Rasmea Odeh—convicted in the murders of Israeli university students Edward Joffe and Leon Kanner in 1969—smiling at cheers from attendees at the Jewish Voice for Peace's convention in 2017. An organizer of an International Women's Strike in the latter year (which called for the "decolonization of Palestine," among other things), she had been invited to speak just before her deportation to Jordan after an immigration fraud plea deal. *The New York Times* would white-wash Odeh, describing her as "controversial" rather than accurately as a murderer. ABC-TV's Peter Jennings had excused the 1972 Olympics killers as "desperate." The *Times* likewise sanitized Odeh as simply someone about whom opinions differed. Understandable, since the dead were merely Jews and Israelis at that.

When not exhibiting the smug certainty of which Justice Scalia spoke, such faces are contorted in screams of hate. In neither condition are they rational, reasonable or humane. Their expressions recall those in newsreels of Gamal Abdel Nasser in May, 1967 declaring, "We intend to open a general assault against Israel. This will be total war. Our basic aim is the destruction of Israel," and the Egyptian masses enthusiastically screaming back to him. The latter were being rhetorically flagellated by the former into an anticipatory ecstasy of mass murder of the Jews. Centuries separated the emotion of Egyptian masses from those of medieval and Renaissance mobs instigated by Catholic clergy and chronic rumor to kill the Jews, but the feeling itself was nearly identical. Nasser had previewed this rhetoric 11 years earlier, in an Oct. 14, 1956 speech explaining his escalation before that year's Suez War, after illegally closing the Straits of Tiran to Israeli shipping, sponsoring terrorist attacks against Israel and shortly before taking military command of an Egyptian, Syrian, Jordanian alliance:

> I am not fighting solely against Israel itself. My task is to deliver the Arab world from destruction through Israel's intrigue, which has its roots abroad. Our hatred is very strong. There is no sense in talking about peace with Israel. There is not even the smallest place for negotiations.[18]

In medieval times, it was believed demonic Jews threatened Christendom. For Nasser and his hearers, intriguing Israel threatened the

---

18 *Middle Eastern Affairs*, December, 1956, page 461.

Arab world. It was the Jews, as always, pursuing their sinister compulsions.

In the 20th century haters of this sort were fascists, Nazis, Communists or pan-Arabists, variations on the totalitarian theme, lock-step in their march from and against individual freedom and democratic self-rule. In the 21st century their heirs also substitute ideology for religion, or, in the case of Islamists, base ideology in their religion. They likewise think in slogans and justify those who talk in bullets, especially those who aim at Jews.

When it comes to governments, their post-modernism is quite pre-modern: Functionally it's neo-royalist or absolutist authoritarian. Their new monarchs or dictators rule by a sort of divine—that is, unquestionable—right, one energized in no small measure by hatred of Jews and their state. That they justify intolerance of those they would oppress in the name of those they describe as oppressed amounts to a minor variation on Albert Camus' observation that "the welfare of humanity is always the alibi of tyrants."

But aren't these eruptions anti-Zionist, not antisemitic? Not in the sense one could, for example, oppose U.S. immigration policy without opposing the existence of the United States or decry American materialism without denying a genuine American identity, a legitimate American nation. Via the three "D's" of anti-Zionist antisemitism, ancient hatred merges with new, or more accurately renewed passions.

Double standards, demonization and delegitimization grease the Palestine lie's spread. Its diffusion in turn excuses, even sanctifies anti-Israeli, anti-Jewish crimes as justified acts of "resistance" born of "frustration," "humiliation" and "despair." Such pop psychology pervades Western news media coverage of Arab-Israeli affairs while missing or excusing Arab-Islamic culture's still powerful "shame-and-honor" motivations. By such superficial psychology and distortion of law Jewish protests and Israeli counter-attacks against lethal "resistance" automatically become hateful, even criminal. This anti-ethical loop increasingly resembles a noose. It is the final solution to the Jewish question.

"Violence against Jews surges; Antisemitic attacks increased 40 percent worldwide last year" announced a *USA Today* headline in 2015. A study by Tel Aviv University found 766 recorded violent acts against Jews in 2014, up from 554 the year before. Assaults in France rose from 141 in 2013 to 164 in 2014; in the United Kingdom from 41 to 95; Germany 36 to 76.

"The overall feeling among many Jewish people is one of living in an intensifying anti-Jewish environment that has become not only insulting and threatening, but outright dangerous, and that they are facing an explosion of hatred toward them as individuals, their communities and Israel, as a Jewish state," the study reported. "If you are a father or mother and you bring your children to school that is like a fortress protected by police and the army with machine guns, you may have doubts about whether you want these kids to remain in such an environment," *USA Today* quoted Roger Cukierman, president of CRIF, a Jewish-French umbrella organization, as saying.[19]

Such social-cultural environmental degradation has been spreading since well before Sept. 11, 2001. Subsequent anti-Zionist, antisemitic fabrication boosted intimidation of the sort that drove Jews from Malmo, Sweden, the country's third-largest city. "I never thought I would see this hatred again in my lifetime, not in Sweden anyway," said Judith Popinski, a Holocaust survivor quoted by a British daily nine years after al-Qaeda's strikes in the United States. The 86-year-old widow added that "Muslim schoolchildren often ignore me now when I talk about my experiences in the camps. It is because of what their parents tell them about Jews. The hatreds of the Middle East have come to Malmo. Schools in Muslim areas of the city simply won't invite Holocaust survivors to speak anymore."[20]

The newspaper reported that Malmo's Jews, however, did not just point the finger at bigoted Muslims and their fellow racists in the country's neo-Nazi fringe. They also accused Ilmar Reepalu, the left-wing mayor, of failing to protect them. Reepalu said, as paraphrased by the report, that "what Jews perceive as naked antisemitism is in fact just a sad, but understandable consequence of Israeli policy in the Middle East."[21] Certainly, to protest against Israel in Scandinavia, burn a synagogue, desecrate a cemetery and let masked men in the streets chant "Hitler!" at passing Jews.

Such anti-Zionist antisemitism has fueled verbal and physical assaults against Jews on U.S. campuses from Brooklyn College and Columbia University in New York to the University of California at Berkeley and Irvine. The toxic spill of antisemitic anti-Zionism goes back to 1975 and the U.N. General Assembly's "Zionism-is-racism" resolution, as highlighted by historian Robert Wistrich's observation with which

---

19 "Violence against Jews surges," *USA Today*, April 16, 2015.

20 "Jews leave Swedish city after sharp rise in antisemitic hate crime," *The Telegraph* (U.K.), Feb. 21, 2010.

21 Ibid.

this work opens. But even that was not its taproot.

CHAPTER TEN

The Less Things Change, the More They Look New

Think of the Palestine lie—especially in its essential parts, including the al-Dura and al-Aqsa libels, the "right of return" claim and "the occupation" indictment—in celebrity terms. In his 1961 best-seller *The Image; A Guide to Pseudo-Events in America* (1992 edition) historian Daniel Boorstein famously observed that among many distortions in 20th century American culture, one featured the celebrity increasingly displacing the hero. A hero's fame rested on his or her deeds. But a celebrity's status stemmed from his celebrity. Boorstein noted that a celebrity's a person well-known for being well-known. Heroic acts were hardly necessary. In fact, the concept of heroism itself came to be seen as dated. Heroes were flawed, self-interested, provincial, even delusional. Instead of worshipping heroes, who—whatever their weakness, or even despite them—accomplished great things, Boorstein's "graphic revolution" of mass media enabled if not propelled people to became fascinated with celebrities. Two such—men of limited and decidedly non-heroic accomplishments, Barack Obama and Donald Trump—became successive presidents of the United States. Boorstein's celebrities' were people whose very flaws, whose mundane coarseness, made them more typical. For example, "The Real Housewives of Beverly Hills," as one "reality" television show billed them. Such obviously unexemplary celebrities supposedly were therefore more authentic and easier for audiences to identify with.

The Palestine narrative, "branded" in American marketing terms as "The Real Victims of the Middle East," is widely taught, quite generally reported, but too little questioned. "Jihad Jane's" story exemplifies its attraction for romantically inclined drifters, perhaps especially those with a history of abuse. In Colleen LaRose's case, reportedly physical. In many other, apparently psychological or intellectual. Jihad Jane—the name LaRose gave herself—"was living with a boyfriend in 2007 when a romantic encounter with a Muslim man sparked an interest in Islam. After months of learning online, LaRose said, she converted to Islam and later watched videos of alleged U.S. and Israeli atrocities against Palestinian children that radicalized her. By 2008, prosecutors said, 'she had managed to align herself with violent terrorists who valued her ability and persistence as their online predator' recruiting new fighters.

"'I just loved my brothers so much, when they would tell me stuff, I would listen to them, no matter what,' LaRose told Reuters. 'And I also was … lost.'" That's how she came to join a 2009 al-Qaeda plot and flew to Europe to help kill Lars Vilks, one of the Swedish cartoonists who had had the temerity to lampoon the Islamic prophet.[1] LaRose received a 10-year sentence in federal court for terrorism-related crimes.

She was radicalized in part by staged videos of illusory American and Israeli atrocities against Palestinian children, examples of the emotive "proof" fueling the Palestinian narrative. That such proofs are counter-factual allegations rooted in propagandistic inversions does not matter. Neither do actual Palestinian Arab atrocities from the 1920s to the present, hundreds of which have been committed against Jewish and Israeli children and adults, individuals and groups. The Palestinian narrative makes development and maintenance of Israel, a prosperous, democratic state under constant siege by neighbors neither prosperous nor democratic—an actually heroic story—seem dated and false.

The Palestine lie in this sense functions as a political-diplomatic equivalent of celebrity notoriety. Consider Paris Hilton and Kim Kardashian. Here were young women with little talent beyond a surreal naturalness when naked or nearly so in front of cameras. Early in the 21st century, thanks to the Internet, they garnered literally millions of "followers" worldwide. They were famous for their fame, based on little more than those usually highly stylized images and incessantly reported personal behavior that a generation or two earlier would have been considered infamous. Could they sing, dance, act or perform in some other artistic manner normally associated with such celebrity? To ask the question was to misunderstand the phenomenon.

1 "After delays, 'Jihad Jane' to be sentenced in murder plot," Reuters in *The Baltimore Sun*, Jan. 2, 2014.

So too with the lie of Palestine. Is it supported by history or current events? Does that matter? These are—in a post-modern, anti-empirical culture—the wrong questions.

With the election of real estate mogul and celebrity television star Donald J. Trump as president of the United States in 2016, pundits, politicians and professors suddenly became alert to the phenomenon of allegedly fake news (while often contorting themselves to avoid confronting real examples of biased journalism). But Internet-enabled false news—information or disinformation considered newsworthy because it is presented as newsworthy—often is just the contemporary, if widespread, version of news in its earlier, pre-print, pre-journalistic form: village and market-place gossip. That is, it amounts to broadly disseminated though frequently unverified or unverifiable rumor.

The desire for news, it should be understood, is a human constant, no doubt as old as humankind itself, as Mitchell Stephens, a New York University associate professor of journalism and communications wrote in *The History of News; From the Drum to the Satellite*. But journalism dates more formally to the political, cultural and artistic journals of 18th century England. It was accelerated by the telegraph and widely disseminated by the rotary press in 19th century America and professionalized in the West in the early in the 20th century with promulgation of print standards—or at least aspirations. These, according to various journalism codes, included accuracy, objectivity, balance, context, comprehensiveness, absence of conflicts of interest and willingness to correct mistakes. But print-based standards, like print news media themselves, have been increasingly displaced in the 21st century.

Beginning about 1990, with the adoption of the home computer, e-mail and list-serves, the digital age destroyed print journalism's advertising revenue-based business model. And print journalism generally had set standards for and the agendas of its usually more time-constrained and therefore often more superficial radio and television broadcast competitors. But as print shriveled, rumor, and propaganda— as disinformation and misinformation—began to return to the fore. *Izvestia* and *Pravda*, the government and Communist Party newspapers, respectively, of the Soviet Union, had dominated that country's news media. But their external influence had been limited, especially outside the Soviet bloc.

However, post-print, as outlets such as RT (Russia Today television and Web sites) and Iran's English-language Press TV exemplify, propaganda can more convincingly and widely be presented as news while instructing in fakery. The influence of such outlets does not remain on the fringe but thanks to the interconnected speed of digital data flow, rushes rather than seeps via "new media" sources from *Vox, Vice, The Intercept, BuzzFeed, Huffington Post, The Daily Beast, Infowars* and countless other Web sites into what was journalism's "mainstream." This Vladimir Putin's Russia banked on with its information operations targeting the credibility Western countries could extend to their own elections, including the 2016 U.S. presidential campaign.

Well before 2016, China's communist rulers, with their Xinhua News Agency, the Soviets with TASS, and the PLO with its WAFA wire service, among other such movements, regularly disseminated fake news. Their purpose, in contrast with their ostensible format, was propaganda. To be useful, to appear credible enough to be quoted and recirculated, their product had to be and often was factual enough to seem plausible, to appear newsworthy, while through deft omission or subtle if false insertion being fully misleading.

In its early years especially, the Al-Jazeera satellite television network often was described in the West as "the Arabic CNN." This was false, that is fake. It was also nonsense, that is, misinformation. Al-Jazeera's use by its owners—Qatar's ruling family—as a means to further Qatari foreign policy and via Islamist program hosts and guests to widely disseminate extremist messages passed with little Western comment. So did CNN's own left-of-center tilt, made obvious by direct comparison with the later arrival of plainly right-of-center Fox News.

So too with BBC and NPR coverage of Israeli-Palestinian affairs that virtually always cast Israelis as perpetrators, Arabs as victims. If the events being reported were not themselves false, then by omission of key facts, neglect or inversion of cause-and-effect, and exaggeration of minor to the denigration of major elements, many of their accounts were misleading. Coverage like NPR's report on Israel's Park Hotel Passover seder massacre in 2002, in which 29 people were murdered, was typical. It made the attack passive, the direct responsibility of no one in particular. Palestinian Arabs didn't kill; rather a bomb exploded. NPR depersonalized the Jewish victims; unnamed people—thereby excluded from the privileged category of "the Other"—died. And the bulk of the segment overturned the sequence's significance; instead of focusing on the atrocity of the attack, the report featured named Palestinian Arabs worrying about Israeli reprisals. If not fake news, then a news fake. This approach epitomized NPR's reporting on the second Palestinian intifada, and much news media miscoverage and malfeasance in regard to

Arab-Israeli stories in general.

What great, heroic act—by their own definition—thrust the Palestinian case directly before the Western TV-viewing public and made it the functional equivalent of a news media celebrity? The 1972 Munich Olympic Games massacre of Israeli athletes. A true horror, this mass murder, as massaged by mass media, simultaneously was news and fit Boorstein's definition of a "pseudo-event." Real enough as a crime and tragedy for the victims, their families, friends and nation, it was false in its subsequent propagandistic telling and retelling. It ultimately became entertainment, which is a primary form of education in the graphic/digital eras, in Stephen Spielberg's morally ambiguous *Munich*. Something similar would occur, for example, with the opera *The Death of Klinghoffer* (more below) staged, for example, by New York City's Metropolitan Opera Co. in 1991 and again in 2013.

The 1972 Munich Olympics massacre in reality featured torturing, castrating terrorists who savaged nine Israeli captives for hours and murdered two others. Not that the Games stopped while this was going on. The athletes and coaches were Israelis, Jews, so their brutalization was not that important. The surviving nine Israelis and five terrorists died in a botched West German rescue attempt at the airport.

With the passage of time, via Palestinian spin and media complicity, sadistic blood-shedders became freedom fighters; polemics supplanted history; and advocacy trumped news. So long as the Palestinian narrative, the Palestine lie targets the "occupiers," the "racists," "enemies of Islam," Zionists—that is to say, the Jews—this fable amounts to a celebrity equivalent that draws celebrities. Pink Floyd member Roger Waters; actress Vanessa Redgrave; the profoundly antisemitic, anti-Zionist Portuguese novelist and Nobel Prize for Literature recipient Jose Saramago, among many others, spring to mind. This celebrity narrative rebrands anti-Zionism as popular and supposedly progressive, simultaneously reducing antisemitism's disreputability. In truth, it certifies the reactionary nature of today's progressivism. But popularized, it floats above reproach, especially for those who harbor the old-new hatred.

Speaking of floating, Waters—insisting he was not antisemitic, just anti-Zionist—performed in 2015 with a large, inflatable pig adorned with a Star of David decorating his stage. In antisemitic medieval German iconography, historian Paul Johnson has noted, the *judensau* was the "Jews'-pig." In a classic example of Jew-hatred obscenely inverting reality, an animal off-limits to Jews became an object of Jewish veneration.

Such imagery played a central role in Germany and beyond, as Joshua Trachtenberg detailed in *The Devil and the Jews; The Medieval Conception of the Jew and Its Relation to Modern Antisemitism.* As noted above, the book was published in 1943, in the face of the Holocaust. Dissatisfied with largely nationalist, economic, political or even "racial" explanations of Nazi antisemitism and its 20th century influence, Trachtenberg went back through Christian supersessionism to classical antiquity and belief in Jewish magic. He found Solomon and Moses portrayed not only as master law-givers but also master magicians, epitomizing the Jews' supposed ability to draw on the dark arts. In medieval Europe, as exemplified in popular passion and mystery plays, the Jew was in league with demons, with Satan himself, whose malign presence daily occupied the minds of the literate as well as the illiterate. Often the Jew not only partnered with demons, he became one himself. Hence the Jews' resort to extreme measures—highlighted by the supposed need to consume non-Jewish blood—to appear as human.

In Jewish state hating, land designated under international law, beginning with the League of Nations' Palestine Mandate and confirmed in the U.N. Charter, for Jewish settlement, becomes "occupied Arab territory." For anti-Zionist antisemites like Waters, the medieval *judensau* seamlessly becomes the *Zionistsau.* The more radical the progressive, the more reactionary the ideology and behavior.

Trachtenberg relates how medieval Christians believed the demonic Jews, in league with the devil, chronically attempted to desecrate the host (the wafer believed to become, through transubstantiation, the body of Christ during the communion ceremony). In allegedly doing so, the Jews meant to destroy Christendom itself. Rumors of such attempts led to repeated massacres of Jewish communities.

Ben-Dror Yemini introduces his *Industry of Lies: Media, Academia and the Arab-Israeli Conflict,* with the story of two pleasant young women protesting a pro-Israel event in Boston a few years ago. They carried signs decrying Israel's "genocide" of the Palestinian Arabs. When he asked them how many Arabs Israel had killed in that genocide, one guessed "millions."

Host desecration to destroy Christianity. Genocide to eliminate the Palestinian Arabs. The fantastical crimes born of satanic desires of the Jews then and Zionists now are threads in the same fabric.

Al-Aqsa is not in danger, at least not from Jews. Neither are Palestinian Arabs, whose non-combatant deaths at the hands of Palestinian Jews and later Israelis numbers not in the millions, not in the hundreds of thousands but in the thousands, comparable to the deaths of Jews at the hands of Palestinian Arabs. But Jews and their state are in danger from people who believe Jews threaten al-Aqsa and Palestinian Arabs.

Fabrications, Fables and Agit-Prop

The highly-schooled, articulate Prof. Penny Gross wanted the West to bomb Israel to stop its non-existent "massacres" of Palestinian Arabs, whose population and standard of living continued to grow. Yet Israelis are not, despite the anti-Zionist, antisemitic matrix, analogous to Serbians bloodily attempting to hold onto Kosovo, bombed into relinquishing it by NATO under the leadership of President Bill Clinton. Even during that bombing campaign, no one spoke of "the question of Serbia" or called for its destruction. The Western professoriate and U.N. bodies could not be moved to indict Russia for its massacres in Chechnya and devastation of its capital, Grozny or slaughter in Syria by its client, President Bashar al-Assad and destruction of Aleppo, including targeting of hospitals in rebel-held territory. Despite its large-scale deadly failures, there was no talk of "the question of Syria." Likewise no rumination over the question of Russia. Even at the height of the international campaign against the apartheid regime of white minority ruled South Africa, neither was "the question of South Africa" debated. But virtually all who insist on its urgency understand that "the question of Palestine" (the question of Israel) is really "the Jewish question." Will the Jews continued to be allowed sovereign equality, or returned to their normative, stateless inferiority?

Israel recurrently is charged with ethnic cleansing and apartheid. The charges presume Israelis defending themselves on part of the ancient Jewish homeland must be Nazis, their country the new Third Reich. Cato the Elder invariably reminded the Roman Senate, regardless of the subject under discussion, "*Ceterum censeo Carthaginem esse delendam*"; "Furthermore, I consider that Carthage must be destroyed." For Cato's Palestinianist successors, regardless of the facts at issue or the issues themselves, so too must Israel be destroyed.

As observed, what starts with the Jews often does not end with them. Jews frequently function—regardless of their own desire—as miners' canaries for all sorts of societies. The longshoreman-turned-philosopher Eric Hoffer, authored *The True Believer*, an influential mid-twentieth century examination of self-righteous religious and political fanaticism of the type that would underpin Palestinianism. He wrote, "I have a premonition that will not leave me; as it goes with Israel so will it go with all of us. Should Israel perish, the Holocaust will be upon us all."[2] Hoffer made this prediction in 1968. He was recalling Israel's international isolation that preceded its miraculous Six-Day War victory a year earlier. He wrote decades before Islamists shot up a Parisian music hall, a Brussels airport, ran down Londoners with cars and trucks and before Iranian-Pakistani-North Korean cooperation on nuclear arms.

Those who delegitimize the Jewish state, who would not much regret the disappearance of the Jewish people are, like the Nazis were, enemies of the "civilizational principle." Hoffer made the point without adornment:

> The Jews are a peculiar people: things permitted to other nations are forbidden to the Jews.

> Other nations drive out thousands, even millions of people and there is no refugee problem. Russia did it, Poland and Czechoslovakia did it. Turkey drove out a million Greeks and Algeria a million Frenchman. Indonesia threw out heaven knows how many Chinese—and no one says a word about refugees.

> But in the case of Israel, the displaced Arabs have become eternal refugees. Everyone insists that Israel must take back every single Arab. Arnold Toynbee [a once-influential British historian] calls the displacement of the Arabs an atrocity greater than any committed by the Nazis.

> Other nations when victorious on the battlefield dictate peace terms. But when Israel is victorious, it must sue for peace. Everyone expects the Jews to be the only real Christians in this world.

> Other nations, when they are defeated, survive and recover, but should Israel be defeated it would be destroyed. Had Nasser triumphed last June [1967], he would have wiped Israel off the map, and no one would have lifted a finger to save the Jews.

---

2 "Israel's Peculiar Position," *Los Angeles Times*, May 26, 1968.

202 co *Jews Make the Best Demons*

No commitment to the Jews by any government, including our own, is worth the paper it is written on. There is a cry of outrage all over the world when people die in Vietnam or when two Negroes are executed in Rhodesia [today's Zimbabwe, then a white minority-ruled country]. But when Hitler slaughtered Jews no one remonstrated with him.

The Swedes, who are ready to break off diplomatic relations with America because of what we do in Vietnam, did not let out a peep when Hitler was slaughtering Jews. They sent Hitler choice iron ore and ball bearings, and serviced his troop trains to Norway.

The Jews are alone in the world. If Israel survives it will be solely because of Jewish efforts. And Jewish resources.

Yet at this moment, Israel is our only reliable and unconditional ally. We can rely more on Israel than Israel can rely on us. And one has only to imagine what would have happened last summer had the Arabs and their Russian backers won the war to realize how vital the survival of Israel is to America and the West in general.[3]

Can Israel rely ultimately, on the United States? When Secretary of State John Kerry finally acknowledged early in 2016 that critics of the Iran nuclear deal were correct, that at least some of the $100 billion or more in Iranian assets unfrozen by the agreement would subsidize terrorism and military expansionism, "he conceded some of that could go to groups considered terrorists, saying there was nothing the U.S. could do to prevent that. 'I think that some of it will end up in the hands of the IRGC [Iran's Islamic Revolutionary Guard Corps] or other entities, some of which are labeled terrorists,' he said .... 'You know, to some degree, I'm not going to sit here and tell you that every component of that can be prevented.' But he added that 'right now, we are not seeing the early delivery of funds going to that kind of endeavor at this point in time.'"[4] Kerry groped for conditional language to acknowledge Tehran's

---

3 "Israel's Peculiar Position," From Eric Hoffer: *The Longshoreman Philosopher*, by Tom Bethell, Hoover Institution Press, 2011.

4 "John Kerry: Some sanctions relief money for Iran will go to terrorism," CNN, Jan. 21, 2016.

transgression without conceding a concurrent obligation to defeat Iranian (or Palestinian) aims.

This grandson of a man who went from Kohn to Kerry, Jewish to Catholic, before leaving Austria for the United States, conjectured further. Speaking softly while carrying the smallest of sticks he said, "[T]here are such great demands on the Iranian government to develop the country that 'there is no way they can succeed in what they want to do if they are very busy funding a lot of terrorism.' He continued, 'If we catch them funding terrorism, they are going to have a problem with the United States Congress and other people, obviously.'"

Kerry continued, "'We are confident that this will not result in an increase somehow in the threat to any partner or any friend in the region.'"[5] Who might those partners or friends be? He did not specify. The source of such confidence? The intellectuals' flight from the reality of the civilizational threat posed by Islamic triumphalism, from the civilizational poison of resurgent anti-Zionist antisemitism. From the reality that Iran's Islamic revolutionary government funds a great deal of terrorism, and ballistic missile and nuclear research and development because what it wants to do is destroy the Little Satan and defeat the Great Satan.

Two years later Israel's ambassador to the United Nations, Danny Danon, told a Security Council meeting he was revealing classified information "to convey what he claimed are Iran's plans to dominate Syria." Danon charged that Tehran was turning Syria into "the world's largest military base" with 82,000 fighters from various militia, the Lebanese Hezbollah, the Iranian Islamic Revolutionary Guard Corps and other groups under Iranian control. Iran could fund these efforts thanks in large part to the nuclear deal Kerry negotiated on behalf of the Obama administration. According to Danon, in 2014 (the year before the agreement), 17 percent of Iranian government spending went to the military. In 2017, the figure rose to 22 percent of a larger budget.[6] Reduced international sanctions, cash unfrozen by the Obama administration and increased trade with Europe paved the way.

Paul Berman located the delusional source of confidence by members of the intelligentsia such as Kerry and Obama in improved Iranian behavior after the nuclear deal in "a moral peculiarity of the modern age. This is the lure of avoidance—the multi-motivated disinclination to discuss or even think about the very largest of crimes. The urge to look

---

5 Ibid.

6 "Israel claims 82,000 fighters under Iranian control in Syria," CNN, Jan. 25, 2018.

somewhere else—to look anywhere at all, except at the main thing."[7]

In this case the main thing being, as fueled by the Palestine lie, demonization of Israel, delegitimation of the Jews as a people and the reopening of the Jewish question. Such moral avoidance, Berman details, applies to, among other things, the direct connection between Haj Amin al-Husseini, Adolf Hitler, Muslim Brotherhood founder Hassan al-Banna, and the post-World War II survival and growth in Arab and Islamic countries of genocidal Jew hatred. "...al-Husseini was Adolf Hitler's most prolix and prominent champion in the Arab world, and ... al-Banna was, in turn, the mufti's most powerful supporter."[8] The result was a "very unusual intellectual atmosphere that came to dominate the Arab lands after the Second World War.

"In other parts of the world, the educated public took in the revelations about Hitler and the Nazis and a great many people saw in those revelations a serious argument, surely the weightiest argument of all, in favor of Zionism. It was the argument to the effect that, in the modern world, Jews did need a homeland of their own, just as the Zionists had always said. The Jews could not rely on the rest of the world to protect them. And the world needed a Jewish state, if only in order to solve a practical exigency of the immediate post-bellum period—namely, the question of where to put masses of homeless inmates of the Nazi camps, the surviving remnant [hundreds of thousands of people], who, having been rescued at last, were languishing miserably in a further set of camps, the DP camps (for 'displaced persons'), which were sometimes the old [concentration] camps. ... [T]his would make for a practical and just solution to a difficult problem—so long as the Palestinian Arabs likewise ended up with a state of their own. And so, there needed to be two states, side-by-side. The partition that had been proposed in 1937, which then was reproposed in 1947 and 1948.

"And yet, all of this, which seemed logical to a good many people in other parts of the world, posed a vexing problem to the journalists and political thinkers of the Arab countries. ... In the Arab world, where the old wartime superstitions about the invisible and demonic power of evil Jews never did come under challenge, even the best-educated of readers, a great many of them, appear to have reacted to the news from Europe in a spirit of wary suspiciousness." So, "the skeptics set about constructing alternative interpretations" and constantly updated them in the following decades.

---

7 *The Flight of the Intellectuals*, Melville House, copyright 2010, 2011, page 115.
8 Ibid., page 120.

"Thus, the Nazis slaughtered the Jews, but did so in self-defense, and were right to have done so. Or, the Nazis slaughtered the Jews, which was wrong, but the Zionists exaggerated the numbers, and Jewish suffering was not really especially terrible. Or, the Nazis slaughtered the Jews, but the Zionist movement was secretly complicit with the Nazis, and Nazism and Zionism were equally criminal. Or, whatever the Nazis may have done to European Jews, the Zionists were doing the same to the Palestinian Arabs. ... Or, the whole story of genocide in Europe was a lie invented by the Zionists and the Nazis never did slaughter the Jews.
...

"But all of those arguments pointed to the same conclusion. This was the belief that, whatever may have happened in Europe, the Arab world had no reason to give the matter any thought."[9] Of course, the opposite was true. "After the war, al-Husseini recalled that his attempts to keep Jews from escaping [Nazi-occupied Europe] had a 'positive effect' for the Palestinian cause."[10] They certainly did, from the mufti's viewpoint. Hundreds of thousands if not millions of Jews who could have lived in Mandatory Palestine died in Europe.

"Al-Husseini's advocacy of the mass murder of Jews convinced the Nazi leadership this would be popular among Muslims not only in the Middle East but also in the USSR and the Balkans. ... While genocide against the Jews was a high priority for al-Husseini and his radical nationalist and Islamist colleagues, their main goal was to help Germany win the war" and thus free the Middle East from British and French control and open it to their own rule. "Al-Husseini gave extensive aid and comfort to the Nazi cause, raising forces that delayed the war's end and thus increased the number of victims."[11]

Not only did the mufti's wartime efforts in Berlin, working with top Nazi leadership, ultimately help enable and broaden the Holocaust, but so did his activities from the 1920s and '30s. The anti-Jewish massacres and later anti-British riots he instigated, which were funded by fascist Italy and Nazi Germany, contributed to London virtually halting Jewish immigration to the nascent Jewish national home in Palestine in the 1930s. Palestinian Arab and broader Arab nationalist and Islamist leadership—merged in and epitomized by al-Husseini—first kept Jews from Mandatory Palestine when Hitler still was considering ousting

9 Ibid., pages 121-123.

10 *Nazis, Islamists and the Making of the Modern Middle East,* Barry Rubin and Wolfgang Schwanitz, Yale University Press, 2014, page 166.

11 Ibid., page 167.

them from the Third Reich and then made sure they were confined in Europe as *Der Fuehrer* settled on genocide. Al-Husseini succeeded, in effect, with Arab occupation by preemption of Jewish land.

And when Nazi Germany crumbled, the dominant views among Arab academics, writers and clergy that the Holocaust had nothing to do with them meant that post-World War II Arab governments would be particularly hospitable to ex-Nazis. In fact, the new leaders of such regimes sometimes employed their wartime contacts to continue their old propaganda, secret police and military specialties, safe from extradition.

Kerry on Iran specifically and Berman's European and North American intellectuals in general exemplify the intelligentsia's moral peculiarity of avoidance. The intellectuals savaged critics of Islamic triumphalism like Ayaan Hirsi Ali (a bogeyman for U.S. campus progressives) to maintain their image of Tariq Ramadan. Ramadan was Hassan al-Banna's admiring grandson and in the 1990s and 2000s perhaps European intellectuals' most highly-regarded "progressive" Islamic thinker. Berman's intellectuals, fleeing the most important questions, warmed to Ramadan's contorted, evasive apologias for Islamist theory. Some imagined in him a guide to a reformed, modern Islam.

Eric Hoffer, on the other hand, though a self-made intellectual—or perhaps because of it—possessed the true intellectual's ability to confront honestly the big things. In doing so, he contrasted not only with the intelligentsia under Berman's microscope but also with their spiritual father, Edward Said, an avatar of the post-modern intelligentsia.

Lee Smith observed that "Said's litmus test for intellectual good faith was the Palestinian cause. [Fouad] Ajami and [Kanan] Makiya had at one time been safely within the fold, but then became preoccupied with their own concerns, which had nothing to do with Palestine and Israel or even the West." That is, their intellectual inquiries and searches for truth were too profound to be stifled by intersectionality. "Ajami [author of *Dream Palace of the Arabs*, which relates Arab intellectuals' failed attempts to promote secular modernization], a Lebanese Shia, became concerned with the outrages of Sunni supremacism, while the Iraqi Makiya [author of *Republic of Fear: The Politics of Modern Iraq*] dedicated himself to fighting Saddam Hussein, but from Said's point of view all they'd done by exposing rifts in the Arab consensus was to confirm for Americans the bad things that they had wanted to believe about Arabs, and Said's strategy was to credit Western intellectuals with all the sins they wanted attributed to themselves."

European theorists and politicians loathed their countries' earlier—ultimately unsustainable—colonialism and imperialism. To atone for it they undertook in the 1960s and 1970s a program by which they imagined they could regain self-esteem while retaining influence if not control in Arab countries. This great purification would come at the cost of European culture and ethnicity—of Christian influence and traditional ethno-national cultures—and with renewed hostility to the Jews, first by delegitimizing the Jewish state.

Bat Ye'or, author of *The Dhimmi: Jews and Christians under Islam* (Farleigh Dickinson University Press, 1985) and *Islam and Dhimmitude; Where Civilizations Collide,* (Farleigh Dickinson, 2001), summarized Europe's surrender to "Palestinianism" and return to anti-Jewish mythomania this way:

*1966-1973: France's Charles de Gaulle instituted a policy "of funding French pro-Arab movements to bind together the two shores of the Mediterranean Sea";

*1970-1973: "the extension of this policy under French pressure as a coordinated European Community [now European Union] policy regarding Israel"; and

*1973-1993: "creation of an unofficial body, the Euro-Arab Dialogue, with specialized and coordinated commissions implemented throughout the European Community and funded by the European Commission. This body triggered two integrated and interrelated movements: the European Community's anti-Israel policy and a Muslim immigration policy within Europe."[12] Its European proponents believed that increased Muslim immigration would support linkage of the European and North African/Near Eastern shores of the Mediterranean and, diminishing Europe's Christian and ethnic histories and culture, advance globalized government.[13] One price for improved Arab-European relations would be Europe's support for the Arab League's pro-Palestinian, anti-Israeli positions.

Bolstering these developments were ex-Nazi converts to Islam in Egypt and Syria, and reactionary European Christians who fought the Vatican's Second Ecumenical Council (1962-'65) and its rejection of Church antisemitism. "Arab [Christian] clerics were utilized by Arab states wishing to maintain the traditional opprobrium of the Jewish peo-

---

12 "Antisemitism/Anti-Zionism: Primal Pillars in Europe's Decay," *Anti-Judaism, Antisemitism and Delegitimizing Israel,* edited by Robert S. Wistrich, University of Nebraska Press, 2016, page 25.

13 Ibid., page 26.

ple in Christian teaching. ... Arab Christians and Europeans went as far as identifying Palestine as the embodiment of a Muslim-Christian Jesus crucified by Israel on the Cross. This was a figure of Christ-like adoration in which Islam and Christianity could mystically unite in oneness against an imagined Jewish 'conspiracy.'"[14]

The compulsion to maintain the old Jew-hatred, to see the Jews' "anti-Christ" state expunged, ran deep. It could be seen in tactically expedient, ultimately self-defeating behavior of Arab Christian leaders. Their churches "made the criminalization of Zionism in the West a basic and essential condition for Muslim-Christian rapprochement. Serving their Muslim masters, they became the major instruments for spreading anti-Zionism in Europe. Elimination of the Jewish state became a priority more important than defending their own Christian communities."[15] They followed closely and echoed "countless ex-Nazis and collaborationist officials, former ministers, diplomats and intellectuals who had recycled themselves" into influential post-war positions in Europe and provided apologias for Palestinian terrorism.[16]

The 56 Muslim-majority countries of the Organization of the Islamic Conference (organized in 1969, plus "Palestine" for a total of 57 members) threatened to punish any country that kept its embassy in Jerusalem. The OIC has sought "to deny any trace of Judaism in the lands of the Bible and to prove its Arab and Muslim character since the third millennium B.C. The Jews are accused of 'Judaizing' the biblical prophets who were, in fact, Muslims, and of usurping the antiquity of other peoples since the Jews have no history of their own. The same could be said of the Christians, who have usurped Jesus ... supposedly a Muslim prophet."

The result? "The war waged against the Jews in World War II did not stop in 1945: its ideology and tactics continued through other channels."[17] "Antisemitism, as we know, has many facets. Today it is a movement molded by the characteristics of our age: it is global. Europe is no longer its only source, although European states and particularly the European Union, gives it abundant funding as well as media, cultural, political and strategic support. In fact its main source is the OIC, which by its numerous commissions and sub-commissions, infiltrates

---

14 Ibid., page 27.
15 Ibid. page 27.
16 Ibid., page 30.
17 Ibid., page 30.

and pressures all international U.N. bodies."[18] When UNESCO declared the Tomb of the Patriarchs (Cave of Machpelah) in Hebron a Palestinian historic site, it "ratified the Islamization of the Hebrew patriarchs, an allegation contrary to all rationality, which relies solely on the Koran. Such a decision has serious consequences not only for Jews but also for the Christian world whose roots have been Islamized. Moreover, it proclaims to the whole world, Muslim and non-Muslim, that the word of the Koran is the truth and supersedes all historical evidence and objective truth."[19]

The EU tolerates this anti-empirical, totalitarian outlook that denies Jewish and Christian history since it parallels the community's leaders' own "rejection of European national identities" and promotion of "multiculturalism ... in compliance with the continuous flow of an immigration linked to Muslim culture, history and values."[20]

In North America, academia advanced the campaign politicians and diplomats promoted in Europe. According to Lee Smith, "intolerance of dissenting Arab opinion wasn't the only characteristic Said's work shared with Arab nationalism. Like many of the doctrine's major ideologues, he saw the Arab world as defined, largely, by the West and in its opposition to it. ... [T]he reason Said wrote about Western views of the Middle East, rather than about the region itself, was because, as he wrote, 'I have no interest in, much less capacity for, showing what the true Orient and Islam really are.'" But for Smith, Said's one-time admiring student, "the notion that it is impossible to describe things as they 'really are' was a postmodernist escape hatch that appealed to the book's more sophisticated readers.

"... But consider how strange that line is: the person who, perhaps more than anyone else, has shaped the contemporary Western understanding of Arabism and Islam was uninterested in showing what the Arab world was really like." As a result, Said "glided over the diversity, conflicts, and tensions among Arab themselves, and painted a picture of an Arab community unified by Western oppression, a worldview derived from Arab nationalism."[21] And like a miniature portrait distilled from that larger, false picture, the Palestinian narrative is worn, metaphorically, as a locket containing the image of a loved one around the

---

18 Ibid., page 35.

19 Ibid., page 35.

20 Ibid., page 32.

21 *The Strong Horse: Power, Politics, and the Clash of Arab Civilizations,* by Lee Smith, 2010, Anchor Books paperback edition, 2011, page 39.

neck of self-righteous anti-Zionists, self-justifying antisemites every-where. It epitomizes post-liberal left, progressive virtue signaling. And it allows the virtue signaler to share the fringe of celebrity limelight focused on the Palestinian Arabs.

Not by accident, as Rubenstein, Herf, Rubin and Schwanitz have shown, has so much Arab and particularly Palestinian propaganda sounded like Third Reich demonization of Jews. Al-Husseini and Hitler sang from the same lyrics. After the war, some senior and mid-level Nazis found refuge in Arab countries and went to work for their governments. Arab leaders who'd grown up listening to al-Husseini and took fascist parties as models reflected their words and deeds.

The more emotional and passionate Jew-hatred becomes—in post-modern elevation of subjective over objective, emotional over rational—the more authenticity it's granted. Anti-Zionist, antisemitic fascism, whether from right or left, trumps knowledge and the self-restraint that separates adulthood from adolescence, that distinguished America's revolutionary Founders from France's revolutionary murderers, Liberty Trees from the guillotine. So liberated—anti-democratic "liberation" invariably opposes individual liberty—anti-Zionist antisemitism would authorize a renewed slaughter of the oldest object of sacred human sacrifice.

Prof. Edward Said's largely successful "lit-crit" discrediting of traditional Middle East studies on grounds of allegedly insufficient empathy with Arabs and Muslims helped open the door to replacement by its mirror image. Instead of "orientalist ethnocentrism" came revisionist apologia for the unblemished Other. It appeared cloaked as new, critical studies that often assumed, when they did not feature, the Palestinian narrative. In place of attempted objective examination by non-Arab, non-Muslim specialists as well as by those personally connected to the region came subjective "contextualizations" and self-justifying defenses.

This helped legitimize Palestinian Arab grievances, real or imagined and regardless of their causes. The proper target of righteous Palestinian rage, "frustration" and of a "humiliation" to be expiated by bloodshed, became the Israeli. That is to say, the Zionist, the Jew, delegitimized and bound on the contemporary sacrificial altar. Every era has such altars, and many groups and peoples and imagined peoples including Irish, Armenians, Kurds and Tutsi, including kulaks, infidels, class enemies and witches have been strapped to them.

But perpetual scapegoat status adheres only to the Jews. This nearly universal indictment makes both determined Jewish resistance and mere Jewish persistence, not just reactionary, but also criminal. "Palestinianism" is essentially a pretext for the enduring, underlying cause. "What is ghoulishly fascinating," Thomas Cahill speculates, "about the history of Christian depictions of Jews (even as early as the fourth century A.D. in the elegantly vicious sermons of John Chrysostom) is that the people being excoriated are presumed to exhibit the unyielding qualities of God himself—the same God whom Christians claimed to worship and whose sacred scriptures they revered. A good case can be made that medieval anti-Hebraism and its modern offspring antisemitism are both forms of God-hatred, masquerading as self-justifying intolerance. The hatred of Christians for Jews may have its ultimate source in hatred of God, a hatred that the hater must carefully keep himself from knowing about. Why would one hate God? To find the answer we probably need to look no further than the stark, unyielding Ten [the Ten Commandments]."[22]

The damned Jews and their damned "thou shall" and "thou shall not."

The damned Israelis and their blatantly successful state.

Chosen/choosing people and their promised/promising land.

So for the Jew, his or her identity and the message that comes with it is itself an admonition, rebuke, crime. That makes Jewish self-defense aggression. It's an old story, the oldest, in new if transparent anti-Zionist garb.

Not coincidentally, another academic influential on the post-liberal (that is, anti-empirical) left, though hardly of Said's stature, was an anti-Zionist Israeli and Said follower. This was one-time University of Haifa historian Ilan Pappe. Benny Morris, himself a lapsed "post-Zionist" or "new" Israeli historian, reviewing Pappe's *A History of Modern Palestine; One Land, Two Peoples*, (Cambridge University Press, 2003) advised, "This is truly an appalling book. Anyone interested in the real history of Palestine/Israel and the Palestinian/Israel conflict would do well to run vigorously in the opposite direction."[23]

No matter. Pappe served as *éminence grise* in a case that in its path to the Israeli Supreme Court epitomized the intellectual and moral bankruptcy of Arab-Israeli revisionists—some Israeli and American Jews among them. A useful source for those compelled to believe Israel was born in sin, Pappe explained his dismissal of academic objectivity

---

22 *The Gifts of the Jews, How a Tribe of Desert Nomads changed the Way Everyone Thinks and Feels*, by Thomas Cahill, Nan Talese/Doubleday, 1998, pages 152-153.

23 "Politics by Other Means," by Benny Morris, *The New Republic*, March 22, 2004.

this way: "There is no historian in the world who is objective. I am not as interested in what happened as in how people see what's happened."[24] In other words, Pappe, in the post-modern vocabulary, privileged perception over reality.

"I admit that my ideology influences my historical writings," he added. "Indeed, the struggle is about ideology, not about facts. Who knows what facts are? We try to convince as many people as we can that our interpretation of the facts is the correct one, and we do it because of ideological reasons, not because we are truth-seekers."[25]

If, as he implies, facts are not knowable and all is historical relativism, then what Pappe calls his interpretation of them is more likely invention when not merely distortion. His "history" is a soft-core product of *1984*'s ministry of truth. It has, as Lord Acton might have put it, no worth or dignity. When Henry Ford declared, "History is more or less bunk," he was speaking as a pre-Pappe Pappist. To give the American automaker his due in this regard, his full quote as reported by *The Chicago Tribune* in 1916 continued, history "is tradition. We don't want tradition. We want to live in the present, and the only history that is worth a tinker's damn is the history that we make today." Since history and tradition were "more or less bunk," Ford was able to publish the notoriously antisemitic *Dearborn Independent* and distribute hundreds of thousands copies of the English-language version of *The Protocols of the Learned Elders of Zion*. *The Protocols* are, as noted above, a forged meta-text alleging an international Jewish conspiracy to control the world. Nazi propaganda drew on its allegations and the work remains widely distributed in Arabic translations throughout the Middle East.

Pappe, an ideologue, preferred indoctrination to history. So the only history worth Henry Ford's damn to Ilan Pappe was that distorted or invented to serve his efforts. Truth-seeking becomes an obstacle. Such an approach would be disbarred in the hard sciences, at a minimum to uphold the ancient injunction, "Physician, first do no harm." Patients would run vigorously from doctors who, presented with worrisome symptoms, replied, "Who knows what the facts are?" But in the "soft sciences," the humanities, where Keynes' mad scribblers distill murderous self-justifying ideologies, such "ideology *über alles*" propagandizing has led, from Hitler to Stalin, Mao to Pol Pot, bin Laden to Khomeini, to literally tens of millions of deaths. Illuminatingly, Pappe's approach literally was thrown out of court.

24 *Le Soir* (Belgium), Nov. 29, 1999.
25 Ibid.

Summarizing the matter: Theodore Katz alleged in a 1998 Haifa University master's thesis that after the village of Tantura surrendered to them in 1948, Israeli forces massacred 200 Arabs. He claimed to base his research on interviews with 60 Tantura residents and dedicated his thesis to "my teacher and friend," Pappe. In 2000, Israel's then-largest newspaper, *Ma'ariv*, promoted Katz's allegations in a five-page article. So much for what Pappe and like-minded Israeli anti-Zionists claimed was Israeli suppression of dark criticism.

Veterans of the Haganah unit that conquered Tantura, the 33rd Battalion of the Alexandroni Brigade, insisted what had occurred in Tantura was a battle to prevent the Haifa-Tel Aviv road from being cut. Fourteen members of the battalion and approximately 40 Arabs died in street fighting. By the time the massacre allegedly took place, said the veterans, nearly all the villagers already had been transferred from Tantura—the women to the nearby Arab village of Faradis, male fighters to the police station in the adjacent Jewish town of Zikron Ya'akov. The veterans filed suit, and in a December 2000 trial their attorney, Giora Erdinast, a Peace Now activist but also son-in-law of one of the battalion members, discredited Katz's evidence. He demonstrated that Katz's taped interviews with villagers contained none of the purported quotes the university graduate student had used in his thesis.[26]

Under oath, Katz claimed he had been misunderstood and never believed the battalion massacred villagers. Ordered by the court, he published a formal apology. Katz quickly recanted however, insisting he was sure a massacre had taken place "even if I can't know because I wasn't there." That was, to say the least, a strange position for a would-be historian. The trial judge rejected Katz's retraction. Israeli Supreme Court judges, sitting as the High Court of Justice, dismissed his appeal.

In addition, a Haifa University committee (approximately 20 percent of Haifa's students and faculty are Arabs) examined Katz's thesis and, discovering fabrication and distortions of quotes, disqualified it. Katz accepted the school's offer to revise his work, but in 2002 a new, five-member board of examiners did not pass the updated effort. The university awarded Katz a "non-research" degree, functionally closing his career as an academic.

However, that was not the end of the "Tantura massacre." Like so many variants of the blood libel, it was too good for too many not to be "true"—at least in the "higher" sense of the Palestinian narrative. As if

26 "The Academic Blacklisting of Israel, the Tantura Affair and Ilan Pappe," by Ricki Hollander, CAMERA, Oct. 13, 2005.

to confirm Eric Hoffer's 1971 observation that "intellectuals cannot operate at room temperature," Pappe insisted in an article for the *Journal of Palestine Studies*—a fun-house mirror of what scholarly journals aspired to before post-modern dismissal of academic rigor in the humanities— on the historical worth of Katz's thesis. He even expanded its original claims. Pappe also attacked Haifa University for rejecting "a solid and convincing piece of work whose essential validity is in no way marred by its shortcomings." In other words, Your Honor, my client's essential innocence is in no way marred by the fact he stabbed the victim.

The *Journal of Palestine Studies'* introduction to Pappe's article held that "though the researcher, Teddy Katz, is himself a Zionist, the case sheds light on the extent to which mainstream Zionism is prepared to go in discouraging research that brings to the fore such aspects of the 1948 war as 'ethnic cleansing.'" Or perhaps the extent to which those who insist on historical accuracy and truth as a defense against libel are prepared to go—at least occasionally—in upholding traditional standards of academic honesty.

Pappe, exhibiting a classic case of anti-Zionist, anti-Israel obsessive-compulsive disorder, could not stop there. He then wrote to American and British historical and Middle Eastern studies associations, urging them to pressure Haifa University to reverse its disqualification of Katz's thesis. His former student, Pappe insisted, had revealed "one of the worst massacres in the [1948] war." Comedians have illustrated the Yiddish word *chutzpah* (unmitigated gall) by the man who murders his parents and then throws himself on the mercy of the court since he's an orphan. Similarly, Pappe charged that "Israeli academics cannot find in themselves the courage to remain loyal to the basic rules of academic research and freedom." The letter and Pappe's public criticism and personal abuse of his colleagues led the university's dean of humanities to seek his dismissal. He was not fired, though the school took note of Pappe's "transgression of all common ethical standards of academic life."

Pappe may have lost the battle over the battle of Tantura, but he bolstered the enemy in the larger war to delegitimize Israeli institutions and the Jewish state itself. In 2005, his letter charging his own institution with attempting to quash academic freedom was one of the points of "evidence" when the executive council of the 40,000-member British Association of University Teachers voted to cut all ties with Haifa University and Bar Ilan University outside Tel Aviv and circulate to its local associations a call by Palestinian organizations for an academic boycott of all Israeli universities. The AUT president, claiming a lack of time, refused to let anyone challenge the motion.

Internal and international criticism led the council to reconvene and rescind its boycott resolution the next month. Nevertheless, the campaign advocating boycotts, divestments and sanctions (BDS) against Israel on the usual but specious grounds of "illegal occupation," "ethnic cleansing" and "racist imperialism" continued unabated. If not with short-term success—Israel's economy and international trade has continued to show remarkable growth and a number of state legislatures in America have barred governmental compliance with BDS aims—then with unflagging commitment as boycotters pursue their ultimate anti-Zionist, antisemitic goals. These are first isolating and silencing Israel's defenders, then enabling destruction of the Jewish state.

Artistic collaborators

The Tantura lie rippled all the way to Washington, D.C., illustrating the Palestinian narrative's termite-like ability to undermine not only academia but also portions of the Israeli and diaspora Jewish cultural intelligentsia. In 2014, Theater J, a professional company attached to the District of Columbia Jewish Community Center, staged *The Admission*, by Israeli playwright Motti Lerner. As this author wrote at the time, the play insinuated a slaughter by Jewish troops of non-combatants in the Arab village of "Tantur" in 1948 and its destructive reverberations generations later.[27] Unable at the time to get *The Admission* staged in Israel, Lerner collaborated with Ari Roth, then Theater J's artistic director.

Though the DCJCC was subsidized in part by the Jewish Federation of Greater Washington, Roth repeatedly had presented anti-Israel works that typically inverted Arab-Israeli history to make moral cripples if not outright villains of Jewish characters and Christological suffering servants of Palestinian Arabs. Roth's Palestinianism played with antisemitism in a sort of theatrical pornography, as in 2009 when Theater J offered staged readings of British playwright Caryl Churchill's anti-Zionist rant, *Seven Jewish Children*. Journalist James Kirchick charged the 10-minute screed "draws a straight line from Nazi Germany's mass murder of European Jewry to Israel's treatment of the Palestinians, an old trope in the quiver of rabid Israel haters."[28]

In another example, in 2011 Roth featured Israeli playwright Boaz

---

27 "Liberating Theater J from Diva Ari Roth," by Eric Rozenman, Jewish News Service, Dec. 22, 2014.

28 "Self-loathing on J Street," by James Kirchick, *The Washington Times*, April 8, 2009.

Gaon's *Return to Haifa*. Based on a novella by Ghassan Kanafani, the play pivots on the false equation of Arab aggression with Jewish resistance in 1948. Kanafani had been a senior member of the Popular Front for the Liberation of Palestine, second-largest faction in the PLO and a U.S.-designated terrorist organization. The PFLP pioneered airliner hijackings in the 1970s, assassinated Palestinian moderates and subsequently imitated Palestinian fundamentalist groups like Hamas and Palestinian Islamic Jihad by launching suicide bombings.

Kanafani himself was assassinated shortly after being photographed in his Beirut office with members of the Japanese Red Army. The latter group, working for the PFLP, murdered 26 people and wounded 80 others in a 1972 attack at Israel's Ben-Gurion International Airport. Yet in its supportive coverage of Roth and the play, *The Washington Post* managed only to describe Kanafani as a "onetime spokesman" of the PFLP, without describing either the scope of his work or the Popular Front's history. Instead, the newspaper sanitized the aims of the BDS campaign and invoked the phantom of Israeli rightists and their U.S. supporters trying to censor artistic freedom.

An acolyte, conscious or otherwise of Said, Pappe and moral/historical relativism in general, artistic post-modernism in particular, Roth had defended *Seven Jewish Children*. He claimed it was an "elusive, evocate, wispy play that has mysteries in it, and we are trying to decode them in a public discussion." Replied Herman Taube, Holocaust escapee, poet and novelist, "We have some Jews who, you spit in their face, and they say it's raining." Roth was still detecting rain (in the unvarnished Yiddish original, spit is piss) in his face when forced to defend production of *The Admission*. The play, in essence, theatrically resuscitated the discredited Tantura libel. It had to be staged in the name of intellectual and artistic freedom, Roth claimed, because "there is a debate that needs to be convened and not stifled."

Never mind that the debate had been convened, the charge publicly aired, the facts thoroughly examined and the verdict—contrary to *The Admission's* innuendoes—rendered. It was that verdict Roth, his supporters and admiring reviewers at *The Washington Post* tried to stifle. When it comes to the Jewish state and the justice of its case, "debate" there must be until the only allowable court, that of the Palestinianists, imposes the only allowable decision—"Guilty!"—facts be damned. Alice in Wonderland's Red Queen presides incognito as one of the *bien pensant*.

A small but vocal, ad hoc group, COPMA (Committee Opposed to

Propaganda Masquerading as Art, which included several friends of this writer) criticized Theater J's staging of *The Admission*, and the Washington Jewish federation's indirect funding of it through support of the DC-JCC. Yet *The Washington Post*, in three major articles on the issue, could not bring itself to provide readers with a straightforward account of the Tantura massacre thesis and libel case. In one it actively obfuscated, its reviewer falsely claiming that instead of a libel verdict the case had "a messy ending that has never been fully cleaned up."

Playwright Lerner said his neighbors and family member all knew about the purported Tantura massacre. DCJCC officials defended *The Admission* as "opening a conversation" about Israel. As if such a one-sided "conversation"—too often an academic/artistic monologue—had not been blaring for years. Where were the plays, readings or exhibitions "opening a conversation" about Arab-Islamic rejectionism, supremacism and hate-mongering that in the post-World War II era led to tens of thousands of Jewish and Arab deaths, hundreds of thousands of Arab-on-Arab killings? That conversation the Israeli-Jewish-American left, reflecting the larger post-modern, post-liberal constellation of which it is a noisy sliver, somehow never seems to hold.

As for Lerner's claim of Israelis "knowing all about the massacre" that didn't happen, this author wrote at the time that "and MacBird was based on some people 'knowing all about' Lyndon Johnson's role in John F. Kennedy's assassination. Its theatrical presentation answered a need to 'open a conversation' about that conspiracy theory." Self-justification, like breathing, drinking and eating, is a primary human impulse.

Early in 2015, after 18 years at Theater J, Roth was dismissed by DCJCC officials. They cited not his chronic weakness for anti-Israel agitprop but rather institutional chain-of-command "insubordination." Artistic directors at theaters across the United States, including big names like Michael Kahn from Washington's Shakespeare Theater Company, leaped to Roth's support. They bemoaned his departure as "censorship" and imposed "cultural conformity." So, following Lord Acton, the lie of Palestine, lacking dignity and worth but congealed into an overarching framework, exercises its corrupting power. In the tradition of modern propaganda, it hardens into an incontrovertible, energizing truth. In other words, the narrative becomes a central article of faith in the old/new anti-Jewish religion.

The Palestine lie epitomizes the big lie. Small untruths easily can be disputed, those so large as to seem overwhelming must be valid, as Hitler and his chief propagandist Joseph Goebbels taught. Especially if big lies are ceaseless reiterated. "If you repeat a lie a thousand times, people are bound to start believing it," Goebbels explained.

The Protocols Repeat as Opera!

Repeating a lie a thousand times: *The Times of London* exposed *The Protocols of the Learned Elders of Zion* as a czarist forgery more than 50 years before the U.N.'s "Zionism-is-racism" libel. That hardly stopped the dissemination and spread of the purported exposé of an alleged Jewish conspiracy for world domination through much of Europe after the 1975 General Assembly vote. Rutgers University Prof. Stephen Eric Bronner notes that in 1934 leaders of the Swiss Jewish community won a suit against promoters of *The Protocols* in their country under laws against libel and "smut literature": "The defendants were, obviously, in a difficult position: they had to authenticate what they themselves knew was a fraudulent document. They chose not to call witnesses of their own and instead they concentrated on demeaning the plaintiffs and their supporters."[29]

Nazi Germany did not officially intervene. However, it hired "the fiercely antisemitic publicist Ulrich Fleischauer to organize support for the defendants.... Fleischauer increasingly took charge of the proceedings and his 'expert' report to the court on the 'inner truth' of *The Protocols* became an antisemitic classic.... Basically, the defense came down to a tautology: *The Protocols* are authentic because the Jews are evil. The Jews are evil because the pamphlet [*The Protocols*] says so."[30] This "inner truth" was of a piece of today's progressive true lies as highlighted above by Victor Davis Hanson.

In the same vein of "higher truths" than truth, in 2014 New York's Metropolitan Opera Company restaged the John Adams and Alice Goodman production *The Death of Klinghoffer*. The work had premiered in New York and Brussels in 1991. It pivots on, though hardly represents, the murder of a wheelchair-bound American tourist, Leon Klinghoffer, by terrorists from the Palestine Liberation Front. They shot Klinghoffer and dumped his body overboard during their 1985 hijacking of the Italian Achille Lauro cruise ship. The title, *Death of Klinghoffer*, begged a question: Why not the more accurate *Murder of Klinghoffer*, or at least *Killing of Klinghoffer*? As in the Met's 2014 revival, the

29 *A Rumor About the Jews; Antisemitism, Conspiracy, and the Protocols of Zion*, Stephen Eric Bronner, 2000, Oxford University Press, page 119.
30 Ibid., page 120.

opera trafficked in anti-Zionist, antisemitic canards. It did so contrary to some reviewers' attempt to spit in readers' faces and tell them it was raining by invoking the production's nonexistent nuance and superficial empathy for both sides.

Protests, inspired in no small measure by open letters to Met General Manager Peter Gelb from my former CAMERA colleague and opera aficionado Myron Kaplan, led the company to cancel simulcasts to theater screens around the world. But its stage performances went on. More than 1,000 people demonstrated against the production outside the Met's Lincoln Center home on opening night.

Kaplan noted that while *Klinghoffer* might, as *The New York Times* claimed, indict "the gruesome cruelty of the terrorists," it more broadly defamed an entire ethnic/religious group, Jews and Israelis. Nowhere, though, did it criticize Arabs or Muslims collectively. Sample Protocol-like lines from the libretto, sung by a self-justifying hijacker:

"Wherever poor men/Are gathered they can/Find Jews getting fat/ You know how to cheat/The simple, exploit/The virgin, pollute/Where you have exploited/Defame those you cheated/And break your own law/ With idolatry." Similar indictments of the Jew blared from Nazi publications of the 1930s, allegations channeling *The Protocols'* caricature Jewish conspirators.

Elsewhere *Klinghoffer* lyrics humanize the terrorist who sings of his mother and brother:

"She was killed/With the old men/And children in/Camps at Sabra/And Shatilla/Where Almighty God/In His mercy showed/My decapitated/Brother to me/And in His mercy/Allowed me to close/My brother's eyes/And wipe his face."

Put aside the artistic embellishment of decapitation at Sabra and Shatilla. Opera does not have to be historical, of course. But unknowing audiences might find it difficult to identify agit-prop when it's staged as drama. In 1982 members of the Lebanese Christian Phalange militia— allowed to enter Beirut's Sabra and Shatilla Palestinian refugee districts by the Israeli army, which had besieged the PLO in the city that summer—committed a massacre. Lebanese police estimated 460 dead, Israeli intelligence calculated 700 to 800. Some international news media and anti-Israel sources put the number killed at several times the Israeli estimate. According to the Lebanese tally, 35 were women and children, the rest men including Lebanese, Palestinians, Pakistanis, Syrians, Iranians and Algerians. For what purpose had the non-Palestinians come to the camps? The opera's higher truths did not say, but the PLO had operated from those locations, in which it built bunkers, stored ammunition and mobilized personnel.

In Israel, approximately 300,000 people—roughly eight percent of the country's total population then—demonstrated to protest the murders. An official committee of inquiry found the military indirectly responsible, and Defense Minister Ariel Sharon resigned. Gen. Raful Eitan was dismissed. In Arab countries there was little public reaction but in the West, Israel faced vehement criticism over Sabra and Shatilla.

The Phalangist massacre had come in retribution for the assassination by bomb two days earlier of the country's Christian president-elect, Bashir Gemayel and 25 others and previous mass killings of Christian Lebanese by the PLO and Muslim allies. These were part of the Lebanese civil war that lasted from 1975 to 1990 and by 1982 had resulted in approximately 95,000 dead in a country of four million. In 1985, Muslim militiamen killed an estimated 635 people in the Shatilla and Burj el-Barajneh Palestinian camps, causing few international protests.

While writing *Klinghoffer*, librettist Goodman apparently had undergone an identity crisis. She discarded her American Jewish heritage, joined the Anglican Church—known at the time for its hostility to Israel—and subsequently became a parish priest in England. "Whatever the reasons," Kaplan and I wrote in 2014, "whether psychological, theological, or political she produced lyrics that rehearsed traditional antisemitic stereotypes and married them to anti-Zionist slogans while exculpating, even dignifying Arab terrorism."[31]

The Boston Globe disagreed. It editorialized that the Met "embarrasses itself and cheats its audience by canceling" the *Klinghoffer* simulcast. Doing so "violates the vital notion that difficult ideas can be confronted and discussed through the arts." As if the opera did that. Leon Klinghoffer's daughters, Ilsa and Lisa, replied that the production's "rationalization of terrorism and false moral equivalencies provide no thoughtfulness, and no insight."

The New York Times, like *The Globe,* criticized the Met's simulcast cancellation, noting that Klinghoffer "has been widely praised" and "art can be provocative and controversial." Not that *The Times* championed controversial art when the subject lampooned one of its taboos. For example, in reporting world-wide controversy over publication by the Danish newspaper *Jyllands-Posten* in 2005 of 12 provocative cartoons of the Islamic prophet Mohammed, *The Times*—like virtually all major

---

31 "*New York Times, Boston Globe* Defend Anti-Israel 'Death of Klinghoffer' Opera," by Myron Kaplan and Eric Rozenman, CAMERA, June 22, 2014.

U.S. news outlets including *The Washington Post* (post-Trump election slogan: "Democracy Dies in Darkness")—failed to reprint or broadcast a single one. Original publication of the images had led to deadly riots in several Muslim-majority countries and assassination plots and attempts against *Jyllands-Posten* staff and terrorist threats toward Denmark. Like the intentionally provocative, even sacrilegious drawings featured by the French satirical paper *Charlie Hebdo*—struck in 2015 by Islamic fundamentalists who murdered 12 staff members, 11 men and one woman singled out for death because she was Jewish—the Danish cartoons caused many advocates of anti-Zionist, anti-Jewish free speech like *The New York Times* to discover prudent self-imposed restrictions on artistic expression. If such expression might not be appreciated by enemies of the Jews and of the West in general, perhaps it was both not quite artistic enough and also too controversial for America's most famous newspaper to defend.

Crusading for artistic freedom against offended Jews and Israelis comes cheap. Likewise against Mormons, as in the case of the commercially successful, widely produced musical parody, *The Book of Mormon*. Yet that show's creators, also the originators of the television cartoon series *South Park*, collapsed when warned by the New York City-based "Revolution Muslim" Web site that "they will probably wind up like Theo van Gogh for airing this show."[32] The episode included a character said to be Mohammed—but hidden in a bear's costume. Van Gogh had been murdered in 2004 on a street in Amsterdam, shot and stabbed by a Dutch-Moroccan enraged over a short film, *Submission*, he'd produced about suppression of women in Islamic societies. According to *The Times*, one of Revolution Muslim's members "tied the group's complaints about 'South Park' to larger frustrations about American support for Israel and the wars in Iraq and Afghanistan."

"South Park" creators Trey Parker and Matt Stone previously had mocked Moses, Jesus and Buddha. But Mohammed? Oh no, intimidated artists and journalists suddenly got religion, and not their own. The program's network, Comedy Central, featured shows and performers ostentatiously parodying a wide range of people and subjects—mostly political conservatives, Christians and on occasion on Jon Stewart's (Jonathan Stuart Leibowitz) "Daily Show," Israel. But it censored a 2006 "South Park" episode in which the producers "wanted to weigh in on a controversy that erupted after *Jyllands-Posten* … published cartoons

---

32 "'South Park' Episode Altered After Muslim Group's Warning," *The New York Times*, April 22, 2010.

satirizing Muhammad...."

The Boston Globe and *New York Times* did not rush to buck up Parker and Stone in those cases. But when Israel is attacked by artists and other members of the intelligentsia, ostensibly on behalf of Palestinian Arabs—including by Jews and Israelis themselves—that's another matter. The attackers may experience a self-ennobling sensation. They see themselves standing above "parochialism" or "tribalism"—above the very identity politics for themselves that they endorse for others.

However, challenging the beliefs, superstitions, stereotypes or simple errors passionately held by the enemies of Jews and Israelis requires something more than spurning group loyalty. It requires individual courage, intellectual, moral and physical. The images of Van Gogh—dead on the street, a knife pinning a note in Arabic slammed through his chest, the note quoting the Qur'an against "unbelievers"; the slaughter at Charlie Hebdo; the 2008 Mumbai massacre by the Pakistani terrorist group *Lashkar-e-Taiba* (Army of the Pure) in which 162 people were murdered at random and two others, a young rabbi and his pregnant wife, were specifically sought and tortured before being killed—are powerful propaganda. They silence and paralyze by example.

After Comedy Central's self-censorship, Nina Shea, director of the Hudson Institute's Center for Religious Freedom and former member of the U.S. Commission on International Religious Freedom, noted "the chilling effect" of threats against, or even pre-emptive fears by those who might satirize or criticize Islam. In a National Public Radio commentary, she observed that pillars of America's intellectual and artistic communities including Yale University Press, Random House Publishers and New York's Metropolitan Museum of Art, among others, already had committed self-censorship in similar circumstances.[33] The vaunted although evanescent power of Zionists to manipulate media—including outlets disproportionately employing Jews—in their favor is nothing compared to Western fear and trembling in the face of Islamist intolerance.

"The only thing necessary for evil to triumph is for good men to do nothing," attributed fragmentarily to Edmund Burke and John Stuart Mill, applies. To do nothing, beginning with refusing to identify and anathematize evil. And worse, for media and academia disgusted by their own cowardice, the compulsion to redeem themselves, in their own eyes, by attacking Israel for its periodic bursts of self-defense.

---

33 "National Review: An uncensored look at 'South Park,'" NPR, April 27, 2010.

Yet more 'massacres'

Jewish and Israeli self-flagellation over massacres that didn't happen, and leftist, including Jewish, defense of agitprop productions based on murders of Jews and Israelis that did occur reconfirms Western intellectuals' neurotically dysfunctional relationship with moral truths. It also takes the race of decent people from Tantura via *The Death of Klinghoffer* to the 1948 War of Independence "massacres" of Lydda and Deir Yassin. These too lie under the dark cloud of the Palestinian narrative that insists on the "original sin" of Israel's birth.

In 2013 Israeli journalist Ari Shavit produced a best-seller with *My Promised Land: The Triumph and Tragedy of Israel*. Some of the book's early and widespread publicity stemmed from a portion excerpted in *The New Yorker* magazine (Oct. 21, 2013) under the headline "Lydda, 1948." Shavit, a reporter and commentator for *Ha'aretz* newspaper, the long-time if shrinking voice of the Israeli establishment left, had a record of relative balance and style when writing about his native country. But in *The New Yorker* article and the section of his book dealing with Lydda, 1948 he failed thoroughly.

According to Shavit, in the 1948 war an Israeli unit led by Lt. Col. Moshe Dayan, using "a giant armored vehicle mounted with a cannon, menacing half-tracks and machine-gun-equipped jeeps" joined other Israeli forces attacking Lydda (Lod, site of present-day Ben-Gurion International Airport) and nearby Ramle between Jerusalem and Tel Aviv. On July 11 they occupied "key positions" (but by no means all) of Lydda. The next day fighting resumed and "in thirty minutes, two hundred and fifty Palestinians were killed. Zionism had carried out a massacre in the city of Lydda."

Zionism carried out a massacre in Lydda? Like "Americanism" carried out a massacre at Kings' Mountain during the Revolutionary War? Really?

King's Mountain was an American victory in battle against British and Loyalist sympathizers in the aftermath of which little or no quarter was granted. Bodies littered the battlefield days later. At Lydda, sporadic fighting took place over two days between an over-extended Israeli force, soldiers of the Transjordanian Legion and Arab irregulars, including locals. The "giant armored vehicle" the Israelis fielded was a South African-made Marmon-Herrington, used by Allied forces in World War II. It can be seen today at the Israeli Armored Corps Museum in Latrun. It's a lightly armored scout car about the size of a Ford Expedition. The

224   *Jews Make the Best Demons*

British transferred some of them to the Jordanian Arab Legion and Dayan's unit recovered this particular model abandoned in a ditch just before the battle.[34]

Outnumbered, the Israeli forces initially attacked with speed and surprise and parts of Lydda—a small city of about 20,000 people plus another 20,000 Arab refugees from Jaffa and elsewhere—surrendered. According to historian Dan Kurzman in *Genesis, 1948,* the overall Israeli commander, Lt. Col. Moshe Kelman, met with local Christian and Muslim leaders. He called for the surrender of all fighting personnel and their weapons within 24 hours. If so, the citizens could remain peacefully. If not, the Israelis would take further action.

After the initial fighting and apparent agreement by local leaders to Kelman's terms, the hard-pressed Israelis sent some of their troops, including Dayan's, to fight elsewhere, as Dayan records in his autobiography, *Story of My Life.* But the next day, July 12, a Jordanian patrol including a tank and two armored cars reached the outskirts of Lydda, firing on the Israelis. The patrol ran into trouble and had to shoot its way out. Townspeople, apparently thinking the Jordanians were trying to retake Lydda, attacked the remaining 500 Israeli troops. Another battle took place, including house-to-house fighting. Within an hour, the Israelis had regained most of the town.

But some Arab fighters still held the Dahmash mosque, outside of which four or five Israeli troops had been killed. Non-combatants also were inside the mosque. Instead of a frontal assault, the Israelis attempted to breach the walls with a PIAT (projector, infantry, anti-tank, a British weapon) that fired a 2.5-pound shell. Kurzman writes that after the PIAT exploded and the Israelis rushed the building they found the defenders dead, killed by the effects of the blast inside the confined space of the mosque.

Historian Martin Kramer, using Israeli military archives, a later documentary on Lydda that interviewed key participants, and himself interviewing some of those same actors quoted by Shavit, cast doubt on Shavit's methodology and conclusions. Of the mosque assault, Kramer writes that after the PIAT was fired, Israeli troops rushed the building, firing and throwing grenades. Inside, there were wounded as well as dead. What there was not was a massacre, either of 70 people in the mosque or 200 Arabs in all of Lydda.[35]

---

34 "Ari Shavit's Lydda Massacre," by Alex Safian, CAMERA, Oct. 26, 2013.

35 "What Happened at Lydda; In his celebrated new book, Ari Shavit claims that 'Zionism' committed a massacre in July 1948. Can the claim withstand scrutiny?" Martin

Contrary to Shavit in *The New Yorker*, Zionism had not obliterated Lydda. Lydda was not "the black box of Zionism." Jews had not hid from themselves, for decades, a contradiction between their national movement and the taking of Lydda.

The New Yorker had—even at first under Israel-obsessed editor David Remnick—a reputation for fact-checking. Until a later sex abuse scandal, Ari Shavit had enjoyed a reputation as one of Israel's better journalists. But when it came to "the Lydda massacre," the reputations of both ultimately suffered. But not in the short run. Pre- and post-publication promotion of *My Promised Land: The Triumph and Tragedy of Israel*, was incessant and fulsome, often by Jewish American journalists and organizations. It won the National Jewish Book Award, spent six weeks on *The New York Times* best-seller list and inexplicably landed Shavit guest appearances for AIPAC (the American Israel Public Affairs Committee).

Still, one might be tempted to discount Tantura, Lydda, even the row over *The Death of Klinghoffer* as little more than inside baseball, contretemps between two Jewish teams, the "Israel Right or Wrong" squad versus its "Proud Jew but Agonized Zionist" opponents in their chameleon-like variety. But what about Deir Yassin, the infamous slaughter of hundreds of Arab villagers by gunmen under Menachem Begin, the atrocity that was said to have helped spark the Palestinian refugee flight? "Remember Deir Yassin!" has been an international rallying cry for the Palestinian self-dispossessed for decades.

Remember what, exactly?

As late as 2011, *The New York Times* referred to the April, 1948 "massacre by Jewish paramilitary forces of 120 Arab civilians" in Deir Yassin, a village just outside Jerusalem overlooking the road to Tel Aviv. As recently as 2016, the Alliance of Baptists in the United States (its Web site described it as a "faith community ... of diverse sexual orientations, gender identities, theological beliefs, and ministry practices" concerned about "drones, homelessness, the death penalty, racism, education, classism, hunger, poverty, and abuse of all kinds") recalled the "Dier [sic.] Yassin Massacre, which occurred in 1947 [Sic.] ... one of the first in the on-going ethnic cleansing of Palestinians that continues to the present." (There were approximately 1 million Arabs in Mandatory Palestine, including what became Israel, the West Bank and Gaza Strip in 1948. Today there are between 3.5 million and 4.5 million depending on who's counting. Either pre-state Zionist and post-1948 Israeli "ethnic cleansing" has been spectacularly incompetent or, as suggested above, it has not taken place, the Alliance of Baptists' continuing delusion notwithstanding.)

But one sort of "abuse of all kinds," the massacre of Jews by Arabs, was common. Unlike any Zionist-Israeli leaders speaking in reference to Arabs, the secretary-general of the Arab League, Azzam Pasha, memorably predicted regarding Jews on May 15, 1948—the day Israel declared its independence and the armies of five Arab countries invaded—"this will be a war of extermination and a momentous massacre like the Mongolian massacres [in the 13th century] and the Crusades." Pasha wildly exaggerated the scope, but not the technique:

*"Sixty-two Jews were murdered by Arabs in the first week after the U.N. [Palestine] partition plan was passed [in November, 1947], and by May 15, 1948, a total of 1,256 Jews had been killed, most of them civilians. These deaths were caused by Arab militias, gangs, terrorists and army units which attacked every place of Jewish inhabitation in Palestine....

*"Thirty-nine Jews were killed by Arab rioters at Haifa's oil refinery on December 30, 1947.

*"On Jan. 16, 1948, 35 Jews were killed trying to reach Gush Etzion.

*"On February 22, 44 Jews were murdered in a bombing on Jerusalem's Rehov Beh-Yehuda. And on February 29, 23 Jews were killed all across Palestine, eight of them at the Hayotzek iron foundry.

*Seventy-eight Jewish doctors, nurses, patients, faculty members, students, Haganah fighters and one British soldier died in the Mount Scopus attack on a convoy bringing medical and military supplies to Jerusalem's Hadassah Hospital on April 13, 1948.

*"And 127 Jews were massacred at Kfar Etzion on May 15, 1948 after 30 others had died defending the Etzion Bloc. ...

*"[In addition] many small kibbutzim were subjected to attacks....In March and April these attacks culminated with an

assault on Hartuv by 400 Arabs based in the village of Ish-wa and an attack on Kfar Darom by members of the Muslim Brotherhood."[36]

So even before Jewish forces captured the first Arab villages—including Deir Yassin— in April, 1948, 924 Jews had been killed in five months of fighting sparked by Arab rejection of the U.N.'s "two-state" partition plan, which Jewish leadership had accepted.

So there had been numerous Arab massacres of Jews. Did Jews massacre Arabs at Deir Yassin?

The village, population 750, occupied a hill one mile from Jerusalem. It was one base among many for Arab forces besieging the city and attempting to cut resupply from Tel Aviv. According to Begin, 100 Irgun members attacked Deir Yassin. Other sources say as many as 132, including some from Yitzhak Shamir's—another future Israeli prime minister—Lehi group. The Jews left open an escape route through which more than 200 residents fled unharmed.[37] Lehi members evacuated another 40 old men, women and children on trucks to a base in Sheikh Bader and then on to eastern Jerusalem. Another source says 70 women and children were removed and turned over to the British.

After the remaining Arabs, including Palestinians and foreign fighters, Iraqi soldiers among them, feigned surrender, then opened fire, a battle ensued that lasted more than four hours. Irgun casualties were four dead, 37 wounded. After the "massacre," the Irgun escorted a Red Cross representative through the village and held a press conference. *The New York Times*' description of the fighting essentially paralleled Begin's, also noting "paradoxically, the Jews say about 250 out of 400 village inhabitants [were killed], while Arab survivors say only 110 out of 1,000."[38] A study by Palestinian researchers at Bir Zeit University, based on discussions with members of each family from Deir Yassin, put the figures at 107 Arab civilians dead, 12 wounded, in addition to 13 fighters killed.[39] Other Arab sources later suggested the number may have been even lower. *The Times*, citing an Irgun source, said about half the Arab dead were women and children. Some women had become targets

---

36 "Ethnic cleansing of Jews in pre-state Israel," *The Jerusalem Post*, Aug. 16, 2007.

37 *History of Israel's War of Independence*. Vol. IV, Uri Milstein, page 262, Lanham: University Press of America, 1999.

38 *Genesis 1948*, Dan Kurzman, page 141, OH: New American Library, Inc., 1970.

39 "Dayr Yassin," Bir Zeit University Research and Documentation Center report, 1987.

because several male Arab fighters had tried to disguise themselves as females.

Ayish Zeidan, an eyewitness to the fighting, was quoted as saying:

> The Arab radio talked of women being killed and raped, but this was not true. … I believe that most of those who were killed were among the fighters and the women and children who helped the fighters. The Arab leaders committed a big mistake. By exaggerating the atrocities they thought they would encourage people to fight back harder. Instead, they created panic and people ran away.[40]

Despite the network's chronic anti-Israeli coverage, a British Broadcasting Corp. series, *Israel and the Arabs: The 50 Year Conflict*, reported that "Hazem Nusseibeh, an editor of the Palestine Broadcasting Service's Arab news in 1948, describes an encounter at the Jaffa Gate of Jerusalem's Old City with Deir Yassin survivors and Palestinian leaders, including Hussein Khalidi, the secretary of the Arab Higher Committee.

> 'I asked Dr. Khalidi how we should cover the story,' recalled Nusseibeh, now living in Amman. 'He said, "We must make the most of this." So we wrote a press release stating that at Deir Yassin children were murdered, pregnant women were raped. All sorts of atrocities.'

> A Deir Yassin survivor identified as Abu Mahmud said the villagers protested at the time. 'We said, "There was no rape."' 'Khalidi said, "We have to say this, so the Arab armies will come to liberate Palestine from the Jews"[41]

Whatever the number, Jewish forces killed Arab civilians in Deir Yassin. The Jewish Agency, soon to become the provisional government of Israel and dominant over the small Irgun and Lehi opposition groups, voiced "horror and disgust" about the attack and expressed disapproval in a letter to King Abdullah of Transjordan.

Less than a week later, Arabs ambushed the Jewish convoy on the way to Hadassah Hospital in Jerusalem. Though the victims included the hospital director, doctors, nurses and patients, nearby British troops

40 *The Daily Telegraph* (U.K.), April 8, 1998.
41 *Jerusalem Report*, April 2, 1998.

did not intervene.

In the Palestinian narrative, the "Deir Yassin Massacre"—shorn of detail, sources and context—epitomizes Israel's 1948-1949 War of Independence. To determined anti-Zionists and gleeful antisemites, it encapsulates Israeli ethnic cleansing. To all who wish to reopen "the Jewish question," Deir Yassin's asserted proof of the Jewish state's inherent racism validates their desired solution. Meanwhile, the number of Metropolitan Opera Co. productions presenting Arab massacres of Jews, the number of artistic "conversations" in the United States, Israel or elsewhere about the recurrent, widespread ethnic cleansing of Middle Eastern minorities by Arabs and Muslims, remains essentially zero.

Antisemitism and anti-Zionism can powerfully deform art and artists, including Jews. In one conspicuous example, anti-Jewish hatred led Russian novelist Boris Pasternak to abandon the faith of his father, Leonid Pasternak, a noted Russian-Jewish painter who had visited Palestine. Reporting Pasternak's 1958 selection as Nobel Prize laureate in literature, the Jewish Telegraphic Agency noted:

"In *Doctor Zhivago*, Pasternak refers to antisemitism. He asks 'For what purpose are these innocent old men and women and children, all the subtle, kind, humane people, mocked and beaten up throughout the centuries?'

"But instead of rebuking the antisemites, Pasternak goes on to ask why the intellectual leaders of Jewry have not 'disbanded this army which keeps fighting and being massacred nobody knows what for.'

"It is concluded from this that Pasternak does not see a purpose in the sacrifice of Jews for survival and feels that Jewry should surrender to antisemitism and disappear. Pasternak's assertion that 'nobody knows' why Jews strive to survive is seen by many readers to reflect an attempt to repudiate Judaism and Jewish values."[42] Neither Pasternak nor JTA apparently examined to what extent, if any, their Judaism made those "subtle, kind, humane people" that way and whether those very traits were the cause of their being mocked and beaten through the centuries.

---

42 "Boris Pasternak's Dr. Zhivago seen as opposing Jewish survival," JTA, Oct. 30, 1958.

CHAPTER ELEVEN

Privileging Jihad as 'Social Justice'

ROM 1980 TO 2000, Israelis received 7,652 patents, compared with 367 for all Arab countries. "In 2008 alone, Israeli inventors applied to register 9,591 new patents. The equivalent figure for Iran was 50 and for all majority Muslim countries in the world [56 such states] 5,657."[1] The population of Iran in 2008 was 73 million; that of Israel, 7.3 million. With a population one-fortieth that of the United States, Israel nevertheless ranked with America as a world leader in high-technology. "To an extent that is truly remarkable for such a small country, Israel is at the cutting edge of scientific and technological innovation," Ferguson observed. "Israel has more scientists and engineers per capita than any other country and produces more scientific papers per capita."

Obsessive—and widespread—antisemitic, anti-Zionist hatred from generations of Muslim Arabs humiliated, enraged and envious of the example of a tiny Jewish state successfully establishing and defending itself and prospering against all odds may be understandable, at least analytically. That speck of a country—overall the size of New Jersey but in its most densely-populated corridor between Tel Aviv and Haifa rarely more than a dozen miles wide—vividly contradicts the Arabic saying "*Filastin arduna wa al Yahud al kelabna*" ("Palestine is our land and the Jews are our dogs"). Cooperation with it—Israel is the world leader in desalinization of sea water, Yemen is short of water, Iran running low—could imply Jewish equality, or even Arab-Islamic inferiority. So what happens when Israeli leaders have the temerity to offer—and insist on—a compromise peace among equals? In Arab societies and econ-

---

1 *Civilization: The West and the Rest*, by Niall Ferguson, 2011, pages 93-94.

omies that, without oil, have stagnated if not collapsed while renewed Islamic fundamentalism surges, what happens is that chronic hatred erupts as rage. Hence Palestinian Arab rejection of repeated "two-state solutions" in exchange for peace with Israel, followed by terrorist violence such as the second intifada.

Arafat said he had to refuse two-state proposals at Camp David in 2000 and Taba in 2001. He told U.S. mediators he would not risk the fate of Egypt's Anwar Sadat, assassinated in 1981 by members of an Egyptian al-Qaeda precursor in part for making peace with Israel. Likewise, Arafat's successor, Mahmoud Abbas, rejected Israeli Prime Minister Ehud Olmert's 2008 offer of a West Bank, Gaza Strip and eastern Jerusalem country in exchange for peace with Israel as a Jewish state. In 2014, as mentioned above, Abbas spurned U.S. Secretary of State John Kerry's proposed "framework" for resumption of negotiations with Israel. He did the same to Vice President Joseph Biden's 2016 initiative for renewed talks aimed at a "two-state solution." Yet such was the influence of the Palestinian narrative that news media, diplomats, politicians, academics and many in the general public—including in Israel—overwhelmingly blamed not Arafat or later Abbas and the Palestinian Authority but Israeli leaders, in particular Prime Minister Benjamin Netanyahu, and their "right-wing" coalitions.

But if the Arab/Muslim conflict with Israel has not been over the nature of a mutually satisfactory peace, not over land and therefore amenable to territorial compromise then Abba Eban was mistaken. His witticism that "the Arabs have never missed an opportunity to miss an opportunity," often cited as axiomatically explanatory, appears to have been ethnocentric and condescending. Israel's adversaries over decades repeatedly have insisted that their conflict is existential, about identity resting on regained "dignity" and "rights." That is, it is about superiority over the Jews and possession of all of what was British Mandatory Palestine and an end thereby to the continued "humiliation" manifested by Israel's existence.

U.S. Secretary of State Colin Powell observed, "The problem is the same problem that has been there for the three years that I have been working this account. And that is terrorism, terrorism that still emanates from Hamas, Palestinian Islamic Jihad, and other organizations that are not interested in peace, not interested in a state for the Palestinian people. They're interested in the destruction of Israel."[2] Not only Hamas and Islamic Jihad on the Islamic fundamentalist side but also the

2 Voice of America News, Oct. 29, 2009.

"more secular" Fatah, repeatedly rejecting two-state peace offers because its over-arching goal was erasing Israel as a Jewish state. Fatah is the dominant movement in the Palestinian Authority, and the PA's school curriculum, for example, incessantly indoctrinates pupils that "Jerusalem is Arab and that Palestine—from north to south, from the [Jordan] River to the [Mediterranean] Sea—is Islamic Palestinian Arab, and will remain so in spite of the damned occupier."[3] And not only during Gen. Powell's 2001 – 2005 tenure as secretary of state did Palestinian officials attempt to delegitimize Zionism and Israel and demonize Jews, but they have done so at least since the British made Haj Amin al-Husseini grand mufti of Jerusalem in the 1920s.

Since that has been the case, then what an educated, articulate, secular Westerner like Eban imagined were opportunities to make peace and open the way to regional prosperity were traps to his assumed interlocutors. If entered they would not only acknowledge Israeli legitimacy and equality but also confirm Arab-Islamic humiliation and subjugation by the lowliest of the low, by their dogs, the Jews.

With each Palestinian rejection, pressure from "the international community" mounted on Israel for more concessions. A more consistent example of political, diplomatic and psychological goal-post moving to its advantage by the "losing" side would be hard to find. And after each realignment, Israel—like hapless Charlie Brown in the "Peanuts" cartoon strip—would be not just invited but more or less compelled by foreign governments—playing the role of the cartoon Lucy—again to try to kick the football of peace that Palestinian leaders would pull away at the last second. All others concerned would thereby send Charlie/Israel to yet another pratfall.

It did not matter that in no instance—not in 2000, 2001, 2008, 2014 or 2016—did the Palestinian side offer a counter to U.S. and Israeli peace proposals. Its intransigence extended an earlier generation's rejection of British partition recommendations in the 1930s, the U.N.'s 1947 partition plan and 1967's "three no's" of Khartoum to Israel's sweeping post-Six-Day War withdrawal offer. The rejectionism was born partly out of leaders' fear of personal retaliation had they "betrayed" the Palestinian cause by making a compromise peace. The fate not only of Egypt's Sadat stood before them. So did that of Jordan's King Abdullah

3 Issa Salman, head of the Jerusalem branch of the General Union of Palestinian Teachers, on official Palestinian Authority TV, Nov 15, 2014 cited in *Palestinian Authority Education: A Recipe for Hate and Terror*, by Itamar Marcus, Nan Jacques Zilberdik and Alona Burger, Palestinian Media Watch, 2015.

I, gunned down outside Jerusalem's al-Aqsa mosque in 1951, in front of his son, the future King Hussein, by a Palestinian Arab incited by rumors of covert talks between Abdullah and the Zionists.

But concern with individual survival was not the only obstacle. Palestinian rejectionism stemmed too from the irredentist nature of the Palestinian cause. Palestinian Arab nationalism has been an almost entirely negative phenomenon. It rests on denial of Jewish nationalism, of Zionism as the Jewish people's modern national liberation movement, on denial of the Jews as equals rather than embodying its own positive, Palestinian Arab state-building impulse. So criticizing Palestinian rejection of a two-state solution, or exposing the boycott, divestment and sanctions (BDS) movement's opposition to a two-state peace, as pro-Israel advocates are wont to do, amounts to a kind of denial itself. Many Israelis, many friends of Israel, many advocates of Arab-Israeli peace persist in a sort of bedrock refusal: They do not acknowledge that beneath the surface clash between fact and fancy lies the other party's deepest, most sincere motivation—at a minimum Jewish resubjugation; at maximum, destruction.

The *"Filastin arduna wa al Yahud al kelabna"* chant accompanied Arab pogroms against Palestinian Jews in the 1920s. Resurrected, it was heard on the streets of San Francisco, Chicago and New York in 2006 at demonstrations against Israel's war with Iranian-backed Hezbollah in Lebanon that summer. Demonstration organizers included International ANSWER and the Council on American Islamic Relations (CAIR). The former is a coalition of old and new hard-left movements, the latter a spin-off of the Muslim Brotherhood. Not that audiences for major American news media would know, given virtually uncritical coverage of CAIR's periodic alarms over rampant "Islamophobia" that federal bias crime reports rarely substantiate. Mentioning the council's status as an unindicted co-conspirator in a major U.S. terrorism funding trial was a virtual taboo for the U.S. press.[4]

Such leftist-Islamist cooperation like that evinced by ANSWER and CAIR reflected, among other things, a diverse, multi-cultural hostility to the Judeo-Christian tradition underlying Western civic culture. This hostility, not uncommon among the college educated, calls to mind the observation often attributed to Orwell that "there are some ideas so absurd only an intellectual could believe them."

---

4 "Special Report—CAIR: Civil Rights or Extremism?" by Meredith Braverman and Eric Rozenman, Committee for Accuracy in Middle East Reporting in America, monograph, second edition, June 2009.

Such was the belief, if not by left-leaning intellectuals, then by many politicians, that the Sept. 11, 2001 attacks by Osama bin Laden's al-Qaeda "changed everything." If so, then only briefly. One change confirmed how many things remained the same: The resurrection of antisemitism, sometimes wearing the fig-leaf of anti-Zionism but frequently naked to those who would see.

The United States has been uniquely hospitable to Jews—it was George Washington who as president promised the Jews of Newport, Rhode Island that the new republic would provide an example of enlarged liberty for all mankind not by merely tolerating minorities. Instead, "happily, the government of the United States, which gives to bigotry no sanction, to persecution no assistance, requires only that they who live under its protection, should demean themselves as good citizens."

Of course, not every American then or in subsequent generations was a good citizen, let alone a Washington. The story of formal and informal antisemitism, including restrictive quotas at Ivy League colleges and "no Jews allowed" signs at hotels and resorts well into the 20th century has been told many times. Today's often violent hostility to Israel and pro-Israel students, faculty and outside speakers is a reiteration, another regression to the mean reflected through the distorting fun-house mirror of reactionary progressivism. Some hatreds are long a-dying. And others, the hardiest of perennials, never do.

But after World War II, after the Holocaust, after Vatican II and the Roman Catholic Church's recognition and abjuration of its own antisemitism, such attitudes appeared to Jewish baby boomers as vestigial, marginal. They appeared to many of their children as ancient history. Especially in the immediate aftermath of Israel's stunning victory in the 1967 war, American Jews—in Israel's reflected glory—seemed not only tolerated but popular, even desirable. As Irving Kristol observed, partially in jest, the problem for Jews was not that non-Jews still wanted to kill them, rather, they wanted to marry them, which created its own problems. Ironically, assimilation in Western diasporas and Israel's growing economic and military strength made the interconnected concepts of Jewish peoplehood and Israel as a refuge as well as a revival appear at last to have been transcended if not simply rendered obsolete.

Yet this golden era of Jewish acceptance and integration, in which Jewish baby boomers went from their 20s to their 40s, began to unravel as early as 1982, as reflected in distorted news media coverage of Israel's war against the Palestine Liberation Organization in Lebanon. If

NBC Television's veteran news correspondent and commentator John Chancellor could compare the Israeli army's encirclement of Yasser Arafat and 10,000 PLO gunmen in Beirut to the Nazis' 1943 siege of the Warsaw ghetto, then the glow was off the 1967 miracle. In December, 1987 pictures of gas mask-wearing, rifle-toting Israeli troops chasing rock-throwing Palestinian Arab youngsters appeared at the start of the first intifada (1987 – 1992). Even though the rock-throwers would soon be augmented by gunmen using them as human shields, the early images further dimmed the Six-Day revelation and its light as reflected onto Diaspora Jewry

Yet for Jews, particularly American Jews and foremost among them committed supporters of the Jewish state, recognition of their changed environment dawned slowly. The academically influential Middle East Studies Association had been a sort of Kremlin of Palestinianism for a generation by the time Jewish organizations, their leaders and major donors publicly acknowledged the threat of anti-Zionist professors and anti-Israeli (even antisemitic) university networks in the 21st century. These include groups such as Students for Justice in Palestine and Jewish Voice for Peace, which proselytized incessantly for the BDS campaign. (Its name notwithstanding, Jewish Voice for Peace's hard-core anti-Zionism consistently flirted with antisemitism. For example, as ADL noted in 2010, JVP approvingly cited Edward Said's simultaneously hyperbolic and obscene equation of the Palestinian Arab *nakba* with the Holocaust, as if that were anything other than a debater's trick to diminish the Holocaust's scope and dilute its Jewish content in favor of Palestinian appropriation, a secular blasphemy.)

The children and grandchildren of such Jewish community leaders and donors, often offspring of one Jewish, one non-Jewish parent and indoctrinated since childhood in multiculturalist theory simultaneously made possible by, yet hostile to Western culture, frequently lacked a sense of American nationalism. They were taught to believe extirpation of the Indians, black slavery and late acceptance of women's rights invalidated the exceptionalism of a continental nation embodying an ever-growing reality of *e pluribus unum*, widespread equality and unprecedented prosperity, not to mention its successful defense of democracy in three world wars—I, II and the Cold War.

So indoctrinated, they could easily confuse cultural Balkanization with diversity of origin. They would disdain the American patriotism that had made possible the lifestyles they took for granted. In such circumstances, then, they could hardly value Jewish national identity.

Members of such a generation, like many in those that immediately preceded them, typically imagined that early Jewish values of social justice were somehow of themselves a natural and independent default position and so could endure non- or supra-Jewishly. Their parents tacitly denied, and they themselves forgot the necessity of a nation of priests shining an ethical light whose source was quite particular but whose glow was universal. Or perhaps they imaged that the universal originated outside the particular in imitation of a divine, asexual conception. Thus rootless, a sort of *pareve*—neither meat nor milk—social justice ethic supposedly superseded its Jewish core.

The "Social Justice" Pitfall

But what Jews of minimal Jewish education or active Jewish participation—the majority—thought *tikkun olam*, perfecting the world, meant and what the Prophet Zechariah originally envisioned were two different things. Until the 1960s, the Episcopal Church was sometimes caricatured as the Republican Party at prayer. In parallel, critics at times denigrated Reform Judaism as the Democratic Party platform with Jewish holidays. Well before the 21st century and the unintentionally self-parodying description of "social justice warrior," the misidentification of *tikkun olam* and Torah-based social justice imperatives with post-liberal left ideological desiderata afflicted the Conservative as well as Reform and Reconstructionist streams of American Judaism. Hence their retranslations and condensations of the traditional, and central, *Aleynu* prayer said three times daily. The original, non-decaffeinated version declares, among other things:

"We therefore hope in Thee, O Lord our God, that we may soon behold the glory of Thy might, when Thou will remove the abominations from the earth and when all idolatry will be abolished. We hope for the day when the world will be perfected under the Kingdom of the Almighty [*al-ken nekaveh lekha . . . le-taken olam be-malkhut Shaddai*] and all mankind will call upon Thy name. . . ." The Sages stressed that "abominations" referred to non-monotheistic pagan practices including child sacrifice. Later Talmudic and mystical Jewish interpretations emphasized *tikkun olam's* more quotidian, particularly Jewish applications. Again, not that numerous Jews who invoke the phrase today recognize the origins or interpretations.[5]

In any case, Jewish social justice warriors had it wrong. *Tikkun*

---

5 "How to Repair the World: Jewish tradition offers three different conceptions of

olam did not rest on efforts to extend day care, raise the minimum wage, build homes for the poor a la Habitat for Humanity or replace "apartheid Israel" with a Palestinian utopia. It meant preparing the way for the Messiah and the Kingdom of God on Earth—the original utopian ideal—by means of ever-expanding observance of *mitzvot*, the 613 divinely-given commandments. Such observance perforce would include fair wages for laborers and charity for the needy, mentioned in the Torah and detailed in the Talmud—but within a traditional Jewish context, not as a redefinition and substitute for it.

Halkin was not the only one attempting to deflate the distorted *tikkun olam* bubble. Rabbi Aaron Starr declared it was "Time to Say Kaddish for Tikkun Olam."[6] *Kaddish* is the Jewish prayer of mourning. In Starr's view, "Synagogue affiliation continues to drop. Jewish ritual practice weakens with every passing year. Parents are far too often choosing for their children to attend soccer and gymnastics over Hebrew school and youth group. Even Israel—that one topic which used to unite the Jewish people—even Israel has become a lightning rod that divides, rather than unites us. Frankly, without a major course correction, the future for non-Orthodox Jews in America appears in jeopardy."[7]

According to Starr, a Conservative rabbi in Southfield, Michigan outside Detroit, it's not that Diaspora Jewry has refused to confront its communal unraveling: "In response to the decline in Jewish life here in America, we have tried to reinvent religious schools and day schools. We have gone through revolutions in prayer styles and published new prayer books. We are ever trying to improve synagogue practices, becoming more welcoming communities and more caring congregations. Yet, somehow, the decline of Conservative and Reform Judaism continues." Of course one faces a crisis in "continuity" if one can't or won't say what one intends to continue, theologically and ideologically, and why one's peculiar particularity matters.

Non-Jews shared the lack of clarity among many Jews about the nature of the late 20th and early 21st century social-cultural environment. Distortion of *tikkun olam*, contortion of social justice and confusion about "Islamophobia" clouded thought and obstructed action. Post-9/11 Western unity and resolve in the face of an enemy that mur-

---

tikkun olam; today's buzz phrase is compatible with none of them," by Hillel Halkin, *Commentary*, July 2008.
6 "Time to Say Kaddish for Tikkun Olam," Rabbi Aaron Starr, *Times of Israel*, Oct. 5, 2016.
7 Ibid.

dered nearly 3,000 people in America in a single day faded quickly. It did so in no small measure because President George W. Bush, like his successor Barack H. Obama, refused to identify the enemy. The adversary was not, as claimed, terrorism, a technique, but rather Islamic triumphalism, a belief system. The latter is a religious-political ideology that comes to America (as to the world) in the words of Omar Ahwad, a co-founder of the Council on American Islamic Relations, "not to make Islam equal with Christianity [and Judaism] but superior, the world's one true religion."[8] The formulation "the world's one true religion," like the phantom of the world's one master race or universal dictatorship of the proletariat before it, means trouble for individuals—Jews and non-Jews—everywhere, including non-triumphalist Muslims.

CAIR, often misdescribed by news media as a Muslim American civil rights group, derives as mentioned from the Muslim Brotherhood and its Palestinian affiliate, the U.S.-designated terrorist organization Hamas. What CAIR's Ahwad echoed of the Brotherhood's call to a supremacist sort of Sunni Islam, Ayatollah Ruhollah Khomeini, founder of Iran's revolutionary Islamic Republic, proclaimed for Shi'ite Islam. Clifford May, a former *New York Times* correspondent and president of the Foundation for Defense of Democracies think tank, has written that Khomeini, a childhood listener to Haj Amin al-Husseini's World War II broadcasts, was "committed to waging *jihad* [holy war] until … 'the writ of Islam is obeyed in every country in the world.'"[9] Bush's declaration of a "war against terrorism" after 9/11 instead of against Islamic supremacism was as misguided as a proclamation by President Franklin D. Roosevelt after Dec. 7, 1941 against sneak attacks instead of Japanese imperialism would have been.

Even if only a relatively small proportion of the world's 1.5 billion Muslims subscribe to Islamic extremism—estimates run as high as 15 percent—then it attracts tens of millions if not one hundred million or more adherents. And though most of them might not act violently towards those they identify as unbelievers if not the enemy, more than a few might support co-religionists who do. These adherents, however fragmented their movements, nevertheless comprise the most dynamic and deadly streams in contemporary Islam. The chronic "honor killings" of women accused of compromising family honor by adopting Western styles and social behaviors, let alone by engaging in non-mari-

---

8 "CAIR: Civil Rights or Extremism?" Braverman and Rozenman, 2009.

9 The search for elusive Iranian moderates; They won't be found among the ruling clerical elite," by Clifford May, *The Washington Times*, Mar. 9, 2016.

tal sex; lynchings—especially in Pakistan—of alleged anti-Islamic "blasphemers"; and of course massacres in London, Madrid, Paris, Baghdad, Kabul, Istanbul, Brussels, Nice, Jerusalem, San Bernardino and Orlando among numerous other places highlight the ideology's vigor. So far its adherents rarely have been opposed effectively by a Muslim Arab "silent majority." The defeat of the Islamic State in Iraq and Syria, for example, depended heavily on U.S. and other Western support and coordination and non-Arab Kurdish fighters, although many Iraqi and Syrian Arabs also fought in the struggle.

The Iranian slogans "Death to Israel!" and "Death to America!" and depictions of the former as "little Satan" and the latter as "great Satan" proclaim and encapsulate an apocalyptic world-view. They have infiltrated Sunni Islam from Shi'ite Tehran, though Saudi Arabian-based Wahhabi Islam prepared the ground. These slogans amount to strategic goals and motivation. In the extreme, or perhaps more pertinent, essential Shi'ite and Sunni ideology there was no place for Jews as a sovereign majority in their own land, no place beyond imposed return to their pre-Enlightenment status as stateless legal and cultural inferiors, existing perpetually at sufferance, vulnerable and popularly derided.

That is also the proper status of Christians. Like Jews, they are "people of the book" and therefore to be protected as *dhimmis*—pre-Islamic monotheists. Protected, that is, from the Muslim majority among whom they live, so long as they pay the *jizyah* poll tax, know their place and keep to their secondary rank. (For introductory reading on this subject, see *The Dhimmi; Jews and Christians Under Islam*, by Bat Ye'or, Farleigh Dickinson University Press, 1985.)

One dangerous weakness of President Obama's foreign policy was its denial of the existence of a Siamese-twinned—Sunni and Shi'ite—global *jihad*. This holy war is dedicated first to imposing a medieval caliphate on the Middle East—an intention dismissed by many Western intellectuals and policy makers and barely comprehended by the public. Dismissed, that is, until made undeniable by al-Qaeda's Sept. 11, 2001 attacks and then the promotional beheading videos produced by the Islamic State in Iraq and Syria. From decapitations in the desert to undermining and ultimately overthrowing the "Crusader" West, that is the path and goal. It would have been clarified for Americans in the 2009 Holy Land Foundation for Relief and Development federal retrial in which five men were convicted of raising and laundering $12 million for Hamas. The FBI introduced into evidence a 1991 document known as "An Explanatory Memorandum: On the General Strategic Goal for the Group in North America." Would have been clarified, that is, had major American news media chosen to analyze and report on the memorandum.

Regardless of that journalistic failure, "the group in North America" was the Muslim Brotherhood and its general goal was "a kind of grand jihad in eliminating and destroying the Western civilization from within and 'sabotaging' its miserable house by their hands and the hands of the believers so that it is eliminated and God's religion is made victorious over all other religions." The Holy Land Foundation trial was that in which CAIR was listed as an unindicted co-conspirator, in which the co-founder of CAIR's Texas chapter received a 65-year prison sentence.

The Explanatory Memorandum was in keeping with Muslim Brotherhood founder Hassan al-Banna's worldview. Al-Banna was a leading promoter of Palestinian Arab nationalism's founding father, Haj Amin al-Husseini—even after and especially because of al-Husseini's World War II collaboration with the Nazis. In 1946, "in a secret bulletin intercepted by [U.S.] OSS agents in Cairo, Al-Banna said of Husseini, 'What a hero, what a miracle of a man. Yes, this hero who challenged an empire [the British] and fought Zionism, with the help of Hitler and Germany. Germany and Hitler are gone, but Amin Al-Husseini will continue the struggle."[10] And after al-Husseini, Arafat; after Arafat, his disciples.

Even before Islamist leader Mohammed Morsi became Egypt's president in 2012, after the Arab spring ouster of Hosni Mubarak, Prof. Jeffrey Herf noted that Brotherhood leaders "have declared their eagerness to foster cooperation with Christians." The chronically oppressed Coptic Christians, descendants of pre-Islamic Egyptians and targets of repeated massacres by al-Qaeda and Islamic State-inspired and affiliated terrorists, comprise at least 10 percent of Egypt's population. "Yet no leading Brotherhood figure has come close to addressing the hostility toward Jews that has long been central to the organization's identity. ... In 1950, Sayyid Qutb, who would go on to become the Brotherhood's chief ideologue, published an influential essay entitled 'Our Struggle with the Jews.' Qutb, like Husseini, placed his Jew-hatred on the foundations of the religious traditions of Islam. The Jews, he wrote, engaged in 'evil-doing' and 'consequently Allah sent against them others of his servants, until the modern period. Then Allah brought Hitler to rule over them. And once again today, the Jews have returned to evil-doing in the form of 'Israel,' which made the Arabs, the owners of the Land,

10 "Scapegoat," by Jeffrey Herf, *The New Republic,* May 12, 2011.

taste of sorrow and woe."[11]

After Egypt's President Nasser had Qutb executed, "the Brotherhood celebrated Qutb as a heroic martyr," Herf observed. Defeating ISIS, the Islamic State in Iraq and Syria, the Taliban in Afghanistan or any other similar jihadist group hardly would change the Islamist-inspired path or goal. It would force tactical and strategic mutations by supporters, as seen when ISIS's Iraqi and Syrian "caliphate" was crushed in 2016-2017, but its members or backers staged terrorist assaults in North Africa, Europe and North America. Defeating jihadism will require defeating the ideology that drives it.

Al-Banna explained, as Prof. Joseph S. Spoerl highlighted, "[T]he Noble Qur'an appoints the Muslims as guardians over humanity in its minority, and grants them the right of suzerainty and dominion over the world in order to carry out this sublime commission. Hence it is our concern, not that of the West, and it pertains to Islamic civilization, not to materialistic civilization."[12] This is Huntington's clash of civilizations.

"[I]t is our duty," al-Banna went on, "to establish sovereignty over the world and to guide all of humanity to the sound precepts of Islam and to its teachings, without which mankind cannot attain happiness."[13]

Spoerl, professor of philosophy at Saint Anselm College, noted that "the founding of the Muslim Brotherhood in 1928 is often explained as a reaction against Western imperialism. This is certainly true. However, one searches in vain in al-Banna's writings for any principled critique of imperialism *per se*. What al-Banna criticizes is non-Muslim, especially Western, imperialism. For Islamic imperialism al-Banna has only the most effusive praise. Imperialism to impose Islamic rule on non-Muslims is altogether to the good. Al-Banna is fully aware that Islam was born not only as a religion but also as an imperialistic ideology mandating the conquest of non-Muslims. The first Islamic conquerors, he writes, 'produced the maximal justice and mercy reported historically of any of the nations.'"[14]

Al-Banna's self-vindicating reading of history was mirage-like. It dismissed the material bounty and spiritual liberty possible under Western democratic-capitalism compared to other political-economic systems. He was threatened by the success of such infidel societies, his "ma-

---

11 Ibid.

12 "The World-View of Hassan al-Banna and the Muslim Brotherhood," by Joseph S. Spoerl, *New English Review,* online, December, 2012.

13 Ibid.

14 Ibid.

terialistic civilizations" to which tens of millions of Muslims immigrated to escape impoverished and stultifying constraints of their own homelands. So al-Banna's musings may sound antique in the digital age. But such denigration would be mistaken; his thoughts remain as immediate as airport body scans and stadium bag checks and the reason for them.

Quoting al-Banna's translator, Charles Wendell, Spoerl adds, "'First of all, it is important to state that by no stretch of the imagination can the movement [the Muslim Brotherhood] be regarded as a more-or-less deviant type of offshoot from Islam like Baha'i, the Ahmadiyya, or American Black Islam [Elijah Mohammad and Louis Farrakhan's Nation of Islam]. In most respects it was if anything ultra-orthodox, and... it had respectable intellectual roots. ... Hassan al-Banna's fundamental conviction that Islam does not accept, or even tolerate, a separation of 'church' and state, or of either from society, is as thoroughly Islamic as it can be.' In other words, the world view of Hassan al-Banna is simply the world view of classical Sunni Islam."[15]

But surely things have changed since 1928? Not so much, not yet. Into the second decade of the 21st century, Western leaders persisted in describing Turkey's former prime minister and later President Recep Tayyip Erdogan as not just an interlocutor but a member, however difficult at times, of their club. At least, they did so until his virtually country-wide suppression of political dissent following an attempted coup in 2016. Erdogan's "purification" of coup plotters and supporters resulted in the arrests of a reported 47,000 people and the dismissal of more than 100,000 from government, academic and other posts.

Erdogan, the leader of a NATO nation, was almost always photographed wearing a suit and tie, and beardless. He looked like other NATO leaders. But he did not sound like they did. Early in his tenure as prime minister, Erdogan commented on the distinction drawn between radical and moderate Islam: "Islam is Islam—there are no modifiers. Democracy is the train we ride to achieve our ultimate objective, which is to make Islam the dominant religion throughout the world."

Again citing Wendell, Hassan al-Banna's translator, Spoerl returns to the general anti-Western threat of what is dryly called "Islamism" or political Islam, distinguished—to the extent possible—from emphatically religious but non-ideological Islam. This recalls us to the lie of Palestine. Spoerl says that in examining Sunni Muslim fundamentalism, "as Wendell puts it, Jews and Christians 'might aspire to nothing higher than a kind of second-class citizenship' under the restoration of clas-

---

15 Ibid.

sical Islamic law envisioned by al-Banna. … [T]o al-Banna's orthodox Muslim mind, 'Nothing could be more hateful than further diminution of the lands traditionally dominated by Islam. I believe that much of the fury and unconcealed hatred of the Zionist state [Israel], which is expressed by the majority of Arabs, will become more comprehensible in light of what *the Islamic domain* [emphasis added] as a concept really meant to the Muslim, seen through the lens of Hassan's exposition.

"'Indeed, implacable opposition to the Zionist project in Palestine was a central preoccupation of al-Banna and the Muslim Brotherhood, and this remains true of the Brotherhood and its Palestinian branch, Hamas, to the present day. The Hamas 'Covenant'—its statement of foundational principles—features a quotation from Hassan al-Banna: 'Israel will exist, and will continue to exist, until Islam abolishes it, as it abolished that which was before it.'"[16] That which was before it refers to the Crusader kingdoms of Jerusalem and Byzantine rule of the Holy Land. It's not only Jewish communities in the disputed West Bank (Judea and Samaria) Hamas opposes, or some fictional Jewish/Arab "apartheid" regime in Israel. It is the possibility—demographic, political, or religious—of a Jewish state in any borders on any land once ruled by Muslims, even if that very land previously was ruled by Jews. In other words, al-Banna's triumphal confiscations closely parallel Soviet leader Leonid Brezhnev's dictum about once-communist ruled territory never yielding to non-communist rule (no matter how communists came by it). Totalitarians echo totalitarianism.

Following al-Banna and Hamas, scholars at Egypt's al-Ahzar University, Sunni Islam's preeminent such institution, were in the late 20th century still debating who lost Andalusia—Spain—500 years earlier. Early in the 21st century, al-Qaeda and other such religio-political sects looked forward to recapturing it. Regardless of the ISIS caliphate's defeat, Spain's social-cultural accommodation to its growing Muslim population continued.

The Muslim Brotherhood did not represent a fringe movement, either before or after the Sept. 11, 2001 terror attacks in New York City and Washington, D.C. Asserting that "most Egyptians are devout, traditional Sunni Muslims," Spoerl notes that "[a]ccording to the Pew Research Center [in a 2011 survey], 85 percent of Egyptian Muslims consider Islamic influence over political life to be a positive thing for their country. Fifty-four percent of Egyptian Muslims support making gender segregation in the workplace the law in Egypt; 82 percent favor

---

16 Ibid.

stoning people who commit adultery; 77 percent support amputation of hands for theft and robbery; and 84 percent favor the death penalty for people who leave the Islamic religion. Seventy-five percent of Egyptians have a favorable opinion of the Muslim Brotherhood. ... A majority of Egyptians (54 percent) say the 1979 peace treaty with Israel should be annulled; only 36 percent say the treaty should be retained."[17]

The Glue of Antisemitism

Given generations of pervasive anti-Israel indoctrination and decades of official "cold peace/cold war" hostility to the 1979 Egyptian-Israeli peace treaty, 36 percent support might be taken as positive, something to build on. This could have been the case even before Egypt's one-year experiment with Brotherhood rule under the increasingly anti-democratic administration of President Mohammed Morsi. Gen. Abdel Fattah el-Sisi overthrew Morsi, the first elected leader in Egypt's 4,000-plus year recorded history, in 2013. Egyptian-Israeli security cooperation intensified as Cairo battled Hamas-supported Islamic State affiliates in the Sinai Peninsula. Nevertheless, 39 years after Anwar as-Sadat and Menachem Begin signed the Egyptian-Israeli peace treaty in 1979, Egyptian tourists could stroll Tel Aviv's beachfront promenade unmolested, on the rare occasions they chose to visit (and risk shunning or worse on their returns home), but not so Jewish Israelis openly attempting to shop in Cairo's bazaars.

Summarizes Spoerl: "The conclusion we must draw is that the rise of the Muslim Brotherhood in Egypt is not a fluke or a mere reflection of disgust with the [former President Hosni] Mubarak regime. It also represents the deep attachment of most Egyptian Muslims to traditional Sunni Islam. In the words of Samer Shehata, a professor of Arab politics at Georgetown University, 'The Brotherhood is the Egyptian Kansas.' Their positions 'reflect rather than oppose what the Egyptian center is thinking.' Wherever one finds conservative, traditional Sunni Muslims, one can expect to find sympathy for the world-view of Hassan al-Banna and the Muslim Brotherhood."[18] And even during the brief "Arab spring" of 2011, the one thing that united Egyptians across the political spectrum from religious reactionaries to many secular liberals, according to journalist James Kirchick, was antisemitism.[19]

---

17 Ibid.
18 Ibid.
19 "Egyptian Liberals Against the Revolution," by James Kirchick, *The American Inter-*

In the early days of "the Arab spring," which in Syria, Yemen, Libya, Egypt and elsewhere became Arab and international catastrophes, perhaps the chief, if not only, glue binding many Arab liberal democrats and Islamic fundamentalists in their rejection of the old order of relatively secular Arab dictatorships was antisemitism. Unsaid was the function of Jew-hatred as cement in Arab orders old and new. The Jewish News Syndicate reported that "prominent Egyptian historian Maged Farag drew headlines when he called for his country to normalize relations with Israel and to ditch support for the Palestinian cause, which he said has caused "nothing but harm" for Egypt.[20] "According to a report by the Middle East Media Research Institute (MEMRI), which translated Farag's appearance on Egypt's Mehwar TV, Farag called on his fellow countrymen to leave 'the old ideology and cultural heritage on which we were raised'—referring to the rampant antisemitism among the Egyptian population—and to embrace Israel out of national interests. Does Farag's statement represent a new realization among Egyptians against the backdrop of new threats, or does rampant societal antisemitism and anti-Zionism still constitute a barrier to normalizing ties with Israel?

"'Anti-Semitism is extremely widespread in Egypt, to say the least,' Samuel Tadros, a senior fellow at [Washington, D.C.-based] Hudson Institute think tank's Center for Religious Freedom, told www.JNS.org. 'It is probably the only ideological component that all Egyptian factions agree on, whether you are Islamist, secular or even those that the West describes as liberals and democrats.'"[21]

In 2007, a Pew Research Center poll of more than 1,000 Muslims living in the United States found "13 percent of all U.S. Muslims felt suicide attacks [against civilians] could be justified often, sometimes or rarely" to "defend Islam." Seventy-eight percent "completely rejected the deadly tactic that has been used by al Qaeda and other militants." But "26 percent of younger Muslims" believed such violence could be justified at times.[22]

Obama, suffering "Islamism denial," refused to recognize in such Sunni groups like Hamas, al-Qaeda and ISIS—plus the Islamic Republic of Iran on the Shi'ite side—committed opponents in the politico-religious equivalent of World War IV (identifying the 44-year Cold War

est, Dec. 22, 2011.

20 "Israel and Egypt grow closer, but antisemitism remains part of the equation," Jewish News Syndicate, June 8, 2015.

21 Ibid.

22 "Poll finds some U.S. Muslim support for suicide attacks," Reuters, May 22, 2007.

as, functionally, World War III). His refusal, like Bush's, enabled their spread. Not long after the president claimed credit for degrading and fragmenting the al-Qaeda of Osama bin Laden, and called the Islamic State terrorism's "junior varsity" team, al-Qaeda's bigger, bloodier off-shoot conquered territory in Iraq and Syria larger than that of Great Britain and proclaimed a caliphate. Al-Qaeda or ISIS affiliates metastasized in Yemen, Libya, Mali and elsewhere. Boko Haram (the name means "Western education is forbidden") continued slaughtering tens of thousands of Christians in Nigeria and neighboring states—to muted reaction by many Western Christians, let alone secularists—and Islamist terrorists struck targets around the world.

Secretary of State John F. Kerry declared, on Sept. 3, 2014, in response to the videotaped beheading by the Islamic State in Iraq and Syria of a Jewish reporter, that "the real face of Islam is not what we saw yesterday, when the world bore witness again to the unfathomable brutality of ISIL [Islamic State in the Levant, an Obama administration-favored acronym for ISIS or the Islamic State] terrorist murderers, when we saw Steven Sotloff, an American journalist who left home in Florida in order to tell the story of brave people in the Middle East—we saw him brutally taken from us in an act of medieval savagery by a coward hiding behind a mask....

"The real face of Islam is a peaceful religion based on the dignity of all human beings. ..."

One didn't know whether to laugh or cry. Such assertions, unconsciously but thoroughly ethnocentric and condescending, came routinely from police chiefs to presidents (few apparently knowledgeable about Islamic theology or Islamist ideology) after each new outrage. In truth, these terrorist attacks were one real face of Islam. One real, fundamentalist face among others—and, as Kerry spoke, the most assertive of them. Whether they represented a demographic minority or not, those who committed them were major actors in an Islam at war internally and externally, in a process of self-definition in the contemporary world. This definition would not to be determined by non-Muslims like Kerry, Obama, Bush, then-British Prime Minister David Cameron, the pope or access-seeking academics and mirror-imaging Western clergy. To pretend otherwise, as a number of commentators pointed out, was to minimize the threat and inhibit assistance to the Islamic triumphalists' rivals within Islam.

The rulers of Iran's Islamic Republic, courted by the Obama administration, signed the Joint Comprehensive Plan of Action with the

United States, United Kingdom, France, Germany, Russia and China in 2015. They also reiterated threats to resume the Holocaust, starting by destroying Israel. The JCPOA was said to temporarily restrict Iran's nuclear weapons programs. Nevertheless, Iranian leaders violated sanctions by testing ballistic missiles, whose primary purpose is to carry nuclear weapons. Of one such test, in March 2016, some news media reported that an Iranian missile carried the slogan "Israel must be destroyed" in Hebrew. Photographs shown on Iranian television and released by Iran confirmed the ballistic inscription. Yet initial reports by major Western news outlets including Cable News Network (CNN) and *The Washington Post* told their audiences such alleged markings could not be verified. Such hesitancy and outright refusal to call things by their proper names are elements in the psychological petri dish in which the lie of Palestine festers. They recall Paul Berman's "moral peculiarity" of refusing to think of "the largest crimes." Such refusal is not new.

In 1942, Jan Karski, a courier from the anti-Nazi Polish underground, met with Western leaders including Lord Selbourne (in charge of covert sabotage in Nazi-occupied Europe) in London and Supreme Court Justice Felix Frankfurter and President Franklin D. Roosevelt in Washington, D.C. He told them of the horrors he'd witnessed on two covert trips into the Warsaw Ghetto and of the Jewish leaders' warnings that Hitler intended to murder all the Jews of Europe. Selbourne did not believe him, Frankfurter could not believe him, and though Roosevelt asked him many questions, they were not about Jews. So Karski went public. His 1944 book, *The Story of a Secret State* was a commercial and critical success. Its message was then quickly forgotten.

Why? University of Massachusetts Prof. David S. Wyman, author of the 1984 best-seller *The Abandonment of the Jews, America and the Holocaust, 1941 – 1945*, "found widespread indifference and hostility to the Jews in Europe, even as their systematic extermination was conclusively documented. He faulted religious organizations, Jewish and non-Jewish; mainstream newspapers and movies; and the anti-Jewish feelings of the public. The federal government was slow to act, enforcing strict immigration quotas and refusing to bomb the concentration camps. It waited until well after the Holocaust had begun to establish a War Refugee Board, then forced the agency to rely mostly on private funding." Wyman charged that "Roosevelt was more concerned about angering antisemites than about helping the Jews."[23]

Hence Gide, as noted at the outset: "Everything that needs to be

23 "David S. Wyman, 89: Writer of 'Abandonment of the Jews,'" by Hillel Italie, Associ-

said has already been said. But since no one was listening, everything must be said again."

Well-documented but little assimilated is the fact the Nazis exported their murderous anti-Jewish incitement to the Arab world as part of the Axis' war effort against the Allies. The Third Reich aimed in particular at the British and French who had colonized or attempted to colonize or otherwise control parts of the Middle East. That such propaganda influenced Arab and Muslim leaders then and later has been shown by Mattias Kuntzel in *Jihad and Jew-Hatred; Islamism, Nazism and the Making of 9/11*, 2007, Herf in *Nazi Propaganda for the Arab World*, 2009, Richard L. Rubenstein, *Jihad and Genocide*, 2010, and Rubin and Schwanitz in *Nazis, Islamists and the Making of the Modern Middle East*, 2014 among others. Herf highlighted the combination of extreme Nazi antisemitism with that of collaborationist Arab nationalists and Islamists, especially from 1941 to 1945 in Berlin. With the admiration and promotion of leaders such as al-Husseini and al-Banna after World War II, this radicalized Jew-hatred continued in the post-war Middle East. Nazism and Islamism have much in common, including mass mobilization of society to the detriment of individuals and human rights, intolerance of minorities, the leader principle and aggressive expansionism. From genocide to *jihad* and *jihad* back to genocide is not far. It is, for example, the route Iran travels in arming Hezbollah and dominating Lebanon, arming Shi'ite militia and maintaining Iran's Islamic Revolutionary Guard in Syria and proclaiming Israel's pending "eradication" while Western countries send trade missions to Tehran.

The Jewish Question, Again

Jews, let alone well-intended non-Jews, have difficulty responding to declarations of "Death to the Jews!" of which "Israel must be destroyed!" is the leading contemporary variant. Perhaps in some cases, like those of Orwell's decent people, they simply cannot comprehend such human viciousness. And maybe in other cases they do not wish to comprehend, since doing so would lead to recognizing a danger that must be confronted. Or perhaps for those merely agnostic about the Jews if not downright tired of hearing about them, it would lead to recognizing a potential outcome one might not seek actively or even consciously acknowledge but would not resist forcefully nor, as time passed, much regret.

ated Press, in *The Washington Post*, March 18, 2018.

The cataclysm al-Qaeda wrought on Sept. 11, 2001 intensified a change already underway. Essayist Jonathan Rosen recognized that the terrorists' success confirmed the reopening of "the Jewish question." It did so by means of a facile answer to the anguished "why do they hate us so much?" self-flagellating query: Because we support Israel.

The question "what must we do with the Jews?" had been urgent previously. Asked, that is, before the Jews got their state. Nineteenth and early 20th century European intellectuals and nationalists raised it recurrently during and after the Napoleonic emancipation of Jews from their ghettos and inferior legal status. Could this stiff-necked people that dwells apart, these Jews, really be assimilated, integrated or trusted? Wasn't it in their nature—as Adams and Goodman's Palestinian terrorists would sing in *Klinghoffer*—to exploit, pollute, subvert and dominate? Antisemitism of the "genteel" sort not uncommon among the British upper classes or the more blatant, "populist" type popular in turn-of-the-century Vienna thrived.

Eventually, Adolf Hitler and Nazi Germany offered not just an answer but *the* answer. Hitler referred specifically to "the Jewish problem" and its "solution" in his oft-cited, ominously revealing speech to the Reichstag on Jan. 30, 1939:

> In the course of my life I have often been a prophet, and have usually been ridiculed for it. During the time of my struggle for power it was in the first instance the Jewish race which only received my prophecies with laughter when I said that I would one day take over the leadership of the State, and with it that of the whole nation, and that I would then among many other things settle the Jewish problem. Their laughter was uproarious, but I think that for some time now they have been laughing on the other side of their face. Today I will once more be a prophet: If the international Jewish financiers in and outside Europe should succeed in plunging the nations once more into a world war, then the result will not be the Bolshevization of the earth, and thus the victory of Jewry, but the annihilation of the Jewish race in Europe!

Why "international Jewish financiers" should seek global impoverishment through "the Bolshevization of the earth"—one of Nazi antisemitism's essential oxymorons—went unexplained. Hitler and the Nazis' nearly total mobilization of German culture, society and economy for war—a war of expansion eastward to provide "living space" for their racially superior people at the expense of inferiors, a war to the death against the phantasmagoric "anti-Aryans," the Jewish-Bolshevik-British world conspiracy—had been underway since shortly after their assumption of power in 1933. The Jew had morphed from anti-Christ to anti-German, anti-volk, just as two generations later he would transform to racist Zionist, anti-Palestinian. The Nazis' aggressive madness was so blatant as to be generally ignored or even denied.

"The Final Solution," in which much of Europe collaborated, actively or passively, was meant to answer the Jewish question or, more bluntly, Hitler's—and much of the West's—"Jewish problem." Aggressive racism, with its hierarchy from superior "Aryan" descending through inferior Slav and Arab, lower still to black African and finally reaching its nadir with the intolerable Jew, was central to the Third Reich's ideology. Its role as primary motivation for World War II cannot be overstated. "At the center of the Nazi vision of protracted war was the 'historic life struggle of the peoples,' which required that 'living space' be secured for the German race. This was neither just a matter of Hitler's ranting in *Mein Kampf* nor some vague metaphor for Nazi war aims; it was a central preoccupation of the Nazi leadership. Germany was overpopulated, could not support a large and growing population within its existing borders, and needed to capture land for agricultural settlement in order to secure the future of the 'race.' That land was to be found in the east, in the Slav territories that stretched out beyond Poland and were in the grip of the supposedly Jewish-dominated Soviet Union."[24]

Nevertheless, as historian Richard Bessel continues, journalists and politicians at the time and scholars subsequently often minimized this compulsion. They emphasized instead more "tangible" explanations including German political and economic turmoil after World War I, resentment at the terms of the Versailles Treaty and the mythical "stab-in-the-back" explanation for Germany's defeat. So, unfashionable truth-tellers like Winston Churchill during Nazism's rise in the 1930s typically were marginalized as reactionary. So too today those who spotlight the genocide-*jihad*-genocide connection and reinforcing anti-Zionist antisemitic feedback loop, who recognize in cries of "Death to the Great Satan!" and "Death to the Little Satan!" "Death to America!" and "Death to Israel!" not only ranting and vague metaphor but also exhortation and policy.

Rutgers' Bronner has written, "antisemitism is the stupid answer

---

24 *Nazism and War*, by Richard Bessel, Orion, 2004, page 57.

to a serious question: How does history happen behind our backs?"[25] Answered stupidly, as it often is, with conspiracy theories at the heart of which operate scheming Jews—or in the case of the Palestinian narrative, scheming Zionists—the question-answer becomes an echo chamber justifying marginalization, subjugation or elimination of the Jewish people. Since the objective was, and for virulent antisemites remains, "the annihilation of the Jewish race," no explanation of Hitler's conflated oxymoron of warlike international Jewish financiers, Bolshevism and world Jewry as aided by Great Britain (and later the United States, both Anglo-Protestant democracies somehow Jewishly-controlled) was necessary. In fact, for antisemitic true believers it wasn't an oxymoron at all but rather a holistic assertion of demonic Jewish manipulation above and beyond ordinary history. So Hitler ordered widespread distribution of *The Protocols* outside Germany in November, 1939 to explain the outbreak of World War II.

And yet, *The Protocols*, this queen of conspiracy theories—covert Jewish control of that which matters—had some real roots. They were sunk ironically in a successful effort by Jews to protect themselves against false conspiracy charges.

In 1839, the Ottoman Turks invaded their nominally subject province of Egypt to quash Mehmet Ali's independence movement. Ali counterattacked through the Holy Land, and his army would leave behind Egyptian settlers who became the ancestors of many of today's Palestinian Arabs. In the midst of the crisis, with British politicians concerned about French penetration of Ottoman lands, leaders of the Damascus Jewish community were convicted of ritual murder—"on the basis of evidence supplied by the French consul. Liberal public opinion in Britain—already excited over slavery—was outraged by the treatment of the Jews, and prominent anti-slavery campaigners such as Sir Thomas Fowell Buxton and the Irish parliamentary leader Daniel O'Connell took up their cause."[26]

"Financially and morally supported by the wealthy [Jewish] diaspora in France and Britain, activists began to target governments and organizations which pursued openly anti-Jewish policies. Thus Moses Montefiore and the Frenchman Adolphe Cremieux went to Alexandria and Constantinople to demand the release of the accused, while

---

25 *A Rumor about the Jews: Anti-Semitism, Conspiracy and the Protocols of Zion*, by Stephen Eric Bronner, Oxford University Press, copyright 2000, page 140.

26 *Europe; The Struggle for Supremacy, from 1453 to the Present*, by Brendan Simms, Basic Books, page 202.

the Rothschilds intervened on behalf of Jews threatened with expulsion from the Russian Pale of Settlement. ... Of course, the Jewish response also helped to create the very phenomenon which it was trying to combat," Prof. Brendan Simms writes. "'The Hebrew nationality is not dead,' the French Catholic newspaper *Univers* thundered in 1840. 'What religious connection is there between the Talmudists of Alsace, Cologne or the East, and Messrs. Rothschild and Cremieux?' It went on to speak of unity [that] binds Jews together, making them act as one man in all parts of the world [so that] by means of their money, they can, when it suits them, control almost the entire press in Europe.' This was the paradox of Jewish internationalism: it raised the cost of discrimination, but it also left Jews everywhere more vulnerable to paranoia and oppression."[27] The paradox of Israeli strength is similar.

At heart, antisemitism is not a Jewish problem but rather a mental illness that too many non-Jews project upon Jews. So paranoia on the part of Europe's peasantry and proletariat and reactionary rulers and Catholic clerics led 50 years later to *The Protocols* and their endlessly metastasizing, lethal conspiracy superstitions. Again, Simms:

"In 1894, Russia authorized a large increase in defense spending to match Germany. Anxieties about the security of the western border areas did not cause, but certainly aggravated, another round of antisemitic riots in 1893, especially in Kishinev. It was in France, however, that the domestic consensus came under greatest strain. As relations with Russia improved, those with the small Jewish community declined. In 1886, Edouard Drumont wrote *La France Juive* which called for the state to confront the Jews, who supposedly constituted a German fifth column. The recovery of Alsace-Lorraine soon gained widespread acceptance not only on the right, but also among many radicals and socialists as well."[28] In 1894 came the Dreyfus case, in which French Army Capt. Alfred Dreyfus, an Alsatian Jew, was wrongly convicted of leaking military secrets to Germany.

In reaction, two years later, Herzl published *Der Judenstaat*, calling for the Jews' own state. European Jewish bankers, including "the Rothschilds, Bismarck's confidant Gerson Bleichroeder" and others already had begun to refuse loans to the czar to protest Russian pogroms, deportations of Jews from Moscow and St. Petersburg and other discriminatory measures. Yet, "the more effectively Jews rallied in their own defense, however, the more antisemites became convinced that they were

---

27 Ibid. pages 206-207.
28 Ibid. page 263.

facing an international conspiracy; these fears soon found expression in the forged *Protocols of the Elders of Zion*, published in 1903 at the instigation of the czarist secret police, which purported to show a Zionist plot to control the world."[29] The most effective demon is damned if he does, damned if he doesn't.

Repeated laments at Holocaust commemorations, including by survivors, and by organizations established originally to fight antisemitism, like the Anti-Defamation League, that Jews have been targeted "only for being Jewish," as if that were somehow a mistake, or an obviously insufficient motivation, miss the point: Jews were and are targeted exactly because they are Jews. Israel is targeted by the *Protocols*-like fictitious Palestinian narrative exactly because it is the Jewish state. Given Judaism's insistence on ethical monotheism, given Jews' repeated and radically disproportionate successes and influence, given Israel's unique accomplishments, nothing more is needed. The dangers from Jews *per se* and the Jewish state incarnate are both individual and mass, immediate and eternal. The point is micro and macro. It's Mark Twain's observation that it would not do well to free this race to recognize its abilities, but absent Twain's humor.

So too now with Israel targeted because it is Israel, the Jewish state. The Israel problem, the Zionist problem, the Jewish problem requires a solution to satisfy the aggressive religious supremacy central to the jihadism of both Sunni and Shi'a Muslim crusaders. It frequently goes discounted when not denied by news media, diplomats, non-Muslim clergy and academics—especially when aimed at Jews and the Jewish state. Holocaust and genocide scholar Prof. Richard L. Rubenstein, among others, makes the connection from the Nazis' Jewish problem to that of Islamists in *Jihad and Genocide*. The work examines genocidal threats from Muslim-led governments, movements, theorists and mobs against non-Muslim minorities from the Armenians a century ago to Israelis today. Yet regarding this threat, too, the main response has been, when not denial, no meaningful response at all. An example in miniature:

In 2016, just outside Washington, D.C., the Annandale, Va. Little River United Methodist Church erected a banner, complete with stylized crucifix, on its property adjacent to a major thoroughfare. The banner—standing two years later—read, "Say no to anti-Muslim bigotry!" But it wasn't anti-Muslim bigotry that had blasted the Pentagon a few miles away or brought down the World Trade Center. It wasn't anti-Muslim

29 Ibid. page 264.

bigotry that in the proceeding five years set the Middle East and North Africa aflame, killing hundreds of thousands of people, mostly Muslims, and intensifying the pre-existing extirpation of ancient Christian communities from their places of origin in the region. It wasn't anti-Muslim bigotry that threatened the Jews of Israel with genocide. Anti-Muslim bigotry hardly was sweeping northern Virginia. In fact, the church stands across Va. Rt. 236 from Northern Virginia Community College, which welcomes countless Muslim students from dozens of countries, and only a couple miles from the Annandale basement in which the Muslim Brotherhood's "Explanatory Memorandum"—to be introduced as evidence in the Holy Land Foundation terrorism trial—was discovered, along with boxes of other related documents.

So why didn't the church banner read "Just say no to bigotry!"? Because doing so would have required thought, discrimination between common interests and "intersectionality," and meaningful action. It would have meant recognizing anti-Christian (and anti-Jewish) bigotry prevalent among more than a few Muslims. That is, it would have required intellectual and moral integrity as opposed to what was primarily a psychological exercise in demonstrative self-affirmation.

~

Many in occupied Europe and more than a few in the Arab Middle East joined in "the Final Solution." Through complementary inaction Great Britain and the United States also contributed to the Holocaust's extent. By deflecting the Jewish refugee issue, as at the 1938 Evian Conference, by not bombing rail lines to the concentration camps, by waiting until most European Jews had been killed before warning Axis leaders they would be held accountable, the Allies gave not formal approval but tacit acquiescence.

Seven months before Germany invaded Poland—before Auschwitz, Treblinka, Bergen-Belsen and the rest of the archipelago of slaughter arose—but after the first concentration camps for Jews and other political prisoners, after the first gas chambers for mentally and physically handicapped and otherwise "undesirable" Germans began operating, Hitler in that January 1939 speech mocked Western democracies. He indicted them for not taking the "infectious, parasitical" Jews off his hands:

In connection with the Jewish question I have this to say: It is a shameful spectacle to see how the whole democratic world is oozing sympathy for the poor, tormented Jewish people, but remains hard-hearted and obdurate when it comes to helping them which is surely, in view of its attitude, an obvious duty.

Acceptance and assimilation then of the Jews, or as refugees any more Jews—persons simultaneously imputed to be inferior and subversive, weak and controlling—came to be seen as difficult or impossible for non-Jewish majorities. In some quarters it was suspect as potentially suicidal, culturally if not physically, for countries that might receive more than a few Jewish refugees.

Arabs in the Middle East, including Palestinian Arabs and their leadership, collaborated in the Holocaust. This fact, of which acknowledgement, not to mention punishment and restitution, has yet to be made, is generally ignored. When asserted, it is denied by adherents of the Palestine lie. But by their riots and massacres of Palestinian Jews in the 1920s and '30s, Palestinian Arabs—subsidized at times by fascist Italy and Nazi Germany—induced the British, in control of the League of Nations' Palestine Mandate, essentially to ban further Jewish immigration. By their often illegal, often ignored migration into the parts of Mandatory Palestine developed by the Jews in those same years, they enlarged the Arab majority. By their numbers they contributed to colonial administrators' belief that the mandate's "carrying capacity" was being reached. (The area now, largely as developed by Israel, supports many times that population and materially in a much more bountiful manner.) For that reason too (an imagined population glut), Jewish immigration had to be severely limited. In a sense this amounted to pre-emptive displacement of what would have been Mandatory Palestine's Jewish majority. It turns out the issue wasn't, and isn't, so much "Israeli ethnic cleansing" and "Jewish occupied Arab land" as Arab occupied Jewish land, not an Arab *nakba* but a Jewish one based in part on de facto ethnic cleansing.

In any case, Jews—the ultimate threat—had to go. They could not be protected in Europe, where their ancestors had lived for nearly two millennia since being expelled from Judea by the Romans. They would not be granted refuge in significant numbers in other countries. And they would be forbidden from emigrating to British Mandatory Palestine, which had been created not on the ruins of any Arab or Muslim "Palestine" but on a fragment of the defeated Ottoman Turkish Empire by the victorious World War I Allies. The League of Nations had confirmed Britain in administration of the Palestine Mandate primarily to permit re-establishment of a Jewish national home. But on the eve of the Holocaust the Jews were left to those who would obliterate them. Such was the "world community's" adherence to international law; such was its humanitarian concern.

What halted the Final Solution after the destruction of half of European Jewry was not revulsion against the Holocaust, powerful though that reaction was among many on the side of the victorious Allies. Liberation of the death camps, incidental to the war's prosecution, stopped the genocide. At least temporarily.

Gen. Dwight D. Eisenhower, supreme commander of Allied forces in Europe, famously cabled Gen. George Marshall, overall U.S. military chief of staff, the following after touring the liberated Ohrdruf concentration camp with Gens. George Patton and Omar Bradley on Apr. 12, 1945:

> [T]he most interesting—although horrible—sight that I encountered during the trip was a visit to a German internment camp near Gotha. The things I saw beggar description. While I was touring the camp I encountered three men who had been inmates and by one ruse or another had made their escape. I interviewed them through an interpreter. The visual evidence and the verbal testimony of starvation, cruelty and bestiality were so overpowering as to leave me a bit sick. In one room, where they were piled up twenty or thirty naked men, killed by starvation, George Patton would not even enter. He said that he would get sick if he did so. I made the visit deliberately, in order to be in a position to give first-hand evidence of these things if ever, in the future, there develops a tendency to charge these allegations merely to 'propaganda.'[30]

According to biographer Michael Korda, Eisenhower remarked after leaving Ohrdruf-Nord "that he 'never at any other time experienced an equal sense of shock.' Over 4,000 prisoners had just been murdered there by the SS guards" before they fled as the Americans approached. "…[B]odies still lay scattered in grotesque heaps. The surviving prison-

30 *Ike: An American Hero*, HarperCollins, 2007; page 574 (HarperCollins paperback, 2008).

ers were emaciated skeletons. Ike was shown the whipping block, the gallows, the ditches crammed with half-naked, decomposing bodies. There were no gas chambers or crematoriums—Ohrdruf-Nord was not a 'death camp' as such, or even one of the major concentrations camps. It was merely one of the thousands of similar 'forced labor' camps large and small in the vast SS concentration camp empire," Korda writes. "But it was enough of a taste of the horrors of Nazi Germany" to cause Eisenhower to urge London and Washington to send immediately a group of newspaper editors to Germany "so that evidence of Nazi atrocities could be 'placed before the British and American publics in a fashion that would leave no room for cynical doubt.'"[31]

Contrary to the implication, though not necessarily the explicit message of ceremonies bringing together aged World War II camp liberators and survivors—including annually in the U.S. Capitol Rotunda—defeat of Nazi Germany, not any effort to rescue Jews, stopped the Holocaust. Almost by accident concentration camp gates were opened and remaining prisoners saved. But soon after, the "tendency to charge these allegations [of mass murder] merely to 'propaganda'" that Eisenhower warned of did emerge. It did so openly in Arab lands of the Middle East and across the Soviet empire, often inspired directly by *Mein Kampf* and *The Protocols of the Learned Elders of Zion*. It did so as well in the West, if at first mostly on the margins.

So though mass murder of Jews stopped, conceptually the Holocaust did not end. Rather, it was interrupted. Its motivation was suppressed, not eliminated. That it did not resume, at least in part, with the destruction of the reborn state of Israel in 1948, in 1967 or 1973 seems due almost as much to miracle as to Israeli determination and inter-Arab cross-purposes. Contrary to the Palestinian narrative's portrayal of Israel as a strategic Western imposition on an Arab-Islamic Middle East, repeatedly—during the 1948-'49 War of Independence, 1967 Six-Day War and at the start of 1973's Yom Kippur War—the Jews and/or their state again were abandoned, or largely so at least temporarily, in the face of long odds.

Today the goal of the demonization of Israel is, for purists, genocide's completion. Hence the functional position of Iranian leaders bent on nuclear weapons: "The Holocaust never happened, and we intend to finish it." For the more expedient, it is the return of the Jews to their proper, pre-Emancipation status as an oppressible if not actually oppressed minority, one that may enjoy certain privileges but not rights,

---

31 Ibid. page 574.

not equality. The Jews, deprived of the Jewish state, are to be returned virtually if not physically to the ghetto and their pre-Napoleonic position—the perpetual "Other," the eternally wandering, rootless and definitely non-sovereign Jew. The cosmic order was rent by the absolutely ahistorical return of an indigenous people to its ancient land, speaking its revived "dead" mother tongue and ruling itself. This people was the properly subservient, if not despised, Jews no less. Restoring cosmic order means Israel now, like Carthage then, must be destroyed.

Revisionism, 'Justice' and the Narrative

After 1945, the Jewish question—temporarily discredited by the gory excess of the Nazi answer—went largely unasked in the West, though this was not the case in Stalin's Soviet Union, its eastern European satellites or post-colonial Arab-Islamic countries. Still, for nearly two generations this query and the antisemitism it expressed remained disreputable in democracies. In them, when World War II veterans or their families—even if not themselves philosemitic—heard antisemites speak, many heard people who sounded like Nazis, like their recent enemy.

Generational turn-over inevitably undermined this interim social-cultural inoculation against doubt, suspicion and hostility about and toward Jews. Its revival waited only a powerful pretext. That pretext would be "the Palestinian narrative." Palestinian revisionism superseded Holocaust revisionism (when it was not outright denial). It thereby became the next link in a long chain. From the classical Christ-killer indictment, medieval blood libels and well-poisoning charges, to late nineteenth century "scientific antisemitism," turn-of-the-century Protocols with its Jewish plots to subvert nations and twentieth century myths of Jewish racial inferiority, the bonds of antisemitism now have been refreshed and extended by the Palestinian narrative.

Palestinian revisionism, nourished by post-modernism's intellectual and moral relativism, its impatience with facts, proportion and context—that is, its impatience with knowledge over feelings—stimulates Holocaust minimization. This can be seen clearly in the Neverland inhabited by "social justice warriors."

Ever since Holocaust denial emerged, Jews and non-Jews have attacked it and its repackaged, sometimes modified variant, Holocaust revisionism. Deniers and revisionists included Palestine Liberation Organization chairman and Palestinian Authority President Mahmoud

Abbas and Iranian President Hassan Rouhani among others. On the far fringes of Western academic and social life such charges were made and repeated, from the late 1940s to the late 1980s, only to be exposed and discredited. Evidence—documentary, photographic, eye-witness, often from Nazis and collaborators themselves—overwhelmed deniers and revisionists. In one celebrated case, historian Deborah Lipstadt successfully defended herself against libel claims by denier David Irving. The affair, recounted in Lipstadt's 1993 book, *History on Trial; My Day in Court with a Holocaust Denier*, contained enough drama to be rendered as a Hollywood movie, *Denial*, in 2016.

But revisionists persisted, if not as open deniers of the Holocaust, of "the lie of the six million," then as advocates of "free inquiry," as minimizers, as if the nature and scope of the Shoah had not been thoroughly documented. The result, after two generations of insinuation, first by neo-Nazis and their apologists, eventually by identity politics progressives and "social justice warriors," allowed the Holocaust to be acknowledged but discounted as merely "white-on-white crime" or, via the astrology of post-colonial studies, misappropriated by a recently minted Palestinian people allegedly subjected to Nazi-like genocide by Israeli Zionists. The perennial nature of "anti-Jewishism," of "Judeo-phobia," bolstered by the defeat of intellectual rigor central to post-modernism, and generational turn-over all befriended and enabled revisionism.

On the denigration of the Holocaust as merely a white-versus-white matter, George Mason University law professor David E. Bernstein offered a tutorial. Commenting at the blog, *The Volokh Conspiracy*, hosted by *The Washington Post*, Bernstein discussed,

[A] Facebook post by a recent Oberlin [College] alumna, clearly a political progressive herself, recounting what she described as various antisemitic incidents she experienced at the school at the hands of the SJW [social justice warrior] left. I noted that I found most remarkable her assertion that multiple students had dismissively referred to the Holocaust as 'white-on-white crime,' as if the 'progressive' students there found it impossible to conceive of horrific racist violence outside the parameters of paradigmatic examples of racist violence in the United States. What's remarkable about the incidents recounted, which range from gross insensitivity to blatant antisemitism, is not that such attitudes exist, nor that they are necessarily serious compared with what other minority students may face at college, but that, if the Facebook post in question is true, some of the most purportedly progressive students, those who are the most acutely sensitive to and active against other forms of racism, ignore antisemitism, belittle it and, in some cases participate in it.

I found the entire Facebook post of great interest, not just as a troubling sign of emerging hostility to Jews and Jewish concerns among self-proclaimed social justice advocates on left-wing campuses, but as an equally troubling sign of the degradation of intellectual discourse at such campuses more generally, as reason, compassion and just plain old decent manners are replaced with shrill sloganeering based on which group can most successfully proclaim itself to be a victim. Nor is there any indication, despite the purported focus on multiculturalism, that the students who engage in these antics have received anything resembling a sound education in world history and cultures, or much of anything else, as everything is shoehorned into simplistic ideological categories that bear no apparent relation to context and reality.[32]

"Shrill sloganeering": Orwell's "streamlined men who think in slogans and talk with bullets." "Which group can most successfully proclaim itself to be a victim?" The Palestinian Arabs, repeatedly self-victimized from the 1920s on by their refusal to treat Palestinian Jews with the same dignity they demanded for themselves, by rejecting from the 1930s forward win-win opportunities between Arabs and Zionists, Muslims and Jews as equals. Unless, of course, "win-win" between Arabs and Zionists, Muslims and Jews is not an opportunity to be seized but rather vehemently resisted as continuing *al-nakba*.

In "reverse racism" (the same old racism with supremacist and suppressed exchanging roles) approved minorities—violating Frankl's paramount distinction between individuals who are decent and individuals who are not—can be only victims, not also perpetrators. Infantilized by assumed lack of choice, of agency, presumed pure by absence of responsibility, such minorities are romanticized as perpetually morally virginal. No matter how numerous or foul their crimes—including those committed against each other—they are perceived to operate un-

---

32 "The Holocaust as 'white on white crime' and other signs of intellectual decay," by David Bernstein, Feb. 5, 2016 *The Washington Post*, online.

der an anti-racist halo.

Intensifying the general collapse of the liberal arts, the oxygen-deprived anti-humanism of the humanities, is the fact that in any case, anti-Jewish racism is *sui generis*. Therefore, anti-Zionist antisemitism, new-old Jew hatred, can be certified as not really racism *per se*. That's because, you see, the Jews, the Zionists, bring it on themselves. Because the Jews must have committed a boundless felony to make the Nazis hate them and so many non-Nazis collaborate against them. If antisemitism is real, and not largely an exaggeration thrown up to justify Jewish special pleading, then it must have real causes, so the implication goes. Hence, the Jews are to be trapped once again in a perfectly closed circle, as they were in most places in the 1930s and early '40s. As they were before Israel's reestablishment in 1948, and as they are becoming once again with the intelligentsia's "privileging" of the Palestinian narrative.

❧

In Arab/Islamic societies—and beyond to the "truthers" of the West—a post-9/11 version of the mythological indictment of secret Jewish plotting emerged: Thousands of Jews/Israelis received a message to stay home from New York's World Trade Center and thus were spared death by Islamic terrorism on Sept. 11, 2001. Candidate Donald Trump's claim during the campaign for the 2016 Republican Party presidential nomination that thousands of Muslims in New Jersey cheered the World Trade Center's collapse on Sept. 11, 2001 met derision. But in much of the Arab-Islamic world and in the fever swamps of the post-liberal left and neo-fascist right those thousands of Israeli-Jews, AWOL from the World Trade Center when al-Qaeda struck, were somehow real. They received a secret e-mail from the Elders, or its equivalent. Of course.

The ancient charge, continually recycled, periodically renewed, of Jewish conceit and cunning is self-proving. To assert it is to confirm it. It stands impervious to evidence, as the 1934 Swiss trial demonstrated. In fact, evidence to the contrary validates the charge. Its very existence demonstrates conspiratorial Jewish cleverness. Information that otherwise would be exculpatory becomes proof of Jewish planning and manipulation. Man's deep-seated need to shift blame, to project, and especially onto Jews, overrides contrary information. This need ever animates the undying, all-purpose tautology of Jew-hatred.

But why is the hatred needed? Russian writer Maxim Gorky put it this way: "Whatever nonsense the antisemites may talk, they dislike the

Jew only because he is obviously better, more adroit, and more capable of work than they are."[33] Political scientist Charles Murray noted that the Jewish mean intelligence quotient is 110, 10 points over the norm. But, "Israelis of all races failed on average to outperform Americans in international tests of eighth-grade math and science skills" in 1999, ranking "just behind Thailand and Moldova" in math.[34] However, *what matters in human accomplishment is not the average performance but the treatment of exceptional performance and the cultivation of genius* [italics added]. The commanding lesson of Jewish accomplishment is that genius trumps everything else," Gilder asserted. He cited Murray for the claim that "the proportion of Jews with IQs of 140 or higher is somewhere around six times the proportion of everyone else. ... Since the 1880s, nearly half of all the world chess champions have been of Jewish heritage."

Even so, "exceptional intelligence is not enough to explain exceptional accomplishment. Qualities such as imagination, ambition, perseverance, and curiosity are decisive in separating the merely smart from the highly productive."[35]

That makes renewed antisemitism, whether disguised by anti-Zionism or plainly connected to older roots, a good fit in today's post-modern intellectual environment. Post-modernism comprises, as suggested above, attitudes increasingly subjective, dismissive of objectivity, impatient with empiricism, materialistically driven and digitally distracted. Above all, post-modern secular fundamentalism behaves—in non-technical fields—like a scavenger fouling its own nest. It is anti-Western, anti-capitalist, anti-American and anti-traditional. Therefore it cannot help being anti-Jewish, since a disproportionate number of Jewish individuals, if not Jews as a group, rise to the top in democratic-capitalist societies. Those afflicted by anti-Zionist antisemitism are, regardless of educational credentials, almost invariably hostile to democracy and capitalism, to social meritocracies. Hence their anti-intellectual hostility to reasoned debate, to the civil, knowledgeable examination of diverse ideas and their furious rejection of Israel.

So it did not, could not matter that many Jews died in the destruction of the World Trade Center and attack on the Pentagon in Washington, D.C. That could not be credited any more than could be the reality

33 *The Israel Test,* by George Gilder, Richard Vigilante Books, 2009, page 32.
34 Ibid, page 33.
35 "Jewish Genius: Jews are extravagantly over-represented in every field of intellectual accomplishment. Why?" by Charles Murray, *Commentary,* April 1, 2007.

that Europe's Black Death in the 14th century claimed many Jews as well as Christians. For those who accused Jews of conspiring with Satan to spread the plague, to poison the wells, the fact of Jewish deaths could not be allowed to register. Assertions of such fatalities must have been false, or at least greatly exaggerated. Similarly, the spectacularly successful terrorist attacks on Sept. 11, 2001 must have been an inside job. It stood to reason that a dozen and a-half partially trained young men, loyal to a religious fanatic hiding in wild Afghan borderlands, simply could not have simultaneously hijacked four U.S. airliners and used them to murder nearly 3,000 people. So devastating a plot must have been known in advance if not actually planned or executed by the FBI, the CIA, the Israeli Mossad, or all three in concert to blacken the reputation of Islam and gin up support for war in the Middle East. Just as President Franklin D. Roosevelt—sometimes disparaged as "Rosenfeld"—allegedly knew of Japanese plans to attack Pearl Harbor but did nothing, hoping to use the resultant national outrage against Japan to help justify war against Hitler's Germany on behalf of the Jews.

Conspiratorial, self-vindicating views like those regarding Jews and/or Israelis and the al-Qaeda attacks helped make explicable seemingly contradictory reactions including a) widespread assertions in Islamic states that no true Muslims could have committed such a crime as 9/11 and b) a surge in popularity of the name "Osama" (after al-Qaeda leader Osama bin Laden) for infant males. When it comes to the Jews and their state, conspiracy theories, no matter how self-refuting, always are in vogue.

Antisemites, anti-Zionists, don't only exaggerate. They deny, invert and invent. They do so "on a scale so immense"—mirroring Hitler's "big lie" technique as implemented by Goebbels—as to place their claims beyond refutation. Facts and logic in defense of the Jews revert to what they were before the Holocaust, irrelevancies. Their assertion becomes again, as Eisenhower feared, "mere propaganda." Especially when the Palestinian narrative suffocates factual assertion.

In the decades immediately after World War II, recognition of the breadth and depth of the Holocaust endangered the oldest bigotry: If the West—finally repelled by the consequences of Jew-hatred, if not by the animus itself—banished the annihilationist dream, then Jews might be accepted at last, tolerated if not always welcomed. Likewise a Jewish country. If the sign of the swastika and the pictures of the camps with their walking skeletons and cordwood-like stacks of corpses at liberation in 1945 permanently demonized Jew-hatred, then the curse of antisemitism might be lifted. If so, then after more than 2,000 years Jew-haters finally would have lost. The Jewish problem would have been solved, the Jewish question closed—to the Jews' advantage. The hatred imposed on Jews would finally wither away. In that case, the possibility the Holocaust could be resumed would have been foreclosed.

This ultimate liberation of Jews from Jew-hatred had to be prevented. Deniers and revisionists therefore fought to keep alive the Jewish question elsewhere, as it was in the Middle East. It had to be reopened, if only a crack, first in Europe and then in North America.

Given the evidence against them, which filled libraries and museums, and the personal experience of so many of the World War II generation, Western "neo-antisemites" made little headway until that generation began to pass from the scene in the 1980s and after. Only then could the fool's gold of the Palestinian narrative begin to supplant the Zionist triumph, restoring and gilding antisemitism in the process.

This process was underway visibly with the 1972 Munich Olympics massacre of Israeli athletes by Palestine Liberation Organization terrorists. The latter were transformed into desperate freedom fighters. Then followed in quick succession the 1973 Yom Kippur War—described by *TIME* magazine as Egypt's effort to regain dignity, PLO leader Yasser Arafat's 1974 speech to the U.N. General Assembly—"I have an olive branch in one hand, a freedom fighter's gun in the other"—and the assembly's subsequent 1975 passage of its Soviet- inspired, Arab League-adopted "Zionist-equals-racism" resolution. Israel's failure to win its 1982 war against the PLO in Lebanon accelerated the trend. By allowing Arafat and his gunmen to sail off under U.S.-endorsed, Vatican-approved international escort, Israel permitted Palestinian rejectionist nationalism, contingent as it was and is on the anti-Zionist psychological war, to fight another day.

As part of that war, the winning entry in a 1982 European contest for best editorial cartoon simply confiscated the famous Holocaust-era photograph of German soldiers rounding up Jews, one pointing a rifle at a Jewish boy wearing a cap, his hands up in surrender. Otherwise unchanged, in the update the cap became a *kefiyeh* and the soldier an Israeli. Viola, Palestinian Arabs as Jews, Israelis as Nazis. First place! Historical confiscation rebranded the Jewish David into the Israeli Goliath and the Arab-Islamic Goliath into the Palestinian David. Such rebranding, from the 1980s on, became a deceit so widespread it was celebrated by many academics and journalists as brutal honesty. Of such fraudulent orthodoxy, Orwell observed, "During times of universal deceit, telling the truth becomes a revolutionary act." The truth was that the cartoon and its "narrative" were false and counter-revolutionary.

CHAPTER TWELVE

Auto-de-Fé, The Sequel

F OR THOSE WHO BELIEVE, for those who hate—for those who believe their hatreds—Jews are always manipulative, always guilty, always evil. In the midst of the Holocaust, Joshua Trachtenberg penned *The Devil and the Jews; The Medieval Conception of the Jew and Its Relation to Modern Antisemitism.* After World War II and the Shoah, John-Paul Sartre wrote of the "satanization of the Jews." Though his postulate of the Jew as lacking a positive civilization and history of his own was at best highly uninformed, at worst itself antisemitic, in writing that if the Jew did not exist the antisemite would have to invent him, he recognized the process. And the process endures: Since Ayatollah Ruhollah Khomeini's Islamic revolutionaries seized power in Iran in 1979, Israel has been, as noted, "the little Satan," the United States "the great Satan." But Westerners with attenuated religious roots have difficulty understanding.

In 2017, a survey in the United Kingdom found non-believers outnumbering believers by the widest margin yet. Over Pope John Paul II's protest the European Union's 2000 constitution ignored Christianity, the religion that shaped the continent's cultural-political identities.[1] Europe's secular materialists imagine they can escape being condemned as satanic by Islamic fundamentalists if they condemn Israel as satanic. Spreading Islamism and repeated terrorist eruptions across the continent confirm their error.

Further, this satanization of Jews and of the West, as the mid-20th

---

1 "*Quo Vadis?* The Philosophical, Spiritual Flounder of Europe in 2017; Where Christianity and cultural identity are declining in tandem," by Garland Tucker, *National Review* online, Oct. 21, 2017.

century writings of Sayyid Qutb and other influential ideologists of Sunni Islamism indicate, is no figurative embellishment. It describes rather the aggressive enemies of Allah and his one true religion, Islam. The slaughter of such enemies therefore amounts to obligatory self-defense for believers. It parallels Nazi belief in a war to the death against its implacable opposite, the international Jew-capitalist-Bolshevik, aided by and manipulating Anglo-American forces.

Such demonization facilitates faith in the Palestinian narrative. As noted, this post-modern folk tale alleges that an old, indigenous Palestinian Arab people was ethnically cleansed from its land by a racist, colonialist, imperialist invasion of foreign Zionist Jews. If anything, the reverse occurred. In large numbers, Arab colonists attracted by Zionist redevelopment occupied land once long inhabited by Jews and newly redesignated for them. They violently prevented European Jews from escaping the Nazi-dominated continent. Other Arabs then caused nearly one million more Jews to flee ethnic cleansing in lands in which Jews had lived for centuries, in some places pre-dating the rise of Islam, lands that became independent countries in large part because of and whose boundaries were drawn by European imperialists. Close to three-quarters of those Middle Eastern Jewish refugees found haven in Israel.

All this is less denied than left unsaid, placed as it were under a taboo. A multi-generational campaign first made insisting on this history "difficult" and "controversial," later attempting to suppress it altogether. That the campaign's underlying Middle Eastern revisionism and denial still reflect Palestinian-Arab-Islamic intolerance of Israel, of Jewish identity, equality and sovereign, was richly illustrated by a clenched fist tantrum PA President Mahmud Abbas threw on Jan. 14, 2018. Addressing the Palestinian Central Council, he returned to the anti-Zionist catechism, slandered Israel as a "colonialist project," implied European Jews chose the Holocaust over emigration to British Mandatory Palestine and claimed Israel's first prime minister, David Ben-Gurion, forced the large Iraqi and Yemeni Jewish communities to move to the Jewish state against their will. Denying the Jews' long history in *eretz Yisrael*, he slandered Israel as "a colonial project that has nothing to do with Judaism" but was imposed to protect European interests. This must explain British, French and other European obstruction of Jewish migration to and state-building in mandate lands from the 1920s through independence in 1948. Abbas' fulmination carried the roots of non-existent "ethnic cleansing" of Arabs and an imagined European desire for a Jewish Middle Eastern outpost backward from Herzl through Napoleon to

Oliver Cromwell, that well-known 17th century British Zionist.[2]

The compulsion to make of the Jews and their state what they are not is assisted by the conformism of the secular fundamentalist academy. It then is reflected via the anti-Zionist antisemitism of the Palestinian narrative. A personal example:

In 1983-1984, I worked as community relations director for the Columbus Jewish Federation. I had inherited a project to get the parents of a local woman listed at Israel's Yad Vashem Holocaust Memorial and Museum as among the "Righteous Gentiles." The designation recognized those non-Jews who had risked their own safety and potentially their own lives to hide or otherwise save Jews from the Nazis and their collaborators.

The woman was the Italian mother-in-law of a prominent local clergyman. My predecessor had advanced the necessary documentation to Jerusalem and essentially all that was required to complete the process was for the daughter in America to approve Yad Vashem's citation of her mother and father. A recognition ceremony in Israel and plaque at the museum would follow. At this point the daughter said no.

Why, I asked, incredulous.

"Because of what the Israelis have done in Lebanon," the minister told me. This was shortly after Israel's 1982 war against the Lebanon-based Palestine Liberation Organization. "My wife thinks they've behaved just as the [Italian] Fascists in World War II, just like the Nazis."

The obscene Israelis-as-Nazis analogy still had some shock value then and was animated by often superficial, sometimes inverted Western news coverage of the fighting in Lebanon. NBC's John Chancellor, with his Beirut-as-Warsaw Ghetto comparison, exemplified such journalistic failures. "That's false," I said. "I'd like to speak with her." I insisted that such a misapprehension was no reason her parents should be denied their rightful place among Yad Vashem's exclusive Righteous Gentiles. They would be recognized as leading members of Frankl's race of decent people.

Despite several requests, I never was permitted to talk with the minister's wife directly. Eventually I came to realize that though we'd played racquetball together at the Jewish Community Center and shared a pleasant lunch or two, the minister was not going to let me speak with his wife, that what he reported as her views on Israeli behavior were in fact his own. It dawned on me, too slowly, that what I'd taken as a pass-

---

2 "Palestinian Leader Sets Out His Thoughts on Zionism: Rewriting history, Abbas calls Israel a 'colonial project' unrelated to Judaism," *Times of Israel*, Jan. 15, 2018.

ing observation, that Zionism was becoming "controversial," was in fact his assertion that Jewish nationalism had been made insupportable. It was an early signpost that the Jews of Israel and their supporters were being neatly severed from their history, both recent and ancient. The Palestinian narrative's inversion, displacing Jews with Palestinian Arabs, making Israelis Nazis enabled the latter to claim the former's birthright and literal grounds of existence.

A Jew can be non- or anti-Zionist without being antisemitic. However, the anti-Zionism of "progressive" Jews like Judith Butler, University of California (Berkeley) philosopher and gender theorist, and Jacqueline Rose, British humanities professor, psychiatrist and feminist literary critic, recirculates antisemitic tropes under anti-Israeli cover. Butler, according to historian Robert Wistrich, "reconnects to the deterministic claim that the Israeli polity is bound to spiritually pervert Judaism." She repeatedly "invokes the false assertion that Israel *deliberately* [emphasis in the original] expelled as many as 700,000 Arabs in 1948. Like so many other 'progressive' Jewish anti-Zionists, she ignores the much larger number of Jews who were persecuted, expropriated, and expelled from Arab lands between 1948 and 1967. Such selective humanism, claiming to speak in the name of a universalistic Diaspora-oriented Judaism, can hardly claim to be 'ethical.'"[3]

As for Rose, Wistrich notes she "has trouble finding words sufficiently trenchant to render the diseased and *demonic* [emphasis added] nature of Zionism. She variously describes the movement as 'bloody,' 'defiled,' 'deadly,' 'cursed,' 'corrupt,' 'cruel,' 'blind,' 'fanatical' and responsible for the ruin of Judaism's moral heritage. ... Virtually no contemporary platitude or libels about the Jewish State are left unmentioned—including the implication that the Israeli army deliberately kills Palestinian children. An innocent reader would scarcely imagine that Israel is an open and thriving democracy surrounded by an imploding Arab world sunk in economic backwardness, mass illiteracy, savage tyranny, civil wars, and religious fanaticism. ... Naturally, this invective is accompanied by the obligatory equation between Zionism and German antisemitism."[4] And naturally, purportedly progressive Jewish intellectuals including Butler, Rose, Ilan Pappe, Noam Chomsky and Norman Finkelstein exhibit "warm feelings for such 'progressive' members of the global left as Hamas and Hezbollah—genocidal antisemitic organiza-

---

3 *Anti-Judaism, Antisemitism, and Delegitimizing Israel,* edited by Robert S. Wistrich, University of Nebraska Press, 2016, page 140.
4 Ibid. page 143.

tions with an Islamic coloring."[5]

A comparative few zealous Jews believe only the coming of the Messiah will herald the rebirth of a legitimate Jewish state. A rather larger number of attenuated Jews insist—against history and holy texts—that Jews are only a religious or—like the late, much honored, much taken with his own particular Jewishness, Philip Roth—even less sustainable, merely a cultural grouping.

But Jews for more than 3,000 years have been a people, "*b'nai Israel.*" The Hebrew phrase means children of Israel, Israel being the patriarch Jacob, literally "one who wrestled with God." Before they were the Jews, followers of a religion, they were the Israelites, a people with an unseen God, Creator of the Universe who, through his prophet Moses, would later reveal their religion to them and lead them back to their promised land. That made them the world's oldest nationality, and, with the Chinese, one of its two longest continuing, still historically significant people. But since the post-national or transnational Left imagines nation-states are obsolete at best, evil at worst, peoplehood—being a nation—constitutes a key indictment against the Jewish state, as Hannah Arendt and more extreme disciples like Butler, Rose et. al. would have it. In fact, the nation-state is the only viable protector yet arisen of individual citizen's rights. Only the United States can guarantee the rights of each American. Only France—not the European Union, not the United Nations—can do so when push comes to shove for the French, should the government in Paris deign to fulfill its responsibility. Likewise the Jewish state for sovereign Jews, people who mean to be free and equal and able to ensure that liberty and equality themselves, when necessary.

In 1960, about six million of the United States' 180 million people, or three percent, identified as Jews. In 2010, an estimated 5.5 million did so out of a total U.S. population of around 310 million, or nearly 1.8 percent. If not for an influx of several hundred thousand Israeli Jews and that many more from the former Soviet Union during those decades, the number would have been significantly smaller. Of the three main American Jewish streams, only the smallest, the most "hard core"—Orthodoxy—has been growing.

So too for Diaspora Jews everywhere. As this author has argued, Hitler lost World War II to the Allies, but he fared better in his struggle against the Jews.[6] In 1939 there were roughly 18 million Jews out

---

5 Ibid. pages 143-144.

6 "Where Are the Rest of Us?" by Eric Rozenman, *Midstream*, September-October, 2005.

of a total world population of about two billion people. At war's end in 1945, the Holocaust suspended, Jews comprised roughly 12 million of humanity's total, still about two billion since wartime births roughly offset the struggle's approximately 55 million deaths. By 2005 more than six billion people inhabited the Earth. According to conservative rates of growth those 12 million Jews from 1945 should have become at least 24 million, and perhaps as many as 36 million. Instead, they numbered an estimated 13-14 million.

Only in two countries had a Jewish population grown. One was Israel, by immigration and natural fertility, from 650,000 in 1947-1948, to roughly five million in 2005. The other, of all places, was Germany, its surviving Jewish population estimated at between 30,000 and 50,000 in 1945 increasing to more than 200,000. This was due largely to the arrival after 1990 of Jews from the former Soviet Union and from Israel itself.

To Ecclesiastes' observation that "of the making of books there is no end" one must concede likewise when it comes to wandering for many Jews. They behave as if almost afraid to sink roots deeply, even or perhaps especially in Israel, as A.B. Yehoshua suggested in *Israel: Between Right and Right* (Doubleday, 1981). Jews could have returned to *eretz Yisrael* in greater numbers than they did long before the state of Israel's establishment in 1948, Yehoshua asserted. They chose not to, not only because of physical difficulties and erratic Turkish rule, he said, but also because of anxiety, of reluctance to once again pick up the burden, as well as embrace the opportunity, of being a nation of priests and a light unto the nations on and from its own soil. Perhaps one reason for the persistence of the Israel question has been so many Jews' significant avoidance of their homeland.

In any case, minimal post-World War II population growth, not beginning to approach pre-Holocaust replacement, was the behavior of a people, in its diaspora majority, not certain it had a reason or desire to continue. It also is the behavior now of most Western European states, their predominant ethnic Italian, Spanish, French, German and English populations reproducing at less-than-replacement rates year after year. For American Jews, new synagogues and community centers in 15 or so U.S. urban/suburban locales did not cancel a contradiction: American Jewish leaders occasionally were given to quoting post-war Jewish philosopher Emil Fackenheim's "614th commandment" (added to the Sages' biblical 613): "No posthumous victories to Hitler." Quoting Fackenheim but—again excluding diaspora Orthodox and Israelis—not heeding him. Late marriages (or no marriages for more than a few), lower-than-replacement fertility rates, out-marriage, superficial Jewish education and ambivalence about or avoidance of attracting and converting non-Jews all pointed to a people undergoing a crisis of faith, in essence an identity crisis.

Jews might proclaim "Never again!" but their actions suggested they did not entirely believe it. The Nazis' destruction of much of the people in one generation left a lingering, often unspoken and sometimes unrecognized intimidated hesitancy in subsequent generations. That and Israel being perpetually under siege, bleeding an estimated 10 percent of its Jewish population back into *galut* made Fackenheim's admonition more honored in the breach. Diaspora communal leaders often earnestly discussed promotion of "Jewish continuity" at the end of the 20th century and beginning of the 21st, of "outreach" to inter-married couples. But they did so without specifying the purpose of such continuity and recruitment. This indicated the depth of the Holocaust's trauma and the weight of Israel's delegitimization.

Yet purpose and opportunity there were. To contribute to and experience Jewish national revival exemplified by the rebirth of Israel, to be "a nation of priests" in a West secularizing faster than its Judeo-Christian ethical base could sustain, the dual purpose and opportunity loomed large. But virtually no non-Orthodox Jewish voices in Diaspora said so publicly, and few among the Orthodox.

Lacking a "mission statement" or, if recognized, a commitment to carrying it out, many conflicted Jews, old and young, proved vulnerable to the lie of Palestine. It obstructed recognition of or desire to seize the opportunity of national rebirth. It provided an excuse not to take center stage in Jewish life and advance cultural, religious and national renewal and the dissemination of ethical monotheism. Or perhaps a compulsion to wander, coupled with denial of the unique opportunity, provided the pretext necessary to continue avoiding the promised land. That and fear of the many enemies of the promised land and chosen people.

This internal challenge to Jewish continuity indirectly recalls the dilemma of early twentieth century Christian Arabs. Unable to insist on the equality of their religious and to some extent ethnic identity in the face of pan-Islamic movements arising in reaction to European colonialism and Zionist resettlement, Christian Arabs helped found and led early pan-Arab movements. Some assisted in pioneering Palestinian Arab nationalism. A few, like the murderous Greek Orthodox physician George Habash, would head terrorist factions, in his case the Popular Front for the Liberation of Palestine.

But pan-Arabism, battered by Israel's defeat of iconic leaders such as Egypt's Gamal Abdel Nasser in 1967 and Syria's Hafez al-Assad in 1973 and American victory over Iraq's Saddam Hussein in 1991, would prove a meager shelter for Middle Eastern Christian communities. Even though these indigenous communities predated Islam itself, as *dhimmi* their members required protection from periodic abrasion and worse in Muslim-majority societies. Significant Arab communities in West Africa and Central and South America, seeded in the nineteenth century by Christian emigrants from parts of the Ottoman Empire that became Lebanon, Syria, Iraq and Palestine, owed their start in no small measure to persecution and economic stagnation at home.

More recently, Christian Arabs faced sectarian furies unleashed among Shi'ites by the fall of the Shah of Iran in 1979 and by the eruption of Sunni extremism exemplified in the seizure of Mecca's Grand Mosque the same year. Pan-Islamic tendencies gathered strength following the American-aided defeat by the *mujahedeen* (holy warriors) of the Soviet Union in Afghanistan by 1988, the U.S.-led coalition's ouster of Saddam in 2003 and "the Arab Spring" of 2011 and its bloody aftermath. As a result, the Christian Arab exodus from Lebanon, Syria, the Holy Land and elsewhere in the Middle East begun in the nineteenth century accelerated in the twenty-first. That is, except for Arab Israelis, whose communities, Muslim as well as Christian, after 1948 enjoyed equal rights alongside the Jewish majority and grew in numbers—contrary to anti-Zionist claims of suppression.

"The Palestinian narrative" of Habash, of long-time PLO leader Yasser Arafat—a Sunni Muslim who invoked pan-Arab, pan-Islamic or Palestinian Arab national themes as circumstances dictated—promotes a thorough-going demonization of Jews, Zionism and Israelis. A compulsion moves from the ancient charge of ritual murder and deicide to the present. It reappeared in conspiracy theory accusations—spread not by medieval gossip but rather its digital reincarnation via the Internet— against the Israel Defense Forces' field hospital dispatched to Haiti as humanitarian relief after the devastating 2010 earthquake.

The IDF hospital was the first and perhaps most efficient such effort, as ABC TV, Cable News Network and other news outlets reported.[7] Yet in only three days this example of Israeli humanitarian aid morphed into an updated, world-wide version of the blood libel. This happened thanks to one anti-Zionist antisemite, the Internet and the widespread,

---

7 "Haiti Day 6—No one but the Israelis have come to help any of our patients that are dying,'" CNN, Jan. 18, 2010.

enduring need to believe the worst of the Jews.

"T. West" of "AfriSynergy Productions" posted a YouTube video suggesting that "the Israel Defense Forces mobile hospital unit in Haiti may be involved in stealing organs."[8] ADL noted that "several anti-Israel Web sites and Middle East news sources have reported as credible" T. West's allegations. Those sources included "PressTV, a state-funded Iranian TV [English-language] propaganda-as-news channel; the Izzedine al-Qassam Brigades, an armed wing of the terrorist group Hamas; and the site of Alex Jones, an American anti-Israel conspiracy theorist." Each of their reports cited West's video, which in addition alleged previous organ thefts from Palestinian Arabs and others by the IDF. Palestinian sources also had charged Israel with snatching organs of "martyrs"—terrorists killed in attempted assaults.

The atmosphere had been prepared the year before by enlightened Swedes. Scandinavia's largest newspaper published a thoroughly false and malicious article alleging Israeli harvesting of Palestinian Arab organs for profit.[9]

T. West, according to ADL, was Theautries West, "a Seattle activist." Activist, like racist, is a word debased by overuse. Generally imprecise, it often is intellectually, though not polemically, useless. West, ADL noted, "has posted a number of anti-Israel and antisemitic videos on YouTube." He "seems to maintain that Zionists and some Jews do not have a legitimate claim to their identity" and "refers to Jews in quotation marks [perhaps a nod to Louis Farrakhan and the Nation of Islam's 'so-called Jews' terminology that attempts to deny contemporary Jews their historical roots] and has called for African-Americans to cut ties with Jews."[10]

Following Orwell's dictum that "we have now sunk to a depth at which the restatement of the obvious is the first duty of intelligent men," ADL properly called the organ harvesting rumors "a new version of the ancient blood libel." Of course. Therein lay its ability to spread world-wide and incite numerous gleeful anti-Israel, anti-Jewish posts and "talk-backs" on a variety of Web sites. When it comes to replacing medieval local priests in inciting an intellectually superstitious peasantry against the Jews, the Internet helps make everything old new again.

8 The Big Lie of Israeli 'Organ Harvesting' Resurfaces as YouTube Video on Haiti Earthquake Goes Global," Anti-Defamation League, Jan. 21, 2010.

9 "Rumors of Israeli organ harvesting in the Palestinian territories spread globally," by Donald Bostrom, *Aftonbladet*, Aug. 17, 2009.

10 "The Big Lie," ADL.

New and much more widespread.

Aftonbladet editors' defense of the organ harvesting invention, and attempt to flip criticism into new "questions" about Israel—that is, re-hashing the previous unsubstantiated attacks—illustrated two mutually reinforcing digital age trends. The first is the difficult if not impossible transition of print-based journalistic standards, or at least aspirations, of objectivity, accuracy, context, balance, willingness to correct mistakes and absence of conflicts of interest, to the Web. The speed of Web-based publishing and its world-wide reach often mean the data disseminated has outraced slower, print-enabled verification that transformed data from rumor to news. The second is the Internet's closely aligned, pre-Gutenberg ability to spread pixelated conspiracy superstitions as breaking news.

A *Wall Street Journal-Europe* Op-Ed dissected the *Aftonbladet* affair. Written by Andrea Levin, executive director and president of the news media watchdog CAMERA, the column noted that the original article "has quickly metastasized to mainstream Muslim media, spawning cartoons of Jews stealing body parts and drinking Arab blood. These have been published in Syria, Qatar, Jordan, the United Arab Emirates and Oman, to name a few. … Algeria's *al-Khabar* newspaper echoed Bostrom in a new fantasy claiming Jewish-directed gangs of Algerians and Moroccans round up Algerian children, spirit them into Morocco and thence to Israel to have their body parts harvested and sold.

"On September 17, Iran's PressTV breathlessly declared 'an international Jewish conspiracy to kidnap children and harvest their organs is gathering momentum.' Hate-filled Web sites have also taken up the theme. Almost invariably, wherever such permutations on the idea of Israeli organ theft appear, *Aftonbladet* is cited. …

"Meanwhile, editors at *Aftonbladet* have neither acknowledged nor corrected any of the factual errors that litter the article, and instead react with indignation to charges of misconduct. In a perversion of journalistic standards, editor-in-chief Jan Helin admitted on his own blog on August 19 that *Aftonbladet* had no evidence for the incendiary charges against Israel. Nevertheless," according to another editor at the paper, cited in the Israeli daily *Ha'aretz* on August 20, the Swedish publication "stands behind the demand for an international inquiry" of Israel's actions.[11]

---

11 "Anatomy of a Swedish Blood Libel; Allegations of Israeli organ theft are ugly, false, harmful—and they spread," by Andrea Levin, *Wall Street Journal-Europe*, Oct. 14, 2009.

The 'Palestinian Narrative': Post-modern is pre-modern

Such double-speak has wings because the post-modern, post-Gut-tenberg age in key aspects also is pre-modern, simultaneously post-lit-erate but pre-literary. Its renewed embrace of subjective over objective—perhaps inevitable in a "therapeutic" culture prizing self-esteem over substance—places emotion above empiricism. Emoticons (hieroglyphs) and abbreviated, nuance-drained text/Twitter-like vocabulary help leverage the digital equivalent of superstition over free inquiry objec-tively pursued and corroborated. Like gossip before or in places without general literacy, it's most prized when confirming existing suspicions. Instructors ask of students how they feel rather than what they know. Something fundamental to the life of the mind is lost in the flight from print to pixels, in migration from contemplation to instant and contin-uous connection.

Arts critic Sven Birkerts made this point early, positing that for most Westerners for half a millennium, roughly 1450 to 1990 (when home computers began to become ubiquitous), the life of the mind was a product of movable type and the Gutenberg epoch. This period per-mitted and required "deep reading" by individuals of texts that could then be discussed and debated. Solitary deep reading, alternating with knowledge-based conversation, helped form the individual Western personality.[12]

Subsequently, the world's libraries have become networked and open, democratized, even universalized. But by the same means so have the false libraries of the anti-mind, of old-new gossip, superstition and credentialed ignorance. Going if not quite gone are the much derided and often discarded "gatekeepers"—librarians, copy editors, scholars and specialists dedicated to inquiry at least over, when not in place of, ideology. Our new masters of information if not intellect too often func-tion as orthodox monks in digital monasteries, online rumor and pro-paganda mills.

Information is more widely and instantaneously available than ever before. So is misinformation, flowing through data networks as in-tellectual waste water. Disinformation and misinformation campaigns operate via the communications networks of Vladimir Putin's Russia; of China under one-party rule behind its "great firewall of China" but with cooperation from corporations like Facebook and Google, unwilling to sacrifice market access for its customers' freedoms; of Qatar-based

---

12 *The Gutenberg Elegies*, Faber and Faber, 1994; Farrar, Straus & Giroux, 2006 reissue.

Al-Jazeera televising leading Islamist preachers like Egyptian-born Sheik Yusuf al-Qaradawi and of the post-modern academic-journalistic-entertainment industrial complex. They work with suppressive vehemence in Western liberal arts departments and post-democratic progressive politics. They often dilute if not corrode the substance of Western news media.

For example, al-Qaradawi, described as a "spiritual leader" of the Egyptian-based Muslim Brotherhood—though not its official "spiritual guide"—returned to Cairo after the ouster of President Hosni Mubarak. On Feb. 18, 2011, he spoke to a crowd estimated by some to include more than one million people at a "Day of Victory" rally. The sheik's bodyguards reportedly denied Wael Ghonim access to the speakers' platform.[13] Ghonim was Google's head of marketing for the Middle East and North Africa, widely credited by Western news media with inspiring the anti-Mubarak movement through Facebook. Foreign press attention notwithstanding, young liberals, social-media savvy, often English-speaking and comparatively secular, who'd help organize the ultimately successful anti-regime demonstrations in Tahrir Square, were not representative Egyptians.

But al-Qaradawi's popular al-Jazeera program "Life and Islamic Law" was watched by tens of millions of Muslims in the Middle East and beyond. He often used it as a platform for anti-Israel, antisemitic incitement. A youthful student of Muslim Brotherhood founder Hassan al-Banna, al-Qaradawi has proven similarly influential. His work, *The Lawful and Prohibited in Islam*, has sold millions of copies in many languages and "is considered the best-selling Muslim book after the Koran."[14] "Al-Qaradawi refers to his religious views as 'moderate Islam,' which seeks to balance intellect and emotion. ... He seeks to unify Muslim minorities to make it possible for them to live under non-Muslim regimes, until the final stage of spreading Islam to the entire world."

In 2003, Qaradawi "issued a fatwa declaring that 'Islam will return to Europe as a victorious conqueror after having been expelled twice. This time it will not be conquest by the sword, but by preaching [*al-dawah*, "the call" or "summons" in Arabic] and spreading [Islamic] ideology. ... The future belongs to Islam. ... The spread of Islam until it conquers the entire world and includes both East and West marks the

---

13 "Egypt protest hero Wael Ghonim barred from stage," Agence France Presse, Feb. 18, 2011.

14 "A Portrait of Muslim Brotherhood's Supreme Authority," Meir Amit Intelligence, Terrorism and Information Center, *The Jerusalem Post*, March 2, 2011.

beginning of the return of the Islamic Caliphate' ..."

As for the Jews and Israel, Qaradawi—perhaps a "modernizing" though not "moderate" Sunni theologian—declared that Muslims should finish what Hitler had started. Though in his 80s at the time, he said he would welcome "martyrdom" in the battle for Jerusalem. An opponent of Iran's Shi'ite expansionism and a critic of al-Qaeda, Qaradawi nonetheless "enthusiastically" supported Palestinian terrorism. "He issued fatwas calling for *jihad* against Israel and the Jews, authorizing suicide bombing attacks even if the victims were women and children."[15]

Qaradawi, was not alone. A Pew Research Center survey in 2013 found that—after two years of inter-Arab and inter-Muslim slaughter in Syria and continuing suicide attacks committed from Western Europe through Israel to the United States—14 percent of Muslims worldwide condoned violence against civilians, including eight percent in the United States. Estimating the global Muslim population at 1.5 billion, 14 percent would be roughly 210 million Muslims, including 320,000 of approximately 4 million in the United States.

The BBC referred to al-Qaradawi as a "moderate Islamist." In doing so it provided one more example of Western mental surrender in the face of Islamic illiberalism highlighted by Paul Berman in *The Flight of the Intellectuals; The Controversy Over Islamism and the Press*. Attempting to cover their retreat with protective fire, they aim at "Islamophobic" critics of those like al-Qaradawi and at "Zionist oppressors."

Substance too often proved too much to convey for Western communications media giddy in their indulgent first blush of the Arab spring over Internet savvy, young Arab liberals.

∾

During the Spanish and Portuguese inquisitions of the 15th century and later, suspected Jews among the "Conversos" underwent interrogatory tortures leading to *auto-de-fé*—processions, masses and related acts of faith. Such tortures, prosecutorially and pornographically barbarous, destroyed the body ostensibly to save the soul. *Aftonbladet* yearned for a modern *auto-de-fé*, perhaps, orchestrated not by the Inquisition but its "lawfare" successors. These include the U.N. Human Rights Council and members of chronically anti-Israel non-governmental organizations (NGOs) and their secular priesthoods, such as those at Human Rights Watch or Amnesty International. The latter organizations' Cold

---

15 Ibid.

War-era "halos" as human rights guardians had been long-tarnished by their critical obsessions with Israel (and other Western democracies) contrasted with two-dimensional concern with post-colonial violators. HRW and AI found in Israel-bashing a justification for continued existence and, exemplified by HRW's Sara Leah Whitson on her 2009 trip to human rights exemplar Saudi Arabia, fund-raising.[16]

The objective of the contemporary anti-Israel *auto-de-fé* would not be Israel's spiritual salvation but ultimately its material elimination. Human Rights Watch's knee-jerk hostility to Israel became so great one of its founders, Robert L. Bernstein—Random House Publishing Co. chairman and president and HRW's board chairman for 20 years—felt compelled to criticize the group publicly. He indicted it for jettisoning its former important distinction between open and closed societies and issuing "far more condemnations of Israel for violations of international law than of any other country in the region." HRW, he added, helped "those who wish to turn Israel into a pariah state."[17]

At *Aftonbladet*, Bostrom in his Inquisitorial prosecution of Israel had spun a "tenuous web of guilt by association among unconnected events, in the classic mode of conspiracy theorists," Andrea Levin charged. This web included multiple errors "concerning Israel, its physicians, laws and military." For one among many, Bostrom asserted that Israel was "'the only Western country with a medical profession that doesn't condemn the illegal organ trade.'" In reality—reality unreported by *Aftonbladet*—"Israel has one of the most stringent laws in the world regarding human organs. It prohibits receiving compensation for organs, bans the sale of organs from the dead as well as the living and minutely defines 'compensation' to prevent evasion of the law. Unlike laws in other countries, it prohibits the use of insurance for pre- and post-operative treatment for those Israelis who go abroad and receive purchased-organ transplant."[18]

During World War II, *Aftonbladet's* sentiments were pro-Nazi. In the great war between good and evil, Sweden itself was neutral. Culturally a Western nation, Sweden also behaved as a Cold War neutral while President John F. Kennedy in his inaugural address was urging Americans to "pay any price, bear any burden, meet any hardship, support

16 "Fundraising Corruption at Human Rights Watch," by Jeffrey Goldberg, *The Atlantic*, July 15, 2009.

17 "Rights Watchdog, Lost in the Mideast," by Robert L. Bernstein, *The New York Times*, Oct. 19, 2009.

18 "Anatomy of a Swedish Blood Libel," Levin.

any friend, oppose any foe to assure the survival and success of liberty" in the struggle between the democratic-capitalist West and communist Soviet bloc.

Today the Swedish government periodically hectors and diplomatically attempts to undermine Israel. So for *Aftonbladet* editors and reporters, regressing to the blood libel via the Palestinian narrative—which now includes alleged organ harvesting from Palestinian "martyrs," Arab children in North Africa and non-Arabs in Haiti—was a short and logical move. How could it be otherwise when today's Jewish state is, above all, racist—the all-purpose, substantively indeterminate, emotionally irrefutable condemnation. Israel is condemned like its predecessors, the Jews of medieval Europe, who were transfigured as not just heretics and blasphemers but essentially inhuman, demonical.

A generation ago the "racist" indictment was not necessary. "Fascist" served. To post-liberal progressives—that is to say, anti-democratic reactionaries—Ronald Reagan was a fascist. Margaret Thatcher was a fascist. Pope John Paul II with his knee-jerk anti-communism might have been a fascist. Menachem Begin definitely was a fascist. In other words, their impeccable democratic credentials notwithstanding, Nazis all. But while the far left found this epithet compelling and the old right recognized it as useful, "fascist" as ultimate accusation did not gain sufficient popular traction.

But "racist" became the all-purpose incantation to conjure with. To be stigmatized as racist by infallible, illiberal orthodoxy was the contemporary version of being declared a heretic by the Inquisition. One so tarred was to be ostracized, interrogated, tortured—on social media at least—and executed—reputationally at a minimum—in this life, condemned to eternal Hellfire in the next.

A descriptive stretch? In *A State Beyond The Pale; Europe's Problem With Israel*, British researcher and writer Robin Shepherd (who makes clear he is neither Jewish nor a Christian Zionist) argues that anti-Israelism is the last stand of the totalitarian left. The United States, bastion of hated democratic capitalism, led the West to victory over the communist Soviet bloc, which collapsed. Even China, looked to with admiration when "reeducating," imprisoning and killing millions under romanticized, idealized Chairman Mao Zedong—a Che Guevara over hundreds of millions of people—later adopted ostensibly capitalist modes to solidify control by a one-party police state.

Shepherd writes that "quite apart from the moral and humanitarian catastrophe of global communism," responsible for the deaths of close to 100 million people, "the core ideological tenets of radical Left thinking have simply been refuted by experience."[19] Yet, like the secular fundamentalist theology it is, radical Left thinking—better, catechism—"is still with us." That is possible because "while it is difficult to subscribe to radical Left ideology in terms of what it has always *supported*, it remains quite possible to subscribe to it in terms of what it has always opposed [italics in the original]." And that is "the liberal-democratic, capitalist system."[20]

However, democratic capitalism not only refused to die but actually triumphed over Marxist-Leninism, turning the workers of the world into consumers who did not just expect free choice in goods and services but reveled in them. A chicken in every pot and a cell phone in every pocket. Let a dozen wireless communications networks bloom! So the hard left "refocus[ed] attention on the revolutionary potential of Third World liberation movements as well as discontented minorities back home. ... If the Western proletariat could no longer be expected to upset the capitalist system perhaps others could. Enter groups like the PLO. ...

"[T]he argument that the radical Left moved against Israel after 1967 because of concerns about human rights and occupation is not credible." After all, Israel was a beacon of human rights in the Middle East, its enemies the enemies of human rights as well. "The real reason for the move against Israel was because a general realignment at around the time of the 1967 war necessitated a reconfiguration of the ideology. Israel had become an enemy not because of anything it had done: Anyone could see that the occupation of the West Bank had followed a war caused by Israel's enemies. Israel had become an enemy in the mind of the radical Left because it was now on the wrong side of the barricades" drawn by writers such as an influential German "critical theorist" of Jewish background, Herbert Marcuse, and the anti-colonialist Frantz Fanon, both more cited than critiqued on college campuses.[21]

So the post-democratic left no longer romanticized the little Jewish land of socialist *kibbutzim* led by a secular Labor Party and threatened by Arab dictators and Muslim religious obscurantists. Instead, it increasingly smeared a militarized ally of the United States that featured growing political participation by Orthodox Jews and a renewed claim

---

19 *A State Beyond the Pale; Europe's Problem with Israel*, by Robin Shepherd, Weidenfeld & Nicolson, 2009, page 218.

20 Ibid.

21 Ibid, page 219.

on Jewish patrimony in Judea and Samaria. The "genocide" hard leftists accused America of carrying out in Vietnam was increasingly mirrored, in left fundamentalist imagination, by Israel's "brutal" occupation of the Palestinian Arabs and suppression of Israeli Arabs.

In fact, standards of living in the West Bank and Gaza Strip—measured by declining infant mortality and rising levels of education, provision of electricity and clean water among other indicators—rose markedly between 1967 and 1987, the initial 20 years of Israeli occupation, compared to those of 1948 – 1967 under Jordanian and Egyptian control. In 2008, a British politician noted that life expectancy in the Gaza Strip exceeded that of East Glasgow.[22] (Higher living standards for Palestinian Arabs in the West Bank and Gaza Strip than Arab brethren in many other parts of the Middle East continued in subsequent decades, as the 2005 U.N. Report on Human Development, noted above, indicated.)

In Israel itself, life expectancy for Arabs in 2010 was 79 years—two years less than for Israeli Jews but one year more than that for the average American, and 10 years more than that for Arabs in other Middle Eastern countries.[23] But facts, as we have seen, are fluid if not gaseous to the post-modern mind. And, as in the pre-modern mind, especially so when it comes to Jews.

Shepherd says that if, pre-1967, Jewish suffering, epitomized by the Holocaust, "had provided ammunition for discrediting 'bourgeois society,'" then subsequently the radical left found its new proletariat, its new revolutionary potential in non- and essentially anti-Western "liberation movements" like the PLO and Islamic extremists. Never mind that these were movements, ideologies and people determined to reimpose Jewish suffering and, among Islamists, eventually an intolerant global theocracy.

As Shepherd notes, "in 1979, the radical French philosopher Michel Foucault [one of the founders of post-modern deconstructionism spotlighted by Victor Davis Hanson] wrote glowingly about the return of Ayatollah Khomeini to Iran…" How, Shepherd asks "can people who have spent their lives campaigning in the West for the rights of women, homosexuals and ethnic minorities, let alone for secularism and pacifism, make common cause with some of the most violent religious big-

---

22 *Industry of Lies; Media, Academia, and the Israeli-Arab Conflict,* Ben-Dror Yemini, Institute for the Study of Global Antisemitism and Policy, 2017, page 276.

23 "Israel's Arab citizens and the struggle for equality," by Joshua Muravchik, *fathom,* Winter, 2014.

ots on the planet?"

The answer is plain, "so long as one is prepared to see the radical Left for what it is rather than for what it has claimed to be. If Islamism's potential was not exactly revolutionary in the sense that there was anything in its positive agenda that resonated with radical Left thinking in the West," then Islamists nevertheless aligned with radical leftists "in terms of what they opposed."[24] Hence the contemporary red-green alliance, the post-liberal left and Islamic triumphalists echoing the red-black front of Soviet Communists and German Nazis from 1939 to 1941 against Europe's liberal democracies.

The PLO understood the potential even before Khomeini's takeover in Iran, which Palestinian leadership celebrated. After Khomeini's rise, the PLO claimed Israel's former embassy in Tehran for itself. As Shepherd notes, point seven of Fatah's 1969 "Seven Points" program (Fatah is the largest PLO constituent group) asserted that "the struggle of the Palestinian People, like that of the Vietnamese people and other peoples of Asia, Africa, and Latin America, is part of the historic process of the liberation of the oppressed peoples from colonialism and imperialism."

This is, of course, an analog of Edward Said's argument in *Orientalism*, a derivative from Frantz Fanon's playbook and by diffusion part of critical studies jargon everywhere. The more unrestrained their pursuit of "liberation," the bloodier—that is, the more "revolutionary"—PLO attacks, the more Palestinian Arabs were understood to be a people oppressed by imperialism. So understood, they became the premier and sainted example of the romanticized "Other."

In attacking New York's World Trade Center, al-Qaeda struck a nerve center of Western capitalism in the most powerful "Crusader nation." "As for Israel," Shepherd writes, "the Jewish state not only stands right on the front line of the battle but it is also symbolic for Islamism of everything it feels insulted by. Israel is capitalist. It is democratic. It is Western. And, it is in their face."[25]

For the anti-democratic left, "to make common cause with the most effective possible opponents of Western capitalism and not to make common cause with virulent hostility to Israel would make no sense." Hence the "large overlap here between opposition to Israel and anti-Americanism. ... Israel, denounced also as a colonialist enterprise reminiscent of the imperialism of the European past and the American

24 *A State Beyond the Pale*, Shepherd, page 222.
25 Ibid. page 223.

present, can never be right in the manner of its self-defense. Islamism, the new, great ally in the struggle against the West, has declared that it has no right to exist. The Left has followed suit."[26]

Here anti-Zionism and antisemitism plainly merge, along with anti-Western, particularly anti-American hatreds. Though Shepherd sees antisemitism as secondary to a totalitarian ideology that pivots on a Manichean world view and feeds on demonized enemies, he spotlights the connection: "The Leftist anti-globalization activist Naomi Klein has made the point explicitly. Calling for an anti-apartheid-style boycott of Israel in 2009 she said, 'Why single out Israel when the U.S., Britain and other western countries do the same things in Iraq and Afghanistan?' Why? Because 'boycott is not a dogma; it is a tactic. The reason the strategy should be tried [against Israel but not the United Kingdom or United States] is practical: in a country so small and trade-dependent, it could actually work.'"[27]

Contrary to Klein, what really have the United States, Great Britain and other Western countries done in Iraq and Afghanistan? In the former, fought a ruthless dictator responsible for hundreds of thousands of deaths in his own and neighboring countries and attempted, however poorly informed, to build if not a democracy then at least a minimally repressive bi- or tri-sectarian state; in the latter, dethroned advocates of an imagined seventh century Islamic utopia who kill those in their way, whether at home, in the greater Middle East, New York City or London, making no distinction between combatant and non-combatant anywhere. Western states have made that distinction, attempting to minimize collateral damage, including non-combatant fatalities, with often quite restrictive rules of engagement. This is as Israel has done, even more successfully in terms of limiting non-combatant deaths, fighting Hezbollah in Lebanon and Hamas in the Gaza Strip.

Then-U.S. Chairman of the Joint Chiefs of Staff Gen. Martin Dempsey put it this way in a New York City appearance a few months after the 2014 Israel-Hamas war:

"I actually do think that Israel went to extraordinary lengths to limit collateral damage and civilian casualties. ... In this kind of conflict, where you are held to standards that your enemy is not held to you're going to be criticized for civilian casualties." Dempsey added that "the IDF [Israel Defense Forces] is not interested in creating civilian casualties. They're interested in stopping the shooting of rockets and missiles

26 Ibid. page 224.
27 Ibid. page 235.

out of the Gaza Strip into Israel."[28]

In fact, the Pentagon sent a "lessons learned" team to Israel to investigate whether measures Israelis took to minimize non-combatant casualties and collateral damage could be integrated with similar American efforts in Afghanistan and Iraq. No matter. Human Rights Watch and Amnesty International, among others, predictably attacked Israel for military transgressions in the fighting in which approximately 2,100 Gaza Arabs died. That a majority were males of combat age, heavily overrepresented compared with their proportion of the general population—which would not have been the case if the IDF had conducted indiscriminate attacks, let alone targeted civilians—generally was too much for the self-described human rights monitors and their media echo chambers to digest. It could not matter for anti-Zionist antisemites, for whom Israel's fundamental illegitimacy makes its self-defense unarguably criminal.

Jews returning to their ancient homeland are colonialists the way Hitler's phantasm-like Jewish financiers were Bolsheviks. So targeting the Jewish state for destruction in the name of anti-colonialism—when not so targeting Great Britain, France or even the United States reveals all three facets of anti-Zionist antisemitism: double standards, demonization and delegitimization. Therefore, Shepherd acknowledges, "it is worth considering one final thought about Liberal Left ideological hostility to Israel. For there is something deep inside *secularist* [italics in the original] 'progressive' thinking, in particular in Europe" which helps explain the "visceral disdain with which many on the Liberal Left relate to Israel and indeed to Jews anywhere whose identity is wrapped around an affinity with the Jewish state."[29] Quoting Anglican Church Canon Giles Fraser, Shepherd notes, "'Like it or not, the very identity and existence of the State of Israel is bound up with Judaism. Israel makes no sense without the Hebrew Scriptures. But because a large part of the Left has so wedded itself to the belief that progress comes with secularization, it cannot accept a religious explanation for anything; so it immediately thinks of it as a form of prejudice."[30]

Bigotry is as bigots do. The prejudice is in the minds of the anti-Zionist antisemites. "Self-declared progressives are practically silent on the Islamic foundations of a whole host of countries around the world,"

---

28 "Israel tried to limit civilian casualties in Gaza: U.S. military chief," by David Alexander, Reuters, Nov. 6, 2014.

29 *A State Beyond the Pale*, Shepherd, page 235.

30 Ibid. page 234.

Shepherd writes. "The anti-religious dimension of Liberal Left progressive thinking is only unleashed as a tool for leveraging hostility to people, nations and projects who have already been designated as part of the 'reactionary' camp." That is, hostility to countries and movements rooted in predominately Christian or Jewish cultures, but not hostility to reactionary Islamic regimes and movements rooted in Islamic fundamentalism. This helps explain also why the otherwise tainted origins of many Arab and some non-Arab Islamic countries in colonialism passes unremarked. But for the British there would have been no 20th century Iraq and Kuwait, among others. But for the French, no Syria or Lebanon. Without European imperialism in general, few African states in their post-colonial guises. Yet for the illiberal left, only Israel, especially in the Middle East, is an intolerable product of Marx's catch-all explanation for international affairs, imperialism.

Hence, says Shepherd, "the mocking tones in which Jews and Israelis are characterized when they offer biblical justification for the re-creation of the Jewish state in Palestine. The lurid obsession of many on the Left with scriptural references to the Jews as the 'chosen people' is part and parcel of the same agenda," Shepherd believes. So "antisemitism and anti-Zionism become conceptually indistinguishable" for some on the anti-democratic left. "The deepest roots of Jewish identity are inextricably bound up with the Jewish religion even, via the cultural inheritance, for Jews who regard themselves as secular. When a political project such as Zionism—designated reactionary for other reasons as well—derives its ultimate justification from religious foundations, hostility towards it is redoubled."[31]

---

31 Ibid. page 237.

CHAPTER THIRTEEN

'Semites', Antisemites and Jew-Haters

THE URGE TO MARGINALIZE, ghettoize, expel and expunge the Jews never dies. Given what the anti-Jew, anti-Zionist believes are the Jews' inherent, essentially anti-human characteristics, it should not die. This is what Stephen Eric Bronner—otherwise misled about contemporary Israel and Judaism by his Marxist inclinations—identifies as antisemitism's chameleon-like nature.[1] Unlike other group hatreds, it is enduringly and endlessly adaptable. The Jewish enemy can be rich or poor, civilized or crude, weak or powerful—and all simultaneously. The antisemite's Jew explains everything, especially the Jew-hater's own failures and those of his or her society. Unlike other such prejudices, whether anti-women, anti-black, anti-Catholic, anti-gay and so on, it makes of its targets not just alleged inferiors or subverters of contemporary order but rather demon individuals and a demon people, standing outside humanity as a whole. Since there is no end to the threats posed by its mythological Jew, antisemitism has no limits.

This means that when it comes to Israel and the Jews, the Jewish state and Jewish people, apparent double standards become unchallengeable absolute standards. The more plausible-sounding the excuse, the more it can be popularized. The more popular it can become the more Jews die, in medieval massacres, Renaissance inquisitions and expulsions, 19th century pogroms and the 20th century's Holocaust.

Today's equivalent of the Inquisition for the Jews and their country is rooted in a modern, superficially legalistic libel, the aforementioned U.N. resolution equating Zionism with racism. In classical antisemitic

---

1 *A Rumor About the Jews; Antisemitism, Conspiracy, and The Protocols of Zion*, by Stephen Eric Bronner, Oxford University Press, 2000, page 145.

288 Jews Make the Best Demons

fashion, the Jewish people's political response to pervasive antisemitic racism becomes, viola! racist itself. "Racist" in this context is, as noted, the secular-contemporary equivalent of "Christ-killer" and "heretic." To save themselves Jews must deny, if not Judaism as in the Inquisition, then at least Zionism and Israel.

So pro-Israel students, faculty and outside speakers have found on many university campuses: Speech about Israel—and, increasingly, Jews in general—is welcomed, when hostile. It's prohibited, by campus speech and/or "sensitivity" codes or, if necessary, mob veto, when it would be supportive and especially when it would criticize and condemn Jew-haters and Israel-haters. Facebook, YouTube and Twitter repeatedly limit or suspend factual pro-Israel or anti-Palestinian posts while chronically expressing surprise and *ex post facto* regret at floods of antisemitism on their platforms.

Pre-World War II quotas—*numerus clausus*—curtailed Jewish and other minority enrollment on campuses. "Gentlemen's Agreements" and deed restrictions did likewise in employment and housing. Now the restrictions, psychologically more crippling, are social-cultural. Self-abasing Jews are endorsed. "Generic" Jews, tolerated. Proud, self-identifying Jews, suppressed.

Under U.S. pressure—organized by John Bolton, later a national security advisor to President Trump, then Assistant Secretary of State for International Organizations and with the approval of President George H.W. Bush—the United Nations repealed the Zionism-is-racism measure in 1991. This occurred during that brief interlude marked by the collapse of the Soviet Union and resultant supremacy of the United States and its closest democratic allies following their ouster of Iraqi forces from Kuwait. This short period exemplified the so-called "end of history" and supposed triumph of Western liberal democracy discerned by Francis Fukuyama and other theorists.

Though Kuwait had hosted Palestinian leaders and a significant Palestinian Arab population, the PLO and many followers had cheered Saddam Hussein's 1990 takeover. As a result, Kuwait's restored rulers expelled several hundred thousand Palestinian Arabs—"ethnic cleansing" barely noticed, since neither Israel nor the United States were involved. The United States behaved as if repeal of the 1975 "Zionism-is-racism" resolution ended the matter. Rather, it opened a potential counter-attack. U.N. agencies continue to disseminate Zionism-is-racism propaganda, led by the Committee on the Inalienable Rights of the Palestinian People, the U.N. Human Rights Council and related institutions. The boycott, divestment and sanctions (BDS) movement, which sought to label Israel an "apartheid" state and have it isolated and undermined as had been South Africa under its actual apartheid regime, stemmed from and has been continuously fostered by these U.N. activities.

Just as medieval blood libels helped prepare the way for Jewish massacres, the "Zionism-is-racism" charge has been invoked countless times in the past 40 years until its iteration has become a virtual loyalty oath for and functional "two-minute hate" in the worlds of Islamic triumphalism and anti-democratic left, neo-Marxist intolerance. Look at the enraged, contorted expressions on the faces of indoctrinated anti-Israel demonstrators: "Two-minute hate" precisely describes their activity, simultaneously impassioned and robotic. Except for their lack of matching uniforms, participants act, as noted, like *Hitlerjugend* or Komsomol members in moments of frenzy. Hatred of this sort, left unresisted—as administrators from Columbia University through Oberlin College to the University of California at Berkeley at times have left it—would prepare the way for a new a great pogrom, the elimination of Israel, and resubordination of diaspora Jews.

The "Zionism-is-racism" resolution itself originated not with Arab delegates but the Soviet Union. The Soviet Communist Party's effort to tar Jewish nationalism in particular with retrograde attributes went back to early Bolshevik days. Lenin frequently repeated the German Marxist-socialist saying that antisemitism is "the socialism of fools," but Marxist-Leninism rejected nationalism as well as religion. So Jewish nationalism was, *ipso facto*, doubly threatening to the communist project. In that spirit, Marx's collaborator, Friedrich Engels, had urged the physical annihilation of many of Europe's numerous such small ethno-religious groups.

The allegedly atavistic attachments of small religious, ethnic and/ or national identities were disdained as reactionary impediments to idealized proletarian consciousness and unity. In other words, genuine multi-culturalism and diversity threatened Marxist-Leninist visions of an undifferentiated mentality on the part of the world's workers. Today, it contradicts the "raised consciousness," the "woke" conformity of reactionary progressives whenever they attempt to impose one view and one voice—the false "universality" of the radical Left—on all individuals within a group. It matters not at all whether, for example, the "identity groups" are women, blacks, white nationalists or Arabs.

Jewish nationalism rankled in particular and seemed to contradict the universalism claimed by the communist movement. This might have been particularly so since the movement included many Jews or Jewish apostates as leaders—Leon Trotsky (Lev Davidovich Bronshtein), Grigori Zinoviev and Lev Kamenev among other functional "*conversos*"— and as followers. Or it did before their decline following the Red-White civil war in the early 1920s and Stalin's purges in the 1930s. Jews had been oppressed previously by the reactionary czarist-Russian Orthodox Church and targeted by its pogromist "Black Hundreds" allies. Jews had looked for revolutionary salvation—again not unlike Arab Christians seeking integration via pan-Arabism in a region dominated by exclusionary pan-Islamic culture. As Tevye's wife Golde says in *Fiddler on the Roof*, if the revolutionaries are right, the Jews will stay in a new, more hospitable Russia, and if the Zionists prove correct, they'll emigrate to the Jewish homeland in Palestine. The czar's regime and Bolshevik leaders both feared Zionism as a potential disrupter of the docility of Russia's several million Jews, if not competitor for their loyalty.

Such hostility continued after World War II. Stalin infamously orchestrated "The Night of the Murdered Poets," Aug. 12, 1952 when leading Jewish cultural figures were killed. He also attempted to resolve his "Jewish question" with the Potemkin Village-like autonomous Jewish region of Birobidzhan, which was neither very Jewish nor autonomous. At the time of his fatal stroke in 1953, Stalin was planning a wide-ranging purge of Soviet Jews.

Golda Meir's visit to Moscow as Israeli foreign minister in 1948, traveling on the renewed Jewish state's first passport, drew approximately 50,000 people to catch a glimpse of her near Moscow's Choral Synagogue. These masses reconfirmed their suppressed identity and symbolically expressed a sentiment that would help shake the foundations of Soviet communism. Israel's defeat of the Kremlin's Arab clients in 1967 made the sentiment more than symbolic. Through non-Jewish dissidents like physicist Andrei Sakharov (winner of Lenin and Stalin prizes for his work on the Soviet hydrogen bomb and later the Nobel Peace Prize for human rights campaigning), Jewish *refuseniks* like Natan Sharansky, and bolstered by U.S. leverage via the Jackson-Vanik amendment linking increased trade with freer emigration, the general Russian and particular Russian Jewish human rights movement helped erode Soviet control. The Soviets made teaching Hebrew a crime; Russian Jewish dissidents persevered and went to jail for it. And they demanded the right of emigration, specifically for Jews to move to the Jewish state.

This resurgent Jewish identification unsettled Kremlin leaders, not only on its own but by fear of potential contagion to other suppressed

Soviet nationalities. Eventually, it would come to pass that Trotsky—who declared "Zionism is incapable of resolving the Jewish question" and was murdered in Mexican exile by Stalin—would have a great-grandson named David Axelrod. Axelrod lived in Israel as a member of a religious kibbutz on the West Bank (Judea and Samaria).

The Kremlin was not interested in historical irony, especially not after Israel's second victory over Moscow's Syrian and Egyptian allies, in the 1973 Yom Kippur War. It needed to recoup. If the Jewish state could not be beaten by conventional military means, it would have to be targeted by unconventional warfare—terrorism, in which the Soviet-backed PLO took the lead—and psychological warfare—in which smearing Israel as "colonialist" and "racist" proved invaluable. The PLO, with Chinese and then Soviet backing, leveraged virtually every organ of the United Nations in doing so. Of course, when it comes to colonialist, it's difficult if not impossible to surpass the Duchy of Moscow, which expanded in 300 years to cover 11 times zones and much of a continent while subordinating by force scores of nationalities and ethnic groups. But saying so would be historical and factual; better, and certainly more convenient, to obsess about the Jews and their (at its maximum) 50-mile-wide state.

Following Israel's sweeping triumph in 1967, Soviet leader Leonid Brezhnev had urged Arab leaders to pursue a strategy aimed at liquidating the consequences of the war with no Israeli gains. In other words, figure out how first to recover all the lost territory—the Jordanian-occupied West Bank and eastern Jerusalem, the Egyptian-occupied Gaza Strip and Egypt's Sinai Peninsula, and the Syrian Golan Heights (originally part of Great Britain's Palestine Mandate) without recognizing Israel or making peace with it. Then later return to the offensive against a Jewish state back in its highly vulnerable post-'49 and '50 armistice lines.

In his memorable speech at the United Nations three days into the 1967 Six-Day War, Israeli Foreign Minister Abba Eban noted that just the day before he had seen Jordanian artillery shells striking Jerusalem. "Every house and street" in the city "came into the range of fire as a result of Jordan's adherence to this pact [with Egypt]; so also was the crowded and *pathetically narrow* [emphasis added] coastal strip in which so much of Israel's life and population is concentrated."[2] Eban emphasized the tempting vulnerability of Israel's pre-1967 boundaries—less than

2 19, Statement to the Security Council by Foreign Minister Eban-6 June 1967, Israel Ministry of Foreign Affairs, Volumes 1-2: 1947-1974.

nine miles wide just north of Tel Aviv, four miles wide at Jerusalem's
western municipal limits—to a West German magazine two years later:

> We have openly said that the map will never again be the
> same as on June 4, 1967. For us, this is a matter of security
> and principles. The June map is for us equivalent to insecu-
> rity and danger. I do not exaggerate when I say that it has for
> us something of a memory of Auschwitz. This is a situation
> which will never be repeated in history.[3]

Hence the Arab League's August, 1967 "three 'no's' of Khartoum."
Israel, as Defense Minister Moshe Dayan famously put it, was "waiting for a telephone call" from Arab leaders to offer peace on generous
terms—most of the captured territories except, particularly, eastern Jerusalem in exchange for recognition and no more war. The Arab League,
with PLO encouragement, in response vowed no recognition, no negotiations, no peace.

The psychological war against Israel would become co-equal with,
if not paramount over the military war. On the psych-war battlefields,
the Palestinian narrative, pivoting on the demonization of Israel as "racist" and—another elastic Marxist-Leninist category—"imperialist" and
making Palestinian Arabs the latest blood libel victim, proved central.

The PLO would institutionalize Brezhnev's advice and the "three
no's" after Israel's victory in the 1973 Yom Kippur War. It turned from
focusing mainly on destroying Israel by using terrorist/guerrilla attacks
in hope of igniting a general Arab-Israeli war to a Kremlin-inspired
blend of terrorism, diplomacy and propaganda. It did so by adopting
the "plan of stages" or "phased plan" in 1974. The plan's advocate was
Salah Khalaf, as noted above one of the founders—with Arafat—of Fatah (Movement for the [Total] Liberation of Palestine), the largest PLO
faction. Exemplifying the "salami tactic," cutting away one slice at a
time until the salami of Israel vanished, Khalaf's plan called for pock-
eting Israeli concessions and then, instead of making peace, raising the
ante Israel must pay for any future "progress" while the Palestinian side
continued the struggle from its newly-improved position. Palestinian
Authority President Mahmoud Abbas' repeated rejection of direct talks
with Israel, talks assuming reciprocal concessions, upheld the phased
plan's utterly one-sided tactical diplomacy.

___
3 *Der Spiegel*, Nov. 5, 1969.

The Palestinian narrative links and extends history's bloody chain of anti-Jewish libels. It continues to rely on omission, distortion, inversion and invention in doing so. For example, news media periodically treat readers and viewers to recurrent coverage of alleged Israeli theft of Arab water. A classic in the genre was promoted by *National Geographic* magazine.[4] In addition to mistaking the history of how Lake Tiberias (Sea of Galilee), one of Israel's key water sources, came to be inside the Jewish state rather than somehow shared with Syria, it also claimed that Israeli wells in the West Bank mostly supplied Israel when in fact they pumped no water into Israel proper. Instead, the flow went the other way: water from inside Israel was piped into the West Bank for both Israeli and Palestinian communities. Among other key errors of omission, National Geographic failed to tell readers that Israel recycled most of its waste water, and most of that was reused for agriculture. By ignoring this fact, the magazine doubled-counted Israel consumption, allowing it to falsely claim Israelis used four times as much water as Palestinian Arabs.[5]

Overall, from 1967 to 1995, West Bank Arabs increased domestic water use 640 percent. During the same period, Israeli domestic usage grew 142 percent. The huge Palestinian increase occurred after Israel drilled or permitted drilling of many new wells, laid hundreds of miles of water mains and connected hundreds of Arab villages towns to them.[6]

But the Jewish state's "theft" of Arab water was a journalistic "evergreen," a formulaic echo of the Jew's eternal need for the blood of Gentiles. So in the spring of 2017, *National Geographic* was back, its television channel repeatedly airing "Parched: Global Water Wars." Half of this one-hour program of "global" reach dealt only with the Israeli-Palestinian conflict. Again, *National Geographic* peddled the false charge that Israel steals Palestinian water. In fact, when Israel conquered the West Bank in the 1967 Six-Day War, only four of the territory's 708 cities, towns and villages had running water and barely 10 percent of the population was connected to a modern plumbing system. Forty-eight years later, thanks to Israel's thieving occupation, 96 percent of the Pal-

---

4 "Parting the Waters," *National Geographic* magazine, April, 2010.

5 "National Geographic, Israel and Water: The Facts," CAMERA, June 16, 2010, at www.camera.org.

6 *Judea-Samaria and the Gaza District—A 16 Year Survey 1967 – 1983, Israel, Ministry of Defense, 1983*; "The Israeli Palestinian Conflict over Water Resources," by Arnon Soffer, *Palestine-Israel Journal*, Vol. 5, No. 1, 1998 and *Statistical Abstract of Israel 1996*, V47.

estinian Arab population had "running water piped to their homes."[7]

Similarly, in 2009 much ink was spilled over, and air-time given to the star-chamber proceedings that resulted in the U.N. Human Rights Council's "Report of the United Nations Fact Finding Mission on the Gaza Conflict." Israel had launched "Operation Cast Lead," its December 2008 – January 2009 war in the Hamas-ruled Gaza Strip, to stop frequent and indiscriminate Palestinian mortar and rocket attacks. Chaired by retired South African Justice Richard Goldstone, the inquiry panel quickly became known as the Goldstone Commission. Its report allowed that Palestinian missile strikes may have been war crimes, but it overwhelmingly asserted, in the words of the U.N.'s official press release, "evidence indicating serious violations of international human rights and humanitarian law were committed by Israel during the Gaza conflict, and that Israel committed actions amounting to war crimes, and possibly crimes against humanity."

Two years later, Goldstone, yet another influential Jew at least temporarily befuddled by the Palestinian narrative, repudiated the main libel of the report, that Israel intentionally had targeted Arab civilians in the Strip. The justice conceded "we know a lot more today about what happened in the Gaza war of 2008-09 than we did when I chaired the fact-finding mission appointed by the U.N. Human Rights Council ...." Regretting Israel's original decision not to cooperate with his panel's inquiry—Jerusalem recognized the Human Rights Council's bias and the open prejudgment of several of its members—Goldstone acknowledged the agency's "history of bias against Israel cannot be doubted." Affirming Israel's right as a sovereign country to self-defense, he also took note of post-conflict Israeli investigations that "indicate civilians were not intentionally targeted as a matter of policy."[8]

But the damage had been done. The libel that Israeli troops intentionally targeted Arab civilians and caused "disproportionate" non-combatant casualties while fighting Hamas, Palestinian Islamic Jihad and other U.S.-government designated terrorist groups in the Gaza Strip gained traction. It would be replayed by international news media during and after the short Israeli-Hamas fighting in November, 2012 ("Operation Pillar of Defense") and more extensively in coverage of the

7 This and other aspects of Israel's world-leading water resource development, including desalination, and conservation, are highlighted in *Let There Be Water*, by Seth Siegel, St. Martin's Press, 2015.

8 "Reconsidering the Goldstone Report on Israel and war crimes," by Richard Goldstone, *The Washington Post*, April 1, 2011.

longer 2014 Israeli-Hamas war ("Operation Protective Edge").

The Goldstone report was another of those U.N./international indictments that reflected in miniature the career of the General Assembly's 1975 "Zionism-is-racism" resolution in macro. Palestinian and other Arab/Muslim speakers and writers including Nonie Darwish, Bassem Eid, Wafa Sultan, Bassam Tawil, Ibn Warraq and other "internal" Arab and/or Muslim critics have similarly exposed central elements of the Palestinian narrative. So, the narrative's true believers targeted them too for marginalization.

The European Union's 2015 call to label, in effect to boycott, products from Jewish communities in the disputed territories—endorsed by the United States via an Obama administration regulatory action—recalled Nazi economic boycotts of Jews and their businesses in the 1930s. Anti-Israel boycotts began with the newly-formed Arab League's attempt, starting in 1945, to abort Jewish settlement in British Mandatory Palestine economically even before the state of Israel itself was born. In fact, waging economic warfare against the Zionist enterprise was a key motive behind establishment of the league. Members formally declared that "Jewish products and manufactured goods shall be considered undesirable" in the Arab countries and all Arab "institutions, organizations, merchants, commission agents and individuals" were "to refuse to deal in, distribute, or consume Zionist products or manufactured goods." To their enemies, "Jewish" and "Zionist" already were synonymous, nearly three years before Israel's establishment.

The U.S. Congress outlawed commercial compliance with the Arab League's anti-Israel boycott in 1977. Signing the legislation, President Jimmy Carter took note of "the divisive effects on American life of foreign boycotts aimed at Jewish members of our society." The Arab League's threats, sometimes implemented, not to trade with companies doing business with Israel, went "to the very heart of free trade among nations," Carter said. Just so the BDS movement's similar efforts to ghettoize and choke the Jewish state. Not all anti-Zionists are anti-Jewish, at least not in theory, religious or philosophical. But all who demand the destruction of Israel for behavior common to other countries certainly are in practice.

By the time Congress barred compliance with the Arab League boycott, the effort had stunted Israel's economic growth. It also had retarded commercial and technological progress in the boycotting countries. The latter, however, did not acknowledge the cut-off-our-noses-to-spite-our-faces effect, since strangling the Jewish state, not building up

Arab League members, was the overriding goal. Today's BDS campaign would continue the Arab League's racist campaign in word and deed.

The countless condemnations of Israel by the U.N. Human Rights Commission, and it successor the U.N. Human Rights Council, for fabricated transgressions amounted to an inquisition of sorts, in which boycotts were one instrument. In the fifteenth and sixteenth century, the Spanish version of the Roman Catholic Church's Inquisition rooted out *conversos*. Contemporary U.N. inquisitions attempt to root out Zionists, Jewish Israelis with the temerity to insist on the right to a nation-state and to defend themselves in it when necessary. This is the same right exercised without question by the United Nation's 192 other members, many of whose roots in the land they occupy are shallower and whose national identity of more recent origin than that of Jews in Israel. It is a right the world body acknowledged for the Jewish state in 1949, one it now aggressively regrets in numerous ways, including the annual November 29 "Day of International Solidarity with Palestine."

November 29 is the anniversary of U.N. General Assembly Resolution 181 (1947), the partition recommendation that Arab delegations and Palestinian Arab leaders rejected but the Zionist leadership of the Jewish Agency for Palestine accepted. Resolution 181 called for two tiny states, one Arab, one Jewish, in the western remnant of the U.N.'s British-held Palestine Mandate. As noted, the first Arab state in Palestine, Jordan (originally Trans-Jordan) had been carved out of the three-fourths of the mandatory lands east of the Jordan River in 1921 and Jews were forbidden to settle there.

U.N.-led delegitimization and demonization of Israel certifies widespread efforts elsewhere to exorcise the demon embodied by the Jewish state. Simultaneously, and not coincidentally, antisemitic devils are rehabilitated exactly because their targets are Jews and their state. For example, social media comments by two dozen University of Texas students and graduates in 2017 "have likened Israel to Nazi Germany, called for violence against Jews and both denied and championed the Holocaust in Facebook and Twitter posts."[9]

"The posts all come from members of the school's chapters of Students for Justice in Palestine (SJP) and Muslim Student Association (MSA), according to Canary Mission, a group that "anonymously monitors anti-American, anti-Israel and antisemitic activity on U.S. college

---

9 "'Stuff Jews In the Oven' Among Antisemitic Social Media Posts Flooding Pages of University of Texas-Arlington Students, Covert Campus Watchdog Finds," *The Algemeiner*, Feb. 15, 2017.

campuses." Comparisons of Israeli Prime Minister Benjamin Netanyahu to Adolf Hitler and Israeli soldiers to Nazis, a reference to the Holocaust as "#LiesToldInSchool" and a BDS supporter retweeting the riddle "How many Jews died in the Holocaust? Not enough. HAHAHA" neatly mirrored the conjoined triplets of this hatred—anti-Jew, anti-Israel and impassioned mindlessness. To such dangerous simpletons, the Nazi genocide is a lie, it didn't murder enough Jews and Israelis are Nazis.

Months before, Brandeis University's Steinhardt Social Research Institute at the Cohen Center for Modern Jewish Studies had reported a survey of 50 American universities. The review included 34 campuses with active SJP chapters. "Jewish students' discomfort talking about Israel … is closely related to the presence" of an SJP chapter. "Brooklyn College, Northwestern University and many schools in the University of California system are hotbeds of antisemitism and anti-Zionism," the report asserted. "Most Jewish students at the schools in question 'perceive a hostile environment towards Israel, and over one quarter perceived a general environment of hostility toward Jews on their campus.'" At universities including Illinois, Wisconsin and Rutgers, "hostility to and harassment of Jewish students" was rated "relatively high" but did "not seem to be highly connected to criticism of Israel." Instead, "more traditional antisemitic stereotypes and tropes … seem to be driving the perceived hostility towards Jews."[10]

Of course, such warnings by institutions like the Steinhardt Institute for Social Research at Brandeis University's Cohen Center for Jewish Studies can be dismissed by "progressives" and the "alt-right" alike as mere "Jew-splaining." Women can talk about sexual abuse, blacks can speak of racial discrimination, homosexuals about anti-gay bigotry but Jews properly may be ignored when they warn of antisemitism. Such are the post-modern hierarchies of aristocratic privilege.

As Palestinian terrorism of the 1970s was the gateway drug to Islamist terrorism of the 1990s, anti-Zionism has proved the gateway drug to renewed antisemitism. "Tis education forms the common mind, Just as the as the twig is bent the tree's inclined," wrote Alexander Pope in 1732 in "Epistles to Several Persons." And miseducation, too. When it comes to Israel and the Jews, miseducation—propaganda, psychological warfare and censorship—seems nearly inescapable. Such is the genius of the Palestinian narrative, the lie of Palestine.

Arabs cannot be antisemites since they too are Semites. So it is

---

10 "Brooklyn College, Northwestern, U of California Among Top 'Hotspots' of Campus Jew-Hatred, New Study Finds," *The Algemeiner*, Oct. 20, 2016.

sometimes claimed. Anti-Zionists similarly insist at times that they are not antisemitic since they're not anti-Arab, or even not anti-Jewish, just anti-Israel. Only those unaware of the origin of the terms "Semite" and antisemite sincerely repeat such clichés.

In January, 2016, the first German version of Hitler's *Mein Kampf* (My Struggle) in 70 years went on sale in Germany. The Associated Press reported, in a dispatch from Munich, that "many hope [the new volume, *Hitler, Mein Kampf: A Critical Edition*] will help demystify the book and debunk the Nazi leader's writing." It "'sets out as far as possible Hitler's sources, rooted in the German racist tradition of the late 19th century,'" said Andreas Wirsching, director of Munich's Institute for Contemporary History, publisher of the heavily annotated book. That racist tradition, which "scientifically" labeled Jews as inferior, symbiotically connected to Hitler's extreme German nationalism and anti-communism. It "would culminate in the Holocaust and World War II," AP recalled. Destruction of European Jewry—and, if success of arms had permitted, the Jews of the Middle East and beyond—was not secondary to the Third Reich's launching of World War II but rather intrinsic to its aggressive global war.

The very term "antisemitism" was minted in Germany in 1879 by Wilhelm Marrih, an anarchist pamphleteer who founded the Anti-Semitic League. "Antisemitic" gave religiously-based German Jew-hatred a more up-to-date, intellectual-sounding name. Marrih drew on the academically-inflected word "Semitic." It too is of German origin, as David Shipler noted in his 1987 Pulitzer Prize-winning *Arab and Jew; Wounded Spirits in a Promised Land*: "The term 'Semitic' was coined in 1781 by the German scholar A. L. von Schlozer to identify a family of related languages, including Hebrew, Arabic, Aramaic and others. He derived the word from Shem, the name of one of Noah's three sons, *giving the unintended impression that all those who spoke Semitic languages shared a common ancestry, thereby setting in motion a process that may have distorted biblical history and anthropology* [emphasis added]."

That is, Arabs and Jews, particularly Palestinian Arabs and Israeli Jews, are not brothers just because the former speak Arabic and the latter Hebrew, two related tongues. Modern DNA testing suggests that Jews have maintained unusually close genetic connections for more than 2,000 years, and in some cases roughly 3,000. It also suggests that their closest relatives, also of Middle Eastern origin, are not Arabs but Kurds.[11] The Kurds, an estimated 35 million people, straddle the bor-

---

11 "The Genetic Bonds Between Kurds and Jews," by Kevin Alan Brook, ww-

ders of Iran, Turkey, Iraq and Syria. They claim descent from the ancient Medes, who preceded Assyrians and Babylonians as rulers of the northern Fertile Crescent. It was among them, the Bible tells us, that the first Hebrew, Abraham, sojourned with his family on his divinely-directed journey from Ur of the Chaldees to Canaan sometime early in the second millennium B.C.E. It was in Mosul—adjacent to the site of ancient Nineveh, which the prophet Jonah found himself compelled against his will to warn and thereby save—where Jewish American troops held a Passover seder in 2003 in one of the "palaces" liberated from Saddam Hussein.

Given America's often short strategic attention span, Mosul also was seized by fanatics of the Islamic State in Iraq and Syria in 2014, threatening the nearby Iraqi Kurdish Autonomous Area. Combined Iraqi government, pro-Iranian Shi'ite militia and American-supported Kurds freed Mosul from the Islamic State three years later. But not before ISIS had blown up the Mosque of the Prophet Yunus, in Christian and Islamic tradition Jonah's burial place, as part of its campaign against pre-, non- or "anti-Islamic" shrines and historic places.

Though a sovereign Kurdistan has as strong or stronger historical, territorial and demographic claims than many nation-states, since World War I the prospect of such a country has unnerved Arab, Iranian and Turkish heads of state and world leaders and been betrayed repeatedly by the latter, including Americans. The same is true in varying degrees for other ancient peoples from Tibet through Chechnya to Corsica. Why is the creation of an independent Baluchistan—perhaps 16 million or more people living in an area larger than France on both sides of the British-drawn colonial border between Pakistan and Iran—not an urgent international issue? Yet somehow the demand for a second Palestinian Arab-majority state (in addition to Jordan), for a 22nd Arab country to serve five or six million people—the large majority of whom are Sunni Muslim Arabs closely related to neighboring Lebanese, Syrian, Jordanian, Saudi and Egyptian Sunni Muslim Arabs—has become preeminent. Why? In no small measure, because it ultimately might be, given the irredentist nature of Palestinian Arab nationalism, at the expense of the one Jewish state. Because then those driven to resume the "final solution" to answer "the Jewish question" would be halfway home.

Some, assuming Arabs and Jews both to be "Semites," insist their hostility to Jews alone doesn't make them antisemitic. How could it, since they have nothing against Arabs? Such people are misled or mis-

---

w.2001translations.com/Kurds.htm, among other articles and posts.

leading. There is nothing "Semitic," except a language group, to be "anti" to. Antisemitism has one sensible meaning, its original: hatred of Jews.

In 18th and 19th century Germany and Austria, where and when "Semitic" and "anti-Semitic" were coined, Jew-hatred "still had a ferocious religious base," Paul Johnson writes in *A History of the Jews*. "[A]t the popular level it was symbolized by the *Judensau*. But the further you went up the social scale, the more secular, cultural and racial it became; so baptism did not work" as a means of escape.

"In the nineteenth century, German hatred of the Jews acquired a *volkisch* basis." This ideology "drew a crucial distinction between 'culture' (benign, organic, natural) and 'civilization' (corrupt, artificial, sterile)." German culture, in that case, Johnson observes, "was in perpetual enmity with civilization, which was cosmopolitan and alien. [The assertion of perpetual enmity and war between the *ummah*, the community of true Muslim believers and the rest of humanity, the *jahiliyya* or world of ignorance, found in the writings of Islamist ideologues like the Muslim Brotherhood's Sayyid Qutb, loudly echoes this sort of Manichean obsession.] Who represented the civilization principle? Why, the one race which had no country, no landscape, no culture of their own: the Jews! The argument was typical of those which caught the Jews whatever they did. If they clung to ghetto Judaism, they were alien for that reason; if they secularized and 'enlightened' themselves, they became part of alien civilization."[12]

"Volkisch rejection of the Jews took many forms," Johnson says. Among them, "a conservationist movement, ancestor of contemporary Green political parties, which rejected industry and high finance (the Rothschilds) and especially the ever-expanding big cities, breeding grounds of the cosmopolitan Jews."[13] Today, anti-capitalist, anti-globalization boycott advocates like Naomi Klein reflect that original Green bias. Such German antisemitism "was hydra-headed, contradictory, uncoordinated, ubiquitous." Novelists, historians, the German Farmers' Union, scientists and pseudo-scientists who created a "social Darwinian" survival of the fittest struggle of the races, all promoted it. Antisemitism became "a new element of German neo-paganism."

A neo-pagan leader, Paul de Lagarde, "rejected Christianity, which had been corruptly invented by the Jew, St. Paul, and wished it replaced by a specifically German Volk religion, which would conduct a crusade to drive the Jews, with their internationalist materialist conspiracy, from

---

12 *A History of the Jews*, by Paul Johnson, Harper & Row, 1987, page 392.
13 Ibid. page 393.

the sacred German soil; he predicted a German-Jew armageddon."[14]

A late 20th century American bumper sticker, "Born-Again Pagan" hinted, probably unconsciously, at the difficulty of fighting antisemitism (and supporting Israel) in increasingly post-Christian societies: If the revelation at Sinai with its universal obligations is overthrown, Judeo-Christian ethics will rest not on something transcendent but rather on mere aesthetic choice. In that case they can bind no one but those who choose to be bound, fluid associations of individuals not committed to communities or nations. They will provide no overarching obstacle to false witness, robbery and murder in societies that embrace or succumb to radical personal autonomy. As Dostoyevsky suggests through the character of Ivan Karamazov in *The Brothers Karamazov*, where there is no God, nothing is prohibited. If human dignity is not inherent, not God-given, then might alone can well make right. The anti-Zionist drive to render Jews as a people again powerless, without either might or right, is, in this context, the means. The antisemitic compulsion to suppress if not eliminate the Jews is the end.

Polling during the 2016 U.S. presidential election, which found 20 percent of respondents with no religious affiliation, up from 12 percent in 2012, might prove significant. Twenty-five percent of registered Democrats or Democratic-leaning voters were "religious nones."[15] Exit polling that November indicated "most weekly churchgoers backed [Donald] Trump over [Hillary] Clinton, 56 percent to 50 percent. ... Those who said they don't attend religious services at all backed Clinton over Trump by a 31-point margin (62 percent to 31 percent)."[16] Eighty percent of white, evangelical Christians said they voted for Trump, according to the Pew survey.

Another Pew canvass in 2013 showed 80 percent of American evangelicals believe God gave the Holy Land to the Jewish people. Remarkably, the survey found only 40 percent of American Jews agreed. Hence the targeting of U.S. Christian supporters by promoters of the new blood libel and the otherwise ludicrous insistence on Jesus Christ's "Palestinian" identity.

Historically, when it came to anti-Jewish, neo-pagan romanticism, there was composer Richard Wagner and his influential circle. They had

14 Ibid.

15 "The non-religious are now the country's largest religious voting bloc," *The Washington Post*, July 14, 2016.

16 "How the faithful voted: A preliminary 2016 analysis," Pew Research Center, Nov. 9, 2016.

"absorbed the race teachings of [Comte Joseph de] Gobineau and, later, of Houston Stewart Chamberlain, and drew a powerful artistic contrast between the 'purity' of German-pagan folk culture and the Judaic-infected corruption of the cosmopolitan idea," according to Johnson. "The violence with which these views were presented was horrifying. De Lagarde ... demanded a physical campaign against Jewish 'vermin': 'with trichinae and bacilli one does not negotiate, nor are trichinae and bacilli subject to education. They are exterminated as quickly and as thoroughly as possible."[17]

Hitler's first written comment on "the Jewish question" echoed De Lagarde's "bacilli" analogy, though it did not yet call for "extermination." On Sept. 16, 1919, nearly 20 years before his Reichstag speech cited above, Hitler described the Jewish presence in Germany and Austria as a "race-tuberculosis of the peoples." He said the initial goal should be discriminatory legislation against Jews. The "ultimate goal must definitely be the removal of the Jews altogether."[18] Removal altogether would become, cross-pollinated by al-Husseini's Islamist supremacism and enabled by Allied indifference, genocide.

In May and the opening days of June, 1967, Egyptian President Gamal Abdul Nasser expelled U.N. peace-keepers from the Gaza Strip and sent 100,000 troops with 1,000 tanks to Israel's southwestern border in the Sinai Peninsula. Nasser vowed to eliminate "the cancer" of the Jewish state. Forty-five years later Iran's supreme leader, Ayatollah Ali Khamenei told worshippers that Israel is a "cancerous tumor that should be and will be cut." He pledged that "from now on, in any place, if any nation or any group confronts the Zionist regime, we will endorse and we will help. We have no fear expressing this."[19] Vermin, bacilli, tuberculosis, cancer; in describing the Jews or their state as an infestation to be extirpated, the brutal repetition of aggressive bigotry varies little.

---

17 Johnson, pages 393-394.

18 "Adolf Hitler Issues Comment on the 'Jewish Question," U.S. Holocaust Memorial Museum, "Timeline of Events (Before 1933)," at www.ushmm.org.

19 "Iran: We will help 'cut out the cancer of Israel," *The Telegraph* [U.K.], Feb. 3, 2012.

CHAPTER FOURTEEN

English Lessons, the United Kingdom, the United States

COMPOSER RICHARD WAGNER, historian Paul Johnson noted, advocated, somewhat like Paul De Lagarde, the *Untergang* (downfall) of the Jews. "I regard the Jewish race as the born enemy of pure humanity and everything that is noble in it ...." The great composer's writings "provoked the furious outpourings of Eugen Duhring, who throughout the 1880s published a succession of widely read racial attacks on the Jews: the 'Jewish question,' he declared, should be 'solved' by 'killing and extirpation.' The attack came from all sides: from the left, from the right; from aristocrats and populists; from industry, from the farms; from the academy and from the gutter; from music and literature and, not least, from science."[1]

Given such demonization—its parallel in France led to the 1895 Dreyfus trial—and following the Russian pogroms of 1881-1882, Jewish thinkers like Leon Pinsker despaired of assimilation. The Viennese journalist and playwright Theodore Herzl "began to abandon his assimilationist position." Witnessing the public degradation of Captain Louis Dreyfus, falsely convicted of treason, Herzl, Johnson says, saw the officer as "the archetypal sufferer in the new ghetto. If even France turned against the Jew, where in Europe could he look for acceptance?"

The same question could be asked today, again starting in but not limited to France. Herzl's answer, to *eretz Yisrael*, to a new Jewish state on the old Jewish land, launched the formal movement of political Zionism, though its antecedents went back more than half a century, to

---

1 *A History of the Jews*, by Paul Johnson, Harper & Row, 1987, page 394.

Rabbi Shlomo Alkali in Serbia with his 1834 pamphlet *Shema Yisrael* (Hear, O Israel) and, after the 1840 Damascus blood libel, the assertion "that for security and freedom, the Jewish people must look to a life of its own, within its ancestral land."[2]

Others, including Rabbi Zvi Hirsch Kalischer in Poland and Moses Hess in Germany and France, were writing Zionist introductions before Herzl's Zionism. Hess moved from his earlier romantic socialism to write, in his 1862 work *Rome and Jerusalem*, "After twenty years of estrangement I have returned to my people. Once again I am sharing in its festivals of joy and days of sorrow, in its hopes and memories. ... The Jews have lived and labored among the nations for almost two thousand years, but nonetheless they cannot become rooted organically within them. A sentiment which I believed I had suppressed beyond recall is alive once again. It is the thought of my nationality, which is inseparably connected with my ancestral heritage, with the Holy Land and the eternal City, the birthplace of the belief in the divine unity of life and of the hope for the ultimate brotherhood of all men." Of the Damascus blood libel, Hess said "Once again we were face to face with the ignorance and credulity of the mobs of Asia and Europe, which are as ready today as they have been for the past two thousand years to believe any calumny directed against the Jews."[3]

And today against the Jewish state. Membership in the mobs has expanded, adding to the ignorant many with academic, legal and artistic credentials. In the 20th century the answer to the Jewish question, to the question of where could and should the Jews go, would lead to Israel's establishment in 1948. But given the primordial staying power of antisemitism and its obsessional drive, many in Europe, in the West in general and areas influenced by the West would rebel against such an answer. After all, it was positive—it let the Jews live and prosper—when a negative solution was desired. In the end, "with trichinae and bacilli one does not negotiate," reason or compromise. One exterminates.

The Atlantic magazine's April 2015 edition featured an article by Editor-in-Chief Jeffrey Goldberg headlined "Is It Time for the Jews to Leave Europe?" The subhead read: "For half a century, memories of the Holocaust limited antisemitism on the Continent. That period has ended—the recent fatal attacks in Paris and Copenhagen are merely the latest examples of rising violence against Jews. Renewed vitriol among

---

2 *The Zionist Idea: A Historical Analysis and Reader*, edited by Arthur Hertzberg, Atheneum/MacMillian Publishing, Jewish Publication Society, 1959, page 104.

3 Ibid. page 119.

right-wing fascists and new threats from radicalized Islamists have created a crisis, confronting Jews with an agonizing choice." Be that as it
may for European Jews, the displacement of one historical period by
another affects not just the Continent. The subhead simply could have
read "The post-Holocaust era is over. Anti-Zionist antisemitism confronts Jews with the ultimate demand: Get out of Israel and get out of
the Diaspora!"

Zionism and its state would not, as Herzl envisioned, at long last
"normalize" the Jews. That may not be possible—or desirable—for
a chosen people with their promised land, for a people destined or
self-destined to be a nation of priests whose Torah containing the word
of God is to go forth from Zion and Jerusalem as a light to all peoples.
To be "normalized" in the sense Herzl intended, to be Jewish citizens of
a Jewish state like Greeks in Greece or Italians in Italy may be possible in
daily life. It certainly feels like it at a table in a Tel Aviv café a few blocks
from the Mediterranean beach. But it may not be tenable as the national calling. In any case, Israel's very successes as a nation-state would,
contrary to Herzl, reinvigorate antisemitism through jealous, resentful
anti-Zionism.

Anti-Zionism is then, in part and in effect, a compulsion to reghet-
toize the Jews, at least at first. The means would be familiar: The Judensau visually separated the German Jew from German society, and
extended the dehumanization of the Jews that Nazi propaganda would
complete. Rock performer Roger Waters' pig balloon with the Star of
David clarifies that the new/old scapegoating with "racist!" and "imperialist!" replacing or perhaps only disguising "swine!" and "bacilli!" has
been invoked to do the same to Zionism, Israelis and their state.

'Permission to poison'

Old imagined Jewish crimes are made new again. In one blatant
example among many, Palestinian Authority President Mahmoud Abbas in 2016 revived the medieval antisemitic charge of poisoning the
wells. On June 19, 2016, the PA's foreign ministry warned that thousands of West Bank Arabs faced dying of thirst as a result of a campaign
by Jewish settlers, sanctioned and incited by Israeli rabbis, to poison
wells and other water sources throughout the territories. The PA cas-
tigated "the international community" for failure to intervene on behalf of endangered Palestinian masses. On June 20, official PA television
news amplified the accusation, reporting that "an Israeli human rights

organization has exposed a religious ruling issued by Rabbi Shlomo Melamed, chairman of the Council of Settlement Rabbis, that gave the settlers permission to poison the drinking water and the natural wells in the [Palestinian] villages and towns throughout the West Bank."

In truth, there was no exposé by an Israeli human rights organization. There was no Rabbi Melamed, no Council of Settlement Rabbis, no permission to poison.[4] In fact, Jewish settlers and West Bank Arabs rely on many of the same water sources. Palestinian Arabs were not threatened by Israel with death by thirst; rather, Israel compensated for Palestinian failures at conservation and sewage control by over-supplying water. All of which Abbas and the Palestinian Authority knew. Jewish communities during Europe's Black Plague relied on the same wells as their non-Jewish neighbors, the same wells they were accused of poisoning. Regardless, on that pretext they were massacred. The reality of Israeli and Palestinian water usage notwithstanding, Palestinian propaganda incites, when massacres aren't possible, acts of individual violence. It also keeps alive the hatred that might someday result in massacres.

Samuel Johnson famously advised James Boswell, when the latter arrived in London more than two centuries ago, to "clear your mind of cant." In the deconstructed, post-modern, post-factual present, when truth collides with orthodoxy and facts prove inconvenient to ideological touchstones, cant prospers. Neither the particular Palestinian fabrication of well-poisoning—faced with a rare outburst of Western disgust, Abbas recanted—nor countless others like it would be allowed to undermine the general description of the Palestinian president (then in the 11th year of a four-year term) and his PA as a "peace partner" with Israel. At least not until the Trump administration began penalizing Palestinian rejectionism by withholding a portion of U.S. funding in late 2017 and early 2018 and relocating America's embassy in Israel from Tel Aviv to Jerusalem. Even so, revived blood libels—accusations of organ theft, water theft, culture and land theft—would not be permitted to cast doubt on the big lie itself, the Palestinian narrative.

Deeply-rooted European antisemitism and Islamic fundamentalism running through the continent's large North African and Middle Eastern immigrant communities have made odd but real political bedfellows. A sort of neo-paganism, growing in North America as well as Western Europe, cultivates the soil for replanted antisemitism. It helps

---

4 "PA Libel: Israeli rabbis called to poison all Palestinian wells," Palestinian Media Watch Bulletin, June 21, 2016.

power hostility to Western civilization's Judeo-Christian ethical base and enables hatred of the Jew and the Jewish state to grow and merge on the secular fundamentalist, multi-cultural left. It also weakens liberal European politics and culture in the face of Islamic triumphalism. Only Israel's military readiness has forced the inversion of the "first the Saturday people, then the Sunday people" sequence of Muslim fanatics. Weakness has made easier targets of Christian communities in Lebanon, Egypt, Iraq, Syria, the Gaza Strip and West Bank from the 1970s to the present. And in terrorist massacres in the West, "the Sunday people" and their "no-day" children find themselves targeted but often unwilling to understand why.

Anti-Israel terror seeks to drive Jews out of the Middle East, as if they were a foreign implant rather than an indigenous people returned. "Aryan" naturalism sought to overthrow what it derided as stultifying European culture with its degenerate, foreign Jewish influences and replace it with what it insisted were authentic German folk traditions and purified, superior ethnicity. Yet as Eric Hoffer reminded readers, what is done to the Jews later would be done to others. The Rev. Martin Niemoller, who spent 1939 – 1945 in Nazi concentration camps, famously observed, "First they came for the Socialists, and I did not speak out—Because I was not a Socialist. Then they came for the Trade Unionists, and I did not speak out—Because I was not a Trade Unionist. Then they came for the Jews, and I did not speak out—Because I was not a Jew. Then they came for me—and there was no one left to speak for me." Neimoller publicly regretted his own earlier antisemitism. His warning remains literal and timeless.

In the Middle East, the intolerant, the purist, the fascist ought to be a true multi-culturalist's opposite. Islamic supremacists or Arab nationalists turned on "the Sunday people," Arab Christians, as primary targets after being unable, at least temporarily, to extirpate "the Saturday people," Israeli Jews. That is, just as today, the Islamic Republic of Iran, led by reactionary mullahs, targets first the "Little Satan," Israel while continuing to demonize and prepare for the "Great Satan," the United States. But secular Western elites and their followers who rarely entertain thoughts of Satan or satanic concepts fail to take seriously those who do. So they have little concern for Arab Christians and other Middle Eastern minorities, including especially Israeli Jews, threatened with expulsion or extinction. Their eyes and moral outrage focus on one ostensibly victimized minority that by its fetishized elevation never can be recognized as a victimizer: the Palestinian Arabs. Of course, another name for selective outrage is hypocrisy.

When the rock singer Sting reopened Paris' Bataclan concert hall, site of the November 2015 torture-massacre of 90 people (the torture little-reported by news media), a year later, he said, in an imagined spirit of perseverance, "We need a return to normalcy." But secular, materialist Parisian normality represents the sort of blasphemy against Allah and satanic aggression against Islam that the terrorists of Bataclan and those inspired by them mean to eliminate. Not long after the Sept. 11, 2001 terrorist strikes in New York City and Washington, D.C., the novelist Salman Rushdie highlighted the obstruction to such normality. Rushdie was already under a fatwa issued by Iran's first "supreme leader," Ayatollah Ruhollah Khomeini that called for his murder on grounds of blaspheming Islam. Said Rushdie:

> 'This isn't about Islam.' The world's leaders have been repeating this mantra for weeks .... The trouble with this necessary disclaimer is that it isn't true. If this isn't about Islam, why the worldwide Muslim demonstrations in support of Osama bin Laden and al-Qaeda? .... Why the routine antisemitism of the much-repeated Islamic slander that 'the Jews' arranged the hits on the World Trade Center and the Pentagon, with the oddly self-deprecating explanation offered by the Taliban leadership, among others, that Muslims could not have the technological know-how or organizational sophistication to pull off such a feat? ... Why all the talk about American military infidels desecrating the sacred soil of Saudi Arabia if some sort of definition of what is sacred is not at the heart of the present discontents?[5]

Calling for a personal, depoliticized, "secular-humanist" modern Islam, Rushdie insisted that "it would be absurd to deny that this self-exculpatory, paranoiac Islam" of the Islamists "is an ideology with widespread appeal." That appealing ideology, he said loathes "modern society in general, riddled as it is with music, godlessness and sex" and fears its own lands "could be taken over—'Westoxicated'—by the liberal Western-style way of life." So calls like Sting's for a return to Paris' self-idealized normality, assertions like John Kerry's that ISIS beheadings didn't represent one true and dynamic face of Islam amount to dangerous denial.

---

5 "Yes, This Is About Islam," by Salman Rushdie, *The New York Times*, Nov. 2, 2001.

The mirror-imaging folly of such "enlightened" attitudes appeared simultaneously with Khomeini's takeover of the Iranian revolution. Epitomizing Paul Berman's intellectuals in flight, President Jimmy Carter's U.N. ambassador, Andrew Young, asserted it would be "impossible to have a fundamentalist Islamic state" in Iran because "too much Western idealism has infiltrated that movement." He said accurately that "Islam is a vibrant cultural force in today's world and not something that died with the Middle Ages" without comprehending the medieval direction of that vibrant force. "Although he acknowledged that Ayatollah Khomeini had been accused of anti-Christian and antisemitic remarks, Young, who is an ordained minister in the United Church of Christ, predicted that 'Khomeini will be somewhat of a saint when we get over the panic.' While anticipating 'a rough year ahead' in United States-Iranian relations, the United Nations delegate predicted that 'in two years, our relations with Iran will be on a pretty even keel.'"[6] France and the West, with Israel as spear tip, need something other than denial and eye-of-the-hurricane calm if they mean to return to, or claim for the first time, Western civil normality. That something is awareness of the enemy coupled with determination and a strategy by which to prevail.

That strategy will recognize three tendencies linked by "the Palestinian narrative"—European antisemitism, Islamic fundamentalism and Western anti- or post-national, anti-religious (anti-Judeo-Christian) secularism. The latter includes a self-loathing form of European post-colonial guilt, the self-loathing psychologically cleansed by projecting the guilt onto Israel. Jeremy Corbyn, a long-time back-bencher from the fringe of Great Britain's Labor Party, surprisingly elected leader in 2015, nearly elected prime minister in 2017, personified such linkage.

A man of the post-liberal, fundamentally anti-democratic left—a former columnist for the *Socialist Morningstar*, close to British Communists—he "is an enthusiastic backer of some of the most violent, oppressive, and bigoted regimes and movements in the world," wrote London-based journalist Jonathan Foreman. Those movements have included the Irish Republican Army, Hugo Chavez and his Chavistas who impoverished Venezuela while imprisoning opponents and destroying Venezuelan democracy in the name of a Latin socialism, Cuba's Castro brothers, Russia's Vladimir Putin and, not surprisingly, Hamas, whose representatives Corbyn hosted at the House of Commons, and Hezbollah, to whom he extended an invitation. "If that weren't enough,

6 "Young Praises Islam as 'Vibrant' And Calls the Ayatollah 'a Saint,'" *The New York Times*, Feb. 8, 1979.

he also invited Raed Salah to tea" at the Commons. This "even though the Palestinian activist whom Corbyn called 'an honored citizen ... who represents his people very well' has promoted the blood libel that Jews drink the blood of non-Jewish children."[7] Saleh, head of the northern branch of Israel's Islamic Movement, served a two-year prison sentence for helping fund Hamas and having contact with an Iranian agent. The Muslim Brotherhood-influenced Islamic Movement was banned in late 2015 for anti-Israel incitement during the violence of the Palestinian 2015-2016 "stabbing intifada."

To dispel accusations of antisemitism, Corbyn addressed the Labor Friends of Israel. But he did so "without ever using the word Israel. It may not be the case that Corbyn himself is an antisemite—of course he denies being one—but he is certainly comfortable spending lots of quality time with them."[8]

Not only Corbyn but apparently the majority of Britain's Labor Party. "Surveying the horrifying news from Labour's [2016] Party conference, one would have been forgiven for thinking that the biggest question facing Britain is a Jewish one. The place of Jews in the party and in Great Britain altogether seemed to dominate the proceedings," wrote Douglas Murray, associate editor of *The Spectator* (U.K.) and associate director of Great Britain's Henry Jackson Society.[9] Among other examples, "Ruth Smeeth, a Jewish member of parliament, found it necessary to bring a bodyguard to protect her from potentially violent anti-Semitic members of her own party."

The trend was evident more than a dozen years earlier. "In September 2002, three Jewish leftists who marched in a Stop the War demonstration [against British participation under Labor Prime Minister Tony Blair's government in the U.S.-led anti-Saddam Hussein coalition in Iraq] described ... how they became increasingly uncomfortable with the 'anti-Israel and anti-Jewish imagery' of their comrades. ... The open link between leftist politics and the defenders of antisemitic terror in the Middle East was made clear by the way that the Coalition for Nuclear Disarmament, a Cold War-era radical leftist group, allied itself with the Muslim Brotherhood to form the Stop the War coalition, one of whose

---

7 "Jeremy Corbyn and the End of the West," by Jonathan Foreman, *Commentary*, January, 2016.

8 Ibid.

9 "The Party of Left-Wing Anti-Semitism; The shocking decline and fall of Labour," by Douglas Murray, *Commentary*, November 2016.

leaders was Jeremy Corbyn."[10]

In the United States, Rabbi Michael Lerner, founder of *Tikkun* magazine, experienced something similar in 2003. A figure on the Jewish post-liberal left since his student days as a leader of the University of California at Berkeley's Free Speech Movement in the 1960s and his federal trial in the "Seattle Seven" case (a contempt of court conviction was overturned, incitement charges later dropped), Lerner had published a book titled *The Socialism of Fools: Anti-Semitism on the Left* in 1992. A harsh and regular critic of Israel and apologist for misguided anti-Israel icons like Rachel Corrie, killed while apparently obstructing an Israeli bulldozer clearing buildings used by Palestinian terrorists in the Gaza Strip, Lerner nevertheless insisted on both his pro-Zionism and hostility to antisemitism.

Yet like many self-regarding Jewish progressives, he continued to allow himself to be fooled. In 2003, he criticized the far-left ANSWER coalition for antisemitism exhibited at its demonstrations against the second Iraq war. But Lerner would not recognize who or what he was dealing with. The ANSWER Coalition, which included his "Tikkun Community" but featured neo-Trotskyites and Muslim Brotherhood affiliates and exemplified the "red-green" anti-Jewish convergence, prevented him from speaking at its rallies. Opposing "U.S. imperialism" was not to be good enough; one must also denounce "racist Zionism." Again, these are two sides of the same counterfeit passed by today's progressives.

Corbyn, challenged from within over Labor's then low standing with British voters and its now blatant anti-Zionist antisemitism, nevertheless prevailed in mid-2016 as party leader. After he surprisingly almost won election as prime minister in June, 2017 blogger Marc Goldberg wrote that Labor's antisemitism had not stopped the British electorate from voting for the party in its millions. "Even on election day a woman was filmed at a polling booth in a Jewish area calling on people to vote Labor 'to get the Jews out.'" British Jews had "assumed the reporting of incidents of antisemitism would disgust their fellow citizens enough to put them off Corbyn," Goldberg observed.[11] Instead, numerous voters came to believe the reports were part of a plot to smear the Labor leader.

"Many people lecture Jews about what they're allowed to believe,

10 Ibid.

11 "The irrelevance of anti-Semitism," by Marc Goldberg, *Times of Israel*, June 12, 2017.

what they're allowed to be offended by, what they're allowed to be concerned by, what does and does not constitute antisemitism against them and few are listening to what Jews are saying about it," he wrote. "Furthermore, many people are shocked and appalled, not by the antisemitism, but by the attempts by Jews to defend against it. … Now the Jews will be the spoilers, the ones ruining everyone else's good time when they talk about their antisemitism problems. It was bad enough before, now it will be impossible to point them out without being shouted down."[12]

Antisemitism, best described not decorously as antisemitism but unflinchingly as Jew hatred, is doubly pernicious since it deforms not only those who hate the Jews but also at times Jews themselves. Sen. Bernard Sanders (I-Vermont), showed himself a lesser Corbyn as he fought former secretary of state, senator and first lady Hillary Clinton for the 2016 Democratic presidential nomination. Himself a Jew, Sanders was a 1960's Bourbon-style leftist. Of the French and Spanish Bourbon dynasties restored to their thrones after Napoleon's defeat it was famously observed that their retrograde members had "learned nothing and forgot nothing." Sanders, a 1960's Brooklyn socialist, continued to speak in counter-cultural, anti-capitalist, anti-imperialist clichés, making him a sort of a bobble-head souvenir of reactionary progressivism. So it was no surprise that he uttered erroneous anti-Israel statements throughout the primary season, parroting disproven charges of "disproportionate" non-combatant casualties in Israel's 2014 Gaza Strip war against Hamas. He insisted on inclusion of proponents of the Palestinian narrative such as Prof. Cornel West and Arab American leader James Zogby as party platform writers. Special guests Sanders' invited to the Democratic convention in July, 2016 in Philadelphia included Paul Bustinduy, a leader of Spain's far-left, antisemitic Podemos Party. In 2017, Sanders actually worked for Corbyn's election. Birds of a feather and all that.

"There are two reasons why Sanders would campaign for an antisemite: 1) He has allowed Corbyn's socialism to blind him to his antisemitism; 2) he doesn't care about Corbyn's antisemitism because it is not important enough to him," Harvard University Law School Prof. Emeritus Alan Dershowitz charged. "Sanders' support for this anti-Jewish bigot reminds me of the Jews who supported Stalin despite his overt antisemitism because they supported his communist agenda."[13]

Dershowitz asserted "it is clear that if Corbyn were anti-black, an-

---

12 Ibid.

13 "Bernie Sanders: Knave or Fool?" by Alan Dershowitz, *The Gatestone Institute*, June 10, 2017.

ti-women, anti-Muslim or anti-gay, Sanders would not have campaigned for him. ... Increasingly, the 'progressive wing' of the Democratic Party and other self-identifying 'progressives,' subscribe to the pseudo-academic theory of intersectionality, which holds that all forms of social oppression are inexorably linked. This type of 'ideological packaging' has become code for anti-American, anti-Western, anti-Israel and antisemitic bigotry. Indeed, those who consider themselves 'progressives'—but who are actually regressives—tolerate antisemitism as long as it comes from those who espouse other views that they approve of. This form of 'identity politics' has forced artificial coalitions between causes that have nothing to do with each other except a hatred for those who are 'privileged' because they are white, heterosexual, male and especially Jewish."[14]

Sanders exemplified a condition not uncommon among many Jewish critics of Israel, including those in Israel as well as the Diaspora. Again, this does not refer to those, Jews or non-Jews, who criticize particular Israeli policies on factual grounds. Rather, it applies to those whose opposition, even enmity, either holds Israel to double standards or simply denies its legitimacy in the first place. As Rabbi Jonathan Sacks put it, one can oppose specific actions by the British government without objecting to Great Britain as a nation-state. Objecting to (often mischaracterized) Israeli policies as a means of attacking Israel's existence is something else. That something else is anti-Zionism serving the cause of antisemitism.

Sanders' misinformed criticism of Israel reflected a syndrome well-known among those active in Jewish affairs. A correspondent once asked the Lubavitcher Rebbe, Menachem Schneerson, how to encourage a formerly observant Jew who had drifted from his old convictions to return to the faith. In providing his correspondent with some practical advice, the Rebbe also observed that his own experience had convinced him "in most cases such as you describe, the true reason for the weakening in the convictions was not the result of a more profound study or deeper insight, but rather on the contrary, it came as a result of the fact that the convictions which one has held have proved an obstacle to the enjoyment of certain material aspects in life. And, human nature being what it is, one wishes to appease one's troublesome conscience by trying to find faults with the convictions and spiritual aspects."

Jews whose identity and social-cultural inclinations—apart from the practice of Judaism and support for Zionism—mirror those of the

---

14 Ibid.

post-liberal or secular fundamentalist left, sometimes appease their troublesome progressive consciences by finding fault with their faith and the Jewish state. Not infrequently, they trumpet their self-purifying anguish over their discovery of the unbearable fact that Israel is not perfect, that Israeli leaders are flawed human beings, that in so many ways—except the one that counts most—Herzl's *alteneuland* is normal. Doing so is less disorienting than examining their own gods that have failed.

It's in the Language. Always

Of publication of a critical, highly-annotated version of *Mein Kampf* in German in 2016, one commentator observed that though Hitler's 1925 autobiography does not mention concentration camps or gas chambers, it repeatedly suggests the answer to the Jewish problem: extermination, preferably by chemical means.

Today Jewish national destruction and genocide germinate in the words of the Palestinian Hamas and Fatah. They spread through the BDS movement and advocates including Jewish Voice for Peace, a voice for anti-Zionism and therefore neither Jewish nor for peace, and Students for Justice in Palestine, who want no justice for Jews. The more the post-liberal left invokes god-words like "peace, "justice" and "equality," especially in promotion of the Palestinian narrative, the more those actually committed to peace, justice and equality should grow suspicious. The inherent deception-by-double-standard makes current Orwell's *Animal Farm* caution that "all animals are equal but some animals are more equal than others." And the least equal, simultaneously the most evil and inferior, according to such advocates of "equality," are the Jews.

Not only does Hamas' Islamic fundamentalist charter call for the destruction of Israel and genocide of the Jews. The Palestine Liberation Organization's "covenant" also chauvinistically denies Jewish peoplehood and therefore any claim by Jews to a state. It declares Zionism "a political movement organically linked to world imperialism and hostile to all movements of liberation and progress in the world" as well as "racist and fanatical" in formation, "fascist and Nazi in its methods." That is, it parrots old Bolshevik and Soviet tropes that the post-liberal left imagines are new and insightful.

Israel also, the PLO charter asserts, constitutes "a constant threat to peace in the Middle East and the entire world." Like the danger posed by Jews and Judaism to general culture in the eyes of 19th century European antisemites. This underlying view of a sovereign Jewish state remained unchanged by the 1990's Israeli-Palestinian Oslo peace process—which, among other things, formally committed both sides to ending incitement and educating their peoples for peaceful co-existence. It is disseminated, blatantly and incessantly, through the schools, mosques and communications media of the Fatah-dominated Palestinian Authority. It was but a few weeks in 2017 between PA President Abbas telling U.S. President Donald Trump in the White House that Palestinian children were educated for peace and Trump, apparently newly-enlightened on the matter, berating Abbas in Bethlehem for lying.

Similar or identical slogans about Israel as the ultimate enemy of Arabs, of Muslims, of humanity echo the language of Lebanese Hezbollah and its masters, the mullahs of Tehran. Instigated, funded, trained and armed by Iran, Hezbollah killed more Americans, beginning with the U.S. embassy and Marine barracks bombings in Beirut in 1983, than any other terrorist organization until al-Qaeda's Sept. 11, 2001 attacks. Its agents blew up the Israeli embassy in Buenos Aires, Argentina in 1992 and the Jewish community headquarters building there in 1994, murdering more than 100, including many non-Jews, and injuring more than 300. In the Syrian civil wars beginning in 2011, Hezbollah on behalf of Iran fought to bolster beleaguered dictator Bashar al-Assad, a key Iranian and Russian ally. By the second decade of the 21st Century, Hezbollah was a leading element of the Lebanese government, its Iranian- and Syrian-armed militia stronger than the U.S.-backed Lebanese national army. Hezbollah's leader, Sheik Hassan Nasrallah, infamously observed that "if Jews all gather in Israel, it will save us the trouble of going after them worldwide."[15] He also characterized Jews—"notice I do not say Israelis"—as the world's most "despicable" people, "cowardly, feeble in body, mind and psyche."[16]

Here anti-Zionist antisemitism shows itself irreducibly as one. It commits actual war crimes and promises more. Nasrallah's threat, and much other incitement from Iran, Hezbollah, Hamas, Fatah and related anti-Israeli, anti-Jewish sources would seem to violate the United Nations' 1951 Convention on the Prevention and Punishment of the Crime of Genocide. The convention calls for punishment of, among other things, "direct and public incitement to commit genocide." It defines genocide as "acts committed with intent to destroy, in whole or in part,

---

15 "Nasrallah alleges 'Christian Zionist' plot," *The Daily Star* (Beirut), Oct. 23, 2002.

16 "In the Party of God; Are terrorists in Lebanon planning for a larger war?" *New Yorker*, Oct. 14, 2002.

a national, ethnical, racial or religious group."

Not that what is often mindlessly referred to as "the international community" can be roused to respond. This "community" was barely able in 2014 to rescue some, but not all, of a few thousand Yazidis trapped on an Iraqi mountain and threatened with slavery or death by ISIS. It proved unable that same year to find and free several hundred girls and young women kidnapped by Nigeria's Islamist Boko Haram. In the latter case much news media attention was lavished and accompanying warm sensations felt, if not at the time of the initial kidnapping then three weeks later for a fatuous and futile Twitter hashtag campaign. "#Bring Back Our Girls" was endorsed by no less than First Lady Michelle Obama. It quickly recorded nearly 2 million retweets and more than a quarter-million Instagram posts, not that any children were freed as a result. An Israel *in extremis*, or diaspora Jews similarly beleaguered, should expect no more and not be surprised by less.

Since Hezbollah's 33-day war with Israel in 2006, Nasrallah has led "the Party of God" largely from hiding, by means of pre-recorded broadcasts. Regardless, by 2017, Hezbollah possessed an estimated 150,000 mostly Iranian-supplied short- and medium-range missiles, some reportedly with sophisticated guidance systems. This was roughly nine or 10 times more than it deployed a decade earlier. Hezbollah held the weapons in violation of U.N. Security Council Resolution 1701, which helped end the 2006 war and reaffirmed the movement's pre-existing requirement under Security Council Resolution 1559, adopted in 2004, to disarm. Further, "the Party of God" based its rockets and missiles illegally among Lebanese civilians and—another violation of international law—aimed the missiles on Iran's behalf mostly at Israeli non-combatants.

No matter; blatant and repeated violations of the genocide convention were not permitted to block the unfreezing of up to $150 billion in Iranian assets as part of the 2015 nuclear deal with the United States, Great Britain, France, Germany, Russia and China. That was so even if some of that money, as U.S. officials including Secretary of State John Kerry tardily conceded, likely would go to funding Iran's terrorist partners, including Hezbollah. Such is the influence of the Palestinian narrative, with its robotic assertions of Israeli violations of international law, that actual ruptures of international law—when anti-Israeli and antisemitic—do not matter.

When hearing Hezbollah and Hamas—or their interpreters and apologists—historical context is vital. They echo, with only slight variations, Haj Amin al-Husseini's bargain with Hitler, as the grand mufti of Jerusalem himself recalled it after World War II and as cited previously, "a free hand to eradicate every last Jew from Palestine and the Arab world" and thereby "solve the Jewish problem".

Solve "the Jewish problem" by "eradicating every last Jew." Anti-Zionist? Of course. Antisemitic? Undeniably.

The Jews often, the Israelis occasionally have been reassured that their enemies don't really mean their hateful, annihilationist words. Or if they do, in their dreams but not right now, not in reality. Or that it's all just politics, for domestic consumption. This too will pass, if you don't over-react. As advice for the ghetto Jew put it, stay still, don't rock the boat. Not in Israel, not in the United States, not in England or France. Know your place and keep it. But much can be learned to the contrary, beginning in France, home of the Enlightenment and scene of the Dreyfus affair.

CHAPTER FIFTEEN

French Lessons: Hatred and Decency

I N APRIL, 2015, two leaders of the extreme-right Czech National Democracy Party left a note on the grave of Anezka Hruzova, "a Czech girl whose killing in 1899 was falsely blamed on a Jew named Leopold Hilsner. Hilsner was accused of committing a 'ritual Jewish murder.'" The note stated, according to a local Czech news Web site *Britske listy*, that Hruzova's death "brought the Czech nation together and showed that it is urgent to tackle the Jewish question. To this day, the Jewish question has not yet been solved satisfactorily." Czech authorities charged two right-wing activists with "incitement and racism" over the content of the note.[1]

A pair of Czech extremists hardly made a trend. But remarks by then-French President Francois Hollande three days after the duo's indictment suggested they were part of something bigger. Hollande, "expressed dismay" that French Jews "feel the need to 'hide.'"

"'It is intolerable that in our country citizens should feel so upset and under assault because of their religious choice that they would conclude that they have to hide,'" he said, "two days after an assault on a kippah-wearing Jewish man in Marseille [by a man] with a machete."[2] The French president "was reacting to the public debate in the Marseille Jewish community on whether Jews should hide their kippahs following the stabbings of several Jews there....

"Tzvi Amar, president of the local office of the Consistoire, the

---

1 *Britsky listy*, cited by *The Algemeiner* Jewish online newspaper, Jan. 10, 2016.
2 "Hollande: 'Intolerable' that French Jews feel they need to hide," Jewish Telegraphic Agency, Jan. 13, 2016.

French Jewish community's organization responsible for religious services, said Jews should 'remove the kippah during these troubled times'
because 'the preservation of life is sacrosanct.'" But "Michele Teboul,
president of the local branch of CRIF—an umbrella group that represents French Jewish communities politically as a lobby—told JTA that
she 'could not support a measure which dials back hundreds of years
during which Jews were able to practice their faiths and live freely as
citizens of the French Republic.'"[3]

Hundreds of years? Such is the Jewish compulsion to remember
things the way Jews wish they had been and—as with the Israeli-Palestinian Oslo "peace process"—imagine a future as they expect it should
be. Actually, French Jews lived more or less free and equally not for
hundreds of years but rather the two decades between world wars and
three or four after the second one ended. In the 1980s, deadly Palestinian terrorist attacks in France brought armed guards to synagogue
doors. Then-Prime Minister Raymond Barre no doubt inadvertently voiced the residual French-versus-Jewish distinction when, after a
bomb killed four people in Paris in 1980, he referred to "a despicable
attack that sought to target Jews who were in this synagogue and that
struck innocent Frenchmen crossing the Rue Copernicus." Jews in a
synagogue versus innocent Frenchmen on the street. The only thing
missing to complete the thought was the word "instead" at the end of
the sentence. Shortly before his death in 2007, Barre blamed "the Jewish
lobby" for criticism of his 1980 comment and "described Maurice Pa-
pon, a high-ranking civil servant convicted as a Nazi collaborator, as 'a
scapegoat.'"[4] Scapegoat, or discomfiting symbol?

~

If the "three no's of Khartoum," coming just after Israel's triumph
in the 1967 Six-Day War, were the Arabs' national rejection of Israel and
therefore of peace with it, then Durban in 2001 was the Arab-Islamist
and secular fundamentalist left's intersected rejection of Jews and Judaism along with the Jewish state. What such rejection of the "little Satan"
meant for the "great Satan" was brought home on Sept. 11, 2001, only a
week after the U.N.'s Durban conference. Al-Qaeda's destruction of New
York City's World Trade Center and attack on the Pentagon in Washing-

3 Ibid.
4 "Raymond Barre, Former French Prime Minister, Dies at 83," *The New York Times*,
Aug. 27, 2007.

ton, D.C. were Durban's intersected manifestos made manifest.

Purportedly against "racism, racial discrimination, xenophobia and related intolerance" (organizers, including Iran, conspicuously omitted antisemitism from the title), the Durban conclave reached a morally and intellectually hijacked end. In the name of fighting racism, Durban's parallel NGO (non-governmental organizations) conference boldly proclaimed death to the Jewish state and, by extension, those who supported it. Arab groups distributed posters of Jews with big noses and bloody fangs, copies of *The Protocols of the Elders of Zion* were sold on conference grounds, the usual unimaginative but potentially lethal "apartheid Israel" tropes were constant.[5]

Anne Bayefsky, representing the International Association of Jewish Lawyers and Jurists at the NGO meeting, said, "Like all Jewish participants, I felt concern for my safety. The Jewish Center in Durban was forced to close because of threats of violence." Bayefsky was asked by delegates from other "human rights groups" to leave a discussion about Palestinian Arabs since "as a representative of a Jewish organization, I was biased and couldn't be counted on to act in the interest of general human rights"[6] (that concept which, according Malaysian Prime Minister Mahathir, Jews invented). According to anti-Jewish group-think, Jews must shut up about antisemitism. A delegate from B'nai B'rith International, the Jewish humanitarian and human rights organization—for which this writer worked at the time—said the open antisemitism at Durban recalled for him the atmosphere in pre-Holocaust Vienna.

Echoing Nazi-style rhetoric, the Durban participants—the U.S. and Israeli delegations eventually walked out—were not only motivated by the U.N.'s 1975 Zionism-is-racism resolution, regardless of its 1991 revocation, but also justified by it. The hate-fest in South Africa, with Iran's significant role in pre-conference preparation, networked anti-Israel, anti-Jewish individuals and movements including some that would reappear in the boycott, sanction and divestment (BDS) campaign.

Since Durban and al-Qaeda's Sept.11, 2001 attacks, more anti-Jewish assaults, including murders, by Arab-Muslim immigrants or their French-born children, have led to many more guards at many more French Jewish community institutions than Palestinian terrorism

---

5 "United Nations: UN World Conference against Racism, Racial Discrimination, Xenophobia and Related Intolerance—Durban, South Africa," Jewish Virtual Library, www. Jewishvirtuallibrary.org/durbain-i-un-conference-against-racism-2001.

6 "The Racism Walkout: The Overview: U.S. And Israelis Quit Racism Talks Over Denunciation," *The New York Times*, Sept. 4, 2001.

in 1980s France. A French intellectual, not far removed from former Prime Minister Barre's mindset, renewed—no doubt unintentionally—Orwell's observation that "some ideas are so foolish only intellectuals believe them." He did so in 2016 by suggesting that the wearing of kipot (skullcaps), a religious requirement for observant Jewish men, indicated affiliation with "diabolical" Israel. And so, implicitly, justified assaults on the wearers. 'Diabolical" Israel recalls Trachtenberg's analysis, borrowed imprecisely by Sartre, of the "satanization" of the Jews. Or at least of their state.

Updating the medieval Devil-Jews association, so successful has identification of Israel with evil become that a 2014 survey conducted by WIN/Gallup International of public opinion in 68 countries ranked the nations most regarded as threats to world peace as 1) the United States, with 24 percent, 2) Pakistan, eight percent, 3) China, six percent, and 4) Afghanistan, Iran, Israel and North Korea tied at five percent.[7]

Nearly 8,000 French Jews immigrated to Israel in 2015, up from 2014's 7,000.[8] Another 5,000 made the move in 2016 for a total of approximately 40,000 in the previous decade. "Does a gritty ex-cop's move to Israel symbolize the end for France's Jews?" asked a *Times of Israel* headline on Oct. 28, 2015. According to the subhead, "For the past 15 years, retired Paris-area police commissioner Sammy Ghozlan has sounded the alarm over the rising tide of attacks in his beloved France. Now he's relocating to Netanya."

France has been home to half a million Jews, the world's third-largest Jewish community after Israel with six million-plus and the United States with approximately five million. (This does not count the estimated 1.7 million Jews remaining in the 15 countries of the former Soviet Union, including roughly 600,000 in Russia and 300,000 in Ukraine.) But with five million Muslims, many first- or second-generation Arab immigrants from North Africa, a significant number of whom have been radicalized instead of assimilated, France also hosts Europe's largest and often problematic Muslim population.

Ghozlan told *The Times of Israel* that antisemitic attacks, often by French Muslims, accelerated after the outbreak of the second intifada (2000-2005) and French news coverage generally so unquestioningly pro-Palestinian as to vilify Israel and its supporters. Many on the French

---

7 "A new poll says these nations are the top 4 threats to world peace. Guess who's number one?' Public Radio International, Jan. 3, 2014.

8 "Record Number of French Jews Immigrated to Israel in 2015," *Ha'aretz*, Dec. 16, 2015.

left, including communist mayors of municipalities with large Muslim populations, helped propagate slanders which, in Ghozlan's view, amounted to incitement against Jews.

Conditions differed from the early '40s. Then the Vichy France government, collaborating with the Nazis, rounded up 75,000 Jews and sent them to death camps, where nearly all perished. In 2015, police and troops protected synagogues, Jewish schools and other communal institutions from an increasingly hostile public, the former police commissioner noted. That's because, at least in part, Israel and its backers "are seen as detestable," as "Nazis," Ghozlan added.

As historian Wistrich analyzed, justification of Israeli actions as self-defense, for example, or highlighting cutting-edge Israeli high-tech or medical innovations don't count: they are dismissed as propaganda, "Jew-splaining" or perhaps more tolerantly, as the work of Jews who might be living less irritatingly, shorn of sovereignty, in Silicon Valley. Where, in fact, many Israelis can be found in American high-tech companies.

In 1980, the Rue Copernicus bombing killed four. In 1982, an attack on a Jewish restaurant in Paris took six lives. Both atrocities aroused mainstream sympathy, Ghozlan recalled. That may have been because authorities and news media initially thought far-right extremists committed both crimes. In fact, each was the work of Palestinian terrorists.

The fascist inspiration and behavior of post-World War II Arab nationalist leaders, including Palestinian nationalists remains a topic often glossed over by academics and journalists. But as Barry Rubin and Wolfgang Schwanitz spotlighted in *Nazis, Islamists and the Making of the Modern Middle East*, it is essential to understanding contemporary Islamic fundamentalism and Palestinian irredentism and their shared supremacism.

~

In July, 2014 the third Israeli-Hamas war began with Hamas' kidnaping and murder of three young Israelis. It continued through repeated Hamas rejections of Egyptian-mediated Israeli ceasefire offers. The Islamic Resistance Movement and allies such as Palestinian Islamic Jihad fired more than 4,500 mortars and rockets into the Jewish state from the Gaza Strip and attempted to tunnel into Israeli communities to kidnap and massacre more Jews. Each launch, each tunnel constituted a war crime or means to one. During the fighting, a mob of more than 300

Muslim and other anti-war "protestors" besieged several hundred Jews in Paris' Don Isaac Abravenal Synagogue. These "Others" did not attack the Israeli embassy, they besieged a synagogue. They did not shout only "Death to Israel!," they also screamed "Death to the Jews!"

Ghozlan told the *Times of Israel* that he believed had the murder of four Jews at a kosher supermarket in Paris by an Islamic terrorist in January, 2015 not occurred only two days after a pair of Islamic extremists killed 12 at the offices of *Charlie Hebdo*, it would have received little notice. "It's not that there's no future for the Jews in France," Ghozlan had said. "It's that there's no future for the Jews in France that they want." Life under armed guard ultimately is "untenable."

Certainly the torture-murder of Sarah Halimi, a retired Jewish physician, in the Paris suburb of Belleville received little official clarity at the time. According to a news account, on April 4, 2017 an immigrant from Mali, Kada Traore, 27, broke into the apartment of a Malian family at 4:25 a.m. and began reciting Quranic verses. The family lived above Traore's own residence. He then jumped over a balcony, entered the apartment of Halimi, 66, and began beating her savagely. Three police arrived at 4:45 a.m. Hearing Traore shouting "*Allahu Akhbar!*" (usually translated "God is great!" but also meaning "Our god is greater!") and "*Shaitan!*"(Arabic for the Hebrew satan, the angel who serves as prosecutor against humankind in the heavenly court), the police feared a terrorist attack. They called for back-up and waited. Anti-terror officers arrived at 5 a.m., but by then Traore had thrown Halimi from her third-floor balcony and resumed his prayers. He was not taken into custody until nearly 6 a.m.[9]

> Shock over the barbaric nature of the murder has been compounded by the reluctance of both the media and French authorities to recognize it as an antisemitic hate crime—even after a silent march of remembrance on the Sunday after the murder was met by local youths chanting 'Death to the Jews' and 'We Own Kalashnikovs'. In an open letter to new French Interior Minister Gerard Collomb, Alexandra Laignel-Lavastine—a French journalist and expert on antisemitism—charged that 'in the advanced decadence that reigns today in the country of (antisemitic comedian) Dieudonne' [M'Bala M'Bala], for whom 'the Jews are dogs,' (and people laugh hys-

9 "French Jewish Anger Grows Over Savage Antisemitic Murder of Pensioner at Hands of Muslim in Paris Suburb," Jewish Telegraphic Agency, May 29, 2017.

terically), it seems that a run-over dog deserves more attention than a murdered Jewish woman.'"[10]

By coincidence, Halimi was the family name of another Parisian Jew, Ilan Halimi, 26, who was kidnapped, tortured off-and-on for three weeks by a group of young French Muslims calling themselves "the Gang of Barbarians" in 2006. Believing all Jews to be rich, members repeatedly called Halimi's family, demanding a large ransom. Halimi died after being found, nearly naked, along a railroad track. By no coincidence, French authorities had been reluctant to acknowledge this crime too as born of antisemitism.

Shaitan, the Jew as devil, as demon. The Jews as dogs, a comedic punch line pulled from *"Filastin arduna wa al Yahud al kelabna"*—"Palestine is our land and the Jews are our dogs". The spirit of Haj Amin al-Husseini, relocated from World War II Berlin and work as indefatigable Nazi propagandist to 21st century Paris as both stand-up comic and murdering immigrant. Both constitute old-new catapults in anti-Zionist antisemitism's effort to hurl the Jews back into their place.

U.S. President Barack Obama made a point of not calling Islamic terrorism by its name. So there was dismay but not surprise when he notably described the murders at Paris' Hyper-Cacher in 2015 as "some folks chosen at random." "Some folks," not Jews. Not marked for death by antisemites purposefully striking a kosher grocery but "chosen at random." Obama's craven syntax, reflecting his thoughts, expunged any need to deal with Islamic triumphalism, with recurrent hostility to Israel, with hatred of Jews. There are countless ways to deny the reality of anti-Zionist antisemitism when one so desires.

The reality extended beyond France. Another Jewish Telegraphic Agency headline, from Jan. 24, 2015 read "Dutch Jews demand troops near synagogues; Following deadly attacks in Paris, Jewish communities ask for protection as attendance rates drop due to insecurity." The article reported "Dutch Jews asked their government to post troops outside synagogues to match security measures in France and Belgium. The plea came in letters addressed to mayors by officials from a number of Jewish communities in the Netherlands following an Islamist's slaying on January 9 of four Jews at a kosher supermarket near Paris. …"

Eleven months after Sarah Halimi's murder, 85-year-old Mireille Knoll, a Holocaust survivor, was found dead in her Paris apartment. She had been stabbed 11 times and her body partially burned. Two

---

10 Ibid.

men—one a neighbor Knoll had known, and hosted at times since he was a boy—were charged with "murder with an antisemitic motive." At a march in her honor, Samuel Cohen, 74, carried a sign reading "In France, we kill grandmothers because they're Jewish." He said "it would be a little exaggerated to say that we are not safe in France today. Yet it's true that we are worried, that it's become hard to practice one's faith in some areas, and that we've reach a new degree of antisemitism with this murder."[11]

Not feeling safe in a country increasingly influenced by anti-Zionist antisemitism from radicalized French Muslims, the far left and the far right, not only had 40,000 or more French Jews emigrated to Israel in the previous decade, but an equal or larger number relocated within France, having "moved from some parts of greater Paris to other parts." And many others "moved to Britain, North America and Australia. The common factor among these migrations is a lack of trust in the future of France—shared, as a matter of fact, by many Christian or secular French. Another incentive is that once you were raised as a proud and happy Jew, you find it difficult to relapse into a near-Marrano status."[12] (Marrano [literally "swine"] was a term applied to suspected secret Jews in Spain of the Inquisition.)

Three months after Knoll was murdered in the French capital, in the German capital a Jewish teenager named Jonathan "was playing an Israeli song—'Tel Aviv,' sung by Omer Adam—in Berlin's Bahnhof Zoo subway station. Three Arab Germans heard the words 'Tel Aviv' and confronted Jonathan and his friends." One Arab man, after confirming Jonathan was Jewish, declared "Seventy years of murdering children! I don't want to hear this Jew s*** here! This is our town, our turf. If I see you here again, I'll slit your throat, you f***ing Jew." The three Arabs then physically attacked Jonathan and his friends, one trying to push Jonathan onto the tracks. When the assailants fled, "the security guards at the station chose not to pursue them." The assault "met for the most part with soggy indifference from Germany's chattering classes."[13]

Such incidents proliferate. As they do, the post- post-Holocaust era comes to resemble in certain respects the pre-Holocaust era. The JTA dispatch detailing the Sarah Halimi case, quoted Frans Timmer-

---

11 "Mirielle Knoll, Murdered Holocaust Survivor, Is Honored in Paris," *The New York Times,* March 28, 2018.

12 "French Jews and the Macron Experiment," by Michel Gufinkiel, *inFOCUS,* Summer, 2018.

13 "German Jewry: A Bleak Future," by Benjamin Weinthal, *inFOCUS,* Summer, 2018.

man, Jewish vice president of the European Commission. Timmerman spoke at a ceremony in Brussels commemorating the victims of the Hyper-Cacher killings: "If there's no future for the Jews in Europe, there's no future for Europe." Certainly not for Europe in the West, Europe of NATO, of the free world. Such constructs, like support for Israel and actual as opposed to theoretical equality for Jews, maybe be too much for post-Christian, post-national, post-modern Europe—in addition receiving millions of refugees and migrants from Muslim-majority countries marked by anti-Zionist antisemitism—to bear.

Former Associated Press reporter Matti Friedman provided an indispensable explanation for Ghozlan's observation that French news coverage in recent decades generally has been so unquestioningly pro-Palestinian as to vilify Israel and its supporters (in that way little different from much other Western European coverage). Friedman worked in AP's Jerusalem bureau from 2006 through 2011. Writing shortly after the 2014 war between Israel and Hamas and its supporters in the Gaza Strip, he referred to an article in *The New Yorker* that "described the summer's events by dedicating one sentence each to the horrors in Nigeria and Ukraine, four sentences to the crazed genocidaires of ISIS, and the rest of the article—30 sentences—to Israel and Gaza."[14] What accounted for such disproportion, the fact that the tilt was almost completely anti-Israel, and that *The New Yorker's* treatment was no aberration but rather epitomized the journalistic (and academic) norm?

Making clear that the Israeli-Palestinian—more specifically the Arab-Israeli or Muslim-Jew—conflict objectively was one of the world's smaller clashes, Friedman wrote that the lasting importance of the Israeli-Hamas 2014 combat "doesn't lie in the war itself. It lies instead in the way the war has been described and responded to abroad, and the way this has laid bare the resurgence of an old, twisted pattern of thought and its migration from the margins to the mainstream of Western discourse—namely, a hostile obsession with Jews. … The world is not responding to events in this country, but rather to the description of these events by news organizations."[15]

According to Friedman, journalism's "severe malfunction" in covering "the international media's Israel story" stems from group-think and "a narrative construct that is largely fiction." It posits Palestinian

---

14 "An Insider's Guide to the Most Important Story on Earth; A former AP correspondent explains how and why reporters get Israel so wrong, and why it matters," *Tablet*, Aug. 26, 2014.

15 Ibid.

Arabs as supporters of a two-state solution and passive victims of Israelis. Reporting provides "nearly no real analysis of Palestinian society or ideologies, profiles of armed Palestinian groups or investigations of Palestinian government. Palestinians are not taken seriously as agents of their own fate." When reality conflicts with the narrative, as it often does, reality goes largely unreported: "The Hamas charter, for example, calls not just for Israel's destruction but for the murder of Jews and blames Jews for engineering the French and Russian revolutions [from *The Protocols of the Learned Elders of Zion*] and both world wars [from Nazi propaganda]; the charter was never mentioned in print when I was at the AP, though Hamas won a Palestinian national election and had become one of the region's most important players."

Conversely, "the fact that Israelis quite recently elected moderate governments that sought reconciliation with the Palestinians, and which were undermined by the Palestinians, is considered unimportant and rarely mentioned." A key example was the information AP reporters gathered on Prime Minister Ehud Olmert's 2008 "significant peace offer to the Palestinian Authority" and on the fact Palestinian leaders nevertheless "deemed it insufficient" and walked away without making a counter-offer. This "should have been one of the biggest stories of the year" but top editors in Jerusalem decided not to publish. Doing so, like examining Hamas in detail "would make that [Palestinian] narrative look like nonsense." Why spike such coverage? "Many of the people deciding what you will read and see from here view their role not as explanatory but as political. Coverage is a weapon to be placed at the disposal of the side they like." That side is not the Jewish state.

Why not? Again, Freidman: "A knowledgeable observer of the Middle East cannot avoid the impression that the region is a volcano and that the lava is radical Islam, an ideology whose various incarnations are now shaping this part of the world." Middle East minorities, including Jews, all "are under intense pressure from Islam. ... But reporters generally cannot see the Israel story in relation to anything else. Instead of describing Israel as one of the villages abutting the volcano, they describe Israel as the volcano."

So, "the Israel story is framed to seem as if it has nothing to do with events nearby because the 'Israel' of international journalism does not exist in the same geo-political universe as Iraq, Syria or Egypt. The Israel story is not about current events. It is about something else.

"For centuries, stateless Jews played the role of a lightning rod for ill will among the majority population. They were a symbol of things that were wrong. Did you want to make the point that greed was bad? Jews were greedy. Cowardice? Jews were cowardly. Were you a Communist? Jews were capitalists. Were you a capitalist? In that case, Jews were communists. *Moral failure was the essential trait of the Jew* [emphasis added]. It was their role in Christian tradition—the only reason European society knew or cared about them in the first place."

Now, when journalists "cover the Jews' war as more worthy of attention than any other, when they portray the Jews of Israel as the party obviously in the wrong, when they omit all possible justifications for the Jews' actions and obscure the true face of their enemies, what they are saying to their readers—whether they intend to or not—is that Jews are the worst people on earth. The Jews are a symbol of the evils that civilized people are taught from an early age to abhor. International press coverage has become a morality play starring a familiar villain. ... You don't need to be a history professor, or a psychiatrist, to understand what's going on. Having rehabilitated themselves against considerable odds in a minute corner of the earth, the descendants of powerless people who were pushed out of Europe and the Islamic Middle East have become what their grandparents were—the pool into which the world spits. The Jews of Israel are the screen onto which it has become socially acceptable to project the things you hate about yourself and your own country. The tool through which this psychological projection is executed is the international press."[16] And in Western academia can be found the roots of the international press' compulsion to project the worst against and about Israel.

Friedman concluded that anti-Zionist antisemitism provides many Westerners "the old comfort of parsing the moral failings of Jews, and the familiar feeling of superiority this brings them, to [avoid] confronting an unhappy and confusing reality." It allows them (as Berman stressed in *The Flight of the Intellectuals*) to avoid facing "the ascendant force" in the Middle East and beyond, which "is not democracy or modernity. It is rather an empowered strain of Islam that assumes different and sometimes conflicting forms, and that is willing to employ extreme violence in a quest to unite the region under its control and confront the West."

The European Union's Timmerman spoke, and Friedman wrote before the November 2015 massacre of 130 people in Paris; before the March, 2016 murders of 28 more in Brussels by Muslim fundamentalists loyal to the Islamic State in Iraq and Syria; before the massacre of

---

16 Ibid.

86 people in Nice in 2016 by a French Muslim driving a 19-ton truck through a crowd celebrating Bastille Day, before the 2017 massacre of concert-goers in Manchester and murders on London Bridge.

On Oct. 29, 2015 a Sudanese Muslim tried to kill an Israeli Jew during an Ethiopian Airways flight. The Jew, an employee of an Israeli communications company working in Africa, said "about 20 minutes before the plane started its descent the passenger sitting behind me identified me as Israeli and Jewish. ... He came up behind my seat and started to choke me with a lot of force ... and at first I couldn't get my voice out and call for help.

"He hit me over the head with a metal tray and shouted 'Allah akh-bar' and 'I will slaughter the Jew.' Only after a few seconds, just before I was about to lose consciousness, did I manage to call out and a flight attendant who saw what was happening summoned colleagues."[17] According to the victim, Arik, "most of the passengers on the half-empty flight refrained from getting involved." After others "pulled him off me he hit me and shouted in Arabic. Some of the flight staff took me to the rear section of the plane and two guarded the attacker during the last part of the flight."

"A Lebanese passenger was one of the few who came to Arik's rescue. Arik says that ... 'After we landed the Lebanese guy told me that ... after they'd overpowered my attacker he said to everyone, 'Let's finish him off.'"

The following day, a New York City television station reported two attacks on Jewish men in Brooklyn. One, reading a prayer from his cell phone while walking to synagogue, was beaten, allegedly by Christian Rojas, 36. Rojas screamed "I hate all Jews" and, while being handcuffed, "I'm fed up with Jews."

The night before, a few blocks away, an off-duty member of Hatzolah, a volunteer emergency medical service active in Jewish communities world-wide, sustained non life-threatening injuries when stabbed by someone dressed in black and wearing a black-and-white hockey mask.[18]

Similar assaults occurred in New York City in December. In the first a "Middle Eastern-looking" man reportedly struck a Chasidic Jew repeatedly in the face in the lobby of a Midtown office building. A wit-

---

17 "Sudanese citizen tried to kill Israeli on international flight," Ynetnews.com (English-language Web site of Israeli Hebrew daily *Yediot Aharnot*, Nov. 3, 2015.

18 "Attacks on Hasidic Man Heading to Synagogue, Off-Duty Hatzolah EMT Investigated as Hate Crimes," NBC Channel 4, New York City, Nov. 4, 2015.

ness told *The Algemeiner* that a security guard and passers-by watched but did not intervene or call police. In Brooklyn, according to WABC Channel 7 Television's "Eyewitness News," a black man at Medgar Evers Community College punched a Jew wearing a yarmulke in the face and stomach, said "I don't like white and Jewish," then fled. A Muslim woman reportedly came to the victim's aid.

Two months later a Jewish man, 25, was stabbed by a black man in Brooklyn's Crown Heights, a neighborhood in which the Chabad Lubavitch Chasidic enclave is surrounded by a larger African American population. The assault, which reportedly was not a robbery attempt, appeared to have been unprovoked, unless the fact that the victim was identifiably Jewish was a provocation.

At the University of Texas system's Austin flagship campus, Israel Studies Prof. Ami Pedahzur said he was compelled to get around incognito for fear of his own and his family's safety after students from the Palestine Solidarity Committee disrupted a lecture he was hosting and launched a smear campaign against him.[19] The "activists" leading the confrontation against Pedahzur wore *kefiyeh*s, the badge of anti-Israel honor and, as noted above, a post- post-Holocaust cloth swastika.

At the University of California-Irvine a mob chased a pro-Israel student, forcing her to take refuge in a campus building.

The Jewish federations of Nashville and Middle Tennessee, Memphis, Chattanooga and Knoxville all expressed "anger, disappointment and worry" at the "tepid response" of university administrators to antisemitism and racism at the University of Tennessee's flagship Knoxville campus. In a 2016 letter, they urged Chancellor Jimmy Cheek to stop downplaying evidence of rampant Jew-hatred and anti-Zionism at the school. Such examples—disruption of events, verbal and physical intimidation, social media posts praising Hitler—could be multiplied endlessly, and since the 2001 Durban conference, have been doing so. In the name of "Palestine," Holocaust jokes and assertions that Jews must die appear online like toadstools from ancient spoor.

Epitomizing the academy's retreat before the "new" antisemitism was Yale University's abandonment of the Yale Initiative for the Interdisciplinary Study of Antisemitism. The initiative began in 2006 at the behest of the Institute for the Study of Global Antisemitism and Policy, itself then only two years old. YIISA attracted well-known scholars and began graduate and post-doctoral programs. But in 2010 it sinned

---

19 "Israeli Studies Professor Forced to Wear Disguise at University of Texas After Being Pursued by Anti-Israel Activists," Dec. 1, 2015, *The Daily Wire.com*.

against progressive orthodoxy and was banished.

That year it held a conference in New York City with more than 100 speakers from 20-plus countries. More than 500 people attended. Only two of the 23 panel discussions examined antisemitism stemming from Arab-Islamic sources and, in the words of the *Connecticut Jewish Ledger*, "noted the clear and present genocidal danger" radical Islam presented to Israel and the Jewish people. But that proved to be two panel discussions too many. Palestinian spokesmen in Washington, D.C. objected. A member of Yale's board of corporators found discussions of antisemitism and Islamism offensive. YIISA shortly was pushed off campus, replaced by the Yale Program for the Study of Antisemitism.

Illustrating how many cannot bear too much truth, especially about Jews and those who hate them, the new program focused not on contemporary Jew-hatred and its sources but rather the history of such bigotry in 19th century France. Even so, Yale's supposedly sanitized new look at antisemitism foundered on what Alan Dershowitz has called today's yet-to-be-completed anti-Jewish genocide. One of its conferences collided with the similarities between 19th century French antisemitism and the Jew-hatred of Muslims in 21st century France. Parsing the 2012 murder of four children and a rabbi at a Jewish school in Toulouse by an Arab resident of France, Yale academics—one resists using the term scholars—"asserted ... that Islamist antisemitism for the most part ought to be considered a 'metaphor' and unworthy of real concern."[20] Such was the rhetorical prestidigitation of craven intellectuals avoiding confrontation with Berman's "ascendant force" of their time and "the largest crimes."

Subsequently, free-standing ISGAP has grown into an important source of research and publication regarding contemporary hatred of Jews. Meanwhile, on the subject of anti-Zionist antisemitism, numerous colleges and universities increasingly resemble medieval monasteries as fonts not of learning but rather of simultaneously vacuous and vicious neo-superstition.

Forty years after philosopher Eric Hoffer's elemental warning, historian Robert Wistrich spotlighted the nexus of Islamic triumphalism, the Palestinian narrative and resurgent Jew-hatred. His analysis appeared just days before his death of a heart attack at 70. Wistrich was director of the Vidal Sassoon International Center for the Study of Anti-Semitism at Jerusalem's Hebrew University. His trenchant commen-

20 "Welcome ISGAP: Institute for the Study of Global Antisemitism and Policy," editorial, *Connecticut Jewish Ledger*, Oct. 23, 2012 online.

tary remains worth citing at length. Referring to the need for Jews "to free ourselves from certain outdated myths," he wrote:

> [E]ven today, Jews in Israel and the Diaspora are fixated on the dangers of far-right traditional antisemitism—whether racist, religious or nationalist. While neo-fascism has not altogether disappeared, it is in most cases a secondary threat.
>
> Second, there is an illusory belief that more Holocaust education and memorialization can serve as an effective antidote to contemporary antisemitism. This notion, shared by many governments and well-meaning liberal gentiles, is quite unfounded. On the contrary, today 'Holocaust inversion' (the perverse transformation of Jews into Nazis and Muslims into victimized 'Jews') all-too-often becomes a weapon with which to pillory Israel and denigrate the Jewish people....
>
> Third, we must recognize much more clearly than before that since 1975 (with the passing of the scandalous U.N. resolution condemning Zionism as racism) hatred of Israel has increasingly mutated into the chief vector for the 'new' antisemitism.
>
> By libeling the Jewish state as 'racist,' 'Nazi,' 'apartheid' and founded from its inception on 'ethnic cleansing,' its enemies have turned Zionism into a synonym for criminality and a term of pure opprobrium. Hence, every Jew (or non-Jew) who supports the totally 'illegitimate' or immoral 'Zionist entity' is thereby complicit in a cosmic evil.[21]

That is, a cosmic evil nearly identical with that of the satanized Jews of the early Church fathers and their medieval followers. Wistrich further asserted:

> Fourth, today's antisemitism is a product of a new civic religion that could be termed 'Palestinianism.' The official Palestinian narrative seeks to supplant Israel with a *judenrein* Palestine from the Mediterranean Sea to the Jordan River.

---

21 "Antisemitism and Jewish Destiny," by Robert Wistrich, *The Jerusalem Post*, May 20, 2015.

In the case of Hamas, this intent is absolutely explicit. With Fatah, it is partly veiled for tactical reasons.

But when it comes to the Palestinian ideology and the millions around the world who support it, virtually all actions of self-defense by Israel are instantly classified as 'genocide,' demonized and treated as part of a sinister Jewish-imperialist conspiracy. Not surprisingly, then, pro-Palestine demonstrations, beginning in the summer of 2014, were often accompanied by ugly chants of 'Death to the Jews' and anti-Semitic incidents.[22]

Wistrich insisted his fifth point was "closely related to this reality. Since the turn of the 21st century, antisemitism has undergone a process of growing 'Islamicization,' linked to the terrorist holy war against Jews and other non-Muslims with its truly lethal consequences. Yet most debates skirt around the issues of Iran and radical Islam.

"However, if we do not confront the prime danger posed by radical Islamist and genocidal antisemitism, how can our common struggle hope to succeed? One of the symptoms of this vain policy of appeasement pursued by America and Europe is the almost Pavlovian reflex after every terrorist, anti-Semitic outrage to immediately disconnect it from any link to Islam. Of course, Islamist is not identical with Islam, only a minority of Muslim believers support terrorism, and stigmatization is wrong. Equally, we must empower moderate Muslims wherever we can.

"But denial does not work. Levels of antisemitism among Muslims clearly remain the highest in the world, and the horrific consequences of *jihadi* movements like Islamic State for all minorities are impossible to ignore. Nothing can be gained by sweeping this threat under the carpet. The Islamists are the spearhead of current antisemitism, aided and abetted by the moral relativism of all-too-many naive Western liberals."

His sixth and seventh observations, the historian stressed, related "to the need for Israelis and Diaspora Jews to rediscover, redefine and reassess their Jewish identity, core Jewish values and the depth of their own connection to the Land of Israel as well as to their historic heritage....

"My final reflection flows from this experience. I believe that in an age of Jewish empowerment, living in a sovereign and democratic Israeli

---

22 Ibid.

state, we can and must first clarify for ourselves our vocation, *raison d'être*, moral priorities, and the deeper meaning of our near-miraculous return to the historic homeland. This is the other side of the coin in our essential and relentless fight against antisemitism. ... [L]et us be worthy of the scriptural promise that 'the Torah will come forth from Zion and the word of the Lord from Jerusalem.'

"Here, in the beating heart of the Jewish nation, where its body and soul come together in the City of Peace, we must be true to the national and universal vision of our biblical prophets. Antisemitism, the long shadow which has for so long accompanied our bi-millennial Diasporic tribulations, and nearly 70 years of renewed statehood, is neither 'eternal' nor must it prevent Jews from fulfilling their ultimate destiny to one day become a 'light unto the nations.'"[23]

Of course, rejection of that light—by early Christian supercessionists, later anti-Christian fascists, by Marxists, by secular fundamentalists and neo-pagans, by Islamic supremacists—has been and remains a primary cause of antisemitism. Enemies of the Enlightenment, of natural law, cannot abide the concept of unalienable (that is, God-given) individual rights and, based on them, self-government. So they attack the concept and reality of American exceptionalism, rooted as it is in the belief in unalienable rights and self-rule. Just so, enemies of religious pluralism, or of religion itself, hate and attack Jewish exceptionalism— especially with its elevation of ethical monotheism and its insistence on God-given free will coupled with divinely-required personal responsibility.

But Jews and their non-Jewish supporters, Israelis and their backers, cannot hope to succeed by denying either their mission or the nature of the struggle any more than Americans can cohere and survive let alone triumph by denying their national identity or the reasons for and hostility to that identity from authoritarian and totalitarian enemies. These can be "progressive" or reactionary, foreign or domestic. It is not, as Hitler insisted, mortal combat between the influences of corrupt civilization and natural culture. Neither is it, as al-Husseini charged, an end-of-times clash between the religion of Allah, Islam, and its ultimate enemy, the satanic Jews. Rather, to paraphrase Frankl, it is the conflict between humanity and inhumanity.

From the beginning the Palestinian narrative has been a species of Middle Eastern revisionism and denial. It pushes toward the same goal, whether invoked blatantly by a Khamenei, with sheer implausibil-

---

23 Ibid.

ity by Palestinian Authority President Mahmoud Abbas or former PA chief negotiator, later PLO general-secretary Saeb Erekat, or presented as a "post-Zionist corrective" by journalists, clergy, academics and other apologists. But instead of the ridicule and rebuke reserved for Holocaust revisionists, Middle East revisionism often has achieved its aims, opening the way for destruction of Israel and reghettoizing the Jews.

Success in the struggle between Zionist and anti-Zionist, Jew and Jew-hater, between the race of the decent and its opposite requires, in part, rejecting the Palestinian narrative. The lie of Palestine is the latest reincarnation of the blood libel, which itself stems from and justifies portrayal of the Jew and the Jews as demonic.

In 1943, Joshua Trachtenberg found in Nazi Jew-hatred an extension of medieval Christianity's identification of the Devil and the Jews as a hand-in-glove anti-Christian team, Hitler's extension making them not anti-Christian but anti-human. A half-century later, Joel Carmichael, exploring why hatred of outsiders is commonplace but hostility to the Jews unique, returned to the theological-as-ideological in *The Satanizing of the Jews: Origin and Development of Mystical Antisemitism* (Fromm International Publishing Co., 1992). In Carmichael's analysis, Jews supplanted the Devil, becoming satanic in and of themselves as they denied Christ and through their obstinate disbelief barred His second coming and the (originally Jewish) kingdom of God on Earth. Secularists dispensed with God, Islamists with His promise to the Jews, but for both the Jew, as Zionist and Israel, goes on like Satan, crucifying Palestine. Theirs is the old reaction, in new garments, against the civilizational principle.

Epilogue

JUST AFTER WORLD WAR I, Aunt Frieda, my mother's oldest sister, immigrated with her mother to the United States. There they reunited with my grandfather, Louis (Lemuel ben Yitzhak haCohen) Mandel, in Willard, Ohio. Though quite young when she left Chemenick in the Russian Pale of Settlement (territory that would return to a restored Poland), Aunt Frieda would remember hiding in the kitchen root cellar during Easter weekend. That was when drunken peasants, incited by local priests over "the Jews' crucifixion of Christ," roamed the streets looking for *zhyds* to beat.

In her later years—she died in 2009 at 95—Aunt Frieda, then living in Florida, occasionally spoke by telephone with my sister Cathy in Israel. Like all homes built in Israel after Saddam Hussein's missile attacks, Cathy's attractive duplex had a "safe room" reinforced against small rockets, its metal door and metal-shuttered window lined against gas or chemical weapons. During the 2006 war in Lebanon, a Hezbollah rocket fired 15 miles south into Israel struck 400 yards away, blasting a hole through an undistinguished piece of modern sculpture in a traffic circle.

From drunken peasants hunting Jews to Shi'ite fanatics hunting Zionists, from the second decade of the 20th century to the first decade of the 21st century, from root cellars to safe rooms, the hatred remained unchanged. What was different was the Jews' ability to retaliate from their own sovereign state. In one important respect this intolerable ability helped transform older Jew-hatred into newer anti-Zionist antisemitism. How dare those Jews, previously somehow demonic but weak, now demonic but strong, defend themselves?

In 2007, a disturbed young man—vibrating to an increasingly

powerful frequency of our times—pulled Elie Wiesel from an elevator in an attempt to force him to deny the Holocaust. In 2011, 23 members of parliament—22 from Labor, including future party leader Jeremy Corbyn—proposed changing the name of the United Kingdom's Holocaust Memorial Day to "Genocide Memorial Day." The head of Britain's Holocaust Educational Trust labeled the attempt one of "denial and distortion" since the observance already included other victims of the Holocaust and subsequent genocides and because the Shoah was "a specific crime with antisemitism at its core."[1] Exactly; hence the compulsion to dilute it through misleading universalization as part of the drive to erase the Jewish past, slander the Jewish present and foreclose a Jewish future.

Proofs of such a compulsion multiply incessantly. One small example, quaint in its lack of self-awareness but ominous as a drop in the growing social-cultural stream, came from a Chicago "room-for-rent" listing: "This apartment strives to be a safe space—no sexism, homophobia, zionism, racism, classism, transphobia, xenophobia, fatphobia or other hatred and prejudice is tolerated." Ah yes, the Jewish people's national liberation movement, right there with all the other "hatreds and prejudices," real and imagined, of the contemporary *bien pensant.* After a Jewish woman who described herself as "very progressive and somewhat left-wing" and LGBTQ (lesbian, gay, bisexual, transgender or queer) complained, the international Airbnb tourism rental operation deleted the listing.[2]

About the same time, California state assembly candidate, Democrat Maria Estrada, explained she was "anti-Zionist, not antisemitic." Estrada said she "enjoys" listening to Nation of Islam leader Rev. Louis Farrakhan—one of America's most vocal anti-Jewish bigots—and claimed "Democrats turn a blind eye to the genocide against Palestinians and justify it by bringing up the Holocaust. ... Anyone who believes they are one of 'God's chosen people' automatically feels superior and justified in all they do."[3] Suppress the Holocaust—or hijack it—oppose the Jewish state, take pleasure from Jew-haters and smear Judaism but tell yourself and the world you're not antisemitic. More and more do.

---

1 "Corbyn called for Holocaust Memorial Day to be renamed 'Genocide Memorial Day,'" *The Times of Israel*, Aug. 2, 2018.

2 "Airbnb removes Chicago listing that would not tolerate Zionism," Jewish Telegraphic Agency, July 30, 2018.

3 "Ghettoizing Israel, Reghettoizing the Jews," by Eric Rozenman, Jewish News Syndicate, July 20, 2018.

In August, 2011, as the prosecution at the International Criminal Court summed up its case against Congolese warlord Thomas Lubanga in the first ICC trial to focus exclusively on child soldiers, Benjamin Ferencz asserted that "seizing and training young people to hate and kill presumed adversaries undermines the legal and moral firmament of human society."

He knew what he was talking about. Then 91, Ferencz also had served as an American prosecutor of top Nazis at the Nuremberg war crimes trials in 1945 and 1946. His presence before the ICC was an historical reminder made flesh: Creation of the United Nations, subsidiaries like the ICC and legislation defining crimes against humanity, among them incitement to genocide, originated primarily in revulsion at World War II's slaughter. This slaughter was epitomized by the Holocaust of European Jewry.

According to prosecutors, Lubanga allegedly recruited hundreds of children for the "armed wing"—terrorist branch—of the Union of Congolese Patriots Party. These child soldiers were "to fight in conflicts .... to kill, rape and pillage."

The incitement component of Lubanga's case echoed charges against leaders of the 1994 Rwandan genocide. Conducted by the country's radical Hutu leaders and their followers against Tutsi neighbors and more moderate Hutus, these crimes of organized hatred and dehumanization ended with the murders of 800,000 people.

Use of child soldiers and incitement to mass murder ought to lead the "international community"—that notional collective that stood aside during the Congolese and Rwanda killings, among others—to the descendants of al-Husseini and Arafat, to Abbas & Co., to Iran of the ayatollahs. But misplaced sympathy for Palestinian Arabs as victims of alleged Israeli repression, fear of foreign and domestic Islamists and the desire for Iranian commerce obstructs connection of these otherwise conspicuous dots.

International law bars the use of children under 15 in war. A U.N. treaty adopted by more than 100 countries, including the United States, puts the age at 18. Nevertheless, recruitment, indoctrination and use of Palestinian children in warfare has been carried out not only by Hamas but also by offshoots of Fatah. Hamas and Palestinian Islamic Jihad used children for more than 30 anti-Israeli suicide bombings between 2000 and 2005. The PA's official television, newspapers, mosque sermons, school curriculum and summer camps have—in violation of the 1989 Convention on the Rights of the Child—fomented hatred of Jews, delegitimization of Israel and a cult of "martyrdom" among Palestinian children.

The United Nations has issued annual reports on children in combat. Given the world body's inbred anti-Israel tilt, it was surprising when the 2005 paper finally mentioned Palestinian Arabs. A year earlier, the U.N.'s Special Representative for Children and Armed Conflict, undersecretary general Olara Otunnu, had called "on the Palestinian Authority to do everything within their power to stop all participation by children in the conflict." The PA ignored him, as did virtually all major news media. So Hamas, Palestinian Islamic Jihad and the PA felt free to continue incessant incitement and periodic mobilization of children.

At the time Ferencz helped prosecute warlord Lubanga for similar crimes, official Palestinian television again was glorifying one of the deadliest terrorist attacks in the history of the Jewish state, the 1978 Coast Road Massacre. Perpetrated by Fatah, then led by Arafat with Abbas as a right-hand man, it resulted in the murder of 37 Israeli civilians—men, women and children. Palestinian movements of all stripes still exalt the female leader of the assault, Dalal Mughrabi, as a role model for children and women.

The PA and Hamas were not alone in anti-Israel genocidal incitement. In 2008, a group of international scholars, legislators and genocide survivors from Rwanda and Sudan discussed trying Iran's then-President Mahmoud Ahmadinejad. They recognized that his anti-Israel declarations resembled the coded anti-Tutsi incitement by Hutu leaders in 1994. Like Jan Karski's 1942 warning about Nazi genocide, the idea went nowhere. But it should not be forgotten. Eventually, prerequisite to Israeli-Palestinian reconciliation, the changes—end of incitement, establishment of education for coexistence, extirpation of terrorist organizations—required by the 1990s Oslo accords must occur.

Without the "de-Nazification" of Palestinian leadership, absent trials like that of Lubanga, unable to identify a generation of Palestinian leaders untainted by terrorism—as President George W. Bush required in his 2003 speech formally endorsing a two-state peace—decent people must not equivocate. They will not split a non-equivalent difference or evasively urge a plague on both houses. They will not retreat into deconstructed relativist excuses that deny human equality in order to exonerate the fetishized "other" and condemn the demonized "privileged."

Instead, they will insist on objective history. They will reject subjective narratives. Refusing to slander or delegitimize, they will judge Palestinian Arabs and Israeli Jews by the same standard. And they will recognize in the Palestinian narrative of thieving, murderous Zionists a reincarnation of the blood libel against the Jews. That ought to motivate them to oppose anti-Zionist antisemitism. The self-choosing decent race—including Jews, Muslims, Christians and others—will stand with Israel. It will stand with the Jews, rejecting at long last the lie of the Jew as all-purpose demon.

In this way the decent race also will help rescue the entwined civilizational principles of sacredness of human life, free will, ethical choice and equality among individual human beings. Insisting on the humanizing power of ethical choice incidentally could help Palestinian Arabs free themselves from crippling self-victimization, help free Islamists of poisonous intolerance—should they want to be liberated. Such insistence would release both a unique minority and humanity at large from an ancient curse, from the oldest hatred.

Two-time Pulitzer Prize-winning historian Barbara W. Tuchman introduced one of her early books, *Bible and Sword: England and Palestine from the Bronze Age to Balfour*, New York University Press, 1956, with this striking observation:

> The history of the Jews is . . . intensely peculiar in the fact of having given the Western world its concept of origins and monotheism, its ethical traditions, and the founder of its prevailing religion, yet suffering dispersion, statelessness and ceaseless persecution, and finally in our times nearly successful genocide, dramatically followed by fulfillment of the never-relinquished dream of return to their homeland. Viewing this strange and singular history one cannot escape the impression that it must contain some special significance for the history of mankind, that in some way, whether one believes in divine purpose or inscrutable circumstance, the Jews have been singled out to carry the tale of human fate.

Frankl's race of decent people appreciate this divinely inscrutable circumstance. Members of his indecent race reject it. Apparently threatened in one way or another by that circumstance, they seek to destroy the Jewish state and people. That much, at least, is clear.

Acknowledgments

I N NOVEMBER 1980, U.S. Representative-elect Robert Shaman-
sky hired me as press secretary. Bob soon was named to the
House Foreign Affairs Committee, Europe and the Middle East sub-
committee. So began my 35-year-plus education in American Middle
Eastern policy, Israel and Jewish affairs. In 1984, M.J. Rosenberg took
me on as assistant editor of *Near East Report*, and I succeeded him as
editor two years later. Shoshana Bryen at the Jewish Institute for National Security Affairs; Leonard "Doc" Kapiloff and his son, Jonathan,
at the *Washington Jewish Week*; B'nai B'rith International's Harvey
Berk and Dan Mariaschin, and Andrea Levin and Carol Greenwald at
CAMERA all opened opportunities that contributed to my instruction.
Without them, I would have not have been able to undertake this work.
From Bertram Korn, Jr. I first heard the indispensable phrase, "secular fundamentalist." Gerald Honigman likewise spotlighted for me the
first partition of British Mandatory Palestine, the one that created the
Arab state of Transjordan. Lenny Ben-David edited my editing of the
1985 and 1989 editions of *Myths and Facts: A Concise Record of the Arab-Israeli Conflict*. My wife, Melinda, helpfully endured many rehearsals
of much of what became this book. Juliana Geran Pilon demonstrated how to corral a non-fiction manuscript. CAMERA colleague Sean
Durns pointed me to key sources. To my editors at New English Review
Press, especially Rebecca Bynum and Kendra Mallock, my gratitude.
Others too numerous to mention also contributed to my understanding along the way. But as always with an undertaking of this sort, the
interpretations, opinions and any errors and omissions are my own.

A Note on Style

I WRITE ANTISEMITISM, not anti-Semitism, unless in direct quotes. As explained in the text, anti-Semitism was a late 19th century German coinage chosen to make Jew-hatred sound more scientific. But there was no "Semitism" to be "anti-." In this I follow scholars such as Robert Wistrich and Alvin Rosenfeld. I also follow American usage, so the British Labour Party is rendered Labor, unless in direct quotes.

SELECTED BIBLIOGRAPHY

Arieh L. Avneri, *The Claim of Dispossession: Jewish Land-Settlement and the Arabs, 1878-1948*, Efal, Israel; New York, Hakibbutz Hameuchad Publishing House, 1980 (Hebrew), 1982 (English).

Paul Berman, *The Flight of the Intellectuals; The Controversy Over Islamism and The Press*, Brooklyn, N.Y., Melville House Publishing, 2010.

Richard Bessel, *Nazism and War*, New York, Modern Library, 2006.

Kai Bird, *The Good Spy; The Life and Death of Robert Ames*, New York, Broadway Books, 2014.

Daniel J. Boorstin, *The Image: A Guide to Pseudo-events in America*, New York, Vintage Books/Random House, Inc., 1992 (Paperback issue of 1987 25th anniversary edition).

Stephen Eric Bronner, *A Rumor About the Jews; Antisemitism, Conspiracy, and the Protocols of Zion*, New York, 2000; Oxford, Oxford University Press, 2003.

Thomas Cahill, *The Gifts of the Jews; How a Tribe of Desert Nomads Changed the Way Everyone Thinks and Feels*, New York, Nan A. Talese (Bantam, Doubleday, Dell), 1998.

Joel Carmichael, *The Satanizing of the Jews; Origin and Development of Mystical Anti-Semitism*, Fromm International Publishing Co., New York, 1992.

Niall Ferguson, *Civilization; The West and the Rest*, New York, The Penguin Group, 2011.

Viktor E. Frankl, *Man's Search for Meaning*, Boston, Beacon Press (with a New Foreword by Harold S. Kushner), 2006. (Original English title, *From Death-Camp to Existentialism*, 1959.)

Lela Gilbert, *Saturday People, Sunday People; Israel Through the Eyes of a Christian Sojourner*, New York, Encounter Books, 2012.

Martin Gilbert, *Churchill and the Jews: A Lifelong Friendship*, New York, Henry Holt and Co., 2007.

George Gilder, *The Israel Test*, Minneapolis, Minn., Richard Vigilante Books, 2009.

Yehoshua Harkabi, *The Palestinian Covenant and its Meaning*, London, Vallentine, Mitchell & Co. Ltd, 1979.

Jeffrey Herf, *Nazi Propaganda for the Arab World*, New Haven and London, Yale University Press, 2009.

Arthur Hertzberg, editor, *The Zionist Idea; A Historical Analysis and Reader*, New York, A Temple Book, Atheneum, 1977. (Originally, Jewish Publication Society, 1959).

Eric Hoffer, *The True Believer, Thoughts on the Nature of Mass Movements*, New York, Perennial Library/Harper & Row, 1951.

Lynn Hunt, Thomas R. Martin, Barbara H. Rosenwein and Bonnie G. Smith, *The Making of the West; Peoples and Cultures; A Concise History*, Boston, New York, Bedford/St. Martin's, Fourth Edition, 2013.

Paul Johnson, *A History of the Jews*, New York, Harper & Row, 1987.

Efraim Karsh, *Palestine Betrayed*, New Haven and London, Yale University Press, 2010.

Michael Korda, *Hero: The Life and Legend of Lawrence of Arabia*, New York, HarperCollins, 2010.

Michael Korda, Ike, *An American Hero*, New York, HarperCollins, 2007.

Bernard Lewis, *The Middle East; A Brief History of the Last 2,000 Years*, New York, Scribner, 1995.

Joshua Muravchik, *Making David Into Goliath: How the World Turned Against Israel*, New York and London, Encounter Books, 2014.

Conor Cruise O'Brien, *The Siege; The Saga of Israel and Zionism,* Touchstone/Simon & Schuster, New York, London, Toronto, Sydney, Tokyo, Singapore, 1986.

Michael B. Oren, *Six Days of War; June 1967 and the Making of the Modern Middle East, Oxford,* New York, Oxford University Press, 2002.

Joan Peters, *From Time Immemorial; The Origins of the Arab-Jewish Conflict Over Palestine,* New York, Harper & Row, 1984.

Dennis Prager and Joseph Telushkin, *Why The Jews? The Reason for Antisemitism,* New York, Touchstone Book/Simon & Schuster, 1983.

Richard L. Rubenstein, *Jihad and Genocide,* Lanham, Boulder, New York, Toronto and Plymouth, U.K., Rowman & Littlefield Publishers, 2010.

Barry Rubin & Wolfgang G. Schwanitz, *Nazis, Islamists, and the Making of the Modern Middle East,* New Haven and London, Yale University Press, 2014.

Binjamin W. Segel, Richard S. Levy, Translator and Editor, *A Lie and A Libel; The History of the Protocols of the Elders of Zion,* Lincoln, Nebraska and London, University of Nebraska Press, 1995. (Based on 1926 German version, *Welt-Krieg, Welt-Revolution, Welt-Verschworung, Welt-Oberregierung* [World War, World Revolution, World Conspiracy, World Super-government].)

Robin Shepherd, *A State Beyond the Pale; Europe's Problem with Israel,* London, Weidenfeld & Nicolson, 2009.

Bernard Simms, *Europe: The Struggle for Supremacy, From 1453 to the Present,* New York, Basic Books, 2014 (first published in the United Kingdom, Allan Lane/Penguin Books, 2013).

Lee Smith, *The Strong Horse: Power, Politics, and the Clash of Arab Civilizations,* Doubleday, New York, 2010 (Cited edition, Anchor Books, New York, 2011.)

Joshua Trachtenberg, *The Devil and the Jews, The Medieval Conception of the Jew and Its Relation to Modern Antisemitism*, Yale University Press, 1943; Cleveland and New York, Meridian Books/Philadelphia, the Jewish Publication Society of America, 1961.

Robert S. Wistrich, editor, *Anti-Judaism, Antisemitism, and Delegitimizing Israel*, Lincoln and London, University of Nebraska Press, 2016.

Ben-Dror Yemini, *Industry of Lies: Media, Academia, and the Israeli-Arab Conflict*, New York, Institute for the Global Study of Antisemitism and Policy, 2017.

Bat Ye'or, *The Dhimmi; Jews and Christians under Islam*, Rutherford, N.J., Fairleigh Dickinson University Press, 1985 (Revised and enlarged English edition.)

INDEX

F

Emil Fackenheim 271
King Faisal 78, 79
James Fallows 146
Frantz Fanon 184, 186, 281, 283
Farhud 161
Louis Farrakhan 242, 274, 337
Fatah 26, 27, 32, 73, 80, 81, 109, 132,
    154, 166, 169, 178, 232, 283,
    292, 314, 315, 333, 338, 339
Salam Fayyad 96
Benjamin Ferencz 338
Fiddler on the Roof 290
The Fixer 140
Henry Ford 78, 212
Michel Foucault 62, 82, 282
France 14, 17, 23, 62, 63, 96, 100,
    140, 146-148, 151, 153, 154,
    172, 178, 191, 207, 210, 247,
    251, 252, 270, 277, 285, 299,
    303, 304, 309, 316-335
France 2 Television 146, 147, 148
Viktor Frankl 142, 169, 172, 177,
    189, 260, 264, 334
Sigmund Freud 57
Matti Friedman 55, 326

G

Galileo 54, 58
gas mask 14, 235
Gaza Strip 26, 28, 32, 33, 38, 40, 51,
    52, 66, 81, 94, 102, 106, 109,
    121, 126-132, 143, 146, 148,
    153-155, 160, 169, 225, 231,
    282, 284, 285, 291, 294, 302,
    307, 311, 312, 322, 326
UN General Assembly 32, 33, 38, 76,
    95, 99, 103, 127, 131, 133-135,
    152, 153, 166, 181, 192, 218,
    264, 295, 296
Fourth Geneva Convention 125, 131
genocide 13, 28, 39, 40, 44, 46, 47,
    64-66, 69, 75, 77, 133, 141,
    142, 164, 165, 174, 179, 180,
    189, 199, 205, 206, 248, 250,
    253-259, 282, 297, 302, 314-
    316, 331, 333, 337-340
Gentlemen's agreements 35
Germany 10, 17, 144, 162, 240, 252,
    298
Sammy Ghozlan 321
André Gide 11
Sir Martin Gilbert 25
George Gilder 21, 50, 51, 104, 262
Newt Gingrich 93-97, 100, 103
Joseph Goebbels 62, 217
Hermann Goering 71, 162
Golan Heights 32, 119, 131, 154, 291
Jeffrey Goldberg 279, 304
Richard Goldstone 294
Goldstone Report 294
Fred M. Gottheil 111
grand mufti (see also Haj Amin
    al-Husseini) 17, 31, 72, 164,
    232, 317
Great Britain 17, 32, 42, 70, 100, 105,
    106, 122-125, 153, 155, 161,
    163, 166, 246, 251, 254, 284,
    285, 291, 303-317
Penny Gross 143, 200
Penny Grunseid 152
Antonio Guterres 13

H

Ahad Ha'am 10, 141
George Habash 272
Hadrian's Wall 42
Haiti 138, 273, 274, 280
Ilan Halimi 324
Sarah Halimi 323, 324, 325
Fathi Hamad 109
Hamas 25-28, 55, 58, 69, 73, 79, 81,
    93, 109, 132, 144, 154, 165,
    170, 178, 179, 182, 216, 231,
    238, 239, 243-245, 269, 274,
    284, 294, 295, 309-316, 322,

I

J

M

Mohamad Mahathir 176
Malmo, Sweden 192
mandatory Palestine 123, 161
Herbert Marcuse 281
martyrdom 57, 58, 146, 168, 278, 339
Marx 76, 182, 286, 289
   Marxism 76, 186
   Marxist 51, 67, 86, 89, 141, 184,
      281, 287, 289, 292
Matzah of Zion 140
Richard Meinertzhagen 102
Mein Kampf 18, 173, 175, 250, 257,
     298, 314
The Prophet Micah 21, 27
Middle East revisionism 83, 335
Mateusz Morawiecki 173
Benny Morris 211
Moses 25, 48, 49, 58, 85, 104, 108,
     172, 174, 185, 199, 221, 251,
     270, 304
Mosque of the Prophet Yunus 299
Mount Sinai 48
Dalal Mughrabi 339
Zahir Muhsein 100
Munich Olympics massacre 97, 198,
     264
Joshua Muravchik 84, 85, 282
Muslim Brotherhood 17, 26, 73-76,
     80, 165, 170, 174, 204, 227,
     233, 238, 240-244, 254, 277,
     300, 310, 311
Myths and Facts: A Concise Record of
   the Arab-Israeli Conflict 37

N

nakba (*al-nakba*) 103, 115, 161, 235,
     255, 260
Sheik Hassan Nasrallah 315
Gamal Abdel Nasser 17, 190, 273
National Committee of the Jews of
   the Land of Israel 158
National Iranian American Council

     65
National Public Radio 55, 222
Nazi 10, 17, 144, 162, 240, 252, 298
Nazi Germany 10, 11, 17, 144, 164,
     205, 206, 215, 218, 249, 255,
     257, 296
Nazism 17, 18, 27, 31, 57, 161, 205,
     248, 250
King Nebuchadnezzar II 106
neo-pagan(ism) 300, 301, 306
Benjamin Netanyahu 104, 162, 169,
     179, 231, 297
New York Times 20, 29, 55, 109, 114,
     126, 127, 129, 130, 131, 157,
     180, 183, 190, 219, 220-222,
     225, 227, 238, 279, 308, 309,
     319, 320, 325
The Night of the Murdered Poets 290
Tal Nitzan 41
Nobel Prize for Literature 11, 198
Nobel Prize winners 21
Non-Aligned Movement 33, 90
Max Nordau 17

O

Barack Obama 121, 178, 194, 324
Conor Cruise O'Brien 37
Rasmea Odeh 80, 190
Ehud Olmert 231, 327
Shrine of Omar 157
Operation Cast Lead 294
Operation Pillar of Defense 294
Operation Protective Edge 295
Max von Oppenheim 18, 74, 167
Organization of the Islamic Confer-
     ence (OIC) 33, 176, 208
George Orwell 47, 82, 89, 189, 233,
     248, 260, 264, 274, 314, 321
Orwellian 13, 59
Oslo accords (peace process) 32, 131,
     154, 169, 181, 315, 319, 339
The Other Side: The Secret Relation-
   ship Between Nazism and

Sayyid Qutb 75, 240, 267, 300

R

Tariq Ramadan 206
Ronald Reagan 122, 131, 280
Vanessa Redgrave 82, 198
Ilmar Reepalu 192
Peter Reitzes 40
Reuters 56, 195, 245, 285
Peretz Reuven 43
revisionism 10, 13, 30, 47, 54, 83,
    106, 108, 160, 258, 259, 267,
    334, 335
Richard Wagner 301, 303
The Right to Maim: Debility, Capacity,
    Disability 40
ritual murder 251, 273
Roman Empire 25, 42, 118
  Romans 23, 109, 117, 119, 156,
    159, 255
Jacqueline Rose 269
Jonathan Rosen 19, 92, 249
Alvin Rosenfeld 22
Eugene Rostow 127
Ari Roth 215
Jean-Jacques Rousseau 48
Rutgers University 218
Rwanda 46, 47, 178, 338, 339
Congressman Leo Ryan 61

S

Sabeel Ecumenical Liberation Theol-
    ogy Center 108
Howard M. Sachar 37
Rabbi Lord Jonathan Sacks 48, 313
Anwar Sadat 77, 127, 160, 231, 232,
    244
safe room 14, 336
Edward Said 82, 84, 86, 99, 165, 206,
    210, 235, 283
Andrei Sakharov 290
Sheik Raed Salah 170
Hasan Salameh 165, 166, 167

Salomon family 169
Philip Carl Salzman 67-69
Samaria 13, 93, 106, 119-121, 125,
    126, 128, 157, 169, 243, 282,
    291, 293
Herbert Samuel 102
Sen. Bernard Sanders 312
San Francisco State University 34
San Remo Treaty 121, 122, 125
Linda Sarsour 80
"great Satan" 28, 84, 239, 266, 319
"little Satan" 28, 51, 84, 239, 266, 319
Satan 11, 143, 150, 199, 203, 239,
    250, 263, 307, 335
Muhammed ibn Saud 74
Saudi Arabia 60, 73, 74, 77, 101, 109,
    112, 152, 163, 180, 279, 308
Antonin Scalia 173
Richard Schifter 122
Menachem Schneerson 313
Scholars for Peace in the Middle East
    40
secular fundamentalist(s) 11, 42, 60,
    76, 86, 145, 268, 281, 307, 314,
    319
UN Security Council 13, 47, 121,
    122, 126-133, 152, 154, 181,
    203, 291, 316
Esther Shapira 147
Natan Sharansky 14, 290
Ariel Sharon 220
Rev. Al Sharpton 139
Ari Shavit 223, 224, 225
Robin Shepherd 280, 281
Daoud Shihad 145
David Shipler 298
Shoah 19, 44, 259, 266, 337
Walid Shoebat 109
Nadav Shragai 104, 105, 113, 155
Ahmed Shukeiry 99
The Siege: The Saga of Israel and
    Zionism 37
Sinai Peninsula 32, 131, 154, 182,
    244, 291, 302

www.ingramcontent.com/pod-product-compliance
Lightning Source LLC
Chambersburg PA
CBHW020454270326
41926CB00008B/599